THE BLACK PRINCE OF FLORENCE

The Divorce of Henry VIII: The Untold Story

The Black Prince of Florence

The Spectacular Life and Treacherous World of
Alessandro de' Medici

CATHERINE FLETCHER

THE BODLEY HEAD
LONDON

3 5 7 9 10 8 6 4 2

The Bodley Head, an imprint of Vintage,
20 Vauxhall Bridge Road,
London SW1V 2SA

The Bodley Head is part of the Penguin Random House group of companies whose
addresses can be found at global.penguinrandomhouse.com

First published by The Bodley Head in 2016

www.vintage-books.co.uk

A CIP catalogue record for this book is available from the British Library

ISBN 9781847922694

Typeset in India by Thomson Digital Pvt Ltd, Noida, Delhi
Printed and bound by Clays Ltd, St Ives plc

Penguin Random House is committed to a sustainable future
for our business, our readers and our planet. This book is made
from Forest Stewardship Council® certified paper.

To my father

CONTENTS

Senior branch of Medici family (selected members)

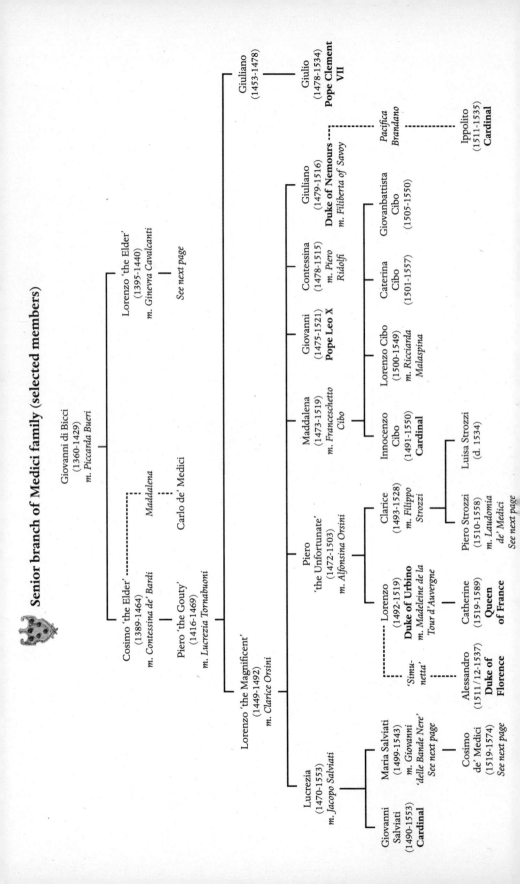

Giovanni di Bicci
(1360-1429)
m. Piccarda Bueri

Cosimo 'the Elder'
(1389-1464)
m. Contessina de' Bardi

Lorenzo 'the Elder'
(1395-1440)
m. Ginevra Cavalcanti

See next page

Maddalena

Carlo de' Medici

Piero 'the Gouty'
(1416-1469)
m. Lucrezia Tornabuoni

Lorenzo 'the Magnificent'
(1449-1492)
m. Clarice Orsini

Piero
'the Unfortunate'
(1472-1503)
m. Alfonsina Orsini

Giuliano
(1453-1478)

Giulio
(1478-1534)
Pope Clement VII

Maddalena
(1473-1519)
m. Franceschetto
Cibo

Giovanni
(1475-1521)
Pope Leo X

Contessina
(1478-1515)
m. Piero
Ridolfi

Giuliano
(1479-1516)
Duke of Nemours
m. Filiberta of Savoy

*Pacifica
Brandano*

Ippolito
(1511-1535)
Cardinal

Innocenzo
Cibo
(1491-1550)
Cardinal

Lorenzo Cibo
(1500-1549)
m. Ricciarda
Malaspina

Caterina
Cibo
(1501-1557)

Giovanbattista
Cibo
(1505-1550)

Clarice
(1493-1528)
m. Filippo
Strozzi

Lorenzo
(1492-1519)
Duke of Urbino
m. Madeleine de la
Tour d'Auvergne

'Simo-
netta'

Alessandro
(1511/12-1537)
**Duke of
Florence**

Catherine
(1519-1589)
**Queen
of France**

Piero Strozzi
(1510-1558)
m. Laudomia
de' Medici
See next page

Luisa Strozzi
(d. 1534)

Lucrezia
(1470-1553)
m. Jacopo Salviati

Giovanni
Salviati
(1490-1553)
Cardinal

Maria Salviati
(1499-1543)
m. Giovanni
'delle Bande Nere'
See next page

Cosimo
de' Medici
(1519-1574)
See next page

Junior branch of Medici family (selected members)

Giovanni di Bicci
(1360-1429)
m. Piccarda Bueri

Cosimo 'the Elder'
(1389-1464)
m. Contessina de' Bardi
See previous page

Lorenzo 'the Elder'
(1395-1440)
m. Ginevra Cavalcanti

Pierfrancesco 'the Elder'
(1431-1476)
m. Laudomia Acciaiuoli

Lorenzo 'il Popolano'
(1463-1503)
m. Semiramide Appiani

Giovanni 'il Popolano'
(1467-1498)
m. Caterina Sforza

Pierfrancesco 'the Younger'
(1487-1525)
m. Maria Soderini

Giovanni 'delle Bande Nere'
(1498-1526)
m. Maria Salviati
See previous page

Lorenzino
(1514-1548)

Laudomia
(1518-1559)
m. Piero Strozzi
See previous page

Cosimo
(1519-1574)
Duke of Florence;
Grand-duke of Tuscany

GLOSSARY OF NAMES

Acciaiuoli, Roberto (1467–1547). A Florentine diplomat, active in city service both before and after the return of the Medici in 1512. Imprisoned during the 1527–30 republic but escaped and held high office in Alessandro's regime, including as one of his first four *consiglieri*. One of the politicians invited by Clement VII to write an opinion on reform of Florentine government.

Aldobrandini, Silvestro (1499–1558). A Florentine lawyer and academic, involved in the revolt against the Medici in 1527. Held office in the 1527–30 republic; cooperated with papal officials at the end of the siege, but was imprisoned. Freed thanks to the intervention of Bartolomeo Valori, he was exiled. He was an advocate for the Florentine exiles during their disputes with Alessandro in Naples and went on to a distinguished legal career.

Aretino, Pietro (1492–1556). An author and satirist, patronised by leading figures of sixteenth-century Italy, including Cardinal Giulio de' Medici (later Clement VII). Spent his early career in Rome but left for Venice after a victim of his satire tried to have him killed and his involvement in the production of pornography landed him in trouble.

Bandini, Giovan. A companion of Alessandro de' Medici, involved in a series of incidents including the attack on Cellini's brother and the duel for the honour of Florence.

Castiglione, Baldassarre (1478–1529). Courtier, diplomat and author, born in Mantua but active at the courts of Urbino and Milan. Best known for his *Book of the Courtier*, a dialogue on proper conduct at court.

Cellini, Benvenuto (1500–1571). A Florentine goldsmith and sculptor, Cellini is also famed for his swashbuckling (and unreliable) autobiography. He produced works for Clement VII, for Alessandro, and for many other patrons.

Charles V, Holy Roman Emperor (1500–1558). King of Spain from 1516; Emperor from 1519. Charles' empire stretched from Spain and southern Italy to the German states and Low Countries. He competed with the king of France for dominance in central and northern Italy but also faced challenges to his eastern dominions from the Ottoman Emperor.

Cibo, Caterina (1501–1557). A niece of Pope Leo X, sister to Cardinal Innocenzo, Lorenzo and Giovanbattista Cibo. Married Giovanni Maria Varano, duke of Camerino, with whom she had a daughter, Giulia; widowed in 1527 and waged a fierce fight to protect her interest in the duchy. Lived in Florence from 1535.

Cibo, Giovanbattista (1505/08–c.1550). Bishop of Mariana in Corsica and (from 1530) bishop of Marseilles. Brother of Cardinal Innocenzo and related to the Medici on his mother's side. A close companion of Ippolito de' Medici.

Cibo, Cardinal Innocenzo (1491–1550). A nephew of Pope Leo X, who promoted him to the cardinalate in 1513; related on his father's side to another pope, Innocent VIII. Held many benefices in the Church; became Pope Clement's representative in Florence.

Cibo, Lorenzo (1500–1549). A military commander in papal service, brother of Cardinal Innocenzo. Married Ricciarda Malaspina in 1520.

Clement VII, Pope (Giulio de' Medici) (1478–1534). The illegitimate son of Giuliano de' Medici, the brother of Lorenzo the Magnificent. His father was assassinated in the Pazzi conspiracy. Giulio was made a cardinal in 1513 following his cousin Giovanni's election as Pope Leo X. He held a number of important offices in Leo's administration and was elected pope in 1523.

Della Rovere, Francesco Maria, duke of Urbino (1490–1538). Ruler of the duchy of Urbino from 1508 to 1516, when he was supplanted by Lorenzo de' Medici, and again after 1521. A *condottiere*, he commanded papal troops and the Venetian army at different points in his career.

Doria, Andrea (1466–1560). A celebrated Genoese naval commander and statesman, Doria fought for various princes but by the mid 1530s was in the service of Charles V.

Este, Alfonso d', duke of Ferrara (1476–1534). Came to power in 1505; had a long-running conflict with the popes over control of the duchies of Ferrara, Modena and Reggio. Allied variously with France and the Holy Roman Empire at different points during the Italian Wars.

Este Gonzaga, Isabella d', marchioness of Mantua (1474–1539). A member of the ruling family of Ferrara, Isabella was married to Francesco II, marquis of Mantua, and was a distinguished political and cultural figure of her time, known in particular for her patronage of the arts. She was widowed in 1519.

Francis I, king of France (1494–1547). Francis came to power in 1515 following the death of his cousin and father-in-law Louis XII. He was the first of the Angoulême branch of the Valois family to rule France. He vied with Charles V for military supremacy in Europe.

Gheri, Goro (1470–1528). Secretary to Lorenzo de' Medici, duke of Urbino, for whom he carried out a variety of political and diplomatic missions.

Giovio, Paolo (c.1486–1552). Physician, philosopher and close adviser to Pope Clement VII, Giovio is also known for his historical writings.

Girolami, Raffaello (1472–1532). Member of a Florentine banking family, he served in city government during the Medici exile of 1494–1512, though was never an advocate for a very broad-based regime. After the return of the Medici in 1512 he continued to hold office, as he did during the republic of 1527–30, when he was one of the more moderate voices in government. From January 1530 to the end of the republic he served as *gonfaloniere*.

Gonzaga, Ercole (1505–1563). Second son of Isabella d'Este and Francesco II Gonzaga, duke of Mantua. He was made cardinal in 1527, following in an uncle's footsteps. Initially preferring a princely lifestyle of hunting and the like, he later took an important role in church reform.

Gonzaga, Federico II, marquis (later duke) of Mantua (1500–1540). Ruler of Mantua from 1519. Eldest son of Isabella d'Este.

Gonzaga, Ferrante (1507–1557). Third son of Isabella d'Este and Francesco II Gonzaga, marquis of Mantua, he joined Charles V's court in Spain at the age of sixteen and spent his adult life in the Imperial military service, quickly rising to high rank.

Gonzaga, Giulia (c.1513–1566). Married at thirteen and widowed at fifteen, Giulia was a member of the Sabbioneta branch of the Gonzaga family. She became the lover of Ippolito de' Medici, but is better known for the religious and spiritual activities to which she turned after the mid 1530s.

Guicciardini, Francesco (1483–1540). Statesman and historian, Guicciardini held senior posts in both the papal and Florentine administrations. Though he was a reluctant supporter of princely rule in Florence, he was one of Alessandro's most important advisers. His *History of Italy* is both an important source for the events of this period and a groundbreaking work of historical writing.

Guicciardini, Luigi (1478–1551). Florentine politician, brother of Francesco. Held a number of offices under the Medici, including *gonfaloniere* (in 1527, when the Medici were exiled) and roles as commissar in Pisa, Arezzo, Pistoia and Castrocaro at different times. Wrote a history of the 1527 Sack of Rome.

Henri, duke of Orléans (1519–1559). Second son of the king of France, Henri was married to Catherine de' Medici in 1533. He unexpectedly became heir to the throne in 1536 after the death of his elder brother, and reigned as Henri II from 1547.

Leo X, Pope (Giovanni de' Medici) (1475–1521). Second son of Lorenzo 'the Magnificent', Giovanni was made a cardinal before his seventeenth birthday. He was elected pope in 1513 but became notorious for his nepotism and worldly lifestyle.

Machiavelli, Niccolò (1469–1527). Political theorist, administrator and writer, Machiavelli was a leading civil servant in the Florentine Republic from 1498 until the return of the Medici in 1512. Although he advised Leo X on the government of Florence, his relations with the Medici family were never comfortable. Best known as the author of *The Prince*, he also wrote a discussion of republics (the *Discourses on Livy*), comedies, poetry and a number of political treatises.

Malaspina Cibo, Ricciarda (1497–1553). Daughter of the marquis of Massa, Ricciarda became the effective ruler of Massa and Carrara following her father's death in 1519. She married Lorenzo Cibo in 1520, and was also the lover of her husband's brother, Cardinal Innocenzo Cibo.

Malaspina, Taddea (1505–1559). Daughter of the marquis of Massa and younger sister of Ricciarda, Taddea was married to Count Giambattista Boiardo da Scandiano but was widowed in her early twenties. In the 1530s she became the mistress of Alessandro de' Medici.

Margaret of Austria (1522–1586). Illegitimate daughter of Charles V and Johanna (Jeanne) van der Gheynst, Margaret is better known as 'Margaret of Parma' after the title of her second husband. Married to Alessandro de' Medici in 1536, she was quickly widowed and married Ottavio Farnese in 1538. She served as governor of the Netherlands from 1559–1567 and from 1578–1582.

Marzi de' Medici, Angelo (1477–1546). Given the name de' Medici through the favour of a minor branch of the family, Angelo Marzi worked in the Florentine chancellery and performed many services for the Medici family. From 1529 he held the position of bishop of Assisi.

Ser Maurizio da Milano. Chancellor to the *Otto di Guardia* ('Eight of Watch', responsible for internal security) during Alessandro's rule of Florence, Ser Maurizio (whose title suggests he was a notary) was a senior civil servant. He gained a reputation for brutality in his enforcement of laws such as the ban on weapons.

Medici, Alfonsina Orsini de' (1472–1520). Mother of Lorenzo, duke of Urbino; grandmother of Alessandro and Catherine. A member of a wealthy and influential Neapolitan family, Alfonsina exercised considerable power in Florence in the years 1515–19, particularly during her son's absences from the city.

Medici, Catherine de' (1519–1589). Daughter of Lorenzo, duke of Urbino and half-sister of Alessandro, Catherine married Henri, duke of Orléans, in 1533. Henri became heir to the throne of France following his elder brother's death in 1536, and king in 1547. Catherine survived him and saw three of her sons rule the kingdom as well as acting as regent of France herself.

Medici, Cosimo de' 'the Elder' (1389–1464). Used his father's banking fortune to establish the Medici in Florentine politics, though not without a brief period of exile in 1433–34 when he was accused of tyranny. Noted cultural and artistic patron. Father of Piero 'the gouty'; grandfather of Lorenzo 'the Magnificent'.

Medici, Cosimo de' (1519–1574). The son of Giovanni de' Medici and Maria Salviati, Cosimo was a member of the junior branch of the Medici family, sometimes known as the 'popolano' branch. He became duke of Florence on the death of his distant cousin Alessandro in 1537, and from 1569 was grand duke of Tuscany.

Medici, Giovanni de' *see* **Leo X**

Medici, Giuliano de', duke of Nemours (1479–1516). Third son of Lorenzo the Magnificent and younger brother of Pope Leo X, Giuliano married Filiberta of Savoy in 1515 and was granted his title by the king of France in the same year. He was the Medici family figurehead in Florence from their return in 1512 until his death. He had one illegitimate son, Ippolito.

Medici, Giulio de' *see* **Clement VII**

Medici, Cardinal Ippolito de' (1511–1535). Illegitimate son of Giuliano de' Medici, Ippolito was the Medici family representative in Florence from 1524 until their expulsion in 1527. He was made a cardinal in 1529 by Pope Clement VII, his cousin once removed.

Medici, Lorenzino de' (1514–1548). A member of the junior 'popolano' branch of the Medici family, Lorenzino joined Alessandro's court in the 1530s. He gained some reputation as a man of letters but is most famous as the Duke's assassin. He was killed in revenge in 1548.

Medici, Lorenzo de', 'the Magnificent' (1449–1492). Effective ruler of Florence from 1469, after his father's untimely death. Survived the Pazzi conspiracy of 1478 in which his brother was murdered; consolidated Medici power in Florence but saw the family bank suffer serious problems.

Medici, Lorenzo de', duke of Urbino (1492–1519). Eldest son of Piero di Lorenzo de' Medici (who was in turn the eldest son of Lorenzo the Magnificent) and Alfonsina Orsini. Made duke of Urbino in 1516, thanks to the patronage of his uncle Pope Leo X; acted for a time as family representative in Florence. Married Madeleine de la Tour d'Auvergne in 1518: they had a daughter, Catherine. Generally acknowledged as the father of Alessandro de' Medici.

Medici, Ottaviano de' (1482–1546). Member of a junior branch of the Medici and husband of Francesca Salviati (daughter of Jacopo

Salviati and Lucrezia de' Medici). Managed Alessandro's household affairs in Florence as well as holding a number of important city offices.

Medici Strozzi, Clarice de' (1493–1528). Niece of Pope Leo X and sister of Lorenzo, duke of Urbino. She married Filippo Strozzi in 1508 and stoutly defended the interests of their children against the illegitimate Medici offspring Alessandro and Ippolito.

Nardi, Jacopo (1476–1563). A politician and historian, Nardi served in Florentine government both before and after the 1512 return of the Medici, but threw his lot in with their opponents after 1527. He was exiled in 1530 and subsequently took a leading role in republican politics, liaising between the oligarchs and the more radical exiles.

Passerini, Silvio, cardinal of Cortona (1469–1529). Brought up with the future Pope Leo X, Passerini was promoted to the cardinalate along with many other Medici friends in 1517. He held a number of lucrative church offices and acted as a guardian to Ippolito de' Medici during his period in Florence in the 1520s.

Paul III, Pope (Alessandro Farnese) (1468–1549). A long-serving cardinal, elected pope on the death of Clement VII in 1534. Paul sought to advance the interests of his Farnese nephews, and successfully established them as dukes of Parma and Piacenza. Responsible for initiating the Council of Trent that oversaw a process of reform within the Roman Catholic Church.

Ridolfi, Cardinal Niccolò (1501–1550). Son of Contessina de' Medici and a nephew of Pope Leo X, Niccolò Ridolfi became a cardinal in 1517 and archbishop of Florence in 1524. He resigned that post in 1532 and supported Ippolito's challenge to Alessandro's rule.

Salviati, Cardinal Giovanni (1490–1553). A nephew of Pope Leo X, son of Jacopo Salviati and Leo's sister Lucrezia de' Medici. Appointed cardinal by his uncle in 1517.

Salviati, Giuliano (d. c.1562). A distant cousin of Cardinal Giovanni Salviati; a companion of Alessandro, who played a central role in the Luisa Strozzi affair.

Salviati, Jacopo (1461–1533). Married to Lucrezia de' Medici (sister of Leo X). Secretary to Pope Clement VII and senior figure at the papal court. Father of Cardinal Giovanni Salviati and of Maria Salviati (mother of the future Duke Cosimo de' Medici).

Schömberg, Cardinal Nicolas (1472–1537). Originally from Meissen in what is now Germany, Schömberg was a Dominican priest who carried out various diplomatic missions for German princes and the Holy Roman Emperor. He was appointed archbishop of Capua by Pope Leo X and made cardinal by Paul III in 1535.

Simunetta. Name commonly given to Alessandro de' Medici's mother, a servant or slave in a Medici household, most likely that of Alfonsina Orsini de' Medici. Also referred to as Anna.

Sforza, Francesco II, duke of Milan (1495–1535). Held the duchy from 1521 until his death, though it was effectively under the control of Spanish troops. Married Christina of Denmark, niece of Charles V, in 1534.

Soderini de' Medici, Maria (1487–1525). A member of the Soderini family, which had been prominent in Florentine government during the exile of the Medici from 1494–1512, Maria married Pierfrancesco the Younger, a member of the cadet branch of the Medici. One of their four children was Lorenzino.

Strozzi, Filippo (1489–1538). A prominent papal banker, married to Clarice de' Medici (sister of Lorenzo, duke of Urbino).

Strozzi, Luisa (d. 1534). Daughter of Filippo Strozzi; her premature death prompted rumours of poisoning.

Strozzi, Piero (c.1510–1558). Son of Filippo Strozzi and cousin to Alessandro and Catherine. Married Lorenzino's sister Laudomia de'

Medici and became a prominent opponent of the Medici regime in Florence. Had a distinguished career in French military service and was a confidant of Catherine de' Medici.

Valori, Bartolomeo (d. 1537). Initially a Medici ally, he supported the family's restoration to power in 1512. Papal commissioner with the Imperial army during the siege of Florence, he served in Florentine government and held the office of governor of the Romagna (in the gift of the papacy). After the death of Clement VII he lost influence in the papal bureaucracy and eventually left Florence. Executed in 1537 after fighting with the rebels at the Battle of Montemurlo.

Varano, Giulia (1523–1547). Heiress to the duchy of Camerino and related to the Medici via her mother (Caterina Cibo). Considered as a possible bride for both Alessandro and Ippolito, Giulia married Guidobaldo II, future duke of Urbino, in 1534.

Vasari, Giorgio (1511–1574). Artist, architect and historian, Vasari studied alongside Alessandro and Ippolito de' Medici, and later worked for both of them. His *Lives of the Artists* is a key source for Renaissance art history.

Vettori, Francesco (1474–1539). Florentine statesman; served in city government both before and after the 1512 return of the Medici in posts including *gonfaloniere* and ambassador. Best known for his correspondence with Niccolò Machiavelli.

Vitelli, Alessandro (d. 1556). Military commander in the service of Charles V. After participating in the siege of Florence, he was appointed as head of Alessandro de' Medici's Florentine guard. Later enjoyed military success in service of Duke Cosimo de' Medici.

TIMELINE

1511/12	Alessandro born
1513	Giovanni de' Medici elected Pope Leo X
1519	Birth of Alessandro's half-sister, Catherine de' Medici
1519	Death of Alessandro's father, Lorenzo, duke of Urbino
1521	Death of Pope Leo X; succeeded by Adrian VI
1522	Alessandro made duke of Penne
1522	Birth of Margaret of Austria, illegitimate daughter of Holy Roman Emperor Charles V
1523	Death of Adrian VI; Giulio de' Medici elected Pope Clement VII
1524	Alessandro's cousin Ippolito made family figurehead in Florence
1525	Alessandro and Catherine sent to Florence; Alessandro lives at Poggio a Caiano villa, just outside city

1527		Sack of Rome; Medici family expelled from Florence and city government taken over by rivals
1529	*January*	Ippolito de' Medici made a cardinal
	June	Treaty of Barcelona between Clement VII and Charles V; Alessandro betrothed to Margaret of Austria
1530	*February*	Coronation of Charles V as Holy Roman Emperor in Bologna
	August	Florentine regime falls after months of siege; pro-Medici faction takes over with Imperial backing
1531	*October–May*	Alessandro travels around German states and Low Countries with court of Charles V
1531	*July*	Alessandro makes entry to Florence
1532	*April*	Ducal authority granted to Alessandro in constitutional reform of Florence
1533	*April*	Margaret of Austria visits Florence before going on to Naples
1534	*July*	Foundation stone of Fortezza da Basso laid
	September	Death of Clement VII
1535	*March*	Delegation of Florentine exiles, Alessandro's opponents, meets Charles in Barcelona
	June	Ippolito de' Medici implicated in plot to assassinate Alessandro
	August	Ippolito de' Medici poisoned
	December	First garrison installed in Fortezza da Basso

1536	*January*	In Naples, Charles V hears cases of Alessandro and the exiled republicans on the government of Florence
	February	Ring ceremony of Alessandro and Margaret
	June	Marriage of Alessandro and Margaret
1537	*January*	Alessandro assassinated by cousin Lorenzino

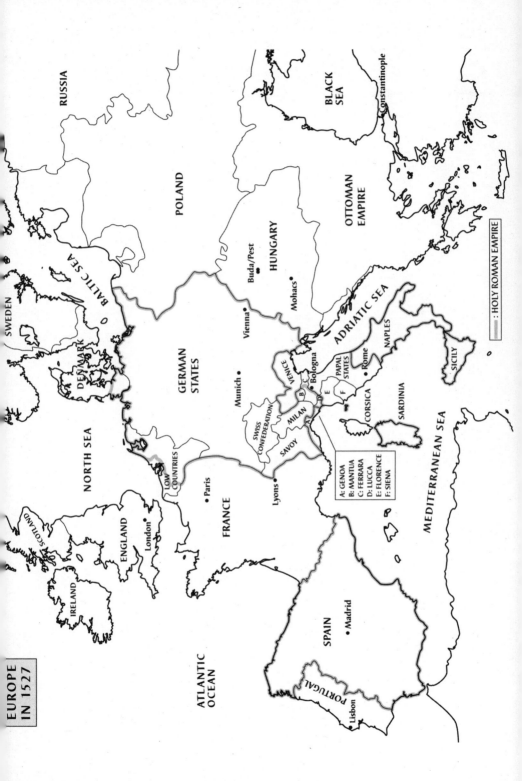

EUROPE IN 1527

ATLANTIC OCEAN

SCOTLAND

IRELAND

ENGLAND

London

NORTH SEA

DENMARK

SWEDEN

BALTIC SEA

RUSSIA

POLAND

GERMAN STATES

Munich

Vienna

HUNGARY

Buda/Pest

Mohacs

BLACK SEA

Constantinople

OTTOMAN EMPIRE

LOW COUNTRIES

Paris

FRANCE

Lyons

SWISS CONFEDERATION

SAVOY

MILAN

VENICE

B

C

D

Bologna

E

F

PAPAL STATES

Rome

ADRIATIC SEA

NAPLES

SICILY

SARDINIA

CORSICA

SPAIN

Madrid

PORTUGAL

Lisbon

MEDITERRANEAN SEA

A: GENOA
B: MANTUA
C: FERRARA
D: LUCCA
E: FLORENCE
F: SIENA

: HOLY ROMAN EMPIRE

A NOTE ON MONEY

A range of coins and currencies circulated in Italy in the sixteenth century. The various city-states on the peninsula issued their own coinage, and exchange rates were not stable, particularly not during periods of war. Most day-to-day transactions were made in silver coins, known in Florence as *grossi* (groats); these were later replaced by the *giulio*. Major (and international) payments were denominated in gold coins such as ducats (the generic term for money of this type) and florins (the Florentine version). These were gradually superseded by the *scudo*, worth about 6 per cent less. A parallel system of *lire*, *soldi* and *denari* (pounds, shillings and pence) was often used for accounting purposes, though *lire* and *soldi* did not exist as coins. In the period covered by this book, a florin was worth somewhere between seven and eight *lire*.

Many people were not paid in cash alone, and reliable price indexes are lacking, so it is hard to estimate the purchasing power of particular sums of money. However, as a rough guide, unskilled labourers could expect to earn 20–22 *scudi* in a year; skilled workers might make twice that. In 1504–5, Michelangelo had a stipend of 120 florins. Soldiers' pay ranged from around thirty ducats a year to over 100 if they had to cover the cost of a horse and followers. Cardinals' annual incomes, on the other hand, ranged in 1521 from 2,000 to 50,000 gold ducats. In 1528, it was estimated that around eighty Florentines had estates worth more than 50,000 florins: Jacopo Salviati, whose estate in Rome was valued at 350,000 florins in 1532, was one of the super-rich. Grain, a staple commodity, was considered expensive when in the 1530s the price of 200 kg reached five ducats, which gives some indication of how extraordinary the incomes of the wealthy were.[1]

THE BLACK PRINCE OF FLORENCE

PROLOGUE

It was the eve of Epiphany, 1537, a night of the most dazzling moonlight. Alessandro de' Medici, duke of Florence, had an assignation. His cousin Lorenzino, little Lorenzo, had promised him the favours of Caterina de' Ginori.

Alessandro's enemies called Lorenzino his pimp.

Caterina, it was said, was beautiful and virtuous. She was married, but tonight her husband was many miles to the south in Naples on business. Lorenzino had assured Alessandro, lord of the city, that Caterina could be persuaded.

After dinner that night, Lorenzino had explained his plan. Caterina lived on the narrow street just behind the Palazzo Medici. Alessandro should make excuses to his friends and head for the privacy of Lorenzino's palace apartment rather than his own. Lorenzino would bring Caterina in discreetly, by the back door, to protect her reputation.

Clad in a cloak of fine Neapolitan silk, lined with sable, the Duke headed out with four friends. In public he usually wore a doublet lined with fine chain mail to protect himself from any enemy quick with a knife. But there was no need for such precautions on a short walk to meet the pretty Caterina. Arriving in the Piazza di San Marco, just a few minutes away from his home, Alessandro dismissed all his companions except one. His servant l'Unghero was to keep watch on the comings and goings at Lorenzino's from the Sostegni house across the road. L'Unghero, lazy and familiar with the Duke's womanising, expected a long wait. He decided not to watch but to take himself off to sleep.

There was a warm fire burning in Lorenzino's chamber. Alessandro took off his sword and threw himself down on the bed. He too had decided to take a nap.

When Lorenzino came into the room and found his cousin asleep he took Alessandro's sword and quickly wound the belt around its hilt, so that it could not easily be drawn from its sheath. He placed it carefully by the bolster, crept out of the chamber and closed the door behind him.

Lorenzino's companion that night was one Piero di Gioannabbate, known by the curious nickname Scoronconcolo, a man of low rank whose ears he had filled with his grievances against a certain unnamed courtier. This courtier, Lorenzino told Scoronconcolo, had cheated him and interfered in his business. Scoronconcolo, who owed Lorenzino favours, had promised to deal with Lorenzino's tormentor, even to kill him. Even if he were a favourite of the Duke's. Even if he were Christ himself.

'My brother,' said Lorenzino, 'now is the time; I have shut that enemy of mine in my chamber, and he is asleep.'

'Let's go,' said Scoronconcolo.

When they reached the landing, Lorenzino turned to Scoronconcolo and said: 'Don't worry that he's a friend of the Duke, just make sure you get his hands.'

'That I'll do,' replied his friend, 'even if he's the Duke himself.'

'Are you ready?' asked Lorenzino cheerfully. 'He can't slip through our fingers now. Let's go.'

'Let's go,' said Scoronconcolo.

Lorenzino tried the latch. The door did not open.

He tried again. This second time, he entered.

'My lord, are you asleep?' he asked, and plunged his sword into Alessandro's stomach.

Alessandro lurched up from the bed and made a dash for the door, seizing a stool to use as a shield, but Scoronconcolo pulled a knife. Slashing down from the left temple, he sliced open the Duke's left cheek.

Lorenzino pushed Alessandro onto the bed. He used the weight of his own body to force the Duke down. He tried to cover Alessandro's mouth so he couldn't scream, but the Duke bit so angrily into his thumb that Lorenzino collapsed beside him.

As the pair grappled, Scoronconcolo drew his sword. Fearful of cutting Lorenzino, he managed only to slash the mattress. Finally he pulled a knife and plunged it into Alessandro's throat.

It was said that for all the time that Alessandro waited, held down by Lorenzino, for Scoronconcolo to strike, he never wept or pleaded for his life. Nor once did he let go of his cousin's thumb.

Lorenzino and Scoronconcolo lifted Alessandro's body from the blood-covered floor, and placed it on the bed. They left it hidden beneath the canopy and went on their way.

The first duke of Florence was dead.[1]

It was the misfortune of Alessandro de' Medici to be assassinated twice: first with a sword, then with a pen. Thanks to Lorenzino, and to the many enemies of the Medici family, Alessandro has gone down in history as a tyrant. Not only did Lorenzino murder the Duke, he wrote an eloquent justification of his actions. He found, too, a sympathetic interviewer in Benedetto Varchi, the historian who later prepared an account of Alessandro's years on the commission of Cosimo I, Alessandro's successor as duke. 'I will recount this death (about which there are various tales and reports) with greater truth,' wrote Varchi, 'having heard it from Lorenzo himself . . . and from Scoronconcolo.'[2] Although the first reports of Alessandro's death were matter-of-fact Varchi's story of Lorenzino's dramatic tyrannicide grips the imagination.

For centuries after Alessandro's assassination, it suited both former allies and enemies to make a villain of him. The enemies were mostly sincere in their dislike. And it was convenient for the Medici family that Alessandro could take the blame for the brutal first years of their rule as princes of Florence. Even the friendlier historians of his rule tell a bloody tale, and it is hard to challenge their version of events because the bulk of Alessandro's papers have disappeared. Perhaps they were lost in the chaos that followed his murder, or perhaps someone decided to destroy the evidence of Alessandro's crimes. We are left with the partisan commentary of the contemporary historians. Alessandro de' Medici has unreliable narrators by the dozen. Writing this book, I have sometimes felt that I have been making a compendium of stories, each told by someone with his (and it is usually his) own reasons for telling. In many cases I have only a single source, and cannot check the facts. In general, I have given a little more weight to the contemporary letters of secretaries and diplomats than to the historians writing with hindsight. I have trusted the keeper of the wardrobe a little more again. (A box of masks is either in its place or not, and if cloth of gold went missing there'd be trouble.) Still, I have more doubts and questions than I would like. Even when a writer is sincere, memory can be faulty. To make this book readable I have avoided interrupting the narrative too often with caveats and qualifications, and I encourage readers who are interested in the detail of the historical sources to consult the notes.

The most famous accounts of Alessandro begin with the tales of his wickedness, in all its bloody glory. His murder, wrote his assassin, was 'a deed incumbent on any good citizen'. He was a tyrant like Nero, Caligula or Phalaris. He was a monster, driven by his 'innate cruelty and savagery'. What do those words allude to? It has long been said that Alessandro was the son of a Moorish slave, or a 'half-Negro' woman.[3] Were Lorenzino's words a racial insult? The answer is not straightforward. Sixteenth-century people thought about the things we now call 'race' and 'class' in very different ways than we do today. Moors – Muslims from North Africa and Spain – were part of the ethnic-religious picture in sixteenth-century Europe, as were Jews, but other racial categories were only just emerging. The Ottoman Empire, which stretched from eastern Hungary through Turkey and along the coast of North Africa, was an ethnically diverse place. Its rulers had themselves portrayed with pale skin, but there were black Turks too, who sometimes appear in the European depictions of the time. In parts of Europe black saints and the black Magus were a feature of sixteenth-century art, where they pointed to the global reach of Christendom. As European slave-trading in West Africa expanded, black Africans were brought to Italy in increasing numbers: they were stereotyped as uncivilised and inferior.

Yet the modern idea of 'race', which emerged with the Atlantic slave trade, is very different from anything that existed in the 1530s. It may be disconcerting to readers who have grown up with today's labels and categories that we do not find them in Alessandro's world. Blood and descent were certainly important; positive qualities were associated with the colour white and negative ones with black.[4] Yet while in Spanish and Portuguese, the European languages most associated at the time with slave-trading, the word *negro* had been used to mean a black person since the fifteenth century, elsewhere in sixteenth-century Europe the equivalent words were only just coming into existence. The French noun *nègre*, meaning a black person, was first recorded in 1516; *negro*, the Italian equivalent, dates to 1532. When Giulio Landi, an Italian author, discussed the Portuguese colony of Madeira in the 1530s, he made a point of explaining the racial categories used there – Moors, Ethiopians, blacks and mulattoes – to his readers.[5] He did not assume they would be familiar. If you went back in time to early sixteenth-century Florence and asked whether any given individual was black or white you would probably get a puzzled look. Adjectives like *moro*, *nero*, and *negro*, variations on 'black', were used to refer to dark- or darker-skinned people but did not define a specific ethnicity.[6] In the sixteenth century 'Moor' was a nickname given to all sorts of people. Among them was Ludovico il Moro – ruler of Milan from 1494 to 1499 – who is not thought to have had African ancestry at all. For mixed-race people the picture is more complex still. The categorisation of people of mixed African and European descent as black – through the 'one-drop rule' – was a phenomenon of early twentieth-century America.[7] We should not expect to find it in Renaissance Italy. In the Florentine piazza, if you used the word *mulatto* (which was used to describe Alessandro) a person would understand you but not in straightforwardly racial terms. *Mulatto* – meaning 'little mule' – was a term applied to bastards. It had a connotation of species-mixing: a mule is a cross between a horse and a donkey. But it was not necessarily associated with race. (A more detailed discussion of this issue can be found in the Afterword.)

It was not until the nineteenth and early twentieth centuries that discussion of Alessandro's 'race' came into its own – and then not in a good way. Scientific racism provided the intellectual backdrop against which historians of the Medici judged Alessandro's rule. But Alessandro also attracted the attention of scholars seeking to challenge racism. In 1931, in the United States, Arturo Alfonso Schomburg, co-founder of the Negro Society for Historical Research and creator of one of the most important collections of sources for African history, wrote an article about him for *The Crisis*, the magazine of the US-based National Association for the Advancement of Colored People. Still, while the story may have been known in the USA, it was far from visible to me as a traveller to Florence, which I had visited three times before I heard it. When I did, I found it not in the city's galleries, but in an academic book chapter in the University of London library.[8] In the museums of Florence itself there was scanty evidence even for Alessandro's existence. A few years ago, when I visited the Uffizi Gallery, his portrait was not on display. To prove to friends that he was real, I was reduced to apologetic leafing through old exhibition catalogues in the gallery bookshop. A friend who had spent a decade studying sociology at the University of Florence knew nothing of the tales of Alessandro's ethnicity. Nor did my Florentine landlady, who had lived in the city for years. She smelt a conspiracy. In the past ten years or so, there has been greater acknowledgement – both in academic literature and in the art world – of the likelihood that Alessandro was mixed-race.[9] Yet he is still very far from a well-known historical figure.

Probably the only black person in the western popular imagination to exist before the seventeenth century is fictional. Shakespeare's Othello is a timeless character, often transplanted out of the sixteenth-century context, but the text gives us important clues to how Europeans saw Africans in this period, not least the ambiguity of their language. Shakespeare calls Othello 'the Moor of Venice', but we cannot tell from the text whether Othello is meant to be from North Africa, or further south. The insults directed at Othello sometimes point in the direction of Arab ancestry ('Barbary horse'), and some-times to sub-Saharan origins ('old black ram', 'thick lips', 'sooty bosom' and simply 'black Othello'). Different productions make different choices. Othello is a former slave, captured by his enemies then redeemed. When Brabantio says angrily that if Othello gets away with marrying Desdemona 'bondslaves and pagans shall our statesmen be' his concern is with Othello's status and (supposed) lack of Christian religion. Othello himself emphasises his 'free condition'. The writers who insult Alessandro do so by saying that his mother was a peasant and a former slave. Yet, as we will discover, perhaps a more telling parallel between *Othello* and the story of the Medici lies in Shakespeare's portrayal of a man – Iago – who like Alessandro's cousin and rival for the dukedom of Florence Ippolito de' Medici believes he has been passed over for a promotion he deserves.

For a very long time, the city of Florence has been mythologised as the symbolic heart of European culture, the cradle of western civilisation. It abounds with the images and stories of great men: Dante, Botticelli, Lorenzo de' Medici, Michelangelo, Galileo. The Renaissance was the first period – so the traditional history went – in which we could truly speak of the great individual, of the 'Renaissance man'. Alessandro's story reminds us that Renaissance men may not always have been white. Alongside the art and poetry, the scheming, intriguing, bloody side of Renaissance politics is well known too. As Orson Welles famously riffed, 'In Italy for 30 years under the Borgias they had warfare, terror, murder, and bloodshed, but they produced Michelangelo, Leonardo da Vinci, and the Renaissance.' To terror, murder, and bloodshed, Alessandro's story adds slavery and the seeds of racism. That said, I have tried to tell it on its own terms, and to avoid imposing a modern mentality of 'race' that he and his contemporaries did not share.

Alessandro's story is a challenge to the way we think of the Renaissance and Florence. His is an exceptional life, and that is why we know so much about it. It is not always a heroic life. Alessandro de' Medici is not a fine example of princely virtue. He may well have been responsible for murder. But you could say much the same of many contemporaries in European politics. For centuries, Alessandro's story has been distorted and overlooked. There is good reason to rediscover it. It would be no bad thing to hang his portrait a little more prominently on Florence's gallery walls.

BOOK ONE
The Bastard Son

1

It was February 1518, and Lorenzo de' Medici, duke of Urbino and de facto ruler of Florence, had another boil on his leg. It caused him some discomfort, but not enough to prevent his travel to France a few months later for his wedding. Lorenzo, the last legitimate heir in the main line of the Medici family, was to marry Madeleine de la Tour d'Auvergne, an heiress and a distant relative of the French royal family. Within a couple of months, Madeleine was pregnant. She made her entry to Florence on 7 September. 'May God grant long life to the Duke and to her,' wrote Goro Gheri, Lorenzo's secretary, 'and many children.'[1]

By November, Lorenzo's health had begun to waver. He had a little tertian fever, 'a small thing,' his secretary insisted. A month later, though he appeared better, he still could not deal with business. His health deteriorated. In February, seeing no improvement, he rode out to his country villa but the journey did him more harm than good. He was now suffering fever and joint pains, and had trouble with his voice. By April he was struggling to sleep and eat.[2]

The duchess' pregnancy, in contrast, went well. On 13 April, she gave birth to a daughter, Catherine. She had a little fever afterwards, but that was normal, said her ladies. Ten days later, the fever had worsened. On 26 April, the physicians turned to holy oil. They held out little hope. On 28 April 1519, the duchess died. The news did little for the Duke's health. 'Every hour [his condition] seems more serious and more dangerous,' wrote Gheri to Cardinal Giulio de' Medici, Lorenzo's cousin. Not only was the Duke's life now at risk: Gheri feared a rising against the Medici in Florence. He sent for Vitello Vitelli, one of the family's favoured commanders, and a squadron of troops.[3]

On 4 May, Lorenzo died of syphilis. He was twenty-six. The troops were not needed, in the end. The city stayed quiet. But with Madeleine's child a girl, and Lorenzo gone, the Medici had no legitimate male heir. The dynasty's future lay with two small boys: eight-year-old Ippolito, illegitimate son of a noblewoman, and his seven-year-old cousin Alessandro, dark-skinned and said to be the illegitimate son of a slave. As one historian has put it: 'The gods were briefly standing up for bastards.'[4]

In 1519, no one imagined that Alessandro de' Medici would become duke of Florence. That he did so, observed one sixteenth-century historian, was 'indeed a great and singular prodigy of Fortune'.[5] On his childhood before Lorenzo's death, the vast Medici archives are silent. Perhaps somewhere in Rome there is a record of his baptism, but the absence is telling. The son of a slave is a non-person. Only after Lorenzo was gone, when the Medici desperately needed any heirs they could get, did Alessandro come to be one of the family.

He had been born in 1511 or 1512, the son of Lorenzo de' Medici and a woman referred to as either Anna or Simunetta. Lorenzo later became the duke of Urbino, a small, beautiful cultural centre in the Marche, towards the Adriatic coast, but he is most famous as a dedicatee of Niccolò Machiavelli's The Prince. At the time of Alessandro's birth, the Medici family were in exile from their native city of Florence in north-central Italy. They had been expelled in 1494. As a French army had marched down through Italy, their opponents had taken the chance to seize power and had forced Lorenzo's father Piero, nicknamed 'The Unfortunate', into exile. Piero died in 1503, leaving the family reliant for its fortune and social status on his brother, Cardinal Giovanni de' Medici (later Pope Leo X), and his power base in the Church.

A few writers of Alessandro's own time claimed his real father was Giulio de' Medici, Lorenzo's illegitimate cousin and the future Pope Clement VII. Others, more malicious, said that since his mother had slept with not only Lorenzo but Giulio and her own husband, a coachman, too, it was impossible to be certain. But most accepted him as Lorenzo's son.[6] It was also widely agreed that Alessandro's mother was a servant or slave in a Medici household – either Lorenzo's own house or that of his mother, Alfonsina. (It is often hard to distinguish servants from slaves in records of this period: the same words could be used for both.)[7]

Other commentators focused not on her position in the household but on the lowness of her birth. Jacopo Nardi, an opponent of the Medici, and Benedetto Varchi (Cosimo de' Medici's official historian and likewise no friend of Alessandro) referred to her *viltà*, a word best translated as 'baseness' (as in the Shakespearean 'base-born'). As we will see, Varchi describes her as a 'poor peasant woman' of Collevecchio. (The location probably comes from Lorenzino, whom he interviewed.) Another of Varchi's informants said she was a housekeeper. There was a castle belonging to Alfonsina's family, the Orsini, in Collevecchio: perhaps she worked there, or in a family property nearby. It is likely that rather few people knew the full facts. Of those who probably did, Lorenzo and his mother Alfonsina were dead by 1520, while Leo X died the following year. When his enemies taunted Alessandro for his low birth, he joked that he appreciated them telling him where he was born, because he didn't know himself.[8] There may have been some truth in that retort.

Since the 1880s it has been assumed that Alessandro's mother was the woman who wrote the following letter to the 'Magnificent Lord Alessandro' in 1528 or 1529, when he would have been around seventeen years old:

> Magnificent Lord Alessandro, dearest son
>
> Extremity leads me to write to you, and forces me with this visit to beg you and, as far as I can, prevail upon you, that for the love of God you should not abandon me in the necessity in which I now find myself. I have two little children, and I don't have the means to feed them. Even if I make economies, I still can't even relieve their hunger with bread once a month. My own [hunger] means nothing to me. . . . Less than nothing, if I should have to sell such little holdings as I have, so as to sustain myself and not die of hunger. Even if I could sell them, there is no grain to buy. On account of this, my son, were it not for this last

hope remaining to me only in Your Magnificence, I should have nowhere to turn, no recourse. So I beseech you, for such love as you bear for God, not to forget me in such necessity and extremity. The bearer of this letter is my husband, who I recommend to you, as I do myself, and these two poor children.

In Collevecchio on the 12 February 1529
Your dear mother
Simunetta[9]

Taking it at face value, the letter confirms that Simunetta came from Collevecchio – as reported by Lorenzino and Varchi. It confirms that she was married – as Lorenzino wrote in his justification of Alessandro's murder. It confirms what we would expect to hear about food shortages in war-torn Italy. It places her as a small property-holder, with two other children. If she had been a servant or slave in the Medici household, this letter suggests that by the 1520s she had left (or been freed) and granted a settlement. Given what we know about Simunetta, the chances she wrote it herself are slim. Few lower-class women were literate, but she may have found someone to dictate it to. But her letter also raises many questions. Most of Alessandro's papers were known by his first biographer, the eighteenth-century writer Modesto Rastrelli. This letter was not. There have long been doubts about its authenticity, and the only copy has gone missing from the archive, so it cannot be checked.[10]

If Alessandro's mother did work for Alfonsina, there might be some reference to her in household documents. Most of these records do not survive, but Alfonsina's will, made shortly before her death in February 1520, listed a series of women servants who were to receive legacies. To the house-girl went 100 florins, according to Florentine custom. The wet-nurse was to be given a dowry and married off; Madonna Fioraliza, who looked after the little girl (presumably Alessandro's half-sister Catherine), was given 150 gold ducats; to Senoera went fifty gold ducats, so that she could buy land at the 'Castello'.[11] Might this Senoera – whose position in the household is not explained – be Alessandro's mother? The castle mentioned here is probably the Castello Santo Angelo in Tivoli, part of Alfonsina's dowry and a property that Alessandro would eventually claim as his own. A later reference to Alessandro's mother, from 1535, describes her as 'poor, currently living near certain castles of Rome, and she begs, leading a miserable life'.[12] That is certainly compatible with the story of a woman who in 1520 received a legacy allowing her to buy land near the Castello Santo Angelo but subsequently struggled through periods of war and difficult harvests. The absence of any detail about Senoera's role in the household is also intriguing. It would fit with a desire for discretion. Senoera is not a standard Italian name, which, in light of the questions about Alessandro's ethnicity, makes her more interesting still. (It is tempting to read the name as a corruption of the Spanish Señora or Portuguese Senhora.) But this single document is all we have and it is not enough to draw firm conclusions.

Whether servant, slave or poor countrywoman, Simunetta fits the typical pattern of the mother of an illegitimate child. Women from all three categories were easy prey for wealthy men. In a mid fifteenth-century survey of Florence over one-third of the bastard children whose mother was named were children of slaves. Another 20 per cent had a servant mother. Sexual violence against lower-status women was very common in this society, to the point that many probably saw it as 'normal'.[13] Whether or not there was violence in this case (and there was always a continuous threat of violence against runaway slaves) there was an enormous imbalance of power between Simunetta and the man whose child she bore. At any rate, she was far from the first woman to find herself in such a situation. There were precedents for slave mistresses in the Medici family. Cosimo the Elder, Alessandro's great-great-great-grandfather, had a son with an enslaved Circassian woman named Maddalena. (Circassia is a region on the north-east coast of the Black Sea, now part of Russia.) Born around 1428, the child was christened Carlo. He was brought up with Cosimo's legitimate heirs and had a career in the Church. He held important papal offices in Tuscany, and helped pave the way for later Medici sons to become cardinals. Cosimo's son, Giovanni, also had an enslaved Circassian mistress,[14] while Giulio de' Medici – who became Clement VII – was himself illegitimate, son of a woman known as Fioretta from a family of modest means. In cases like these, where paternity was acknowledged, there was presumably enough exclusivity in the arrangement for the master to be relatively sure that the child was his.

Between about 1 and 1½ per cent of the eleven million people in sixteenth- to seventeenth-century Italy were enslaved.[15] As the Circassian cases show, slaves were of varying ethnicities but by the beginning of the sixteenth century slave-trading with these eastern territories was in decline. The Atlantic trade, in contrast, was growing. Unlike the Spanish and Portuguese, Italians were never central to the trade in slaves from West Africa to the Americas, though some Genoese merchants were involved, and Sicily (for its proximity to Spanish trading posts in the Mediterranean) had a high percentage of black African slaves. During the first half of the sixteenth century the ethnic composition of the slave population in Italy was very mixed. Wars in the Mediterranean had increased demand for galley slaves. The majority now came from Ottoman territories: Turkey, the Balkans, the Middle East and North Africa. Most were Muslims but some were Jews. Black Africans were a 'modest percentage' of the total. Enslaving people from Western Christendom, members of the Roman Catholic communion, was forbidden, though some unscrupulous traders tried it. Once enslaved, though, conversion to Christianity did not mean automatic freedom for the person concerned. That said, slavery in Renaissance Italy had a different character to the Atlantic slave trade. It was normal for slaves to be freed after a period of service, or on the death of their master.[16] Simunetta may have been the daughter of a free African.

The Medici family is not associated with the purchase of enslaved Africans to the same extent as some other Renaissance rulers. Still, an African archer is depicted in the mid fifteenth-century fresco of their family chapel in the Palazzo Medici-Riccardi. Piero di Cosimo's painting of *The Liberation of Andromeda*, commissioned in 1513 as an allegory of Duke Lorenzo's return to Florence, shows at least two black Africans, albeit in a fantastic mythological scene. (Andromeda, though shown as white in the painting, was supposed to have been an Ethiopian princess.)[17] Alfonsina Orsini de' Medici came from the Neapolitan branch of the Orsini family, and black Africans formed the majority of the slave population of late fifteenth-century Naples.[18] It is well within the bounds of possibility that Alfonsina's household included enslaved African women.

The second bastard child in the Medici family in 1519, Ippolito de' Medici, was the son of Giuliano, duke of Nemours (the brother of Cardinal Giovanni/Pope Leo), and Pacifica Brandani, a gentlewoman of Urbino. Baptised on 19 April 1511 in Urbino, he was probably born earlier that year. He was older than Alessandro and his mother was of higher social status. Of the two illegitimate Medici offspring, he was the senior.[19]

Shortly after the birth of both boys, the fortunes of the Medici had changed for the better. Exiled from Florence since 1494, they had built their power in Rome and the Church. In 1512 they fought their way back, led by the brothers Cardinal Giovanni de' Medici and Duke Giuliano. Unsure of their forces against the city militia, with the help of Spanish troops they instead attacked the smaller town of Prato, north-west of Florence. Perhaps two thousand people died; there was mass rape; citizens were tortured. It was a terrible and effective piece of psychological warfare. The Florentines panicked and came to terms. The following year, there was more good news for the Medici. Cardinal Giovanni was elected Pope Leo X. Sometime in the autumn of 1513, Ippolito was taken to Rome.[20]

The popes of the early sixteenth century were very different to their modern counterparts. As heads of the Western Church they were – until religious division took hold with the Reformation – considered to be the representative of Christ on earth. European monarchs would seek the pope's approval for seizures of power, for conquests of new territory, for marriage and (less often) divorce. But the popes were also rulers of a large part of Italy, stretching from Rome north to Bologna and across to Ravenna on the Adriatic coast, with all the usual responsibilities of government (and conflicts with neighbouring states) that entailed. Their incomes came from land-owning, from taxes on church office-holders, from the sale of church offices (controversially), and from more surprising sources such as a monopoly on alum, a chemical compound vital to the textile industry. It was sometimes hard to distinguish them from any other European monarch. Pope Leo X, for example, took every opportunity to celebrate his family. In September 1513, he honoured his brother Giuliano, duke of Nemours, and nephew Lorenzo, duke of Urbino, with the citizenship of Rome. He had a temporary theatre seating over a thousand constructed on the Capitoline Hill, and held a twenty-course banquet for the assembled dignitaries. They watched a performance of Plautus' comedy, *Poenulus* or *The Puny Punic*, a moderately racy tale of a young man in love with a prostitute who has to rescue her from her pimp. It was performed in Latin but had sufficient slapstick to keep the less scholarly entertained. Giuliano, meanwhile, used his relationship with the Pope to bolster Ippolito's prospects: he hoped to secure a rich property in papal territory near the northern Italian city of Parma for the three-year-old.[21]

Giuliano was now the chief representative of the Medici in Florence, responsible for maintaining their party's grip on government, and his life looked promising indeed. In February 1515 he married the duke of Savoy's daughter Filiberta, the first of his family to enjoy such an international aristocratic match. Later that year, on 30 November, Leo X made a spectacular ceremonial entrance to Florence. His *entrata* was an opportunity to celebrate his family's power in the city. Seven great triumphal arches, each depicting one of the Virtues, and an eighth showing all seven Virtues together, were set up along his route. Prudence, constancy, honesty, sobriety, chastity, modesty and abstinence were not, perhaps, qualities associated with the reality of Leo's rule – his was a fleshy, worldly papacy – but they were certainly part of his rhetoric.[22] The crowds greeting Leo are portrayed in a fresco in the Palazzo Vecchio, Florence (then known as the Palazzo della Signoria). In Vasari's image a group of women, kneeling with their children, beg absolution from the pope for their sins. One of them, an indistinct figure, holds the hand of a small, dark-skinned child. Vasari gives no name to this figure, but it is easy for a viewer to imagine it is the future Duke Alessandro, still outside the family, his mother seeking to atone for having borne an illegitimate son.

A year later, aged just thirty-seven, and without a legitimate heir, Giuliano died. Lorenzo de' Medici had been made duke of Urbino in 1516 in a manoeuvre that saw Pope Leo X oust a nephew of his predecessor, Pope Julius II, from the tiny state in favour of one of his own. Now, as the sole heir to the family fortune and with his mother Alfonsina in tow, Lorenzo took over the Florentine government.[23] That left Ippolito as the second-ranking layman in the family. His prospects continued to improve. In 1517 he was created archbishop of the rich diocese of Avignon, with a dispensation for his tender age. It was usually expected that a bishop should be thirty.[24] The acquisition of church benefices – bishoprics, legateships, abbacies and the like – was a route to a substantial income. At another point Pope Leo planned for a marriage between Ippolito and a daughter of the Colonna family, Roman barons allied to Spain. He obtained a lordship in the realm of Naples – a part of Italy then under Spanish control – for Ippolito, giving his nephew an income of 6,300 ducats a year. (That was, in fact, a bribe from the king of Spain, Charles, to ensure Leo's support for his efforts to be elected Holy Roman Emperor.)[25]

Whether Alessandro grew up alongside his cousin Ippolito is not clear, but it was not unusual for rich parents to find a slave or servant child to act as their own child's companion, so it is possible that he did. The Strozzi family of Florence discussed buying a slave girl or Moorish boy to be a friend for their own toddler son. The Medici, like other noble parents of this period, took a great deal of interest in the proper rearing of their children. Like little Catherine de' Medici, Lorenzo's daughter, very young children would have had a wet-nurse. Country girls were preferred. Once a little older, they were placed in the care of tutors and nursemaids. Some religious training of children was entrusted to women, but for the most part education was the responsibility of fathers. Education was preparation for the masculine sphere of political life. In the case of orphans, it fell to uncles or in-laws to make decisions on schooling. Study began early. Even two-year-olds might be taught their alphabet. One family memoir records how parents would carve letters out of fruit: if a child guessed correctly, he could eat the fruit as a reward. From the age of five, boys would have a tutor, charged with beginning their formal education. Yet while three-year-old 'Ippolitino' – little Ippolito – was numbered among the guests at a 1514 wedding in Rome, his status as Giuliano's son acknow-ledged in the list, Alessandro was not. If he was living in the household at the time, it was not as a child of nobility.[26]

Unlike Giuliano, Lorenzo does not seem to have taken much of an interest in his son. Lorenzo acknowledged Ippolito. He even gave him a horse with a black velvet saddle and cover in 1517. In contrast, the records say nothing to indicate a relationship with his own son, Alessandro. A 1518 letter from his secretary noted that 'His Holiness has another nephew, that is, Ippolitino.' It made no reference to Alessandro, whose absence from the records in these years is striking. Later observers noted Alessandro's 'lack of learning' (whereas Ippolito was widely praised on this account). That story would fit with a late start to his education.[27] At the beginning of 1519, Alessandro de' Medici was still nowhere near the rank of duke. Probably he was not even acknowledged by his father.

Lorenzo was now the principal Medici representative in Florence, though he was not the most popular of leaders. He teetered too close to ruling like an absolute lord. Criticism was greeted with draconian punishment. In one incident, a local who described him not as 'Lorenzo the Magnificent' but as 'Lorenzo the Shit' was sentenced to exile for eight years. Heavy taxes and a lack of consultation with other leading families caused tension. His decision to leave his Neapolitan mother Alfonsina in charge of the city while he went off on campaign prompted great disquiet. The Florentines disapproved of a woman, and worse a foreigner, taking charge of city business.[28]

(That hostility towards female rule also explains why Catherine de' Medici was not a potential ruler for Florence. Though she would become one of the most powerful women of her age as queen and queen mother of France, in Florence women were almost entirely excluded from public life. Even by the standards of the time this was a notably male-dominated society.)[29]

When Lorenzo, duke of Urbino, died in May 1519, Leo and his ministers moved fast. On the very day of the Duke's death, they legitimised Ippolito de' Medici. He was now the main hope for securing the dynasty.[30]

It is possible that Alessandro was legitimised at the same time, but there is no firm evidence for the date of this process, and it may have happened somewhat later; his name does, however, appear in a late seventeenth-century record of legitimised Florentine bastards, now in the city's state archive. His mother's social status mattered here. In fifteenth-century Florence children of slaves were less likely to be legitimised than those of higher-ranking mothers. While legitimisation allowed a child to inherit, it could not remove the 'stain' of dishonour that came from conception outside marriage. Nor could it change what one historian has called 'the quality of blood that flowed in the child's veins'. In Venice the children of servants and slaves were excluded from entering the nobility.[31] Indeed, a Venetian ambassador, writing from Rome about the death of Duke Lorenzo, did not even seem to know of Alessandro's existence. 'There's not a single legitimate son left in the house of Medici, say the Pope's men,' he wrote, 'except a natural son of the late Magnifico Giuliano.' That was Ippolito.[32]

The ambassador's apparent ignorance of Lorenzo's bastard confirms that Alessandro's profile had been low. Diplomats were expected to know such details. But Alessandro was rapidly discovered. A few days earlier, a better-informed private correspondent to Venice had written that 'there are two little bastards, one of this Duke Lorenzo and one of the Magnifico Giuliano.' And by the end of the month the ambassadors had more information on Leo's plans: 'the Pope will raise up, it's said, a natural son of Giuliano, and will put Lorenzo's son into the Church.'[33] As with Carlo de' Medici the century before, a clerical role was a likely option for the illegitimate son of a serving-woman. No direct comment from Alessandro on his illegitimacy survives, but a later story about his life, written for his own bastard daughter, hints at how he may have felt. As duke of Florence, hearing the case of a man who claimed an illegitimate nephew could not inherit, Alessandro asked: 'For all that he's a bastard, is he not made of flesh, and born of man and woman, like you? . . . And for all that he's a bastard, does he not have soul and body like all those legitimately born?'[34]

Leo also looked to political solutions for the problems that now faced the Medici. In the early sixteenth century, the Italian peninsula was divided into numerous different states. There were five large ones: the Papal States, Naples, Florence, Venice and Milan. There were many smaller polities: for example Siena, Lucca, Urbino, Mantua and Ferrara. Some of the Italian states were ruled by a prince – in the terminology of the period the word 'prince' was applied to a range of aristocratic title-holders including dukes, marquises and lords. Other states, including Florence, Venice and Genoa, had an elected head of government, though generally on a very limited franchise of elite citizens. Florence, therefore, was formally a republic, though the Medici had become more and more princely in their style of government. Leo now commissioned Niccolò Machiavelli to write a report on the best options for Medici rule of Florence.

Machiavelli's relationship with the Medici was difficult. He had held office in Florence during their exile and had been removed from his positions when the Medici returned in 1512. His rehabilitation had been slow. Now, for Leo, he explained that the Medici needed to choose between a republic (his preference) and a principality. Either would be more stable than a hybrid solution. He proposed that the Medici and their allies in Florence institute a radical reform of the city's political institutions, in which power would be shared between the aristocracy, the middle ranks and the people, but ensured that the Medici would be able to control appointments.[35]

However, the political complexities facing them extended well beyond Florence itself. Since 1494 the larger European powers had been fighting sporadic wars on the peninsula in alliance with various Italian states. This was essentially a struggle for power between the kings of France and the Holy Roman Emperor (ruler of various German states, not yet united into a single country, Austria, the Netherlands and after an accident of inheritance Spain too). In this context of conflict, states could be lost as easily as won. Even before the deaths of Lorenzo and Madeleine, the Medici had struggled to hold the duchy of Urbino. A year before, the city had been attacked by its former rulers, the della Rovere relatives of Pope Julius II. With Lorenzo gone, the ousted Duke Francesco Maria della Rovere saw his chance. His troops advanced; Lorenzo's infant daughter and bastard son were hardly serious rivals. The Medici had lost Urbino. Would they lose Florence too?

With Giuliano and Lorenzo dead, and with no heir of sufficient age to govern, responsibility for the city now fell to Leo's cousin, Cardinal Giulio de' Medici. He was its third ruler in seven years.

Adopted into the family as a last resort, to 'reinforce a family line that was disappearing', as Paolo Giovio (a well-established adviser to Pope Leo) put it, there were now significant changes in Alessandro's life. For a start, he was afforded a 'refined education' in the household of his grandmother Alfonsina in Rome.[36] Here, as the 'spare' to the heir, Ippolito, Alessandro de' Medici had ample time to observe and absorb the spectacle of the splendid, decadent world of the Leonine court.

2

The court of Leo X was one of glitter, colour, glamour and spectacle. Leo went hunting most days. He kept a menagerie in the grounds of the Vatican. Foreign envoys competed to provide him with the next, most exotic gift. He had an elephant, Hanno, a gift from the king of Portugal; the king tried to send him a rhinoceros, but it drowned en route. Perhaps its story made an impression on the young Alessandro. Later he made the rhinoceros his emblem. Behind the scenes, Leo had a household staff of almost seven hundred people, not including the artists and poets, or the military officials (though an astrologer and a jester were accounted for). Many of Leo's cardinals openly favoured mistresses. Cardinal Dovizi da Bibbiena, one of his closest lieutenants, commissioned Raphael to design erotic frescoes for his Vatican bathroom. Attitudes towards papal and indeed clerical celibacy were relaxed. The point of the celibacy rule was that priests' children should not inherit – and that the Church could thereby keep control of its property. But if Leo's court looked brilliant to his admirers, to his critics it was worldly and licentious. Amid deepening wars on the Italian peninsula and calls for reform further north, Leo's government was little short of irresponsible.[1]

Like many wealthy families, the Medici had decided that dispatching a second son into the Church would be a useful means of advancement. The best bishoprics brought with them substantial landholdings and rich incomes through taxation and rents. Senior Church positions also brought political clout. Leo's election in 1513 had been the culmination of long efforts by the Medici to expand their influence in Rome. He continued the efforts of his predecessors to assert the personal power of the pope in the Church against those clerics who advocated a less authoritarian system. Yet power and money also drove conspiracy. In the summer of 1517 it had been announced that a plan to assassinate

Leo had been uncovered. No fewer than five cardinals were implicated, chief among them the Sienese Cardinal Petrucci, accused with two henchmen of scheming to poison Leo. Arrested along with Petrucci were cardinals Riario, Sauli, Castellesi and Soderini. The evidence for the plot was shaky at best. Careless conversation could be proven, but little more. Some supposed that Leo had framed his enemies: the plot was suspiciously convenient for the Pope.[2]

In the autumn of 1517, prompted by nervousness at Giuliano's death the previous year, concern to secure the Medici succession and fear (perhaps justified) of further conspiracy, Leo had diluted the power of the old guard in the College of Cardinals, promoting a staggering thirty-one new men. Among them were nephews and relatives by marriage: Giovanni Salviati, son of his sister Lucrezia; Niccolò Ridolfi, son of his sister Contessina; Luigi de' Rossi, a cousin. Leo's approach in the College of Cardinals mirrored his family's long-time practice in Florence of governing with a party of allies, their relationships consolidated by intermarriage. But the promotions made Leo enemies among the cardinals who remained. Before, they had shared Church income among barely half that number. Now, the best benefices had to be divided between many more people. And Leo decided who got what.

That said, while nepotism aroused the ire of both jealous rivals and Church reformers, not everyone in the sixteenth century saw it so negatively. Within limits, the desire to do well for one's family was praiseworthy. Leo was hardly the first pope to promote his relatives. In the past sixty years, Pius II had enriched his Sienese clan, the Piccolomini; Alexander VI had done the same for the Borgias; Sixtus IV and Julius II for the della Rovere family. Cesare Borgia, the son of a pope, had featured at length in *The Prince*, Machiavelli's famous, though often ironic, guide to taking and holding power. Cesare had died too young to hold his state in the Romagna, and Machiavelli hinted that his was not an example to follow, but plenty of papal nephews would try. From early in Leo's reign drafts and extracts of *The Prince* were being exchanged in select circles, although it would not be published until 1532, after its author's death.[3]

It was the measure of Leo's papacy that he focused his efforts on favouring friends and tackling enemies in Rome: his priorities were family, legacy and power on the Italian peninsula. But further north in Europe his policies were about to provoke a revolutionary reaction. The Church had long supplemented its finances by selling 'indulgences'. In return for a donation to the Church, purchasers could redeem some sins and spend less time in Purgatory before ascending to Heaven. Cardinal Albrecht von Brandenburg, appointed in 1514, had borrowed heavily from German bankers to pay his 'annates', the year's income that was the effective price of a cardinal's hat, and to make a large donation to the restoration of St Peter's Basilica. Leo authorised the sale of indulgences to pay off the Cardinal's debts. But when one of the Cardinal's salesmen went too far, he found himself in confrontation with a man about to become the most famous theologian in Europe: Martin Luther. From 1517, when Luther's challenge to church doctrine became public, Leo became the target of Protestant propaganda, contrasting his lavish lifestyle with the poverty of Christ. His decadent doings were written up in lurid terms and illustrated in cutting detail by reformers who had decided that the Pope was the Devil on earth.

Leo was slow to grasp the political dimensions of the threat. Indeed, many of those who saw Leo's court would have considered his magnificence to be a virtue. It was quite proper for rulers to display their wealth through costly building projects, art commissions and the like. Pennypinching was not commendable in a prince. The social hierarchy depended on the rich being seen to be rich, and being seen to be generous, with gifts to charity, public festivals and entertainments, endowments for churches and hospitals. Leo's lavish rule continued unabated. The Roman satirists were generally vicious about the Florentines, of which Pope Leo was one. This poem, written after his death, sums it up:

> Contrarians, rebels,
> Sodomites, tyrants,
> Sad little people,
> Usurers, enemies of Christ in Heaven.
>
> When did we ever see
> The seat of Peter so despoiled
> If not when Florence got its hands on the Church.[4]

★

It was entirely in keeping with Leo's regime, therefore, that Alfonsina Orsini de' Medici, his sister-in-law, presided over a magnificent household in Rome, and it was here that Alessandro now found himself. The Medici residence was the grand house now known as Palazzo Madama. Leo's three sisters, Lucrezia, Maddalena and Contessina, stayed there during visits. Alfonsina was a wealthy woman, whose property holdings ranged from this Roman palace to dairy farms in Tuscany.[5] Her daughter Clarice was married to Filippo Strozzi, a banker and close ally of the Medici; they had a son, Piero, who was of an age with Alessandro and Ippolito. Here Alessandro spent the formative years of his childhood.

Renaissance boys were expected to acquire an impressive standard of education, encompassing good manners and sporting prowess as well as academic knowledge. Leo himself had been tutored by the celebrated poet Angelo Poliziano. But, as Baldassarre Castiglione wrote in his advice for the courtier, 'good masters not only teach children their letters but also polite manners and correct bearing in eating, drinking, speaking and walking.' To that could be added hunting, hawking and the other sporting pursuits befitting a young prince. The education of the young Medici boys was entrusted to Pierio Valeriano, one of the star scholars of Leo's court.[6] Here in Rome, Alessandro could watch Leo's conduct of politics, and learn from that too.

On 1 December 1521, Pope Leo X died. In the conclave that followed, Leo's cousin Giulio de' Medici, he who had inherited the late Lorenzo's mantle in Florence, had significant support, but the cardinals were reluctant to follow one Medici pope with another. To avoid the election of a serious rival, Giulio and his fellow cardinal Alessandro Farnese (scion of an old Roman family who owed his promotion to his sister's affair with Pope Alexander VI) manoeuvred an outsider into place. Their dealings were reported to include plans for a marriage between Ippolito and one of Farnese's bastard daughters.[7] Their compromise candidate was a 62-year-old Dutch cardinal, Adriaan Florenszoon Boeyens, head of the Spanish Inquisition and former tutor of the Emperor Charles V. (Charles, king of Spain, had won his election to become Holy Roman Emperor and now ruled the States of Germany and the Netherlands too.) Adriaan was not even present at the conclave. On 9 January 1522, after much wrangling, he was elected. He finally arrived for his coronation in August that year. His serious and impartial approach to papal government sat uneasily with the men who had elected him. His asceticism did not suit the courtiers accustomed to Leo's more worldly style.

Giulio de' Medici still held the important vice-chancellorship of the Church, making him the leading administrator of the Papal States. But his family no longer wielded the same power in Rome, and Giulio now had to operate a little differently. He made a settlement with the rival della Rovere claimants to the duchy of Urbino, effectively acknowledging that the Medici were in no position to revive their claim on the city. He worked to cultivate the support of Charles V, who had already promised him a pension of 10,000 ducats a year from the archbishopric of Toledo. He commissioned another report on the government of Florence, this time from Francesco de' Pazzi. Pazzi took a very different line from Machiavelli, arguing that the Medici could best win support by satisfying the material self-interests of the citizens.[8]

By 1522, although his family's powers were somewhat diminished, Alessandro's personal stock was rising. Having been acknowledged as one of the Medici, he needed the accoutrements of rank, and that year Charles granted him the duchy of Penne, a fief in the realm of Naples, along with the town of Campli, a little way to the north. Penne lies in the eastern foothills of the Apennines, not far from the coastal city of Pescara. This tiny medieval hill town of around seven hundred hearths had been inhabited since long before the Romans and was well fortified. Though Penne was not nearly as grand as Urbino, its grant compensated the Medici a little for the loss of that duchy. Moreover, the towns provided Alessandro with a substantial income: at least 3,000 ducats a year. Most importantly for Alessandro, though, the grant of a duchy 'gave him more reputation'. Dukes, even of minor Imperial fiefs, outranked every other sort of nobleman. Before, he had been a mere 'natural nephew' in the Medici family. Now, Alessandro was styled 'Illustrious Duke of the City of Penne', and as the only duke in the Medici family he was often referred to simply by that title.[9]

Nor were the Medici out of power for long. To the relief of the more worldly cardinals, Adrian was a short-lived pope. He survived barely a year, dying on 14 September 1523. The cardinals quickly reverted to a devil they knew. Cardinal Giulio de' Medici was elected pope. He took the name Clement VII. In control of the Church once again, the Medici were able to contemplate greater projects than ever before. The Pope's nieces and nephews became pawns for dynastic alliances. Early in 1524 they were on show at the papal court. Alessandro was by now twelve or so, his cousin Ippolito a little older, his sister Catherine not quite five. It was Carnival and an observer described the spectacle:

> Plenty of masquerades here. Yesterday there was horse-racing. The Cardinal of Lorraine had a livery made up, with outfits of velvet and gold, and there were four of them, viz. the little nephews and niece of the Pope and their master, all very gallant, and they were praised. The aforesaid cardinal of Lorraine paid for the lot: he spends plenty and quickly throws his money away; he's rich, he can do it. There was another show, of Noah's ark, in which there was some music and they sang about the passing of the flood and they threw birds out of the ark, quite a nice invention from Cardinal Cesarino, but rather cheap.[10]

Giulio's election as pope left a vacancy – again – for the rulership of Florence. Since Lorenzo's death, Giulio had done his best to oversee the city's government, but that was no longer possible. In December 1523 it had been reported that Ippolito might be appointed bishop of Florence, but the benefice went instead to Cardinal Niccolò Ridolfi, a cousin. In April 1524 Silvio Passerini, cardinal of Cortona and another Medici ally, joined Ridolfi in Florence. Later that summer Ippolito, now about thirteen years old, went too. Like Alessandro's appointment to Penne, this was a means of 'giving him reputation'.[11] It put him in line to take on the role of chief family representative and de facto lord of Florence that his father had enjoyed before him.

On 30 August Ippolito arrived in the city on a bay jennet, a small Spanish saddle horse. He was clad in black. His entourage of ten grooms wore red silk and white leather corselets. That this could be described by Varchi as 'without any ceremony' indicates just how extravagant normal life could be. Ahead of their procession rode a ten-year-old black page, on a dappled jennet.[12] Black pages were rather fashionable among the nobility of Renaissance Italy. Although, as we have seen, Europeans did not yet have a fully worked out theory of race, they stereotyped and objectified black Africans in various ways. These children, for example, were treated as exotic objects, through whom a master (or owner) could demonstrate good taste and refinement. Titian had painted Laura Dianti, mistress of the duke of Ferrara, with a black page the year before. Isabella d'Este, marchioness of Mantua, sought to purchase black child slaves, on one occasion sending instructions to her agent to find a girl who was 'as black as possible', most likely in order to provide an aesthetic contrast to the Marchioness' fashionably fair skin.[13]

Ippolito took up residence in the Medici palace in Florence, the long-standing family home commissioned from Michelozzo in the 1450s, located between the Duomo and the Dominican convent of San Marco. Within a year there were rumours that he might be created cardinal. Clement, however, had much grander schemes for his nephew. Charles V, Holy Roman Emperor, had an illegitimate daughter, Margaret. In December 1525, a Venetian ambassador, reporting directly on a conversation with the Pope, wrote: 'As for the alliance that it's said His Holiness will make with the Emperor, viz. to give a natural daughter of the Emperor to Signor Ippolito de' Medici, he says it's not an idle rumour, but he wants to sort out public affairs before private ones.' Margaret was, in any case, only three years old, so marriage was necessarily a long-term plan.[14] For the moment, Ippolito had to establish himself in the political circles of Florence.

On 19 June 1525, Alessandro and his six-year-old half-sister Catherine were sent to join him. Although it was not yet clear whether either of them would take any substantial role in the city government, they needed to become accustomed to Florentine affairs and manners. Their father Lorenzo's regime had suffered as a result of his lack of familiarity with the city's customs; Lorenzo's secretary had emphasised the importance of sending Ippolito to Florence 'as a citizen' (that is, not in too lordly a fashion).[15] Alessandro, however, did not join Ippolito in town. He lived about twelve miles outside the city, at the Medici villa in Poggio a Caiano that had been his father's last retreat. It was a suitably discreet home for a young man of secondary status in the family. Throughout Alessandro's life, Poggio, with its rich hunting grounds, would be his favoured residence. Also in Florence in 1525 was the eleven-year-old Lorenzino de' Medici, scion of a separate, junior branch of the family; the following year he was placed into the care of Cardinal Passerini, along with his cousins.[16]

The illegitimacy of the Medici nephews occasionally prompted comment, not least because Clement VII had been illegitimate too, his parents' secret marriage conveniently discovered long after the supposed event. Michelangelo – no admirer of the Medici – joked that the family holdings should be turned into a Piazza dei Muli, a piazza for mules, playing on the word's use as slang for 'bastard'.[17]

At any rate, despite their differences in rank, to some observers Alessandro and Ippolito were close enough to seem like brothers.[18] A few letters from these teenage years survive. Alessandro wrote from Poggio asking to be recommended to 'the Magnificent Lord' – Ippolito had borrowed the soubriquet used by his father and by Lorenzo the Magnificent before him. He corresponded about silverware, and he began collecting guns. Small matchlock firearms, a relatively new technology, had come into their own in the Italian Wars, proving decisive for the Spanish in more than one battle.[19] Perhaps the young Alessandro had his eye on a military career. That was a likely ambition for an illegitimate son in Renaissance Italy. In terms of government, Alessandro had little to do, as his affairs in his duchy of Penne had been placed in the hands of an experienced governor, Roberto Boschetti.[20]

Alessandro's guardian at Poggio was Giovanni di Bardo Corsi, formerly a member of Giuliano de' Medici's circle. A politician, diplomat and man of letters, Corsi was well-placed to guide the education of the Pope's nephew. In the city, Silvio Passerini, cardinal of Cortona, was Ippolito's political guide, a bad choice, some thought, for his grasp of Florentine politics was poor. Ottaviano de' Medici, member of a junior branch of the family and husband of Leo's niece Francesca Salviati, took responsibility for the households of both nephews.[21]

Alessandro was joined in the schoolroom by Giorgio Vasari. The future author of the *Lives of the Artists* was of an age with the young Duke, and spent two hours a day with him and Ippolito. Pierio Valeriano, their tutor, boasted that under his guidance Ippolito acquired 'perfect' knowledge of Latin and Greek. Jacopo da Pontormo, an up-and-coming artist who had already worked on the decoration of the Poggio villa, painted them on Ottaviano's commission. He showed Ippolito with his favourite dog, Rodon. The dog, said Vasari, was done 'so well and naturally, that he seemed alive'.[22]

Rumours about Clement's plans for his nephews and niece continued to circulate. In May 1526 there was speculation that Ippolito and Catherine might marry as a means of preserving her inheritance for the family. Alessandro was slated to become a cardinal.[23]

Ippolito, now about sixteen, was beginning to take a role in political life. In early 1527 he was to be found greeting a visiting Venetian ambassador and attending meetings of the *Otto di Pratica*, the eight-strong city magistracy that dealt with external and military affairs. When the Viceroy of Naples visited in April of that year, Ippolito led the welcome party.[24] It must have been a tense visit. Florence and Naples were at war. The victories of Charles V against the French had left Clement wary of growing Imperial power on the Italian peninsula. He had established the League of Cognac – an alliance of France, the Papacy, Florence, Venice, England and Milan – to challenge Charles.

There were challenges too within his home city. Since their return in 1512, the Medici had run through four different figureheads: Dukes Giuliano and Lorenzo, Cardinal Giulio and now Ippolito. Over the years, their regime had crept closer to lordship, and that had compounded many small resentments. Now that Ippolito was sixteen, the prospect that he might personally come to dominate government like his precedessors in the family grew closer. Within days of the Viceroy's visit, rebellion broke out.

3

Florence was a city of merchants. 'They most excel in trade,' Pope Pius II had written, 'which philosophers think sordid.' (Pius was from the rival city of Siena, and some hostility was only to be expected.) The wealth of the Medici family was based on the wool trade but most importantly on banking. By the beginning of the fifteenth century they were one of the leading families in Florentine government. In 1421 Giovanni di Bicci de' Medici became *gonfaloniere* – literally, the standard-bearer of the republic, one of the most prestigious offices in the city. He was also a banker to the popes in Rome, and his bank has been called 'the most successful commercial enterprise in Italy'.[1] It was the basis for his son Cosimo the Elder's rise to power.

These fifteenth-century Medici did not rule Florence by dynastic right, but exercised considerable authority as the city's leading oligarchs. In fact, Florence excluded its old noble families, the *grandi*, from government (some even changed their names in order to gain access to power). Instead, the city was controlled by a series of elected committees. Any member of the city's twenty-one guilds who was aged thirty or over was eligible to hold office. Office-holders typically served for very short terms, a couple of months at a time. As well as the nobility, this system of election excluded ordinary people such as day-labourers, who were not eligible for guild membership. Three-quarters of the population had no political rights at all. A handful of families, linked through ties of friendship and marriage, could effectively manipulate the elections. In political or military emergencies, and increasingly under the Medici's sixty-year 'rule', a system of pre-selection of candidates allowed them further control. And with access to city offices came access to power, influence and wealth.

Officially, then, Florence was a republic – and the Medici made good use of the rhetoric of republicanism. But as Pius II put it, Cosimo the Elder was 'king in everything but name,' although (in a backhanded dig at Florentine commerce) 'more cultured than merchants usually are'.[2]

Because the power of the Medici in Florence hovered on the boundary between oligarchy and tyranny, there had been many attempts by their competitors to move against them. The great rivals of the Medici in Florence were the Albizzi family. Their conflict came to a head when in 1433 the Albizzi contrived to have Cosimo arrested. They called a parliament, excluding Medici supporters. But influential customers of the Medici bank – the Republic of Venice, the marquis of Ferrara – came to Cosimo's aid. The Albizzi had hoped for his execution but had to settle instead for his banishment to Padua. The following year, as Florence faltered in a war with Milan, Cosimo's supporters won the city elections. The Medici were back.

Cosimo was succeeded by his son, Piero 'the Gouty'. Piero survived an attempted coup but died in 1469, leaving his twenty-year-old son Lorenzo as head of the family. This Lorenzo – 'the Magnificent' – was the target of the most infamous attack on the Medici, the Pazzi conspiracy of 1478, when assassins succeeded in killing his brother Giuliano. Thanks to Lorenzo's brilliant personal diplomacy, however, the Medici held on to power. In March 1480 Lorenzo returned to Florence, his regime secure. 'If Florence was to have a tyrant,' observed Francesco Guicciardini, 'she could never have found a better or more delightful one.'[3]

The Medici had always ruled a 'rhetorical republic'. Their opponents had constantly accused them of exceeding their power. Back and forth went the power play, the accusations. Lorenzo helped himself to money held in trust for his cousins, the cadet branch of the family, descendants of Cosimo the Elder's brother (another Lorenzo). He took money from the public treasury too. (It was an allegation that would later be repeated against Pope Clement VII, following his spell as the chief Medici representative in Florence: in November 1527 he was deemed to owe the city 212,658 florins.)[4] Lorenzo was a great patron of art – the man who patronised Botticelli and the young Michelangelo – but his grip on the family bank was far less secure than his ancestor's. When King Edward IV of England failed to repay loans owed to the Medici bank, its London branch collapsed. Branches in Milan and Bruges followed: those in Lyons, Rome and Naples were in trouble too. As the bank faltered, the Medici became ever more reliant on the state of Florence for their wealth and position.

Lorenzo died in 1492 and his son Piero proved a weaker ruler. He quarrelled with the cadet branch of the family. In 1494, when French troops marched down through Italy, his rivals in the cadet branch backed the French. Piero surrendered. The city authorities had had enough. The priors slammed the gates of Florence in Piero's face, tolled the great bell, called a parliament and threw the Medici out.

For a while, Girolamo Savonarola, a Dominican monk, ruled a virtual theocratic state. Offending books were burnt, and art, but his populist regime did not last. He was excommunicated and burnt at the stake in 1498. Florence returned to a more conventional republican government, but the Medici stayed in exile. Piero de' Medici died in 1503 while serving with the French army. His successor as head of the family was Cardinal Giovanni de' Medici, the future Pope Leo X. For the next three decades, the fortunes of the Medici would be tied to papal politics. It was thanks to the Cardinal that in 1512 the Medici made their way back to power in Florence. But it should have come as no surprise that their enemies would try to move against them again.

On 26 April 1525, Ippolito de' Medici was out of town at the family villa in Castello. A couple of miles to the north of the city, this elegant country residence with its imposing white front and red-tiled roof belonged to the junior branch of the Medici. Along with three cardinals – Passerini, Ridolfi and Innocenzo Cibo – Ippolito had gone to dine with the duke of Urbino, Francesco Maria della Rovere. Two armies were encamped nearby. The Duke led the army of the League of Cognac but his old rivalry with the Medici over Urbino made him an uneasy ally. His troops faced those of the Holy Roman Empire. A rumour spread in Florence that Ippolito and the Medici had fled the city, fearful of the Emperor's army, fearful that the city would rebel.

Giovanni Agnello, an eyewitness to events, explained what happened next. Having dined, he had joined the cardinals and some Florentine gentlemen on their way back to Florence. 'A stone's throw away from the city, we heard news that the whole place was up in arms, and that the citizens had seized the main square.' Sceptical of the rumours, they went on to the Medici palace. It was 'full of armed men'. As they tried to find out what was happening, Cardinal Cibo's brother Lorenzo and Federico Gonzaga da Bozzolo, one of the mercenary commanders, tried to get closer to the city centre. They were detained and taken prisoner in the Palazzo della Signoria, Florence's seat of government.[5]

The whole city, wrote Marco Foscari, a Venetian ambassador, 'seemed to have turned upside down'. With a band of infantry, the duke of Urbino led the way to the Palazzo, securing the streets against the insurgents as he went. The rebels – mainly disgruntled young men from local families – had not had much time to raise support. The people had barred their doors and stayed inside. The rebels retreated to the Palazzo, sniping from the windows with their arquebuses. They killed seven or eight men, and injured many more, including one of Cardinal Cibo's entourage, Luciano Pallavicino. Michelangelo's statue of David, which stood in the piazza, nearly lost an arm.[6]

Supporters of the Medici brought three pieces of artillery into the piazza 'to clear out the palace and cut everyone inside to pieces'. The Duke, Francesco Maria della Rovere, persuaded them not to fire, though, and instead talked the rebels out. Realising they lacked support, they freed Federico Gonzaga. The Duke secured written agreement from the city authorities that the rebels would not be penalised either personally or by confiscation of property, and they quickly cleared out of the palace. Francesco Guicciardini, a key Medici ally, took a hand in settling things.[7] But, as Agnello explained, the whole affair boded badly for the Medici:

> The real basis for all this, as far as I've been able to gather, is that many gentlemen from the most noble houses of the city, among them the Strozzi, the Salviati, the Martelli, unhappy with the government of their fatherland, feeling that they were being tyrannised and mistreated, took the opportunity of the absence of the three cardinals and Ippolito. Thinking that they could exclude them and take over the city government, they took up arms and began to

shout 'Liberty, liberty, people, people,' to which cry around
two hundred armed men quickly gathered, and these were
the ones who took over the palazzo. And if the lord duke
[of Urbino] hadn't got there so quickly, and made the good
provisions I've described, or if they had begun an hour
earlier, they could have achieved their plan, because the
people had begun to take up arms and go in their favour,
and they would have had the backing of the greater part
of the territory.[8]

In fact, rumour had it that an uprising had been planned for
the following day, only to be scuppered by the spontaneous action
of the 26th.[9] Foscari was more sceptical than Agnello about the
extent of popular support for the rebels; the source of their grievance,
he said, was frustration at not being permitted to carry arms in the
city (a privilege important to wealthy youths but not the most obvious
issue to rouse the people more widely). But Foscari also knew that a
city rebellion would have been especially dangerous if the Emperor's
forces had been encamped nearby. 'It was a good thing that the enemy
[troops] were far away; because, if they'd been near, things would
have gone badly.'[10]

The Medici could take heart, however, because Agnello's report in
fact exaggerated the number of their allies involved. Most had stayed
loyal, including the main branches of the Strozzi and Salviati, traditional allies with whom they were intermarried: Clarice de' Medici to
Filippo Strozzi; Lucrezia de' Medici to Jacopo Salviati; their daughter
Francesca to Ottaviano de' Medici.[11] The Medici had always ruled with
a coalition of families behind them. The loss of their support would
be damaging indeed, but for now it was only rumour. Back in the
Palazzo Medici, surrounded by armed guards, Ippolito and Passerini
waited to see what might happen now.[12]

On 6 May 1527, Giovanni Guiducci, an agent of Cardinal Innocenzo
Cibo, arrived in Florence. He dropped in on Cibo's fellow cardinals
Passerini and Ridolfi, advisers to the young Ippolito, hoping for news.
He found Passerini in bed, with some eye trouble and a fever. Ridolfi
was reading in the study, with its blue-and-white-tiled ceiling that
depicted the twelve months. Good-natured, quiet and virtuous, the

Cardinal loved his Latin and Greek, and was much favoured on a personal level by Pope Clement, if rather less as a political adviser. As far as the pair knew, from a letter of 1 May, Clement was in good spirits. But by the time Guiducci came to pen his report to Cibo (who had presumably left town), the political situation had taken a dramatic turn. Mutinous Spanish soldiers had sacked Rome. The Pope was besieged in his own castle. The news reached Florence on 11 May.[13] Opponents of the Medici saw another chance. They even found support within the Medici family.

There was no love lost between Clarice de' Medici Strozzi, sister of the late Duke Lorenzo, and her cousin Pope Clement. Clarice resented Clement's promotion of his bastard nephews over her legitimate children, and she resented his failure to make her son Piero a cardinal. Worse, Clement had abused her husband Filippo's goodwill. In 1526, troops loyal to the Colonna family had sacked Rome. To guarantee Clement's settlement with them, Filippo Strozzi had offered himself as a hostage and had spent months as prisoner in the Castelnuovo, Naples. (Other supposed Medici loyalists, like Jacopo Salviati, had refused to go.) For months Clement failed to pay his ransom. Strozzi broke with the Pope, agreed with the Colonna to back the expulsion of the Medici from Florence, and began working to convince other traditional Medici allies that the city would be better off without Ippolito and his advisers. When Clarice arrived in Florence on 14 May she advised Cardinal Passerini in no uncertain terms that he and his charge should leave the city. The Cardinal was a peasant, she said, and Ippolito a bastard. Filippo, in her wake, confirmed her message.[14]

Three days later, Ippolito and Passerini made their way through crowds on the Via Larga to the San Gallo gate and into exile. 'Full of fear,' they headed for Poggio a Caiano, there to join Alessandro. Eight-year-old Catherine de' Medici remained with her aunt Clarice, at first in the convent of Santa Caterina, and, from December of that year, at another nunnery, Santissima Annunziata delle Murate. Lorenzino de' Medici, who had been staying with his cousins at Poggio, left their company and travelled with his family to Venice, where he lived through the years of Medici exile.[15]

In Florence, the new form of government was still to be decided. There were tensions between advocates of a broad-based regime, and those who preferred a tighter oligarchy (albeit one without the Medici). The former group gathered support on the streets from a public suspicious that the wealthy *ottimati* (meaning Florence's elite citizens) might betray their revolt. The bell of the Palazzo della Signoria ('della Signoria' means 'of the Lordship' or ruling authority) was tolled to call a parliament; new elections were held for the key committees of Florentine government. Supporters of the Medici were marginalised; some would be arrested and imprisoned.[16]

Alessandro and Ippolito fled west from Florence, and headed first for Pisa, some fifty miles away. They were vulnerable to attack. One eighteenth-century historian even suggests there was a plot to take them prisoner. But it failed, and they moved quickly on to Lucca, a free city a little way to the north. They planned to go to Massa and wait there to see how the war proceeded. Massa, a coastal town with a cliff-top fortress, would have been a secure retreat, but its marchioness, Ricciarda Malaspina, proved reluctant to receive such troublesome guests. After difficult negotiations for safe passage through the lands of the duke of Ferrara, and a strenuous horseback journey over the Apennines, the pair arrived in Parma.[17]

From May to December of 1527 Pope Clement remained a hostage in his own fortress, the Castel Sant'Angelo, Rome, surrounded by Spanish and German troops whose commanders sought ever-higher ransoms for his freedom. Alessandro and Ippolito became pawns in his negotiations with his captors. In November he promised to hand them over as hostages. In the meantime he left three of his cardinals as substitutes. It was a cunning double-cross on Clement's part. He had no intention of delivering his nephews. Ten days later he escaped from the Castel Sant'Angelo and fled some seventy-five miles north to the tiny hilltop town of Orvieto. There, for the next six months, in much reduced circumstances, his court operated in exile. Clement briefly considered a plan to move Ippolito and Alessandro north into Savoy, territory under French control, but once he was settled in Orvieto he agreed that Parma and nearby Piacenza, cities of the Papal States, were safe enough for them. Reports on their whereabouts from 1528 continued to reflect Ippolito's status as senior nephew. On 26

September, Antonio Soriano, a Venetian diplomat, reported their arrival in Parma. He described the pair as 'The Pope's nephews, Signor Ippolito and Signor — di Medici'. Either he, or the person copying down the dispatch, was unsure of Alessandro's name.[18]

Ricciarda Malaspina was not the only person to be cautious about contact with the Medici. Their tutor Pierio Valeriano deserted Ippolito and Alessandro. He fled to his home near Venice, and despite repeated pleas to return did so only in October 1528. In the meantime, he was replaced by Giovanni Antonio Buglio, baron del Burgio, a Sicilian nobleman formerly in the service of Pope Leo X.[19] Buglio's task as tutor was far from easy. As he wrote to the marquis of Mantua, the times were 'so turbulent everywhere'. He constantly assessed how best to keep his charges safe. Parma, where they were currently living, was a walled city on the road between Bologna and Milan, a papal possession with some fine medieval palaces. But Buglio sought the Marquis's assurance that if war or plague forced them to leave, he might bring Ippolito and Alessandro to Mantua.[20]

Despite occasional troubles – lack of staff, lack of the customary luxurious clothing – the nephews left their security to Buglio and instead amused themselves with the usual pursuit of aristocratic young men: hunting. Their letter to the marquis of Mantua reveals far less serious preoccupations:

> Having returned to Parma, we thought it our duty to send this servant to make our reverence to Your Excellency, so that you would know where your most affectionate servants are. And as, Illustrious Lord, we have found this area quite devoid of dogs, we are forced to beg Your Excellency to deign to send us a pair of greyhounds and a pair of beagles, so that in our daily exercise we will enjoy your beneficence.

The Marquis duly sent the dogs. To Buglio he sent a safe-conduct with the assurance that the young Medici would be very welcome in Mantua.[21]

Exchanges of gifts – dogs, horses, hawks, fabrics, food – were part of the political routine in Renaissance Italy. They helped to cement relationships between allies, to confirm friendships, to bestow favour. The nephews responded with the customary polite thank you.

Ippolito's letter to the Marquis about his fascination with hunting is an extravagant, if rather bloodthirsty, example of this genre of writing:

> Every time that Your Excellency has deigned to honour me with presents of horses, hounds and hawks, I have taken the appropriate consolation at being cherished by such a benevolent prince. Nonetheless I have never had a gift that more contented me, nor was more fitted for the occasion, than the two beautiful dogs for big game hunting, newly sent to me by Your Excellency. Next Sunday I have ordered a wolf-hunt in the mountain woods. And I have such hopes that they'll put on a good show that night and day I dream of seeing them attacked and put to the test by various animals.[22]

In fact, Ippolito's fascination with the hunt was such that he wrote an entire treatise on the subject, recording the different types of dog typically used, where one could find wolves, the different types of wolves to be found in Africa and Egypt compared to those in the North and so forth. Alessandro also gave dogs as gifts. Around 1529–30 he gave Benvenuto Cellini, the goldsmith, 'a big shaggy beast, good both for hunting and as a watch-dog'.[23]

While Alessandro and Ippolito spent their months of exile enjoying the hunting-grounds of northern Italy, Pope Clement VII remained with his court in Orvieto. He hoped for a French advance against the Emperor's Spanish and German troops. He continued his dynastic schemes. There were rumours of a possible match between Ippolito and Giulia Gonzaga, a member of the ruling family of Mantua and widow of an Imperial commander. In the summer of 1528, as French troops made progress (or so it seemed) against Imperial forces, Clement felt heartened enough to move south, not yet to Rome but to the spa town of Viterbo. It afforded rather more comfortable accommodations for the cardinals and functionaries of the Curia than Orvieto. By the autumn Clement was able to make his way back to Rome. There Ippolito joined him. Gossip about Ippolito's future floated around diplomatic circles. 'They say the Pope wants to make him a cardinal,' reported the duke of Urbino's envoy in November.[24]

For Clement, the political situation in Italy was far from encouraging. Florence remained in the hands of the anti-Medici party. French prospects were proving illusory. In August they had been routed near Naples, and the king of France cavilled at pouring funds into a losing campaign. The Venetians had taken advantage of Clement's captivity to seize some contested cities from the Papal States, and some devilish inspiration had convinced the king of England to try to abandon his marriage to Catherine of Aragon. Poems pinned to the Pasquino statue, the favourite site for public satire in Rome, showed little sympathy for the Pope's plight. This *pasquinata* sums up the local hostility. (Lino, successor to St Peter and an early Christian martyr, is contrasted in rhyme with the Medici favourite Cardinal Francesco Armellini, notorious for his greediness and imposition of taxes):

> I'm telling you Clement, or rather I'm laughing
> Because if I didn't, I'd not be Pasquino
> And I'm speaking Italian, because with Latin
> You might not get what I'm saying.
>
> The Emperor gives not one fig about you
> And France even less, they're trying to make you
> A martyr like Lino, and that thief Armellino
> Has already made you everyone's enemy
>
> With thousands of sorrows and thousands of schemes
> Taxes and duties he's killing the people
> So everyone longs for your final destruction
> And ruin, so that
> You'll have to rely on charity,
> Stay at San Giovanni
> In a room and kitchen.
>
> From now on, I fear
> Your fortune, O Clement, is:

You'll be back where you started
A nobody.[25]

Clement never could escape allusions to his illegitimate birth.

Under the circumstances it was no surprise that the Pope took to his bed. By January 1529 there were real fears that Clement's fever might cost him his life. His attendant physicians tried their best cures. They gave him rhubarb as a purgative. As Clement thought he was dying, he made one last move to keep the family in power. With Florence beyond his control, he would have to secure the maximum influence in Rome and the Church to sustain what the Venetian ambassador had called Clement's 'infinite desire for Florence'. 'Oppressed by his dangerous infirmity, [fearful of] leaving his heirs beggared and deprived of any defence,' on 10 January 1529, the Pope created a successor. Ippolito de' Medici became a cardinal.[26] His titular church was Santa Prassede, one of the most stunning small basilicas in Rome, its array of eighth-century mosaics and polychrome marble floor an inspiring sight. Yet despite all the possibilities of a rich living in the Church – perhaps one day the papacy – the role of cardinal was not what Ippolito wanted.

And for Alessandro it meant a dramatic and wholly unexpected change to his prospects.

4

Clement's decision to make Ippolito a cardinal was risky. The wealth
to be shared among the church elite was finite, after all. Jacopo Salviati,
husband of Clement's cousin Lucrezia, was said to be opposed to
Ippolito's promotion: he did not want competition for his own son,
Cardinal Giovanni, when it came to the most lucrative benefices. For
the most part, though, Clement's decision to elevate his nephew
aroused relatively little hostility. It was a 'very reasonable' thing to do,
wrote the Mantuan ambassador, while even Salviati observed that 'the
cardinals themselves, having compassion for the pitiful state in which
he was leaving his nephews and house, came to beg His Holiness that
he might be content to make Lord Ippolito a cardinal.'[1]

Had Clement died, as expected, this story might have ended very
differently. But he recovered, to find a family situation dramatically
changed. With Ippolito in the Church, the only candidate for dynastic
alliances was Alessandro. Now seventeen or so, Alessandro had been
acknowledged as part of the family for about ten years. In that time
he had been afforded the best of education. It was probably enough
to overcome the disadvantage of his mother's low birth. Plans for him
to enter the Church were now set aside. Clement quickly started
plotting marriages for his nephew, initially to Giulia Varano, niece of
Cardinal Cibo and heiress of the tiny duchy of Camerino.[2]

Ippolito, however, did not plan on staying a cardinal. He had a
precedent for joining the cardinalate then leaving it: Cesare Borgia,
illegitimate son of Pope Alexander VI, who in 1498 had renounced
his cardinal's hat in the quest to become a prince. Cesare had failed,
thwarted by his own ill health and his father's untimely death and
wily successor. But might Ippolito succeed? His interests lay in the
princely, military side of life and (as a Venetian ambassador put it) he

was 'better-looking and more educated' than his cousin Alessandro. For almost five years, since his arrival in the city of Florence in the summer of 1524, he had been groomed for the role of first citizen. At the end of 1528 it had even been rumoured that he might marry the Emperor's illegitimate daughter.[3]

But those were plans for the future. For the meantime, the new Cardinal needed to look to Church property. He already had the archbishopric of Avignon, to which he had been appointed at the age of just seven. For the richer benefices, he would have to wait until some elder cardinal died. Fortunately the Cardinal of Cortona obliged. His death left an opening as legate to Perugia, a post that Ippolito acquired in May 1529. Later the same year, he became legate to Genoa, commendatory abbot of Sant'Anastasio alle Tre Fontane and, in November, administrator of the see of Casale Monferrato.[4] If he was to acquire the secular power he so desired, the wealth those offices brought would be very useful.

While Ippolito was fuming at his unwanted promotion, his younger cousin was coming of age and covering up murder. So said Benvenuto Cellini, at least. Cellini, some twelve years Alessandro's senior, was a goldsmith and jeweller in Pope Clement's service, who had been held hostage with the papal court during the Sack of Rome.

Not long after Alessandro de' Medici was made duke of Penne, wrote Cellini, he was living in Rome with a group of soldiers trained by Giovanni de' Medici (a distant cousin and celebrated *condottiere* or mercenary commander). Among them was Francesco, Cellini's brother, nicknamed Cecchino or 'Little Frank'. Cecchino had gone to a shop in the Via dei Banchi, a hang-out for Alessandro's men-at-arms. In the same shop was Bernardo 'Cattivanza' degli Strozzi. Strozzi's men got into a fight with a group of city guards who had arrested Captain Cisti, a Lombard and former soldier for Giovanni de' Medici. (Cisti owed Strozzi money.) When one of them was killed, Cecchino intervened.

> He threw himself with all his dash and spirit into the middle
> of the band, and before his man could turn on guard, ran
> him right through the guts, and with the sword's hilt thrust

him to the ground. Then he turned upon the rest with such energy and daring, that his one arm was on the point of putting the whole band to flight, had it not been that, while wheeling round to strike an arquebusier, this man fired in self-defence, and hit the brave unfortunate fellow above the knee of his right leg.

Cecchino's injury was serious.

The doctors who were called in consultation, treated him with medicaments, but could not decide to amputate the leg, which might perhaps have saved him.

As soon as his wound had been dressed, Duke Alessandro appeared and most affectionately greeted him. My brother had not as yet lost consciousness; so he said to the Duke: 'My lord, this only grieves me, that your Excellency is losing a servant than whom you may perchance find men more valiant in the profession of arms, but none more lovingly and loyally devoted to your service than I have been.' The Duke bade him do all he could to keep alive; for the rest, he well knew him to be a man of worth and courage. He then turned to his attendants, ordering them to see that the brave young fellow wanted for nothing.

Cecchino died, and was buried 'with due ceremony in the church of the Florentines'.

Benvenuto Cellini's revenge was still to come. He went to the arquebusier's house, stabbed him in the neck and narrowly avoided arrest. But he knew who might save him.

I made off, and fearing I might be recognised, took refuge in the palace of Duke Alessandro, which was between Piazza Navona and the Rotunda.

This palace was the building completed for the Medici a generation earlier that would later be known as Palazzo Madama.

On my arrival, I asked to see the Duke; who told me that, if I was alone, I need only keep quiet and have no further anxiety, but go on working at the jewel which the Pope had set his heart on, and stay eight days indoors. He gave this advice the more securely, because the soldiers had now arrived who interrupted the completion of my deed; they held the dagger in their hand, and were relating how the matter happened, and the great trouble they had to pull the weapon from the neck and head-bone of the man, whose name they did not know. Just then Giovan Bandini came up, and said to them: 'That knife is mine, and I lent it to Benvenuto, who was bent on revenging his brother.' The soldiers were profuse in their expressions of regret at having interrupted me, although my vengeance had been amply satisfied.[5]

Giovan Bandini was one of Alessandro's closest companions.

This story should be treated with some caution. Cellini was one of the great raconteurs of the later Italian Renaissance. His auto-biography is a swashbuckling tale of adventure, starring the man himself and written with a good deal of hindsight between 1558 and 1563. Cellini – artist, warrior, lover, adventurer and self-confessed killer – gloried in the sometimes notorious reputations of his supporting cast. He knew that his readers would be familiar with the story that Alessandro went on to be a tyrant and that he was ultimately assassinated. Still, Cellini has tales to tell about Alessandro that no one else does, and they shed light on the Duke's private conduct in a way few other accounts do. Whatever the truth of the Cecchino incident, in Cellini's account Alessandro was a man prepared to protect a killer connected to his family. Even if all this is his imagining, half-remembered, misremembered or entirely concocted for effect, it still gives a sense of Alessandro's Rome: the street violence, the ubiquity of swords, the gun-toting guards, and the acceptance of vendetta.

As Cellini's revenge played out on the streets of Rome, Pope Clement VII was coming to accept that he would have to make peace with Charles V. In June 1529, they concluded the Treaty of Barcelona. Charles was the victor in this phase of the Italian Wars: the treaty was on his terms. Pope and Emperor made a deal over restoration of lands to the Papal States. They agreed a league of mutual defence. There were big financial benefits for Charles.[6] But Clement made sure that the treaty took care of Medici interests. Charles would help restore the Medici to power in Florence. His seven-year-old natural daughter, Margaret, would be betrothed to Alessandro. In return Florence would become a bastion for the Empire. Margaret was a far greater prize for Alessandro de' Medici than Giulia Varano. She came with a dowry of 20,000 ducats, part to be derived from lands in the realm of Naples. Their betrothal displeased the marquis of Mantua, who had hoped to have Margaret for himself.[7] It likewise displeased Ippolito.

Like Alessandro, Margaret was the child of a servant. Her mother was Jeanne (Johanna) van der Gheynst, a maid. In 1521, hundreds of miles to the north, Jeanne had found herself entangled with Charles while he was visiting André de Douvrin, cupbearer to his brother Prince Ferdinand, in whose house Jeanne worked. Charles was at this point twenty-one years old and unmarried but he had been elected Holy Roman Emperor in 1519 and was already the most powerful man in Europe. As with Lorenzo and Simunetta, we know nothing of the detail of their encounter but Charles acknowledged Jeanne's daughter as his own.

Margaret was born on 5 July 1522. She was baptised in the parish of Pamele near Oudenaarde, a town famous for its tapestry-making, located in what is now Belgium. The following month, her mother Jeanne was granted a pension of eighty florins a year, and little Margaret was taken to live with the Douvrins.[8] At the age of three or four Margaret was brought to the household of Charles' aunt, Margaret of Austria. Margaret senior was an accomplished Renaissance woman, whose court had become a centre for high culture. She surrounded herself with intellectuals, and her skill as a musician, artist and poet was praised by contemporaries. She took an active role in political life and in 1529 would negotiate with Louise of Savoy, mother of the king of France, a treaty that became known as 'the Ladies' Peace'.[9]

Her Habsburg relatives may have cared for little Margaret. The satirists were not so kind. They called her the 'Spanish mule' for her bastard status, and because, as one poet put it, she was 'neither Flemish nor Spanish'.[10] The eldest of Charles' acknowledged children (her legitimate brother Philip was born five years later, in 1527), Margaret was just four when she first became a pawn in diplomatic negotiations: in the autumn of 1526 there was talk of her marriage to Ercole d'Este, son of the duke of Ferrara. As religious reform picked up pace in the sixteenth century, attitudes changed, but in the 1520s it was still quite possible for an illegitimate child to be used in matrimonial alliances. That said, there were limits to what Margaret could expect. Her legitimate half-sisters would go on to marry princes of similar rank but Margaret could expect to marry the ruler of a smaller or subject state. Alessandro de' Medici was that man.[11]

The deal between Charles and Clement was to be sealed with one of the grandest ceremonies the Church of Rome could offer: an Imperial coronation. The last such event had taken place in 1452. Formally speaking, the coronation symbolised the Emperor's submission to papal authority, but in 1529 the whole of Europe knew Charles had the upper hand in Italy. The coronation would be a chance for him to make a grand appearance on the Italian stage, a performance of his power and magnificence. For Alessandro, these ceremonies offered a first opportunity to impress his future father-in-law. In August 1529 he and Ippolito left Rome, took ship from Piombino, on the coast of Tuscany, and sailed north to Genoa as part of the papal delegation to greet Charles. They received 1,000 gold ducats apiece to cover the cost of their voyage.[12]

Their relationship cannot have been easy. No longer were they hunting companions, exiled together, their respective rank in the family clear. Now Alessandro was to have the splendid dynastic match to which Ippolito had aspired. Clement must have known the delicacy of his family situation, but to outsiders he emphasised the better news. 'The Emperor seems disposed to peace with everyone,' Clement told a Venetian ambassador. 'He has greeted our nephew Count Alessandro de' Medici with good cheer.'[13] Alessandro's rapport with Charles would be crucial to the success of Clement's plans. Royal favour could make or break a potential son-in-law's fortunes.

From Genoa the Imperial party travelled inland, heading north over steep mountain roads to cross the Apennines. They arrived in Piacenza on 6 September. It was raining and Charles had to make his entry beneath an umbrella, but the party was imposing enough. There were three cardinals, three ambassadors and an entourage of perhaps two thousand. On 5 November Alessandro was spotted at the monastery of Certosa, outside Pavia, among a group of five lords travelling with Charles. (Pavia held splendid memories for the Empire: it was there, back in 1525, that Charles' troops had won a great victory, capturing Francis I, king of France.)

On 15 November Alessandro joined Charles for his formal entry into the city of Bologna.[14] Nicknamed 'Bologna la Grassa' – Fat Bologna – for its riches (and perhaps also its succulent meats), it was the second city of the Papal States, a striking place with its red-brick palaces, colonnades and dozens of towers soaring above the skyline. Clement's court had been uprooted from Rome for the occasion, billeted on the city's patrician families. While Charles and Clement lodged in the Palazzo Comunale on Bologna's central square, Alessandro stayed in the Palazzo Manzoli on the narrow Via Zamboni, leading out of the city to the north-eastern gate of San Donato, a billet he had to share with Isabella d'Este, marchioness of Mantua. As Charles' discussions with Clement – and with the numerous diplomats in attendance – wore on, weeks, and then months passed.[15]

For the young men of the papal and Imperial entourages, the long summit in Bologna was an opportunity to kick their heels and kick up trouble. Discontented with his new role as cardinal, Ippolito de' Medici took to carousing around the city late at night, in the company of his cousin Giovanbattista Cibo and Cibo's brother-in-law, the Count of Caiazzo. Keen to show off their skill at arms, while out masquerading one night they got into a fight with some Spaniards. The vendetta escalated. A servant of Giovanbattista's brother Lorenzo stabbed to death a Spaniard who had drawn a sword on his master. Three people had died before Cibo's brother, Cardinal Innocenzo, intervened to prevent further reprisals. It was all too easy for acceptable youthful hi-jinks – a welcome escape from civic responsibility – to tip over into delinquency and disorder. All the more so when carrying swords was a marker of nobility and, besides, everyone carried a personal knife, not least for eating. This was a society where fights could very easily end in bloodletting.[16]

Ippolito was 'infinitely displeased' at developments that winter: Alessandro was gaining the Emperor's favour and it seemed ever more likely that the Florentine rebels would either surrender or face defeat at the hands of Spanish and German troops. He 'found it insupportable that anyone but he should be lord of Florence,' wrote the Cibo family chronicler, 'and was so open about his desires, that both the Pope and the Duke held him in suspicion, and kept their wits about them.'[17] The satirists labelled Ippolito a *bravazzo,* a bravo in spades. One poem began 'Don Clement's the infamy of the church,' continuing through a list of cardinals before getting to Ippolito: 'Medici, little brain morning and night'. Another was quite explicit about his disdain for church politics:

> Now should the Pope die, all these cardinals
> Have schemes and plans for the papacy
> Only Medici, who wants to be a soldier
> Couldn't care less who gets it.[18]

But if Ippolito lacked interest in the Church, he certainly took an interest in the future of Florence. The constant evidence of Alessandro's advancement must have been hard to watch. First, Alessandro needed money to sustain the lifestyle appropriate to an Imperial son-in-law. On 13 November Clement made him governor of Spoleto, a hilltop town in the Papal States,[19] an office that could be delegated to others while still bringing him income. Then, in the Christmas Eve ceremonies Alessandro took one of the most prestigious roles for a layman, carrying water for the papal ablutions,[20] second only to the Emperor in the order of precedence. Given that Alessandro, ruler only of a smallish fief in the realm of Naples, was a relatively low-ranking duke (far lower down the hierarchy than, say, the duke of Milan or Savoy), this would have required some conscious stage-management by the papal functionaries. A few days into the New Year, Clement dispatched an envoy to Flanders to conclude the contract for Alessandro and Margaret's marriage with her guardian, the elder Margaret of Austria, duchess of Savoy.[21] This would be the first of three steps in concluding the marriage, to be followed, once Margaret was of age, with the exchange of rings and finally the marital Mass and consummation. Those who opposed the match could console themselves that the bride was still only seven years old. Plenty might change in that time. Besides, the government of Florence was still to be settled. Clement awaited the arrival of three ambassadors from Florence. This was a last opportunity for the Medici to make a settlement with the city regime.[22] If talks failed, Clement would hold Charles to his promise. There would be war to retake Florence.

At the festival of Candlemas, on 2 February, in a beautiful ceremony, the church filled with dozens of candles, gilded, white and yellow, Alessandro attended the Pope again.[23] Ippolito, who would have sat among the cardinals, could only look on.

5

The coronation of Charles V was immortalised in dozens of eyewitness accounts, one of the most memorable ceremonial occasions of its time. Bologna's cathedral was dressed to replicate the splendour of St Peter's in Rome, the traditional venue for Imperial coronations. Extravagant clothing was the order of the day: magnificence was compulsory. In fact, Charles had not one, but two coronations. In the first, on 22 February 1530, he received the Iron Crown, a symbol of Imperial authority over Italy that had traditionally been granted to Holy Roman emperors in a ceremony in the northern region of Lombardy before their coronation as Emperor by the pope in Rome. Alessandro arrived for this occasion dressed in dark damask lined with wolfskin (Bologna can be cold in winter). This was an intimate, small-scale ceremony. It took place in the chapel of the Palazzo Comunale, where Charles and Clement were staying in adjoining apartments. Alessandro carried the orb, a golden globe adorned with gems dividing it into Asia, Africa and Europe, topped off with a little jewelled cross, topped in turn with a ruby. It signified Charles' claims to global power. Spanish noblemen carried the sceptre and sword, while the marquis of Monferrato, like Alessandro an Italian nobleman courting Imperial support, bore the Iron Crown.[1]

The following day, still more dignitaries arrived for Charles' coronation as Emperor. It was scheduled for 24 February, Charles' thirtieth birthday and the fifth anniversary of the spectacular victory of Imperial troops against the French at the Battle of Pavia. The bishop of Trent came, and the duke of Savoy, with horses, carriages and a guard of archers, favoured by good weather. The following morning, Charles decided to go out to greet them in person. 'On the spur of the moment,' wrote a watching diplomat, 'he left the palace with Duke

Alessandro de' Medici and a few others.'[2] Alessandro – no doubt under the vigilant eye of Pope Clement – was doing an excellent job of establishing himself as one of Charles' companions. Alessandro's skills in languages beyond Italian are unknown, but they would have had little trouble conversing as Charles was fluent in several (though the claim he spoke 'Spanish to God, Italian to women, French to men and German to my horse' is almost certainly a later invention).

Ceremonial etiquette meant that when it came to the Imperial coronation itself, Alessandro had a relatively low profile. The strict order of precedence meant he had to give way to higher-ranking noblemen. There were, nonetheless, ways for Alessandro to highlight his new status: through the luxury of his attendants' dress, for example. His fifteen gentlemen wore a livery of *pavonazzo* – a shimmering peacock purple – and dark, fiery red. In an engraving of the coronation procession, though Alessandro is not named as an individual, his entourage features in a way no other nobleman's does, on horseback, sleeves puffed and slashed, echoing German style, their caps extravagantly feathered. One is carrying a bird, perhaps a hunting hawk.[3] Whether for their spectacular appearance, or for their relationship to the Emperor's future son-in-law, his men attracted attention.

One seventeenth-century historian who wrote a *Life of Charles V* described how Alessandro was present as Charles narrowly escaped injury or death. Three days after the coronation, so his story goes, Charles was on his way to Mass one morning, accompanied only by Alessandro and a few servants. As they were passing beneath a wooden gallery, all of a sudden a great piece of masonry fell at their feet. Had Charles taken another half-pace he would have been dead. Alessandro took great fright at this. Charles simply raised his eyes to the heavens and then, turning to the Duke, said: 'I don't know whether I should say I was born in Ghent or Bologna but whatever my nature, I can say that in the month of February I was born twice.'[4] If the truth of this tale is doubtful, its message is not: Charles was invincible. And he and Alessandro were close.

While the two courts were preparing for the coronations, Clement had been working behind the scenes to convince Charles to back a military offensive to retake Florence for the Medici. There were serious worries that it would be a tough campaign. The Emperor feared the 'complete ruin' of the city, such was the obstinacy of Clement on the one hand and the government of Florence on the other. Since the Medici's forced departure in 1527, the personnel of the Florentine regime had changed. Old allies of the Medici, who had initially stayed in government, had drifted away or been accused of disloyalty and forced into exile. That had left Florence in the hands of more radical republicans, who were reluctant to compromise. The Emperor was also preoccupied by a challenge to his power from the Turks on the Empire's eastern front, a far more serious matter than the domestic politics of an Italian state. In an attempt to persuade Charles there was no other option, Clement agreed to talks with the Florentine ambassadors, but he set his demands high and to no one's surprise the negotiations failed.[5] On 4 February the embassy took its leave. War was now almost inevitable. Barrels of gunpowder were sent up on mules from Bologna over the steep hill roads across the Apennines. Plans were made to attack Florence from three different directions. But by the middle of March the Mantuan envoy in Bologna was reporting that plans for battle had been abandoned in favour of continuing with a siege. 'Thinking to take Florence by force,' he wrote 'is talking the impossible.'[6] Its walls were too strong, those inside too well prepared. The city would not be quickly won.

Throughout all this, Ippolito de' Medici's ambition to rule Florence had not waned in the slightest. In the spring of 1530 there was still a possibility that he might. Clement VII, as Cardinal Giulio de' Medici and Legate to Tuscany, had overseen family affairs in Florence after the death of Duke Lorenzo in 1519, until his election to the papacy in November 1523. Cardinal Ippolito might do the same now. One possible compromise would have made Alessandro the duke of Milan, where he might have replaced the discredited ruler Francesco Sforza.[7] That would have left the government of Florence open to Ippolito, in a parallel to the previous generation, when Ippolito's father Giuliano had ruled Florence, while Alessandro's father Lorenzo had been duke of Urbino. Clement, however, was reluctant to accept Milan (where his family had no established power base) as an alternative to Florence, and it would have been risky for Charles to extend Medici power to a second city.[8] Charles eventually arranged for Sforza's marriage to his niece, Princess Christina of Denmark. Florence – and nowhere else – became Clement's focus. And with no alternative role for Alessandro, the logic was clear: he would rule in Florence while Ippolito stayed in the Church.

All the same, as the siege was prepared, Ippolito put his mind to political affairs. He wrote to Bartolomeo Valori, papal commissioner with the Imperial army, urging him to prevent a sack of Florence. Later, as Legate to Perugia, he would pen a series of maxims on government. They would detail the importance of preparation for power, considering how far exile should be used, the difficulty of maintaining a weak state, the danger of sustaining an army with too little money (or too much). Being insufficiently prepared for war was damaging. In a siege one needed to consider whether provisions would last. It was fairly obvious stuff, but more important than the content is the way the aphorisms would betray Ippolito's interests. He would not be the first cardinal to lead troops. Pope Julius II had become known as the 'warrior pope' for his exploits in battle. Ippolito aspired to do the same.[9]

The battle for Florence was the last to be fought in this phase of the Italian Wars. The city had been surrounded since October 1529 when Philibert of Chalon, prince of Orange, the twenty-seven-year-old Imperial commander, had begun his advance from Figline, on the road from Arezzo, reaching the hills around Florence on the 24th. The Emperor sent 4,000 German infantrymen, 2,500 Spanish and 800 Italian, more than 300 light cavalry and twenty-five artillery pieces. Inside the city, the Florentines – prepared for a siege of several months – hoped the enemies would run out of money. But Imperial troops gradually took control of the surrounding countryside: the towns of Pistoia and Prato, north-west of Florence, part of the city's dominion, surrendered to the Pope; so did Pietrasanta, on the Tuscan coast. The papal-Imperial side tried to buy off Florence's mercenary commanders. Secret negotiations with Malatesta Baglioni came to nothing, but they had better luck with Napoleone Orsini, who took his money from the Florentines then abandoned their cause to make peace with the

Pope and Emperor, taking some of his captains with him. Clement lobbied the king of France to withdraw support for the Florentines, but when he left Bologna for Rome at the end of March there was still little progress in the siege.

As the not-quite-war continued, an extraordinary duel took place outside Bologna. Held on 12 March 1530, this was no fight for individual honour, but a contest staged to determine which of the two sides in the battle for Florence – those in the city, or those in exile – were traitors to their fatherland. (Though some said the real conflict was over a woman.) The challenge had been issued by Lodovico Martelli and Dante da Castiglione, who fought for the city. They were given safe conduct by the Imperial forces for the occasion. Giovan Bandini – the close associate of Alessandro who had been involved in the fracas with Cellini's brother Cecchino – fought for the pro-Medici exiles, along with Bertino Aldobrandini, who had grown up in Cecchino's household. Alessandro watched.

The combatants made a grand departure from Florence, preceded by pages dressed in red and white, on horses in white leather barding. They themselves rode Turkish horses; they wore red satin and silver tissue, and red hats with white feathers, and half a dozen grooms walked beside them as they left the city. The story was recounted in a letter from Bologna to the marquis of Mantua:

> News. Yesterday, the 12th, four Florentines fought, viz., two from outside, and two from inside, over who was a traitor to the fatherland. . . . The four names were put in a box and lots were drawn and it was down to Giovan Bandini to fight the Martellini [sic] man, and Aldobrandini with da Castiglione, and they were not allowed to help one another.

> They entered the field, and four swords and four mail gloves were brought over. Giovan Bandini and Aldobrandini told Martelli and Castiglione that they should strip down to their shirts, and take off their hats, and take a glove and a sword each. That was how they wanted to fight. So they stripped and took a glove and a sword each and were about to come to blows; but before they did Giovan Bandini

twanged his sword and, vibrating, it split in two pieces, and so he asked for another sword.

There was a three-hour stand-off while the four argued over whether Bandini should be allowed a new weapon.

> During that dispute, there were perhaps three thousand people watching from a hill nearby, those from inside Florence mixed with those from outside, and thanks to those from inside, notwithstanding the promises made by one and other side, two heavy artillery shots were fired from that little hill. By some miracle of God no one was hit, though it did take the head off a horse belonging to one of those from inside, and did no other harm.

> The dispute over, another sword was given to Giovan Bandini and they went back to the field and started to attack, such that Bandini wounded Martellini nine times, and the said Martellini retired, and Bandini was untouched.

> Aldobrandini, back in the field, gave Castiglione a great cut on the side of the head, which he tried to stem with his free hand, only to receive such a cut on that arm that it almost took it off clean. And when Dante felt the arm wound with his sword-hand, he put his hand up to support the other arm and so, with his sword straight, he advanced on the enemy and stabbed him in the eye.

With blood flowing down his face, Aldobrandini had to retire. One man from each side had won. Observers hinted that the duel had been staged. The drawing of lots had conveniently paired the stronger man from each side with the weaker man on the other. But staged or not, the three injured men were seriously wounded. Martelli and Aldobrandini died: the combat was declared a draw. Only Bandini emerged untouched. He was expected in Bologna the following day, in the company of Alessandro de' Medici.[10]

★

If the duel for the honour of Florence had left two men dead and one man seriously wounded, the war for Florence itself was quite as brutal. In the city conditions deteriorated. Catherine de' Medici became a target for death threats. Some schemed to use her as a human shield; others to send her to a whorehouse. She had to be moved to a safer location, the convent of Santa Lucia. The young men inside the siege kept up spirits with the traditional Carnival game of football in Piazza Santa Croce, accompanied by trumpeters perched high on the church roof to ensure the besiegers heard them.[11] Late in March the Imperial commanders tried bombarding Florence's defences, to no avail. They had more success in capturing the city's supply lines. Volterra fell first, then Empoli. Economic sanctions were levelled against Florentine merchants in the papal territories, who found their goods confiscated or were arbitrarily imprisoned. Anyone entering the city with provisions faced the death penalty.[12] Shortages of food soon hurt. The Imperial commanders managed to tempt Malatesta Baglioni to a secret meeting and made him elaborate promises of land and wealth if he would betray the city. On 3 August he refused to attack an Imperial camp. There was only a little relief for Florence when the Imperial commander, the Prince of Orange, was killed in the ensuing battle.

On 9 August, as hunger mounted, and the prospect of death in the city grew real, the Florentine authorities agreed to send ambassadors out to Ferrante Gonzaga, Orange's replacement. On 12 August Lorenzo Strozzi, Pierfrancesco Portinari, Bardo Altoviti and Jacopo Morelli signed the capitulations, setting out the terms of Florence's surrender.[13] The magistrates agreed 'out of fear', wrote Francesco Guicciardini (who had initially opposed the return of the Medici but later accepted roles in Clement's papal service and in Florentine government). They accepted that the Emperor would determine the form of government, 'understanding that liberty would be preserved'. Medici supporters would be allowed back into Florence, and their property returned. The sum of 80,000 ducats would be paid to the Imperial army. Fifty hostages would be handed over to Don Ferrante as a guarantee of the city's good faith. Any citizen who wished to leave would be permitted to go to Rome, or wherever, without molestation of property or person. All lands in the Florentine dominion taken by the

Imperial army would be returned to the city's control. The army, once paid, would leave the territory, but if payment took more than eight days the Florentines would supply victuals for the troops. The Pope, his relatives, friends and servants would pardon the injuries done them; no one would be penalised for his service to the Florentine state. In short, there would be no reprisals. Bartolomeo Valori, papal commissioner, summoned a parliament, the traditional assembly of the Florentine people. Pikemen and halbardiers were stationed outside to guarantee a suitable outcome. The parliament elected a *Balìa*, a council of twelve citizens – all Medici supporters – to govern the city.[14]

The siege had badly weakened Florence. Varchi estimated 8,000 soldiers from the city had been killed, and 14,000 of the besiegers. The city was all but bankrupt. Many residents had left; the remaining population was divided. There had been no harvest that year, and no sowing of crops: shortages would inevitably continue. Prices soared. More money left the city to pay for imports of food and livestock than had ever been spent on the war, costly though that had been. 'The misery and ruin of the city and the countryside around are unspeakable, greater than we can possibly imagine,' wrote Guicciardini to a friend. It was a disaster. The future of Florence, 'as I've said a thousand times, depends entirely on the Duke's qualities'. (He was not advocating here that Alessandro should be made duke of Florence, simply using his title as duke of Penne, but it was now apparent that Alessandro was the Medici candidate to lead the city.) Though Alessandro was too young to rule by himself, Guicciardini observed, if he had faith in good counsel there was hope of founding a stable regime. If not, it might prove entirely the opposite.[15]

Hundreds of soldiers had to be demobilised. As they waited for their promised wages, men of different nations squabbled and scrapped. Italian mercenaries attacked the Spanish; the locals came to their aid; the feared German landsknechts intervened. Their commanders struggled to pacify them. Only by some miracle (so it was claimed in Rome) did the Emperor's ambassador Giovanni Antonio Muscettola manage to calm things down. The miracle consisted in large part of the application of money: 40,000 ducats for the Germans; 49,000 (after some negotiating) for the Spanish. The Italians were due 90,000 but had to settle for 48,000 in cash, 12,000 in textiles, and the rest in IOUs. The funds for these settlements were raised through forced loans. Old Medici allies and in-laws – Jacopo Salviati in Rome, Filippo Strozzi in Lucca, Luigi Guicciardini in Pisa – were asked to collect the tax from fellow pro-Medici exiles. One such man, Bernardo Vettori, was alone taxed 35,000 ducats, a sum that would have paid the wages of just under four hundred men-at-arms for a year.[16]

The promise of no reprisals was soon broken. On 28 August forty-eight citizens were arrested and taken to the Palazzo della Signoria. Some were moved to the Bargello, the city prison, interrogated and tortured. Raffaello Girolami, *gonfaloniere* of the republic, was imprisoned for life.[17] Silvestro Aldobrandini, another senior official, escaped execution thanks to the intervention of Bartolomeo Valori but he spent time in prison before being exiled from Florence for three years. Exile was a common punishment for political enemies, and could have serious financial consequences, but the harshest penalties were reserved for the younger, more radical participants in the fallen republic as opposed to the older office-holders. The new regime needed sufficient continuity to ensure stability, while at the same time excluding those opponents who seemed most likely to initiate another uprising. In all, about one hundred and fifty were exiled (this number probably does not include their families).[18]

On the other side of the political divide, Medici backers were enthused by their victory. Piero Salviati wrote to family matriarch Lucrezia de' Medici Salviati, wife of Jacopo, describing his delight at the family's success. Throughout the city, people were shouting 'Palle! Palle! Pane!'[19] *Palle* referred to the six balls of the Medici insignia. *Pane* meant bread. Peace brought the prospect of food and prosperity once again.

Clement decided not to send either of his nephews to the city for now. He preferred to maintain the pretence that none of the reprisals against regime members were on Medici orders. Any action against the republic's supporters – like the eight executions of office-holders in late 1530 – had to seem the ordinary work of the city magistrates.[20] He kept Ippolito in Rome, while Alessandro was sent to join the

Emperor on his travels through Germany. Antonio Soriano, Venetian ambassador to Rome, implied that Clement was concerned that Charles might get cold feet, and that Alessandro's task would be to persuade Charles to send Margaret to Italy as previously agreed. Clement, wrote Soriano, had told him that he didn't want Alessandro to fall into a life of lazy vice in Rome. He hoped that at the Emperor's court Alessandro might acquire some polish. This was to be an educational journey, an opportunity to prepare Alessandro for his new responsibilities. In September Alessandro travelled north via the city of Trent, crossed the Alps on the Brenner Pass and made his way into the German territories.[21] His challenge now was to secure the Medici–Habsburg alliance.

6

By the spring of 1530 Ippolito was out of favour with Pope Clement, and Alessandro was in. 'Ippolito is good-looking and seems very genteel and affable,' Gasparo Contarini, a Venetian diplomat, reported. 'The other one [Alessandro] is little renowned and younger. And it seems to me that His Holiness is more content with Alessandro's cleverness and manners than those of the Cardinal.' By this time Alessandro seems to have compensated for any missed education. 'He did not lack cleverness,' conceded Jacopo Nardi, in a history otherwise very hostile to the Medici.[1] The word these men use is *ingegno*, which besides cleverness has a sense of craft or cunning.

No one praised Alessandro's looks and education in the way they did Ippolito's, but there were other princely qualities he could cultivate: the graceful speech so valued among courtiers, the martial arts of jousting and hunting. An unusually flattering account of Alessandro's rule by one Alessandro Ceccherelli applauded his biting wit and way with words.[2] The absence of comment on Alessandro's appearance, however, raises the question of how those around them might have perceived his looks. Though his contemporaries did not have a clear theory of race, darker skin still had negative associations for them. The most desirable skin colour for a nobleman was pinkish, a combination of red and white. Giovan Battista della Porta, a sixteenth-century theorist of physiognomy, linked a dark complexion to a melancholic, fearful personality.[3]

Exactly what prompted Clement's irritation with his elder nephew is a mystery. In January 1529, when Ippolito had been appointed to the cardinalate, there had been no doubt that he was the Pope's preferred successor as head of the family. The historian Benedetto Varchi observed:

Anyone who really considers the situation in which Clement found himself then will judge that he preferred Ippolito to Alessandro; and indeed Ippolito, besides being older and more gracious in his looks, was already a man of letters, which were of the greatest ornament to him and made him dear and well regarded. It's certain that Clement didn't yet know his lightness and inconstancy, which came after he was made cardinal; he seemed (if he wasn't faking it) to like him better, and to hold him in greater esteem.[4]

Now, however, that esteem had faded. Perhaps that was a consequence of Ippolito's dogged determination to make himself ruler of Florence; perhaps his bordering-on-delinquent bravado on the streets of Bologna had angered the Pope; perhaps Clement thought that Ippolito, by not taking his role as cardinal seriously, was failing in his duty to the family. Ippolito skipped consistory, the regular meeting of the College of Cardinals, preferring to go hunting with friends. Pope Alexander VI might have tolerated his son Cesare Borgia ditching a cardinal's hat to found a new dynastic state, but Pope Clement VII, whose family had an existing state almost in their grasp, would not contemplate such adventures.

Ippolito's resentment of his cousin grew. Ambassadors in Rome gossiped about his ambitions. They noted the parallel with Cesare Borgia, and Borgia's unhappy fate when his schemes had failed.

Yet this was not only personal rivalry. There had been a history of conflict between Alessandro's father and Ippolito's, which had split the extended family. Duke Lorenzo had enjoyed the support of Clement (then Cardinal Giulio de' Medici), of the Cibo family and of his mother Alfonsina. Duke Giuliano had found backing from his sisters Lucrezia Salviati and Contessina Ridolfi, and from other members of the Ridolfi family.[5] Those old alliances had never quite disappeared.

By the end of September, Alessandro was close to Augsburg, the latest stop on Charles' autumn progress through his German territories. Such royal tours were an important tool of sixteenth-century government. In an age when most people never moved more than a few miles from their place of birth, they were a chance to see their ruler in person. For those of higher rank, they were an opportunity for direct contact with the monarch and his courtiers, to seek favour and to parade the riches of their own locality, although putting up an emperor and his entourage did not come cheap. Charles' progress would wend its way north to the Low Countries. Munich was a possible stopping-off point – it had an excellent reputation for the chase – as were Frankfurt and Cologne.

Alessandro joined the court early in October 1530, in the company of Girolamo da Schio, bishop of Vaison, papal nuncio and perhaps something of a chaperone for the eighteen-year-old Duke. Initial reports suggested Alessandro was going to spend 'some days' with Charles' court. In the event, his visit lasted more than six months.[6] It was a round of banqueting, entertainments and hunting, and a chance to learn more about the realities of Imperial government. Charles' wars did not stop for leisure; nor did his extensive responsibilities as Holy Roman Emperor. On 23 October, Charles' younger brother, King Ferdinand, held a banquet for Alessandro, da Schio, and Cardinal Lorenzo Campeggio. After dining the four retired in a small, domestic party with just two or three of the king's gentlemen and the Mantuan ambassador. The talk was of military practicalities for the campaign against the Turks, a matter preoccupying Ferdinand whose Hungarian territories were vulnerable to attack from the east.[7] Destined as he was to be a linchpin of Charles' policy in Italy, and with an eye on a military career, Alessandro would need a good grasp of strategy.

He seemed to have little trouble maintaining Charles' favour. Within a month of his arrival at court, Charles had issued a statement confirming that the Medici family would have perpetual charge of Florence, beginning with Alessandro, who was to marry Margaret, and then their heirs. The subtext was clear enough: this new regime would have Charles' military backing too. Dated 28 October 1530 at Augsburg, it was sent south to the papal court. Garbled versions of these events reached Rome within a few weeks. There was a secret deal to make Alessandro 'king or duke of Tuscany', reported the Venetian ambassador. That was an exaggeration: Charles' agreement was limited to making the Medici 'first among equals' in Florence, maintaining the historic form of government in which the city's leading families shared power. But even that roused Ippolito's ire. The ambassador was certain. 'He won't tolerate it.'[8]

Ippolito was not the only threat to Alessandro's rule. The Florentine authorities had detained former city leader Raffaello Girolami. Suspected of new plots against the regime, he was deemed 'likely to incite disorder'. Girolami was held first in Florence's prison, the Bargello, then transferred to Volterra, a small town in the countryside south-west of Florence, its forbidding fortress extended half a century before by the regime of Lorenzo the Magnificent. On learning of the detention, Ferrante Gonzaga, commander of the victorious Imperial forces, wrote to Florence insisting that holding Girolami or doing him any violence was a breach of the agreement that ended the siege and contrary to both his own and Charles' honour. (Torture was routinely employed in judicial investigations: the reference to violence here was no throwaway comment.) Concerned that Gonzaga might ask the Emperor to intervene in Girolami's favour, the frustrated *Balìa* wrote to Alessandro asking him to raise the issue with Charles. 'Raffaello was not detained for anything that happened before the capitulation,' they wrote, 'but on account of suspicions and indications of new schemes. Your Illustrious Lordship must understand that, if the Emperor should write anything here in Raffaello's favour, it would ruin the reputation of this regime, which has so many enemies in the city, as you know.' Charles had expended authority, men and money to make Florence the state it was: the Emperor now needed to think about maintaining it. The *Balìa* urged Alessandro to speak up. Don Ferrante, they wrote, needed to be reminded not to favour the Emperor's enemies. 'We recommend ourselves to Your Illustrious Lordship; praying that you deign to intervene not only in this matter of Raffaello, but all the other citizens from whom we, in the future, might wish to secure ourselves, as suspects and enemies of ourselves and His Majesty, as is the said Raffaello.'[9] Florence, in these months after the siege, was no comfortable place for anyone whose loyalty to the Medici was suspected. It was also a city that had to accept that the favour of the Emperor mattered in political decisions. Its once-prized liberty was slipping away; its icons and traditions would be remade for this new world of Imperial power.

Having secured Charles' confirmation of his rule in Florence, Alessandro's next task was to convince Charles to send his fiancée Margaret to Italy for her education, which would be an important demonstration of Charles' willingness to honour the marriage agreement. Following visits to Frankfurt and Cologne, after Twelfth Night the court moved on to the ancient spa town of Aachen, a favoured residence of kings and emperors for some eight centuries. On 10 January Charles and Ferdinand made a grand entry. There were two thousand horses, the Emperor and King with their horse guards, forty or fifty gentlemen, and the lesser lords, among them Alessandro. He and the marquis of Villafranca threw coins to the spectators. Seated on two great coursers were pageboys in tunics of gold velvet brocade carrying pennants. Another dozen of Ferdinand's pages wore crimson gowns trimmed with cloth of gold; there followed eighteen of Charles' pages, two heralds, a German count bearing the Imperial sword, and finally Charles and Ferdinand themselves, the Emperor in full armour with an overshirt of gold brocade and a black velvet hat with a little yellow feather. Ferdinand's crimson overshirt was embroidered with pearls and an emblem of F&A for Ferdinand and Anna of Bohemia, his wife. His hat was adorned with white feathers. Behind them followed the Imperial electors, two cardinals, members of the Imperial council, men-at-arms and archers.[10] Such displays underlined the Habsburg rulers' wealth and power. For Alessandro they were a model of princely conduct to add to the ceremonies he already knew from the papal court and his two years on the margins of Florence. From Charles he might also learn how to balance the role of ruler with the sensitivities of city governments: there were many free cities in the Holy Roman Empire, and they guarded their independence jealously.

From Aachen the Imperial party moved on to Brussels, and there, on 25 January, Charles sent Alessandro to meet his fiancée for the first time. Following the death of Charles' aunt, the younger Margaret was now in the care of his sister, Mary of Hungary. Like Charles, Mary was keen on hunting: Alessandro must have fitted comfortably into their circle. The Emperor was known to enjoy the chase and the tournament far more than intellectual pursuits. We know little of Alessandro's first encounter with his future bride. It was most likely formal, constrained, polite. An eyewitness reported that Margaret seemed 'very small, and doesn't look older than nine, but quite pretty and gracious'. In fact, she was only eight. This was not only her first introduction to her fiancé, but also probably the first time she had met her father.[11] But unlike Alessandro, who had not been acknowledged until well past infancy, Margaret had been destined throughout her childhood for a dynastic marriage. She was well prepared.

If Margaret was on show, so was Alessandro. This was the first extended period he had spent away from close family and advisers. Evidence of his conduct – positive and negative – was pored over and reported upon by the assembled agents and correspondents. Late that January a row between two of his servants tipped his household affairs into violence. The first was a steward nicknamed 'Panonto', meaning bread and oil. His real name was probably Domenico Romoli. The second was an unnamed furrier. The pair had words. The furrier took offence. Alessandro turned up and demanded to know what all the noise was about. When Panonto replied with a string of lies, Alessandro was infuriated. He drew a weapon – perhaps a dagger, perhaps a sword – and slashed the steward across the chest. Listed among his possessions, Alessandro's daggers read like art objects. One had an ivory handle; one was inlaid with lapis lazuli, another with jasper, another with agate.[12] Evidently they had more practical uses.

The story got out. Sigismondo della Torre, an agent of the duke of Mantua, wrote about it to his master; a copy reached the Venetians. His version gave only the bare facts of the affair, which he played down, describing it as a 'bit of disorder'. Panonto's wound was not deep: the steward was not badly hurt. Thirty years on, in a book of advice on household management, Panonto would write: 'Always be obedient to your superiors, modest with your equals and pleasant with your inferiors.'[13] Perhaps he had learned from experience. Nonetheless, the incident cannot have reflected well on Alessandro. At best, it might be put down to youthful hotheadedness. At worst, it suggested Alessandro's household was in disarray – and a man who could not manage a household could hardly be trusted to manage a state.

7

Back in Florence, the process of preparing for Alessandro's return continued. On 17 February 1531 he was deemed eligible for election to all the city magistracies, enabling him to take a role in government. Usually such votes went through without dissent. In Alessandro's case, twelve out of eighty-four voters objected to his candidacy.[1] There was palpable unease about Medici intentions.

In Brussels, meanwhile, as Carnival season approached, the festivities became grander. Alessandro's household troubles prompted no further comment. The following week della Torre was penning instead a glowing account of the young Duke's abilities in jousting. Alessandro had acted as *mantenitore* at a contest.[2] It was a dangerous role. The jousting arena was divided in two by a low wall. On one side the *mantenitore* sat still on his horse in full armour. Jousting armour was heavy and protective, a luxury manufacture, often beautifully decorated. Even so there was risk involved. As the *mantenitore* waited, a fully armed knight charged down the other side of the wall, seeking to hit the *mantenitore* with his lance, on the head, upper body or arm. The *mantenitore* would defend himself with his own lance, trying to injure or unseat the challenger over three rounds. Alessandro put in an impressive performance. 'He carried himself so well,' wrote della Torre, 'that he not only deserved commendation as a young man and beginner, but was highly praised as the equal to much better and more experienced competitors.'[3] If observers were reticent about Alessandro's looks, they could certainly laud his athleticism. Another Italian observer wrote from Ghent in April that 'in these jousts here, no one has borne himself better than Duke Alessandro de' Medici, nephew of the Pope and son-in-law of the Emperor's Majesty. It makes me glad to be Italian, especially when I hear the Spanish praise him.' In

Baldassarre Castiglione's *Book of the Courtier*, the jouster was encouraged to be 'as elegant and attractive as he is competent'. The most telling account of Alessandro's accomplishments on this progress came from Lorenzo Bencivenni, an agent of the Orsini family in Rome. After reporting that Alessandro had broken no fewer than fourteen lances in a tournament, he added: 'Many write that the Emperor loves him greatly – and not as a son-in-law but as a son.'[4]

On 3 May, Charles made a second declaration giving the Medici family perpetual charge of Florence. Alessandro left the Imperial court in the middle of the month, 'very well content'. It had been agreed that Margaret would leave the Low Countries at the end of August. She would make her way via Rome to Naples, where she would remain, as the Mantuan ambassador bluntly put it, until she was 'old enough to copulate with the Duke'.[5] Though dynastic brides were often married very young, at fourteen or so, that was still some years off. The Medici would have to ensure they retained Charles' favour, lest he swap Alessandro for a more advantageous match.

As Alessandro prepared to depart he received the customary leaving gift from the Emperor. He got a pair of horses with elaborate harnesses, one made in Italian style, another in Spanish, perhaps a hint at the alliance to come. He was given a Moorish sword too, with a scabbard and a hilt of hammered gold, and a pair of spurs, also in the Moorish style, also of gold. Margaret gave him a gold chain with a large ruby pendant. Observers estimated that as a whole the present – a sign of Charles' liberality and favour – was worth 6 or 7,000 *scudi* (more than the annual income of some cardinals). But its importance was not only in its monetary value. The gifts would be on public show. Throughout his rule of Florence, Alessandro wore a gold chain.[6] If it was this one, its provenance would have been noticed, a powerful sign of the protection Alessandro enjoyed, but also of the allegiance he owed.

While Alessandro was feasting and jousting in the north, his cousin Ippolito was nursing his discontents in Rome. Just four days after the *Balìa* had appointed Alessandro to the Florentine magistracies, Ippolito organised a pageant for Carnival. It featured an entourage of forty, dressed in Turkish, Indian and Spanish styles. 'A lovely sight,' wrote one observer.[7] Ippolito's household was quite an extraordinary collection of people from around the world. Paolo Giovio, who had become one of Clement's close advisers, described it in marvelling tones:

> Ippolito was extremely satisfied that in his dining rooms one might count more than twenty languages spoken by his barbarian guests. Among them were Numidians of royal blood who filled with admiration the eyes of whoever looked at them for their ability to ride and to jump from one horse to another. To them were added some Tartars, incomparable archers, and some Ethiopians, who in wrestling could beat all the strongest wrestlers. There were Indian swimmers and divers – most expert – who were used as teachers, seeking to imitate them because, in his youthful enthusiasm, Ippolito dedicated himself intensely to this activity. The Turks, on the other hand, the army's bravest, he had hunt, and used them day and night as excellent bodyguards.[8]

It is hard to escape the impression that this was something of a human zoo to entertain Ippolito and his friends.

Ippolito's papers are lost – perhaps destroyed – and his motivation for creating such a household remains a mystery. He might have read Hernán Cortés' intrigued account of the humans collected by Aztec ruler Moctezuma, published in 1522. Moctezuma had a room in his aviary for albino people, and beside his animal zoo, with its 'lions, tigers, wolves, foxes and cats' was 'another house where lived many deformed men and women, among which were dwarfs and hunchbacks and others with other deformities'. Animal menageries were a common feature of Renaissance courts. Rulers competed to obtain unusual specimens.[9] Perhaps Ippolito extended this idea to people too. As early as 1524, when he made his teenage entry to Florence, he had a black page in his service. He was far from alone in his fascination with people who – as in this description – were perceived by Europeans as exotic and different. We can only imagine what the people labelled 'barbarian guests' made of Ippolito and his friends. There is no record of their opinion. But it is notable that just as the value of black pages was aesthetic (and not based on skill or learning), the value of these 'guests' to Ippolito lay in their physical rather than intellectual skills: once again, a typical approach of Europeans to peoples they perceived to be inferior.

Ippolito's lavish lifestyle was expensive. He probably thought it was suitable to his status: liberality was a princely virtue. But he and the Pope fell out badly over money. Rumour had it that Clement, infuriated at his nephew's inability to live within his means, had called in Ippolito's major-domo, demanded a list of Ippolito's servants and struck from the roll those he deemed surplus to requirements. When the major-domo had reported the Pope's orders, Ippolito had retorted: 'Our Lord is correct, that I don't need all these servants that he's crossed out; but because they need me, if you care to stay in my good grace, don't sack any of them.' The teller of this tale observed that it was precisely for such princely conduct that Ippolito merited a rich state, rather than a cardinal's hat.[10] His gracious lordship – whether fact or fiction – contrasts with della Torre's story of Alessandro's rough household justice.

On 18 April, Ippolito suddenly left Rome. He headed to Florence with a few trusted men. It was a day's ride, perhaps two. Alessandro was still in Ghent. The risk was that Ippolito might seize the city in his cousin's absence, and manoeuvre himself into government.[11] His departure was quickly discovered. Clement was furious at his nephew's disobedience. It was not for Ippolito to overturn his decisions. He, Pope and head of the family, had decided that Alessandro would govern Florence. He had made him the Emperor's son-in-law. Now Ippolito's actions risked compromising the stability of city government. Clement needed to assure the Emperor of a friendly, stable, allied state in north-central Italy. If Ippolito's insubordination meant he could not deliver that, Clement's entire deal with Charles was at risk.

The Pope dispatched Cardinal Innocenzo Cibo to intercept Ippolito. He sent word to Nicolas Schömberg, his representative in Florence. He ordered Alessandro Vitelli, commander of Florentine forces, to ready his men. He sent a messenger to Luigi Guicciardini, commissar of Pisa, to warn him of Ippolito's plans. On his arrival, Ippolito announced that he had merely come to talk to Alessandro. That was unlikely: he must have known that Alessandro was yet to arrive in Italy. Schömberg played down the affair, emphasising Ippolito's worries about money. By 20 April he was writing that 'every hour the business looks more benign'.[12] Clement's secretary Jacopo Salviati did the same. 'It was evident,' he wrote, that Ippolito had not gone to Florence 'with plans to do anything that might displease His Holiness.' This was pretty close to an outright lie on Salviati's part. But Salviati, father of Piero, had his own ideas about the Medici bastards. He had never been keen on Clement's promotion of his nephews, preferring a broader form of government.[13] He might yet prove an ally against Alessandro.

For Clement's inner circle there was evident interest in assuring the outside world that this was merely a squabble about cash, not a threat to the stability of Florence. Some people bought that story. But there was much wilder speculation. Some said Ippolito had the backing of the king of France and the duke of Ferrara, both determined to cause trouble for the Emperor in Italy. He had planned to seize the fortresses of Pisa and Livorno, they said, and the duke of Ferrara would have come to his aid.[14]

Perhaps realising the futility of a poorly prepared coup d'état, Ippolito slunk back to Rome. In return for his compliance he persuaded the Pope to pay off his debts – between 9 and 12,000 ducats, depending who you believe – and give him an income of 700 or 800 ducats a month, though apparently Ippolito had asked for more. Cardinal Cibo helped out, offering Ippolito two of his smaller benefices. Clement was grateful. 'The roots of the hatred between the aforesaid cardinal and Duke Alessandro go right to the heart,' declared a Venetian ambassador. He speculated that Ippolito was hoping to marry Catherine de' Medici, his cousin once removed. Catherine's dowry would have helped Ippolito's finances considerably. 'It is obvious,' observed an agent of the Orsini family, 'that the Cardinal does not care to be a priest, and aspires to the state of Florence. And that never more can there be union, peace and benevolence between His Lordship and the Lord Duke Alessandro.'[15]

On 3 July 1531, the Venetian Senate gathered at the ducal palace, just off St Mark's Piazza, to hear the report of its ambassador, Antonio Soriano, recently returned from his mission to Rome. Venice was another of the Italian republics. Like Florence, it was built on mercantile wealth, but Venice's was a maritime empire, with a reach across the eastern Mediterranean. This was an occasion for the envoy to provide his colleagues with important political information, but it was also a set piece, a chance for him to show off his skill in rhetoric. Following convention, Soriano began with descriptions of the central players in papal (and Medici) affairs: Pope Clement, Cardinals Cibo, Ridolfi and Salviati. Then he turned to an assessment of the Medici nephews:

> Ippolito is bright enough, and has spent some time studying letters, so that he doesn't come across as ignorant among the cardinals. It's true that he has a lively nature, even rest- less, but perhaps that's allowed, on account of his youth. Up until now he's been unwilling to take holy orders; and the Pope told me this himself, when the cardinal returned from Florence, as I wrote to Your Serenity in my letter of 26 April: at that time the Pope used these precise words: 'He's mad, the devil, he's mad; he doesn't want to be a priest.'

There was little love lost between the Venetians and the Papacy. It is easy to imagine the laughter of Soriano's fellows.

> It's become clear that he's envious of Duke Alessandro. It seems to him that the Pope has done him an injury by setting Duke Alessandro to govern Florence; both because he thinks it belongs to him, because he's older, because he isn't thought to be a bastard (many say he's the legitimate son of a noblewoman of Cagli); but even if he were a bastard, he thinks he's of better condition than Duke Alessandro, who was born to a servant. Besides which, Giuliano was duke before Lorenzo, Alessandro's father. He also thinks he's better liked and loved by the city of Florence, with respect to his father, who the Florentines much loved; on the contrary, they despised Lorenzo, Alessandro's father.

These were arguments that Ippolito would refine and repeat.

Alessandro, on the other hand, 'appears clever, and has this quality: he knows how to accommodate the nature and will of the Pope better than does Cardinal de' Medici. His Holiness has openly shown me that he loves the Duke, and holds him in higher account.' Clement had spoken to Soriano about Alessandro on several occasions.

> He confirmed that it was his will that Alessandro should live in Florence, be the head of the family and govern the *Signoria* as his predecessors did. He has no title from the Emperor, neither Vicar nor Lieutenant. And His Holiness told me that he doesn't want him to have either of those titles, just the status of first in the family. Though it could well be that in time the Emperor will grant him some greater pre-eminence, also with the assent of the Pope, which will change.[16]

As Soriano was speaking to the Senate, the stage was set for Alessandro to make his entrance to Florence. He had travelled the long road south from Ghent and over the Alps. He arrived in Piacenza by 20 June and from there took the hill road via Pontremoli, reaching Massa, on the coast, by the 23rd. Alessandro had planned to go directly to Florence but there was plague in the city that summer and his journey was diverted to the nearby town of Prato. News of his approach was sent ahead to Florence. Two ambassadors, Roberto Acciaiuoli and Luigi Ridolfi, came out to greet him on the road. The city put on a handsome welcome, with trumpeters; tapestries and hangings adorned the Palazzo della Signoria.[17]

The city of Florence lay on either side of the River Arno, its houses, workshops and churches surrounded by high walls that had survived the siege with only limited damage. The enormous dome of Santa Maria del Fiore soared above the rest; the crenellated tower of the Palazzo della Signoria marked out the seat of government. Beyond the walls, hills encircled the city, offering a next line of defence. Alessandro arrived in Florence an hour before sunset on 5 July. (The Florentines measured their day by the number of hours from sundown.) He entered by the Porta a Faenza, to be greeted by a great crowd, and went straight to the Church of the Santissima Annunziata, the great basilica of the Servites on the piazza designed by Brunelleschi. In 1527 a gang of young republicans had gone into the church and knocked down its wax statues of Popes Leo and Clement. Now the Medici could renew their presence there. From Santissima Annunziata,

Alessandro went on to the Palazzo Medici, a few streets away on Via Larga. In the days that followed there were masquerades, fireworks, gun salutes, and 'every other sign of happiness'. The 6th of July was the feast of Saint Romulus of Fiesole. Alessandro, the Imperial envoy Giovanni Antonio Muscettola and the papal nuncio Nicolas Schömberg made their way to the Palazzo della Signoria, accompanied by 'great celebrations and the happiness of the people'. The crowds shouted 'Palle, Palle, Medici, Medici, Viva, Viva,' and even if some of this was manufactured excitement, hopes of a return to good times and an end to war were probably real enough.[18]

The ruling council and magistrates of Florence had gathered in the oldest part of the palace, in what is now the Hall of the Two Hundred. Halfway down the room was a wooden platform carved with lilies, garlands and the city's coat of arms. Flanked by Alessandro and Benedetto Buondelmonti (once in Duke Lorenzo's service, now Florence's *gonfaloniere*), Muscettola took the stage and outlined the Emperor's decision. His speech pulled few punches. He reminded the Florentines present how many privileges they had enjoyed from Emperors beginning with Charlemagne, seven centuries before. He noted their ingratitude and – what was worse – their open enmity to the Empire. It was known from long experience, he said, that their general government had been the cause of continual troubles and was more suited to ruin and revolution than to universal peace in Italy. Nonetheless, the Emperor was prepared to pardon every felony committed against the Empire, and every injury to His Majesty. There was plenty more.

Muscettola then handed the Imperial privilege to Francesco Campana, first secretary and chancellor of the Florentine government, who read it out, announcing that the house of Medici would govern the republic of Florence in perpetuity, beginning with Alessandro, the Emperor's son-in-law and his legitimate and natural sons born of 'Madama Margherita', the Emperor's daughter. Jacopo Salviati reported (rather implausibly) that the declaration was 'accepted with universal satisfaction'. Alessandro received the keys to the city's fortresses. Buondelmonti thanked him on behalf of the city, and Alessandro spoke. He thanked the Emperor, promising him his inviolable faith and perpetual service. To the city of Florence he promised 'entire justice and every best comportment that he owed to his fatherland,

and to a fatherland that had elected him to such honour and to a perpetual dictatorship, and that was so noble, and dignified, and full of such excellent personages and treasures'.[19]

At least, that was one version of events. Alessandro's critics spread quite another. They claimed that the council that greeted Muscettola was small. Many of its members were in exile and others were absent, because they did not agree with Alessandro's installation. Even with three secret ballots, Muscettola could not win the consent of those present to invest Alessandro as head of government. Finally, he demanded an oral vote, and no one dared oppose him. 'Universal satisfaction' of a sort.[20]

Following the ceremony, in a carefully staged sequence of celebrations, Alessandro distributed alms to some religious institutions; fires were lit across the city; an amnesty for all but a tiny handful of prisoners was declared; for three days solemn Masses were said. Francesco Corteccia's motet *Laetare et exsulta* ('Rejoice and be glad') may have been composed for this occasion.[21] Perhaps most important of all, the Duke announced a cut in the price of grain, and hinted at further cuts in the days to come. The people were greatly relieved.

It was said that the following day, when members of the *Signoria* went to Palazzo Medici to greet Duke Alessandro, he kept them waiting for an audience. It was said too that those who sought an audience were the pragmatists: men who preferred the hope of advantage to the certainty of honour. The papal and Imperial officials present squabbled over protocol. Alessandro left them to it and returned to Prato until he could be sure that Florence was clear of the last traces of plague. Even Medici allies felt frustrated at the arguments. Chiarissimo de' Medici, a distant relative who went on to serve in Alessandro's government, told a friend: 'Things cannot stay like this. We can't rule.' Chiarissimo felt as if he were at sea with no sight of shore. He prayed to God for aid. But back in Rome, Pope Clement was delighted at his nephew's success, and told visiting ambassadors so.[22]

On the sixth anniversary of the investiture, 6 July 1537, Pietro Aretino, poet and satirist, observed that in putting Alessandro de' Medici into power against the will of the Fates, Charles V had all but done the impossible.[23] If Alessandro was to hold off Fate, he would need a great deal more of Charles' help.

BOOK TWO
The Obedient Nephew

8

Many years later, long after Alessandro's death, Benvenuto Cellini, sculptor, goldsmith and Alessandro's associate in Rome, reflected on the trouble with Florentine government.

> Those men of Florence have set a young man upon a mettlesome horse; next they have buckled spurs upon his heels, and put the bridle freely in his hands, and turned him out upon a magnificent field, full of flowers and fruits and all delightful things; next they have bidden him not to cross certain indicated limits: now tell me, you, who there is that can hold him back, whenever he has but the mind to cross them? Laws cannot be imposed on him who is the master of the law.[1]

Cellini was not talking about Alessandro, but he might as well have been. Now that he and his heirs had been granted perpetual control of Florentine government, in theory he had ample power to run the city as he wished. But there were many difficulties to overcome first. The city was badly damaged after months of siege. There was rebuilding to manage, a militia to organise. Artisans had left and the alliance with the Emperor risked disrupting historic trade links with France. Alessandro had to sustain – and enhance – what popular support existed for his government. He had local officials to deal with, and anxious citizens to win round.

Condemned as common merchants by others, the Florentines saw themselves as special. They were the quintessence, the fifth vital element of life after water, fire, earth and air, wrote Benedetto Varchi: 'He who wants to destroy the universe should take away the

Florentines.' Florence was a city of perhaps 70,000 people. Encircled within its walls were the great family palaces of the fifteenth century, a university and over a hundred churches. There were convents with their orchards, hospitals and hospices, among them the famous Hospital of the Innocents, providing care for abandoned children. The Florentine territories encompassed Pisa, Volterra, Pistoia, Arezzo, Cortona, Borgo San Sepolcro, and another forty-five market towns, besides dozens of villages. War had badly disrupted agricultural production, but in better times, Tuscany's farmers produced grain, vegetables and oil, while the Chianti region was already famed for its exquisite wines. The war had also hit city revenues from customs duties; from taxes on salt, wine and meat; from stamp duties. Florence had had to rely instead on extraordinary taxes and forced loans. The city's currency had been devalued by 10 per cent in 1530–31, increasing the price of imports and reducing purchasing power.[2]

Alessandro was fortunate to have around him experienced political advisers. Liaising with Clement in Rome, they would make many of the important decisions in city government, leaving Alessandro to enjoy plenty of days out hunting. The new regime included representatives of the families traditionally allied to the Medici, including those who had wavered in the rebellion of 1527. Francesco Guicciardini, later author of a famous *History of Italy*, was one. Francesco Vettori, whose close friend Niccolò Machiavelli had died a few years earlier, was another. The Strozzi family, whose bank underwrote much of Clement's activity as pope, were represented. So were the Capponi, the Valori, the Acciaiuoli. Members of the Ridolfi and Pucci families, who had benefited from Medici largesse when relatives were promoted to the cardinalate, served in Alessandro's government too.

As Machiavelli had noted, 'there is nothing more difficult to execute, nor more dubious of success, nor more dangerous to administer than to introduce a new order of things.'[3] The *Balìa* feared plots against the government, and the most urgent matter on their minds was the defence of the city. Alessandro Vitelli, whose family had long served the Florentine state, was chosen as commander. It was an uncompromising and controversial choice. Vitelli's father Paolo, a *condottiere*, had been employed as captain of the Florentine army at the end of the fifteenth century. He had deliberately prolonged a war with Pisa at the request of the duke of Milan (a move that not incidentally extended his own employment and, consequently, income). His schemes discovered, he had been executed by the Florentine republic in 1499.[4] Kin relations mattered in Renaissance Italy, and hostile Florentines feared Alessandro Vitelli would be no better than his father. The Medici choice for chancellor to the *Otto di Guardia* (the magistracy responsible for security in Florence) was no more welcome. Nicknamed 'the Butcher', Ser Maurizio da Milano was another official appointed from outside the city (his title indicates that he was a notary, though 'Ser' was also used more widely, by artisans). His ruthless enforcement of Alessandro's rule won him few friends. 'He took such delight in tormenting men,' wrote Benedetto Varchi, 'that just the sight of him instilled fear.' These 'foreigners', as they were perceived, became the target of much antagonism. For the regime, though, the appointments made sense. There was a long tradition in Italy of employing outsiders in key city offices. They would be loyal to the current ruler and not to any local family interest or faction.[5]

Alessandro's residence in Florence was the Palazzo Medici, the magnificent house on the Via Larga (now Via Cavour) commissioned by Cosimo the Elder over eighty years before. It is one of the archetypal Renaissance palaces, with an imposing three-storey facade and dramatic overhanging cornice.[6]

The first room on the left of the Palazzo Medici gate was reserved for guests. Ground floor chambers such as this had the advantage of being cooler during the summer heat. It housed a bed with black taffeta hangings, a desk and some spare bedding for servants; on the wall was a work in marquetry. Messer Giovanbattista, the major-domo, head of the household staff, kept the key to this room. Elsewhere on the ground floor lived Don Girolamo and Don Annibale, the chaplains, and Signor Girolamo da Correggio, Alessandro's chamberlain. Girolamo, of an age with Alessandro, was the son of Veronica Gambara, a celebrated poet and stateswoman.[7] He and his colleagues in the ducal chamber might play a number of roles, from assisting with the Duke's toilette to carrying official messages and acting as Alessandro's companions for hunting, hawking and sport. The titles of these men indicate their relative status in the household: 'Messer' was an honorific used for knights and lawyers but also for courtiers more generally, while 'Signor' implied nobility.[8] Then there was Alessandro the *credenziere*, responsible for cold foods and service at table. There were grooms and couriers, trusted to ride with the Duke's messages. Other ground-floor rooms were reserved for Maestro Antonio, the Duke's cook; 'El Giena', custodian of the tableware, and Matteo, the cellarman. The grandest room on the ground floor was that of Angelo Marzi, a long-standing supporter of the Medici who had served Duke Lorenzo and Pope Clement. He had been rewarded for his loyalty late in 1529 with the bishopric of Assisi. Now in his forties he was one of the men tasked with guiding Alessandro into government.

Up a great staircase, famed for its beauty, was the entrance to the main apartments.[9] On the first floor lay what is now the palace's most celebrated room. The chapel decorated by Benozzo Gozzoli is a tiny jewel-box. His splendid portrayal of the procession of the Magi, interspersed with images of the Medici family, winds its way around three walls, surrounding the worshippers present. In the background are scenes of hunting, castles, countryside, angels singing. Gozzoli's frescoes are also testimony to the presence of Africans at the Medici court: a black archer is shown in the foreground of the Medici entourage. They are testimony too to the incorporation of the children of slaves into the family. Just behind the figures of Cosimo the Elder and his legitimate son Piero, Gozzoli had portrayed a man wearing a curious headdress. This was Carlo de' Medici, the bastard son of Cosimo and his enslaved mistress Maddalena.

Near the chapel lay the entrance to Alessandro's apartments. First was his dining room. Already new hangings were being commissioned for its walls. In the next room Alessandro gave audience: it was adorned with seven new arras hangings and a round ebony panel worked with a design of white bone inlay. There were benches, perhaps to accommodate officials or petitioners waiting to be heard. Its gilded ceiling was one of the most stunning features of the palace.[10] An antechamber came next: the pages, boys responsible for running messages and assisting with personal service for the ruler, slept here. In the study a ceiling covered with great blue-and-white tiles showed the passing of the seasons.¹¹ Alessandro himself had the final room of the sequence. The decor reflected his favourite pastime. His chamber was hung with seven arrases depicting hunting scenes; another, with a design of animals, lay on his bed. The room had a damask carpet, four *braccia* wide (a Florentine *braccio*, or arm's length, was about 23 inches, so this was about eight feet) and an inlaid casket for storage. Two images of the Virgin Mary – one a painting on canvas, one a bas-relief, perhaps again part of the Medici inheritance – completed the decor. These saints watched over the people in the rooms, protecting them as they slept and as they went about their daily lives.

The major-domo slept on this first floor too, as did the under-cooks and skivvies, and Messer Cesare, a steward responsible for the meals in the ducal apartments. Up another set of stairs was Signor Mario Colonna, probably another of Alessandro's courtiers, perhaps a son of the Roman condottiere Stefano Colonna who had led the republic's forces during the siege. Also on this level were Messer Giulio da San Gimigniano, Agostino da Gubbio, the tailor, Messer Girolamo d'Ancona, 'El Conte' (responsible for the wine) and Messer Manfredi da Pavia. Nicolò da Cevoli, responsible for the servants' hall, had a room near the tower.¹²

Living alongside the courtiers and servants on the second floor, in a room at the top of the back stairs, was Baccio Bandinelli, the sculptor. The son of a goldsmith, Baccio had been born in Florence in 1493. Among his father's apprentices – Baccio's later rivals – was Benvenuto Cellini. From early in his career Baccio had benefited from Medici patronage. He had made temporary sculptures for Pope Leo X's triumphal entry to Florence in 1515. He was commissioned to make a copy of the famous *Laocoön*, an ancient sculpture unearthed in Rome in 1506, for King Francis I of France, and produced a model of a tomb for Henry VIII of England. Now he was working on a much bigger commission for the Medici: a statue of Hercules and Cacus. His larger room was simply furnished with a trestle bed and bedsheets *da famigli* (for household members) – a term used to indicate lower quality than sheets *da gentiluomo* (for gentlemen). He had a table seven and a half feet long, a desk half the size, a larger trestle table about thirteen feet long, a couple of old stools and a red leather chair. There was an old carpet to lay across one of the tables, as was the fashion; the one arras hanging was in a sad state. In a second, smaller room, where Baccio himself perhaps slept, there was another bed.[13]

Alessandro de' Medici had most of the usual assets of a Renaissance ruler now: a palace, a bride, advisers, artists. Sometime after his return to Florence, he found himself a mistress. Six or seven years Alessandro's elder, Taddea Malaspina was the widow of Count Giambattista Boiardo da Scandiano. She had survived an unhappy marriage. Scared of her husband, at the age of twenty-one Taddea had fled to a convent and begged her mother's relatives to let her stay there. The following year, however, her husband had died, and Taddea had been able to return to her family. One of four sisters, Taddea was well connected and well off. Her father Alberico Antonio, marquis of Massa, had left her a dowry of 6,000 ducats.[14] Her mother, Lucrezia, was a member of the Este family of Ferrara and cousin to Isabella d'Este, marchioness of Mantua. A few miles up the Tuscan coast from the marble quarries of Carrara, their great fortress of Massa – the Rocca – nestled in the cliffs, overlooking the sea. Besides palatial accommodation for the city's rulers, it afforded defence against attacks on the coast.

The lords of Massa had suffered a setback when Alberico and his wife produced no sons and four daughters, but despite a supposed prohibition on women inheriting, first their eldest and then the second daughter, Ricciarda, had managed to hold the marquisate after their father's death in 1519. Ricciarda, eight years Taddea's elder, was married to Lorenzo Cibo, the brother of Cardinal Innocenzo Cibo who had quelled their cousin Ippolito's rowdy behaviour in Bologna and had been sent by the Pope to intercept him as he advanced on Florence. And if Ricciarda's unusual independence was noteworthy, her open affair with her husband's brother Innocenzo made her notorious. Her son Alberico, born in 1534, was widely thought to be the Cardinal's, though he was acknowledged as the legitimate child of her husband.[15]

Taddea became Alessandro's mistress sometime in the early 1530s. They may have met earlier, in 1527, when Alessandro passed by Massa in search of refuge from the Florentine rebellion, or around 1524, when he was at the papal court. Ricciarda was certainly in Rome then. Their affair produced a son, Giulio, and some accounts suggest he was four years old at the time of Alessandro's death at the beginning of 1537, which would suggest a conception date in late 1531 or early 1532. The

Malaspina family records, however, say that Giulio was only three, so the relationship may have started later. A conception date of early 1533 would fit better with Giulio's likely baptism date, December that year.[16] What we do know is that shortly after Alessandro's entry to Florence, Taddea had returned to Massa from the port city of Genoa, some seventy miles to the north. By early August 1531, she, Cardinal Cibo and others were planning to make up a party to go to the baths at Lucca, a convenient spot for a rendezvous within easy travelling distance of both Massa and Florence. For a mixed group of bathers, a spa offered all manner of erotic possibilities.[17]

9

Luxury lodgings and entertaining one's mistress were intrinsic to a princely lifestyle, but there were serious matters of government to address in Florence too. In later histories Alessandro de' Medici would take the blame for his regime's tyranny, but even before his arrival in Florence his ministers were convinced that only severe repression would make the city safe for the Medici party. Francesco Vettori, one of the most senior of Florence's statesmen, complained that Fra Benedetto da Foiano, a republican leader detained in Rome, was not facing tough enough questioning. The lax treatment of men such as Fra Benedetto set a 'bad example'. Francesco Guicciardini, another important figure in government, was accused of particular cruelty in his dealings with opponents.[1] Back in 1527, many of the men who ended up in Alessandro's government – Guicciardini, Vettori, Strozzi and Valori – had flirted with the republic. But like most of the *ottimati* they had fallen under suspicion for their historic ties to the Medici, had left Florence and had broken with the republican regime before the start of the siege. This tension between the elite and the more radical faction of the republicans (the *popolari*) was to haunt those who opposed Medici rule.[2]

The key sanction against political opponents was exile. This was not so straightforward as a simple expulsion from the city. Those deemed enemies of the new regime were constrained to live within a certain distance of a certain town or city, often one long distant from Florence. In Italian they were called *confinati*: literally, 'the confined ones'. If they broke their confinement, they risked losing all their property in the city of Florence. One step up from the *confinati* were the *banditi*, those who had been declared rebels and their property forfeit.[3] Florence, a city of bankers, targeted financial interests to ensure compliance. (Most of those sentences had been handed down in late 1530, when Alessandro was away in Flanders, allowing him to deny any charge that he was taking personal revenge on his family's opponents.) Other measures were used to avoid the removal of resources from Florence. Although it had been agreed after the siege that anyone who wished to leave could do so freely, this offer was quickly revoked. The new regime was not prepared to risk a collapse in population, and with it a collapse in the economy. Nor was it prepared to risk an organised campaign by the exiles. They were deliberately confined in different parts of Italy, so as to make it harder for them to meet.[4] The satirist Pietro Aretino joked that on the gates of Florence were written the words 'Abandon hope all ye who leave.'[5]

Despite the sentences of exile imposed on many opponents there was a collective nervousness in Florence. Entry to and exit from the city was regulated. Men needed permission to leave the city at night, to take post horses. After long years of war, suspicion of spies was rife. In 1527, Cardinal Innocenzo Cibo had fretted that his letters had been intercepted: some opened, some stolen.[6] This was commonplace enough. Information was a saleable commodity. As a consequence, sensitive messages were rarely written down. Wherever possible, they were sent orally by messenger; where not, secretaries cultivated vagueness. Rather than spell out details of a problem, they referred to 'that business with the countess' or 'this issue with the preacher'.

Alessandro and his ministers set up intelligence networks to protect their regime. The accounts of the *Otto di Guardia*, the committee responsible for internal security, show numerous payments to 'secret spies'. Some received just a florin or two for their services; others, commissioned to work outside the Florentine dominion, were paid much greater sums, over a hundred florins in some cases.[7] In his dialogue on the Duke's actions, Alessandro Ceccherelli tells the story of how, shortly after taking control of Florence, Alessandro had richly rewarded a spy. This man pretended to take the side of the *popolari*, and reported back on their activities in the city. When he was denounced publicly, he went to Alessandro, complaining that he'd been called a spy, and demanding that Alessandro set things right. Alessandro replied: 'Don't be surprised: the man who called you that is a man who calls a cat a cat, who tells it like it is.' Hearing the Duke's response, the spy left, doubly mocked.[8] The moral of the tale: he who betrays his friends risks betrayal.

The political ruthlessness of Alessandro's regime was the kind of behaviour that might later be labelled 'Machiavellian'. The most original thinker of Renaissance Florence had died in 1527, but the ghost of Niccolò Machiavelli haunts Alessandro's story. He had been a civil servant and diplomat in the republican government after 1498, while the Medici were in exile. Imprisoned, tortured and then exiled himself after their return in 1512, he had sought to regain their favour. He planned to dedicate his book *The Prince* to Giuliano de' Medici, then seeking a state to rule in Italy. (*The Prince* is a complex text that seemed to advise princes even while undermining the practice of princely government.)[9] For several years, especially via his friend Francesco Vettori, Machiavelli sought a return to government. Finally, after Alessandro's father, Duke Lorenzo's death in 1519, the Medici sought Machiavelli's opinion on the government of Florence. In 1520 Cardinal Giulio de' Medici commissioned him to write the city's history, and in 1526, as war loomed, he sought his advice on Florence's defences.[10] It was not until the summer of 1531, however, four years after Machiavelli's death, that Cardinal Giulio, now Pope Clement VII, granted permission to Antonio Blado, a printer in Rome, to publish three works by Machiavelli: the *Florentine Histories*, the *Discourses on Livy* and *The Prince*. The last of these three had eventually been dedicated to Duke Lorenzo de' Medici, but the printed edition had a new dedicatee: Filippo Strozzi. In a changing political world, there was evidently a market for new ideas. Blado's edition sold well, and the Giunti printing house in Florence saw a lucrative business opportunity. Bernardo Giunti applied to the Pope for a licence to print the book himself, citing the backing of Machiavelli's heirs (which Blado had not secured) and insisting that, as Blado's print run had all but sold out, the Pope could grant him exclusive rights to the works for ten years without compromising his rival's profits. On 20 December 1531, Clement granted Giunti that privilege.[11] Even the story of this book's publication contains a lesson on the reach of papal power.

★

In September 1531, Alessandro went to Rome for his first meeting with Pope Clement since he had left Italy for the Imperial court the previous year. His visit was in large part aimed at seeking his great-uncle's advice on managing Florence and working with its leading politicians. Much had changed in their relationship. Though Clement was still the family patriarch, Alessandro now had independent access to the Florentine treasury, and he could wield his new personal relationship with Charles V.

Alessandro had meetings at least once a day, sometimes twice, with the Pope. They discussed the merits of a new citadel in Florence, to house a personal guard for Alessandro. In 1522, trying to lead the government of Florence, Cardinal Giulio de' Medici, as he then was, had survived a republican conspiracy to assassinate him, uncovered when the plotters' correspondence was intercepted. Pope Clement knew well the dangers of Florentine politics. His advisers, however, were not all convinced that a fortress was the answer.[12]

Three years since he had returned to Rome after his exile in Orvieto and Viterbo, tensions remained between the Pope and the city. Part of the reason was that the Roman countryside had not fully recovered from the recent war and harvests were poor. Another, though, was Clement's determination to pursue his family interests in Florence – whatever the cost to the people of Rome – embodied in the person of Alessandro. Verse six of a satirical poem on the seven joys of the Church, posted on the Pasquino statue, spells out the source of the tension:

> Hail, pure and immaculate dove
> Example to all of patience
> You're starving Rome like never before
> To keep a mule in Florence;
> You've failed in your duty to feed us
> But Strozzi will do penance
> What he should sell for six goes for twenty
> This sixth joy is for the discontented.[13]

The avaricious Strozzi here was Filippo, banker to the Medici, husband of Alessandro's aunt Clarice. The 'mule' was Alessandro, the bastard whose costly campaign to rule Florence was pushing up taxes in Rome.

Alessandro arrived around sunset on 14 September. He made an informal entry, without the grand ceremony that a duke arriving in Rome might demand, but nonetheless with 'many gentlemen and priests'. A large entourage was a good demonstration of power, and the Mantuan ambassador reported that his 'beautiful and flowering' company was welcomed with 'happiness and good cheer'.[14] There was always an impressive welcome for distinguished visitors to Rome. It was known as the 'theatre of the world' for good reason.

The court of Rome watched carefully for clues to the state of Alessandro's relationship with Ippolito. Ippolito had made some effort not to greet his cousin at all, but it could not be avoided. They made a pretence of friendship as they dined together on the Tiber Island but observers were sure that their 'exterior caresses' hid an absence of affection. There was 'hatred and malevolence' between them, wrote the Mantuan envoy. Clement was increasingly unhappy about Ippolito's behaviour, but the Cardinal did little to allay his uncle's fears. Facing down his criticism, on one occasion Ippolito, 'almost as if he didn't care, or was unable to do otherwise, raised his head and shrugged his shoulders.' On the 17th they dined together again, this time in the company of Clement, Catherine and John Stewart, duke of Albany, a relative of Catherine de' Medici's mother Madeleine. Besides Alessandro's role in Florence – which Ippolito saw as rightfully his – there was a vicious squabble over money. Alessandro had an income of some 20,000 ducats from Florence, and Ippolito wanted a share. Clement brokered a deal in which the money would be split equally between them, but Alessandro, confident in his new relationship with Charles V, had his eye on another source of income. He hoped to become Captain-General of the Church: head of the papal armies.[15] It was a role that could bring not only wealth but princely honour.

The other rulers of Italy saw Alessandro very much as Clement's man. If they had a deal to make, they went to Rome, not to Florence. The city's real business was done at the Curia. Nonetheless, Alessandro could and did lobby for his own interests – and those of his most powerful backer. He asked for a cardinal's hat for Nicolas Schömberg, archbishop of Capua, a German cleric who was currently papal representative in Florence. Clement pronounced himself in favour, though he never delivered and Schömberg had to wait for his successor as pope to grant the promotion.[16] Alessandro and Clement, meanwhile, had arranged for the departure of two Florentine ambassadors to the Emperor. Palla Rucellai and Francesco Valori went on behalf of the city to welcome Charles' appointment of Alessandro as the city's governor. Between the formalities, they had a message for Charles: with the Medici in power, he would have a friendlier Florence than with any popular government.[17]

Around 19 October, Alessandro left Rome and headed back to Florence. His ministers were busy with plans for reform of the *monte di pietà*, Florence's public pawnbroker and a key source of credit in the city. Otherwise things were quiet. Ippolito headed south, to Naples and Ischia. Some said he sought a warmer climate and the company of women. Giulia Gonzaga, widowed at fifteen, celebrated for her beauty and learning, and once touted as Ippolito's bride, became his mistress. Others, more suspicious, thought he had his eye on a deal with Cardinal Colonna: he would back Colonna as the next pope, if Colonna would back him over Florence.[18]

When Alessandro had come to Poggio a Caiano as a teenager, in 1525, it had been to live at a discreet distance from the city while his cousin Ippolito learned to govern. When he came back in 1531, the Poggio villa became his retreat from city life and political business. It was one of several Medici properties in the hills that ringed Florence. There were other country houses at Careggi, La Petraia and Castello. The white facade of the villa at Poggio faced south, beneath its red-tiled roof. Half a dozen windows spanned the upper floor. Above the colonnaded entrance with its marble floor was a blue-and-white ceramic frieze, after the same fashion as the tiles in the Palazzo Medici study. It showed an allegory of time, a great serpent consuming its own tail. Time and its passing had been a fascination for the learned men of Lorenzo the Magnificent's court some fifty years before. Images of renewal and regeneration underlined the continuity of the dynasty.[19] Down the straight steps at Poggio, there were formal gardens, an orchard and stables. In the near distance were small hills. There was a view of the mountains, a welcome breeze, calm, stillness, perhaps the chatter of cicadas away from the heat and bustle of the city.

The interior of the villa was a work in progress. In the Hall of Leo X, the family arms were displayed on the ceiling. As yet it had only two of its four planned large frescoes. One, by Franciabigio, depicted the return of the Roman politician Cicero from exile during the time of Julius Caesar, a reference to the return of Cosimo the Elder to Florence in 1434. Since then the Medici had been exiled twice more, in 1494 and 1527, and twice they had returned. The second fresco, by Andrea del Sarto, showed Julius Caesar receiving tribute from Egypt, a reference to gifts sent to Lorenzo the Magnificent by the Sultan of Egypt: a parrot, a goat, a monkey, a giraffe. Jacopo da Pontormo had contributed a fresco for a lunette. It showed the story of Vertumnus and Pomona, a tale from Ovid in which the god of seasons tricked his way into the orchard of the young woman in order to seduce her.[20]

For Alessandro, the hunting grounds were Poggio's main attraction. As ever, he sought out the best stock. He asked Giovanni Borromei, the duke of Mantua's agent, if he could get his hands on some pheasants. They proved to be out of season, but in the meantime the Duke promised to send Alessandro a couple of puppies from the next litter. Besides game birds and hunting dogs they exchanged sparrowhawks, peregrine falcons, a Hungarian horse, their qualities debated in pages of letters between the two courts. Alessandro even had a silver basin made to hold the bait for his falcons. Others were less sanguine about Alessandro's habits. 'The Duke attends to his hunting,' wrote Luigi Guicciardini, an ally, if sometimes a reluctant one, of the Medici, 'and works little.'[21] An epitaph for Alessandro's favourite hunting dog by the poet Francesco Berni hinted at a link between the dog's vicious character and its master's:

> Here lies buried in this dark hole
> A rebel traitor dirty dog
> He was Spite, and called Love
> There was naught good about him –
> He was the Duke's dog.[22]

Though Luigi Guicciardini insinuated that Alessandro was lazy, he acknowledged too that the Duke had political ambitions. Luigi and his younger brother Francesco (the historian and political theorist) were important figures in the Florentine government. They had held numerous offices under the Medici. Luigi had been made commissar of Pisa in 1530, while Francesco had been appointed governor of Bologna, second city of the Papal States, an office in the gift of Clement VII. In November 1531 Luigi wrote to his brother with a long update on Florentine affairs. Alessandro was beginning to make his own political decisions, he reported. He had rejected Clement's preferred choice of ambassador to Rome in favour of Benedetto Buondelmonti. It was not the most significant of matters, but it was a small marker of independence.

The matter of Raffaello Girolami, however, was more concerning. Girolami, the most prominent of the regime's prisoners, was still causing difficulties. He had been transferred to the fortress in Pisa, but Ferrante Gonzaga, the Imperial military commander, continued to offer him his influential support. He had even convinced Clement to give Girolami the freedom to come and go as he liked within the castle walls (with a bond of 20,000 ducats as surety against any plotting against the current government or Clement himself). 'This was no way to put fear into enemies,' wrote Luigi, and he worried that Clement would do the same for others. 'If you don't govern states with the same rigour and rules as those who've held their states long-term,' he wrote, 'you're bound to ruin them. Too much pity is harmful: it can destroy you.' As far as he could tell, Alessandro had not been pleased with the Girolami decision, 'but His Excellency has patience yet.' Luigi blamed others of Alessandro's ministers for the move: Nicolas Schömberg and Ottaviano de' Medici. 'Whoever governs a state like this one, and wants to govern it well, must court fortune, just like its other partisans: otherwise he falls into error, especially when he has to deal with desperate souls like our enemies.' Piety, justice and reason had not won over enemies in the past: there was no reason to think they would in the future.[23]

Yet if Alessandro's ministers were dismissive of his hunting, it was quite *de rigueur* for a European prince, the 'true pastime of great lords'. Half a century before, in the days of Lorenzo the Magnificent, hunting had been a patrician pursuit. One of Lorenzo's most famous poems, 'The Partridge Hunt', conveyed its pleasures: the dawn start, the falconers' banter, the beauty of the countryside. But now, in wartime, the hunt had acquired a different, military value. In *The Prince*, Machiavelli wrote of the importance of hunting as training for war: 'Besides keeping his soldiers well disciplined and trained, [the prince] must always be out hunting, and must accustom his body to hardships in this manner.'[24] The point of hunting was both to learn the shape of his own territory and to understand better how quickly to grasp the lie of the land in another's. Ippolito de' Medici had also written on the links between hunting and warfare. In his *Exhortation to Hunt* he highlighted the parallels between the dextrous hunter and the diligent soldier. 'Good hunters,' he wrote, 'know as soon as they arrive in a place how that plain lies, how that mountain rises, where those valleys lead, where one crosses that river, which roads are shorter, which easier to ride, things that for the most part – no less than other virtues of the captain – are profitable in times of war.' The hunter's mind and body were important too: he should have 'a burning soul, be young in years, and dry and robust in person, so that he's able to rise three or four hours before daybreak to ride.' Conquering injury, thirst, hunger and exhaustion were an 'honourable victory' for the hunter.[25] Alessandro's hunting was not just a matter of pleasure or escapism from political duties. It was part of becoming a prince.

But however appealing country life might be to Alessandro, the dangers of the city were constant. He surrounded himself with guards. According to Benedetto Varchi, the Duke never went out without protective clothing.[26]

10

Itemising the Medici wardrobe in 1537, after Alessandro's assassination, the wardrobe master noted that the Duke had owned 'plenty' of mail. Alessandro's doublets were reinforced with a fine chain mail known as *gazarina*. In April 1532 alone the master of the wardrobe took custody of a mail shirt, a jacket, and collars adorned with black and grey velvet. Another collar was decorated with silver chains and lined with red satin. Alessandro's wardrobe was managed by one Pietro Monferrati da Lucca, nicknamed Pretino, the 'little priest'.[1] It held not only Alessandro's clothing but items for his courtiers, as well as being a storage facility for textiles and other valuables. Pretino monitored the transfer of items from the store to Alessandro's courtiers and in particular to his chamberlain, Girolamo da Correggio. He issued lengths of fabric to the Duke's tailor to be made up into new clothes in the latest styles. This was a post that carried with it considerable responsibility. The rich velvets, silks and satins that clothed the Duke and his courtiers were expensive commodities. When Agostino, Alessandro's tailor, came to pick up fabric, he had to sign it out, noting the length in Pretino's record book.

More generally, Pretino's book records the numerous purchases and commissions of items for the Duke's use, and offers a window onto the luxurious world of Alessandro's court. It details not only clothes and fabrics but other items for the household: in March 1532 the chamberlain handed over for safekeeping forty-nine taffeta standards, in multiple colours, and a swordstick decorated with the arms of Pope and Duke. Weapons feature regularly in these wardrobe accounts. Alessandro owned numerous *stioppi*: matchlock handguns, most imported from Germany, Imperial territory. (Firearms were not yet accurate at long range – although, as Cellini had discovered, they could be lethal close up – but the new matchlock mechanism allowed the gun to be held steady with both hands when firing, which helped to some extent.) One was decorated with gold, as much for showing off as for practical use. There were swords too: some for one hand, some for two, some gilded, some in worked leather scabbards. In February 1532 Federico, a chamberlain, brought in a sword inscribed in French, a Turkish dagger and two *stioppi* designed for use on horseback. Arms and warfare still defined a prince. When Baldassarre Castiglione had written his book on the courtier, published just a few years before, despite his emphasis on the courtier's literary and artistic accomplishments he had made clear that 'the first and true profession of the courtier must be that of arms.'[2]

Alessandro made regular gifts of weapons, too: a new German *stioppo* went to the lord of Monterotondo, father of his courtier Valerio Orsini. Tomaso da Castello got a new sword blade, Captain Fabrizio Maremano a pair of arquebuses and Captain Rosa da Viccio a *stioppo*.[3] The Battle of Pavia – the stunning victory for the Imperial troops at which they had taken the king of France hostage – was said to be the first battle in which small arms were decisive: it had been fought just seven years before. The fact that Alessandro's guns were German hinted at the source of his political power. The fact he owned them at all was also a provocation. At the end of the siege one of the new government's first acts had been to disarm the populace.[4] For his courtiers to enjoy such privileged access to weapons surely aroused resentment.

If weapons had both a symbolic and practical purpose, so did many of the other items in the ducal wardrobe. Here were the makings of an aristocratic household, the piecings together of the Medici collection of old. Some of these objects had once belonged to Lorenzo the Magnificent, in the heyday of Medici pre-eminence in Florence. There were eighty-seven pieces of porcelain, large and small. There were eighteen new arras cloths, some depicting historical events, others with a Deposition from the Cross and the image of Our Lady. Two old panel paintings showed the triumphs of Petrarch (there had once been four). There were red silk bedcovers, beds for the stable-hands, seven portraits and seven relief heads of Medici ancestors. There were little pictures of Saint Sebastian, usually shown pierced with arrows, and Jerome, the scholar, often portrayed in his study or removing a thorn from a lion's paw. There were two globes, one of the earth, one of the heavens, later given away as gifts. There was a lily branch, from the San Giovanni palio, Florence's annual horse race. For learning and leisure there were seventy-four books in Latin and vernacular, a chess set in agate and jasper, and twenty-five masquerading costumes in purple, yellow, green and grey. There was a marble vase with gold handles, and an ancient stone wine-cooler. There was one white skin of a Levantine goat, one cradle, two gilded coffins.[5]

On his travels to Rome in the autumn of 1531, Alessandro had arranged for the dispatch of further goods to Florence. His agents sent up a stunning set of jousting gear: silk, satin and taffeta to dress the horses. They sent horse-tack for jennets; half a dozen sets of spurs; dozens of breastplates. There were velvet saddle-covers, velvet caps, more costumes for the masquerade.[6] A year later, Pretino recorded further additions to the wardrobe: a silver cup with a cover, decorated with reliefs of foliage and enamel roses, newly restored; two more silver-gilt cups; a little silver clock with bas-reliefs of foliage, possibly German (by the turn of the fifteenth to the sixteenth century, artisans could produce clocks small enough to carry on the person or in a bag); a striking sword belt, trimmed with enamel, silver and gold, and a silver-gilt bracelet, adorned with six pearls.[7] This is probably far from the total: these items were recorded by mistake in Pretino's book, crossed out and the entries transferred to another volume which is now lost. The full splendour of Alessandro's court remains to be imagined.

Observers noted that Florentine fashions were changing. Hooded cloaks fell out of vogue, to be replaced by hats of different types. Hair was no longer worn long, to the shoulders, but instead cut short. Beards came in. Alessandro had short hair, but his portraits show only wisps of facial hair. Breeches were now slashed, their taffeta lining made to show through the cuts, a German fashion. There had long been efforts to regulate clothing in Florence through sumptuary laws, and anxiety about citizens adopting foreign styles. Madeleine de la Tour d'Auvergne, duchess of Urbino, had won praise for dressing *all'italiana* – Italian style – in her brief months in Florence. Like the guns, the latest changes in fashions hinted at Alessandro's new diplomatic alliance. They also hinted at a more martial ideal of masculinity in Florence, a product of warfare and siege.[8]

★

As the look of the Florentine people changed, the look of the city changed too. Alessandro began to fortify the city and to rebuild the countryside castles around it. With a faltering city economy, the challenge of rebuilding was all the greater, and the weather was not helping. There had been little rain that year. The grain harvest was poor, the grape harvest worse. Now, the authorities had to avoid a situation where failed crops led farmers to abandon their land and migrate to the city. There were walls and streets to restore, roads to mend. As Varchi put it: 'There's not a single city, castle, town or village, however great, however small and poor, that hasn't been sacked and otherwise cruelly damaged – often more than once.'[9]

Even before Alessandro's return, measures had been taken to address the problems of flooding in the lowest-lying part of Florence, and to begin relaying the major roads out of the city. During the siege itself the city had been fortified, and some buildings demolished, to improve the chances of defence. Houses and workshops in the area immediately outside the city walls had been razed to the ground on the orders of the city authorities, the better to secure the walls. In October 1531, Florence's five Procurators for the Fortification of the City and Countryside issued their first by-laws confirming limits on construction close to the walls. One of the first projects to be undertaken was the rebuilding of the bastion at the Porta alla Giustizia (Gate of Justice), at the eastern limit of the city, just north of the River Arno, so called because it was the site for city executions. Alessandro always put security first, wrote Bernardo Segni in his history of Florence. He wanted a secure retreat in times of trouble, where he could defend himself from popular revolt.[10] He also owed it to the Emperor to provide suitable defences. This fortress had 160 placements for guns, from small arms to eight large cannons, a sizeable defence.

Besides the rebuilding of Florence, there were other towns to consider. Ready access to the ports of Pisa and Livorno was essential if the city's economy was to improve, but this cost money. In July 1532, the local authorities in Pisa raised the price of salt by 50 per cent. Taxes on salt – a vital commodity because of its role in preserving meat – were an important component of public revenues in Renaissance Italy. The plan was to use the money to improve the embankments of the Ozzeri canal, and to do works along the road to Florence. But even with the additional salt tax, the lack of money available for such public works soon caused conflict between Florence and the subject cities. In 1532, the Pisan authorities complained that a promised contribution from Florence to the rebuilding of the Ponte a Stagno, a bridge on the post-road between Pisa and Livorno, had not arrived. The *Otto di Pratica* (the Florentine committee dealing with external affairs) had changed their mind. Citing poor weather that would be bound to increase the cost, and a shortage of money in the city, they wrote: 'You have to consider that we're aiming to save as much as possible. Nonetheless, this being a necessary task we consider that it would be worth doing, but at a time when it can be done more easily and at less expense.'[11]

For Alessandro and his ministers, the priority in Pisa was its fortress, on which in 1533 they spent 8,500 *lire* (about enough to employ fifty labourers for a year). They invested too in restorations in the border towns of Borgo San Sepolcro, where the captain's house was restored, and Cortona, where they spent rather less: 1,000 *lire*.[12] Behind its castle walls and chain-mail jackets, this was a regime that knew it had enemies, and that knew the risk of invasion.

11

Clement VII had intended that Alessandro would govern as 'first citizen' of Florence, following the not-quite-princely fashion of his forebears, though with Charles' official backing for permanent Medici rule the rhetoric of the republic cannot have sounded convincing. Within a few months the Pope was beginning to wonder whether the old style of government was indeed the best solution. Late in 1531, he began to canvass the views of leading pro-Medici politicians on constitutional reform. Francesco Guicciardini and his brother Luigi wrote down their thoughts; so did Roberto Acciaiuoli and Francesco Vettori. They differed in the detail of their views, but all agreed that the preferred form of government would be a narrowly based regime controlled by the Medici and their allies. Even that would be fragile. Twice in the past forty years a Medici regime had fallen. The Medici no longer had the wealth that in the past had won them backers, wrote Vettori. They were entirely dependent on one man, Alessandro, and the loyalty of his guards, wrote Acciaiuoli. Luigi Guicciardini was prepared to accord Alessandro some veto, but not one of the men consulted proposed that he should be duke of Florence. 'I do not see that this would provide (for now) either greater power or more security,' wrote Francesco Guicciardini.[1] Clement ignored them. He decided to make Alessandro a prince – not just of his tiny duchy of Penne but of the city-state of Florence too.

'It is the new principality that causes difficulties,' Machiavelli had written.[2] On 3 April 1532, a council of twelve men was established to carry through the reform, which would establish new constitutional arrangements for the city. It had a month to do so. Among the men chosen were Francesco Guicciardini, Acciaiuoli, Vettori, and members of numerous leading families: the Strozzi, Pucci, Ridolfi and Valori among them. Clement sent Filippo Strozzi, husband to Alessandro's aunt Clarice de' Medici, up from Rome with 'advice from the Pope on the road to be taken'. Cardinal Cibo worked through details of the draft, amending and adjusting, considering the niceties of government, his comments and corrections scribbled in the margins of the text. He considered whether there should be quotas for men living in different parts of the city. He tidied up details of inheritance: the duchy was to pass to Alessandro's son, or nearest male descendant. Only in the absence of children would it pass to the next nearest male blood relative. It is in the small details that the document is revealing about how the old routines of life in Florence were disrupted. The city's musicians were put on half pay, for example. There were changes to protocol for welcome of visiting dignitaries.[3]

On the surface, the 1532 structures of government looked similar to those that had gone before. Florence still had large and small councils, though they were reduced in size to a council of two hundred, and one of forty-eight. The key change was that ultimate authority now rested with a Supreme Magistracy, consisting of the Duke, his lieutenant and four councillors chosen from among the Forty-Eight as advisers to the Duke, who served three-month terms. Two committees of eight, the *Otto di Pratica* and the *Otto di Guardia*, responsible respectively for external affairs and internal security, functioned alongside this structure, and there were other committees with more specific roles, such as the *Capitani di Parte Guelfa*, responsible for the militia and the maintenance of fortifications. Yet by placing the Duke at the centre of government, and giving him the power to select members of the councils, the new structure would inevitably tend towards absolute rule.[4]

Within the month plans were carried through. Alessandro seemed content – or was under orders from Clement – to stand back from the politicking and let his ministers deal. The Florentine ambassador in Rome told his Venetian counterpart that Alessandro had not been involved in the discussions.[5]

An account of Alessandro's rise to power, written by one Tyberio di Alcini (perhaps a member of the Albizzi family), was circulated via a mercenary commander to his masters in Venice:

Your Lordship must know how the *Signoria* of Florence
was reduced to twelve lords with the *gonfaloniere*, and now
is reduced so that the said lords renounce all their jurisdiction, and that of the *Signoria*, to the excellent duke
Alessandro de' Medici, and invest him with all powers, and
elect him their true and legitimate duke and lord, with the
Imperial investiture, so that there will no longer be a
Florentine *Signoria*, but the Duke alone will be lord, and
his heirs. A beautiful triumph is being prepared for him,
for the first day of May, for on that day the Duke will enter
into government and lordship, and there will no longer be
a *gonfaloniere*, nor the Twelve, nor the Forty Lords. We
await the Duchessina [Catherine de' Medici] who is coming
from Rome for this triumph, and will be the bride of a son
of the king of France, so they say, and the Duke will have
the Emperor's daughter for a wife, as has been said many
times. And so the world goes by, and we stand and stare,
and provided we live we will see beautiful things.[6]

The Albizzi were old rivals of the Medici and this flowery write-up
may be ironic. A more explicitly hostile account that, like Alcini's,
ended up in Venice described Clement's 'cruel and inhuman desire'.
The Pope had left Florence exposed to 'tremendous dangers', the prey
of 'inhuman barbarians'. He had tried to deprive the people of their
arms, imposing fines of two hundred *scudi* (ten times the annual wage
of an unskilled worker) on anyone who did not present weapons on
demand. Though the reform made four of the forty-eight elected
officials Alessandro's counsellors, 'the four could do nothing without
Alessandro, and he can do everything without them.'[7]

   Alessandro's officials wasted no time in taking inventory of the
Signoria's property. Antonio Ricasoli, Jacopo Berlinghieri and Guasparre
dal Borgo worked their way through the rooms of the Palazzo, listing
furnishings, valuables and documents. They catalogued the *gonfaloniere*'s papers, the treasurer's books, the keys for the munition room,
a leather bag containing the passwords for the fortresses, a little box
containing the keys to the city gates. After curfew, no one was allowed
in or out without a pass. Room by room, they itemised furniture and

fittings. The *Signoria* employed three bell ringers: Lorenzo, Giovanni and Pierino. Their beds, mattresses, chests and linen were added to the list. So were the brass basins of the barber's room and the chalices from the chapel. One of the dozen silver maces had already been removed by Alessandro's mace-bearer.[8]

On 1 May Alessandro formally took over the government of Florence and Tuscany. 'There was no one to speak the contrary,' wrote Tyberio in a second letter. 'Everyone cried "Duke, duke, Palle, Palle."' Accompanied by soldiers, captains, gentlemen and 'all the people', the Duke went first to hear Mass in the Baptistry, then made his way to the Palazzo della Signoria to meet the Eight, greeted with the sound of gunshots into the air, drumming and trumpets. Alessandro had risen to the occasion with another populist move: he revived the traditional festival of the *Potenze della plebe*. Five local teams fought in this spectacle of arms, each with its own insignia: one had the Prato well, the others a golden mountain, a red city, an armed captain on horseback, a girl at the foot of a medlar tree. The festival had not been held for some years, a consequence of plague, war, shortages and poverty. Now Alessandro had a taffeta standard made up for each of the five squads. Worth sixty gold ducats apiece, they were hung from the windows of the Palazzo Medici on the eve of the extravaganza. On discovering that the 'Emperor' of the Prato team had been imprisoned for a debt of forty ducats, Alessandro paid off the creditors and had the man freed. On 1 May, after the morning meal, the spectacle began.[9]

Tyberio continued: 'Today there was a great feast, and great triumphs and they ran the quintain and did beautiful *moresche* [Moorish dances] and more than two hundred horses raced, all jennets and Turkish, and it was a beautiful sight, and all the heralds of Lucca and Siena came to this triumph.' He enclosed a copy of a poem in Alessandro's praise that had been put up around Florence and on the walls of the Medici palace. 'You who will now be our duke, may the sacred powers always favour you,' it began. The author hoped Alessandro would enjoy peaceful days, that he would live happily and cheerfully.

A week later Alessandro was joined by his thirteen-year-old half-sister. He and his men went out to meet Catherine about twelve miles from Florence, before the little duchess made her way through the crowds to the Palazzo Medici, the streets dressed with tapestries, the air full of shouts and sounds, her arrival once again a reason for feasting, jousting and celebration.[10]

The Medici party was now confident enough to relax the restrictions on their exiled opponents. Provided they did not live within thirty miles of Florence, Rome, Venice, Genoa or Ancona – large cities where they might organise together   the republicans were permitted a little more freedom.[11] There were hints that not too far in the future some of them might be welcomed back. Now and again there was even mercy. In June 1532 Ser Maurizio seized Giovanbattista da Castiglione from his home outside Florence and had him thrown into prison. Everyone expected, wrote Varchi later, that da Castiglione would have had his head cut off. He was implicated in the burning of the Medici villa at Careggi during the siege. To their amazement, Alessandro had him freed. It was an act that simultaneously underlined Alessandro's clemency and made clear that if he wanted to arrest and execute his enemies it was in his power to do so.[12]

Yet if the threat from republican exiles was contained in 1532, it would not stay that way, as another of the artists linked with Alessandro's court, his old Roman acquaintance Benvenuto Cellini, attested. Travelling from Florence to Venice perhaps eighteen months later, in the company of fellow sculptor Tribolo, Cellini ran into two exiles, Niccolò Benintendi and Jacopo Nardi. Nardi had been confined since the end of 1530, first in Petigliolo, a little way out of Florence, and later in Livorno, and Benintendi should have been in Venice, but both had broken their confinement and moved to Ferrara, more politically comfortable territory. (Ferrara's duke, Alfonso d'Este, was a formidable player in Italian politics and no friend of Clement VII, having annexed the city of Modena, which Clement was demanding back; he was happy to make use of the exiles as a bargaining counter in their quarrel.)[13] Though originally from an elite *ottimati* family, Nardi maintained close relations with the more radical *popolari* republicans. He had held office in the 1527–30 regime and unlike other *ottimati* had not broken with it before the siege. He would go on to write one of the most celebrated histories of Florence from the republican perspective.

Whether this particular incident took place exactly as Cellini described is impossible to say (though it may have done). But he sums up the republicans' troubles with his usual bravura: as they passed the exiles, Tribolo, 'who was the most timorous man that I have ever known, kept on saying: "Do not look at them or talk to them, if you care to go back to Florence."'

Cellini took his friend's advice, but Benintendi went out of his way to provoke him. A heated row ended with Benintendi saying, 'They and their duke can fuck right off.'

Cellini pulled his sword. The exiles scattered in disarray. 'In short,' he wrote, 'it was an indescribable confusion; they looked like a herd of swine.'[14]

Cellini – with the benefit of hindsight, of course – was an acute observer here. The exiles' trouble was that they couldn't agree among themselves.

If the regime in Florence was now more sanguine about the threat from the exiles, the situation within the Medici family was worrying. 'The rift between Cardinal de' Medici and Duke Alessandro is worse than ever,' wrote the duke of Urbino's agent from Rome in March. The pair had fallen out over the appointment of a new governor of Perugia, a city in the Papal States. Located near the border with the Florentine territories, Perugia's hilltop location made it an ideal base from which to launch an incursion into Tuscany. Alessandro was unhappy that the post had gone to the Bishop of Sora, a man he thought was 'entirely dependent' on Ippolito. His people were lobbying for the Bishop's removal. In the information economy of Rome, every detail of the affair was scrutinised. Clement, it was said, had sided with Alessandro. Another rumour circulated: Ippolito was planning to leave the cardinalate and would revive his plan to marry Giulia Varano, heiress of Camerino. He would convince Charles V to grant him a fief in Naples, as Alessandro had been granted Penne, and in return Ippolito would promise to stay out of Florentine affairs. But Clement wanted Ippolito to hold off until after he had seen the Emperor, whom he was due to meet later in the year.[15] The Pope had a reputation for indecision, but in his dealings with his nephews he was nothing but consistent. Once he had decided on their futures, he held his line.

Discussions between Ippolito and Clement continued in an effort to reach agreement. The Pope offered his nephew a 'good number of offices' as an alternative to his role in Perugia. The arguments ran on through May and June. Clement apparently agreed not to force Ippolito into holy orders in return for his assurance that he would not quit the cardinalate. (It was not until the twentieth century that cardinals had to be ordained, and the deal left the way open for Ippolito to marry in future, as Cardinal Ferdinando de' Medici would do later in the sixteenth century.) Ippolito agreed to leave the governorship of Perugia provided he was appointed legate to the Marche, a region in eastern Italy, instead. But there Clement's hands were tied, because he had already accepted the sum of 19,000 ducats for the office of legate to Ancona and the Marche from another young and ambitious cardinal, Benedetto Accolti, and the chances of the avaricious Accolti surrendering it were minimal.[16]

Meanwhile, Ippolito grumbled that Alessandro had refused him a loan of 2,000 ducats: hardly surprising, perhaps, given the expenditure Alessandro was incurring in Florence, not only on his own account but in rebuilding a shattered city. Alessandro feared that, granted too many rich benefices, Ippolito might gather sufficient wealth to challenge his power in Florence. He worried that Ippolito was trying to spy on him.[17]

Clement had an unenviable balancing act to perform, but the balance was tipping further in Alessandro's favour as the Pope became more and more frustrated with Ippolito's behaviour. In a letter of 18 June 1532, the duke of Urbino's agent in Rome reported that His Holiness was 'quite discontent': Ippolito was doing nothing but attending to his own ruin, and that of his house. From Clement's point of view, the decision to make Ippolito a cardinal had been a sign of affection; it would have left him head of the family in the event of Clement's death, while Alessandro would have had no support at all. But now Ippolito was complaining, 'as if he were displeased that the Pope hadn't died'.[18]

Clement had other family troubles. Several generations on, the money Lorenzo the Magnificent had taken from the junior branch of the Medici was still the subject of dispute by their descendants. To buy off the cadet branch, Clement granted the governorship of Fano, a town near Urbino on Italy's Adriatic coast, to the eighteen-year-old Lorenzino de' Medici, eldest male representative of that side of the family.[19] Alessandro's new power also came at a price. He – and Florence – was now tied to the fortunes of Charles V. And though the city might be poor, Alessandro, like the other Italian princes in Charles' orbit, was expected to contribute to the Imperial war effort, for example donating equipment for the Imperial expedition east in June 1532.[20] Such expectations placed further strain on Florence's already stretched finances.

Alessandro's position as duke would only be truly secure with his marriage to Margaret of Austria, but Margaret was still in the Netherlands. Alessandro's ambassadors there wrote back to him regularly. She was in good health, and greatly desired to come to Italy, they reassured him. Clement continued to lobby for her early move to Naples. 'It would be a great consolation to His Beatitude if the Illustrious Lady, wife of the Lord Duke Alessandro, might be sent into Italy, as His Imperial Majesty has said he wishes to do,' wrote Jacopo Salviati to Cardinal Lorenzo Campeggio, papal legate to the Emperor. 'His Holiness would like Your Lordship to remind him dextrously now and again and advise us of what he resolves.'[21]

In July, Charles was still making excuses. He told Campeggio that he had initially planned to bring Margaret to Italy himself, so he could present her to the Pope. Then he had considered sending her to Innsbruck but had abandoned that scheme on account of Margaret's age (she was not yet ten), her lack of German and because Charles did not want her acquiring German manners. Finally he said that in light of the 'present tumults' – a reference to the ongoing conflict with the Turks on the Empire's eastern front and in the Mediterranean – he had decided to leave her where she was. He assured Campeggio that he understood Clement's concerns, and that he would speak to his advisers about Margaret's future.[22] Plausible though the excuses were, they offered little comfort to a pope anxious to secure his family's rule.

12

In desperation, Clement decided to remove Ippolito from the Italian scene entirely. Hoping that a spell away from Rome might impart some discipline, he appointed him legate *a latere* (the most powerful rank of legate) against the Turk, and sent him off to join the Imperial army at its eastern front in Hungary. There Charles V's troops were facing down a threat from Ottoman Emperor Süleyman the Magnificent. Ippolito left Rome on 8 July, dressed 'like a soldier, with a red beret, white feathers and a slashed cassock, sword and dagger', a choice that conveyed his rejection of ecclesiastical garb, although a later historian attributed this Hungarian-style dress to a desire to win the hearts and minds of the locals. From Alessandro's point of view, Ippolito's departure was no doubt a relief. In a show of generosity he dispatched 'horses and other things that may be useful' to his cousin. The wardrobe accounts note two bows and two quivers of arrows 'in the Turkish style' that had been given to Cardinal de' Medici, as well as a pair of drums, also *alla turchesca*. The duke of Mantua's agent reported that 'many young noblemen' were leaving Florence to join Ippolito's entourage, though whether their departure indicated support for Ippolito in his rivalry with Alessandro or simply a desire to distinguish themselves in warfare is not clear.[1]

Shortly after Ippolito's departure, the sudden death, age 53, of Cardinal Pompeo Colonna freed up a rich set of benefices, including the vice-chancellorship of the Church and the archbishopric of Monreale.[2] So convenient was Colonna's death for his more ambitious colleagues that rumours of poison were bound to follow. Gregorio Rosso, in his contemporary *History of the Affairs of Naples under the Empire of Charles V*, wrote a dry account simultaneously questioning the rumours and making it entirely clear that Ippolito had had motive, means and opportunity.

The Pope sent Cardinal Ippolito de' Medici [to the Emperor] in person as legate *a latere*, with a large sum of money and many men; the Cardinal, not long before he went as legate to Germany, had secretly been in Naples, under cover of making peace between Cardinal Colonna and the Pope, though many said for some other reason.

Was that an allusion to their deal over the papacy? Or something more sinister? Rosso moved on to discuss another topic but then returned to the Cardinal's fate:

At the beginning of July [in fact on 28 June] Cardinal Pompeo Colonna, viceroy of Naples, died, said to have been poisoned by figs, which he used to eat in his garden at Chiaia, by means of Filippetto, his steward.

If it's true that Cardinal Colonna was poisoned by figs in the garden, it's strange that the count of Policastro didn't die, because they used to walk together, conversing in the garden, and on the morning that the Cardinal is said to have been poisoned, he was with the Count of Policastro, and he ate figs, as did the Cardinal. . . .

As soon as he heard of the death of Cardinal Colonna, the Pope granted the vice-chancellorship of the Roman Church, and the greater share of his benefices, to his nephew Cardinal Ippolito de' Medici, who had gone to Germany.[3]

Under the circumstances, suspicion was bound to fall on Ippolito, but gossip about poison was commonplace and in the absence of evidence not much could or would be done.

Back in Florence, to match his title of duke, Alessandro commissioned the appropriate accoutrements. Since November, the Medici arms had been on display in the *Signoria*'s audience chamber: one coat of arms for Clement VII, one for Alessandro. Now, Domenico di Polo, one of

Florence's leading artists in the art of *pietra dura* (inlaying with semi-precious stones) and gem cutting, made a new seal for him. Cut from dark green chalcedony, it featured the classical hero Hercules armed with a club and crowned with a laurel wreath. Hercules was sometimes said to be the mythical founder of Florence and since the thirteenth century his image had been used on the city's seal. The new duchy employed old symbols to emphasise its continuity with the past.[4]

Other items hinted at different political dynamics. One of the most intriguing costumes in Alessandro's wardrobe is the Turkish outfit that the chamberlain Girolamo da Correggio handed over to the wardrobe master on 28 April. There was a Turkish-style cassock of red cloth, lined in black, a pair of striped silk breeches, likewise Turkish-style, a gypsy scarf or headdress of multicoloured silk, and two pairs of Turkish-style boots. Dressing up as a Turk was a common enough thing to do at the European courts as more-or-less affectionate mockery of military opponents: Henry VIII did it, while at Francis I's court there was a fashion for Egyptian styles.[5] But for a new and controversial duke or his courtiers to invite analogies with the Turks was risky. In Renaissance Italy the military might of the Ottoman sultans was respected, but the Turks were pejoratively called 'bastards, pretenders, usurpers, brigands and thieves'. Dressing up Turkish-style in a political context where the regime stood accused of being at least the first three of those things was either carelessness or very cutting wit. Alessandro's opponents would later declare his rule of Florence 'worse than being in the power of the Turk'. And there was another parallel between the Sultan and Alessandro. The mothers of Ottoman sultans were invariably slaves. Were Alessandro and his courtiers mocking the critics of the Duke's low birth? Striped clothing had associations with both servitude and the 'Oriental': African pages were often portrayed in stripes.[6]

Alessandro's day-to-day clothing was more sober but still luxurious: satins, damasks, velvets, though the predominant colours were black and white. In his book on Alessandro's rule, Alessandro Ceccherelli wrote that the Duke lived 'as if he were a private citizen'. Asked by a member of the household why he hadn't changed his manners with the change of regime, Alessandro replied: 'So that the citizens learn not to exalt themselves on account of holding office, I will not exalt myself on account of the principate.' Ceccherelli's characters praised Alessandro for setting this excellent example. They went on:

> One of his household often told him that it didn't suit a prince of his rank to go about so soberly dressed, citing the example of Aristotle, who thought that princes should dress sumptuously, so that they would be known by their vassals; Alessandro replied that it was more honourable to send his men out dressed in that manner, because it was far better to dress many and deprive himself, than to deprive many so as to dress just him.

Perhaps Alessandro dressed modestly in public, but his wardrobe suggests otherwise. More likely Ceccherelli was trying to make a parallel between Alessandro and Charles V, who was certainly criticised for his sober apparel.[7]

No court in Renaissance Italy would be complete without a resident artist – or several. Alessandro had a long family tradition to live up to: the Medici had been patrons of Botticelli, Ghirlandaio, Michelangelo and many other stellar names of fifteenth-century art. In 1532 Giorgio Vasari, who had been living in Florence and attending lessons with Alessandro and Ippolito before the siege, returned to the city. Vasari had been in Ippolito's service, but with the Cardinal away in Hungary, he needed an alternative patron. Ippolito had introduced Vasari to Clement who in turn dispatched him to Florence, where he arrived in December. Ottaviano de' Medici took him under a fatherly wing and Vasari, who was still only twenty-one, took the opportunity to learn from the masters, studying Michelangelo's work-in-progress in the New Sacristy at the church of San Lorenzo there. Alessandro received him with 'good cheer', he wrote when, much later, he came to pen his own *Life*. Vasari's own first work in Florence was an *Entombment of Christ*, now in the Casa Vasari in Arezzo, which he initially intended for Ippolito. 'I have made a cartoon for a large painting for Your Lordship's chamber,' he wrote to the Cardinal, no doubt hoping that Ippolito would commission him to complete the work. He described the scene he had envisaged: Christ's body borne with reverence by three old men, the three Marys supporting Mary, mother of Christ, as she weeps for her son; in the background the thieves crucified alongside Christ, brought to their tombs too. Ippolito never got his painting. The *Entombment* went to Alessandro instead, and the Duke commissioned a new work from Vasari: a series of frescoes for the Palazzo Medici.[8]

Domestic and political matters were never quite separate in the government of Florence now. In the past, city office-holders had moved away from their families, to live temporarily in the Palazzo della Signoria during their short terms of office. Now, the Duke's household in the Palazzo Medici provided a space for the entertainment of guests but also for receiving petitioners and giving audience. He kept an open room for visitors. His behaviour was a contrast with his father's, who had given audience only reluctantly.[9] It was a sign of access, of the possibility that anyone might seek the Duke's favour. It was also a reminder that these days, the Duke and no one else had the power to grant those requests.

Through August and September business rolled on. The authorities issued new planning regulations preventing the building or restoration of overhanging jetties on Florence's houses. The appearance of a comet prompted comment.[10] This was a period in which heavenly phenomena were regarded as auspicious – for good or ill. Don Pietro di Toledo, newly appointed as viceroy of Naples, made a visit. Naples was Imperial territory; as the Emperor's deputy, Don Pietro was Charles V's most senior appointment on the Italian peninsula. He might prove a useful ally for Alessandro. Alessandro revived the festival of St Cosmas, a saint long associated with the Medici family. On 26 September he, his counsellors and the city's confraternities and priests, held a devotional procession through Florence.[11] Religion was an important part of Florentine civic life, and such events were a way for the new Duke to demonstrate at least an appearance of piety.

Clement recalled his envoy Nicolas Schömberg from Florence, perhaps because he thought it time Alessandro governed independently. It was rumoured in Rome that Alessandro still coveted the role of Captain-General of the Church's armies. Still, it was Clement who headed the family and at times Alessandro had to lobby his great-uncle like any other petitioner. In September 1532, for example, he had written to Jacopo Salviati to recommend that Clement consider a certain candidate for the role of papal secretary.[12] Opening the letter he addressed Salviati as 'come padre', 'like a father', wording that is in part the standard language of courtesy but also perhaps indicates Alessandro's desire to win over an influential elder relative.

Alessandro's little sister Catherine was now thirteen. Clement was considering a French match for her, a counterweight to the Imperial marriage for Alessandro. The only legitimate child in the main line of the family, Catherine could expect a prestigious marriage, and she was growing into a demanding teenager. 'Most Blessed Father,' she wrote to the Pope in October, 'As Your Holiness has sent a jennet to Monsignor Reverendissimo and another to His Excellency the Duke, I think Your Holiness might yet wish to send me the one that you promised.' She was planning to spend eight or ten days at Poggio, and this was her second begging letter in a week. 'I wrote the other day to Your Holiness that I needed a dress and that it was getting cold and I had nothing to wear,' she added as a reminder.[13]

Catherine's absence from the city was well timed. Alessandro and his ministers were about to make a symbolic statement marking irrevocable regime change in Florence. On 12 October 1532, the great bell that for decades had hung in the tower of the Palazzo della Signoria was taken down and broken up. In the past, in times of crisis, the bell of the *Signoria* had been sounded to summon all male citizens over fourteen to form a parliament and elect a *Balia*, an emergency committee to coordinate a response. The Medici had used such parliaments to their own ends, as in 1530, but they had been used against them too. In 1494, when Piero de' Medici had surrendered to the French, the city priors had slammed the gates to the city in his face, tolled the bell, called a parliament and thrown the Medici out. That exile had lasted eighteen years. Now, the bell was melted down, turned into fourpence pieces and artillery, so it could never be rung to summon the citizens again.[14] The fate of Lorenzo, Giovanni and Pierino, the three city bell ringers, is unknown.

How much Alessandro had to do with that decision is debatable. Just two days before the bell's destruction, Giovanni Borromei, an agent of the duke of Mantua, wrote to his master: 'The Duke delights in hunting and every day is out in the hills.'[15]

13

In November 1532, Charles V returned to Italy. He was due to see Clement for the second time in three years. Alessandro went to see him too – as did an embassy from among the Medici's exiled opponents. It was their first formal approach to the Emperor, and they hoped that he might intervene in their favour against Alessandro's regime.[1] In Alessandro's absence, the government of Florence fell to a new legate, Cardinal Innocenzo Cibo. Cibo had been involved in the past, on and off, in Florentine affairs. Now he took a central role.

The Cardinal belonged to an old papal family. Pope Innocent VIII, who ruled from 1484 to 1492, had been a Cibo. His son Franceschetto, product of a youthful liaison before he embarked on an ecclesiastical career, had married Maddalena de' Medici, sister of Pope Leo X. Innocenzo was their child, and he could now count three popes in the family: his grandfather, his maternal uncle, and, in Clement VII, a cousin. He was, in short, extremely well connected, which had no doubt contributed to his promotion to the cardinalate back in September 1513 at the age of just twenty-two. An inventory of the cardinal's possessions, now in the archives at Massa, testifies to his expensive lifestyle, funded through a rich portfolio of benefices (worth perhaps 22,000 ducats a year), but also with loans from his sister-in-law – and lover – Ricciarda Malaspina. The Venetian envoy Soriano thought him 'dedicated to worldly pleasures, and rather lascivious'. As one of Alessandro's elder relatives, the Cardinal seems to have become something of a father figure to the young Duke, just as Charles V had the previous year.[2]

The Cardinal's name, 'Cibo', means 'food' in Italian and proved a gift to satirists. *'Cibo da vermi e da rabbiosi cani'* began one poem: 'Food for worms and rabid dogs'. Cibo had unashamedly sold his homeland to the Spanish, it continued. Giving Cibo (that is, food) to satirists was a bad plan, suggested another: he had the look of a killer. He cared for nothing but his incestuous affair with his sister-in-law; he ought to burn in Hell; his brother Lorenzo was no better, being delighted that Innocenzo was cuckolding him. Other *pasquinate* alluded to Cibo's liking for whores, banquets and dancing, and suggested he had syphilis. It was scurrilous stuff, though no worse than most cardinals could expect from the satirists.[3]

Cibo arrived in Florence in mid November. His journey had been delayed by bad weather. He was, he wrote to Clement, 'very graciously received by His Excellency [Alessandro], and today I was informed by him of all the city's affairs, and his intentions; which believing to be most prudent, I will endeavour to satisfy with all my wisdom and power.' He praised Alessandro's 'great merits,' with which Clement should be 'very well content'.[4]

Cardinal Cibo did not enlarge on the nature of Alessandro's intentions, nor how he intended to satisfy them. But within a few days, Raffaello Girolami, the prominent opponent whose influential supporters, as we have seen, had proven a persistent thorn in the side of the Medici regime, was found dead in the fortress at Pisa. He had been poisoned, so it was said, on Clement's orders. 'Princes must delegate distasteful tasks to others,' Machiavelli had written with more than a little irony, 'pleasant ones they should keep for themselves.' As Luigi Guicciardini, commissar of Pisa, had argued a year before, 'too much pity' risked destruction. Then, his desire for a tougher line on Girolami had been stymied by the lobbying of Imperial commander Ferrante Gonzaga and his ally Nicolas Schömberg. Now, Schömberg was gone, but rumours swirled that Gonzaga planned to ask for a pardon for Girolami.[5] For supporters of the Medici, the risk was that such a move would embolden their opponents, and restore to them a prominent figurehead. Had Alessandro's 'prudent intention' been to dispose of an inconvenient enemy? Such an order would not have been written down, but it was a blunt warning to the exiles, as they prepared to approach the Emperor. On the other hand, it risked crystallising opposition to a tyrannical regime.

The other danger – Ippolito de' Medici – was away in Linz (in what is now Austria). His allies continued to lobby Clement's ministers in his favour. In September 1532, Uberto Gambara, a papal official and diplomat, wrote to Jacopo Salviati, the Pope's secretary (and husband of Ippolito's aunt), in Ippolito's praise. Clement had been worrying – again – about the young cardinal's expenses. Gambara tried to reassure him. 'If His Holiness could see how the Most Reverend Legate [Ippolito] comports himself,' he wrote, 'with what gravity, prudence and religion he makes himself known, and how he is an ornament to his rank and dignity, then the loss in expenses would seem little by comparison to the gain to His Holiness and his illustrious family.'[6]

After Ippolito's aborted coup of April 1531, there were bound to be fears he would try again. In early October 1532, a mutiny broke out among the Emperor's Italian troops. Amid disputes about payments to mercenaries (often late), such events were not uncommon. The mutinous men headed back towards Italy, with the Emperor and Ippolito following behind. When Ippolito headed up the column to join them, accompanied by a band of four hundred arquebusiers, he was immediately suspected of planning to employ the insubordinate soldiers in a march on Florence. At San Vito al Tagliamento, some fifty miles north-east of Venice, he was arrested by Imperial officers.[7]

The affair was highly embarrassing for Clement, who resorted to a diplomatic offensive against the impertinent decision to detain Ippolito. He called in the Imperial ambassadors for an audience, denouncing 'with tears in his eyes' the Emperor's 'lack of respect for the Apostolic See and his own blood'. Ambassador Miguel Mai, well versed in Italian politicking, replied that the arrest had been an error. The Emperor had been unaware of it. But, he pointed out, it was quite justifiable given that the mutiny could well have been prompted by Ippolito's efforts to make trouble in Tuscany 'for which – as the Pope knew – the young man had always had quite a craving'. Clement replied that if his nephew had somehow erred, then the appropriate course was for the Emperor to call him in and leave it to him, the Pope, to chastise him.[8]

Ippolito was quickly freed on the Emperor's orders. He headed to Venice, and there consoled himself in the arms of Angela Zaffetta, a courtesan. He met with Florentine friends and associates who might support him against Alessandro and began to build a coalition.[9] He had not given up.

*

In 1529 Alessandro had gone to greet the Emperor at the spectacular monastery of Certosa di Pavia, south of Milan; this time they met at the lakeside city of Mantua, whose ruler had Charles to thank for his recent promotion from marquis to duke. The wardrobe Alessandro took with him was a truly impressive affair, no doubt aimed at reassuring his future father-in-law of the rich and splendid court into which Margaret was due to marry. In addition, the accounts for November detail a series of lavish outfits that seem to have been made for his courtiers. Almost exclusively monochrome, there were garments in white damask, white taffeta, and silver tissue; there were black satin and velvet doublets lined in white. It would have been a striking look for their appearance at court. Alessandro also went well prepared for hunting and sport. He took with him riding hose, a black velvet hat and riding boots in luxurious Spanish Cordoba leather, besides the vital protective chain-mail sleeves and a glove.[10]

On 13 December, an hour before sunset, Alessandro arrived in Bologna with Charles and the Imperial entourage. Fourteen cardinals went out to the gates to greet the Emperor. Preceded by 3,000 infantrymen (some said 4,000), Charles' gentlemen, herald and horsemen put on a sumptuous show. On one account the entry took nine hours. Alessandro's place in the procession made visible his new rank: he entered alongside his fellow dukes of Milan and Mantua. Then came the marquises and with them the interfering Ferrante Gonzaga. During the Christmas ceremonies, Alessandro's status was evident again. He carried the Imperial orb, just as he had done in the coronation ceremony almost three years before. This time he walked in the company of Alfonso d'Avalos, marquis of Vasto, who carried the sceptre, and the duke of Saxony, who bore the sword.[11] The three embodied the reach of Charles' European power, from Spain, to Italy, to the German states.

Behind the festivities this meeting was the setting for complex diplomatic negotiations. Charles and Clement were busy preparing a league for the defence of Italy. Charles sought to deter any French invasion and to firm up his alliances on the Italian peninsula; Clement could not afford to alienate Charles but nor did he want to burn his bridges with the French. Ambassadors came and went. Charles proposed that Francesco II Sforza, duke of Milan, marry Catherine de' Medici, as an alternative to her French match. Clement demurred. Charles proposed that Ippolito might join him in Spain as papal legate. Ippolito did not favour the idea. Back and forth went the negotiations. Ippolito was learning the trade of a papal diplomat here, alongside his uncle Jacopo Salviati and Francesco Guicciardini.[12] Only time would tell whether he would ever be satisfied with even a senior role in church administration.

Alessandro's stay in Bologna coincided with Carnival. The costumes he took suggest he made the most of the festivities. Packed up in a pair of white leather-covered strongboxes, transported by Il Pistoia the muleteer, were numerous luxury garments, including two masquerading costumes in peacock-coloured and turquoise-blue satin, two matching Hungarian-style turbans and two matching Turkish outfits. Most fascinating, though, is the following entry in Pretino's wardrobe book:

In a box, in which are masks

6 masks for peasants
5 masks for women
3 masks for Moors
one mask for a Moor with a beard
one Turkish-style mask
one mask for a hermit with a big beard
a horse-hair wig
a red beard (*barba rosa*).[13]

All the information we have about Alessandro's Carnival masquerading is this list, but the last item hints at its theme. Barbarossa was an admiral in the Ottoman fleet. Properly known as Hayreddin (or Khair ad-Dīn), he was a major naval rival of Charles V's commanders, and in 1538 managed to establish Ottoman dominance in the Mediterranean, lasting through until 1571. The conflict between the Holy Roman and Ottoman Empires was a popular theme in Imperial entertainments. Charles' younger brother Ferdinand enjoyed 'Hungarian' or 'Hussar' tournaments, played between two teams, one dressed as Christian fighters from Central and Eastern Europe, the other as caricature Turks.[14]

While dressing up was sometimes a matter of fun, it could also be deeply political. During the Italian Wars, for example, the Spanish were subject to similar mockery by locals hostile to their troops' presence in Italy.[15] For Alessandro himself, masquerading was perhaps a brief distraction from weighty responsibilities, but it might also have had political overtones. As Castiglione had observed, for a prince to put on a mask and 'mix with his inferiors as an equal' could also help him show that 'it is not being a prince that accounts for his worth'; this is one way Alessandro's contemporaries might have perceived his dress. But masquerading also had less wholesome associations – with sexual misconduct. In Machiavelli's comedy, La Mandragola, characters quip that a young merchant trying to seduce a married woman would look more suspicious in a mask than out of one; the joke works because of the popular assumption that wearing a mask suggests you may be up to no good. Alessandro's masquerades were open to negative interpretation too.[16]

Away from the entertainments, the political arguments in Bologna were settled with an agreement over money. Clement negotiated down his financial contribution and a league was, finally, concluded between the Emperor, the Pope, the dukes of Milan and Ferrara, and the republics of Genoa, Siena and Lucca. Florence, wrote a Venetian envoy, was understood to be included 'being the Pope's fatherland, and the Duke Alessandro his nephew'. For some observers, at least, Clement remained the power behind Alessandro's ducal throne.[17]

At the end of February 1533 Charles readied himself to depart and prepared to make his way to Genoa. Just as at Brussels, lavish leaving gifts were exchanged. The duke of Urbino presented Charles with two Turkish horses for his travel home. Alessandro gave Charles no fewer than five. Charles, in turn, gave Alessandro a selection of the late Cardinal Colonna's stock. With generous tips to the papal court officials, the Emperor left for Spain. Even as he did, some observers feared that, in the face of Clement's determination to marry Catherine to a French prince, he might abandon the Medici. The Emperor had, wrote Francesco Guicciardini, 'the quite firm intention (so it was said) that if the marriage alliance with the king [of France] went ahead, that of his daughter and Alessandro de' Medici would not take place.' Yet though Charles might have made such threats, he also – finally – fulfilled his agreement of 1529 that Margaret would be brought up in Italy. A message was dispatched to Flanders: the Emperor's daughter was to travel south.[18]

14

In Florence, meanwhile, December had been a rainy month. The River Arno was rising; near the vaults of the Palazzo Spini it was up by nearly two feet. An order went out from the Forty-Eight restricting the slaughter of livestock, so that herds would be reinvigorated and, in the longer term, prices would fall. Amid the troubles, Clement sent a chest full of relics for the feast of Santa Lucia. They went on display in the Basilica of San Lorenzo, in fifty rich silver vases adorned with jewels and precious stones. Those who went to see them and made their confession received a plenary indulgence, remitting them from the earthly punishment due for their sins.[1] Work continued on fitting out the basilica's New Sacristy, where Michelangelo was close to finishing the grand sculptures that would adorn the tombs of Dukes Lorenzo and Giuliano.

While Alessandro was masquerading in Bologna, in Florence there were Christmas celebrations of another sort. On Christmas Eve, a group of young noblemen gathered outside Palazzo Strozzi. Vincenzo and Roberto, sons of Filippo Strozzi and cousins of the absent Duke, took the lead in a riotous ball game. Masked, they led their gang through the city streets. In the Mercato Nuovo, the new market, they started a game of football, heading down Calimara, to the Mercato Vecchio, the old market, with a big, blown-up ball. It was a prime shopping day in Florence. The merchants had their wares on display – fruit and vegetables – and a well-directed shot could do plenty of damage. As the ball flew across the streets, muck and dirt splashed up into faces and spoilt market goods. Unfortunately for the vandals, among their muddied victims was a certain Francesco Antonio Nori, a long-standing city office-holder. He quickly had them arrested. Once unmasked, and their identities revealed, they were released on a promise to make good the damage caused.[2]

In Alessandro's mythology, this casual vandalism – and the resentment the arrests prompted – was the point at which relations between the Strozzi and Medici families began to deteriorate. For others, the problem was that Alessandro opposed a marriage between Strozzi's daughter and the Valori family, leaving the young woman stuck in a convent. In fact, there were multiple reasons. Tensions between the Strozzi and Medici pre-dated Alessandro's rise to power, going back at least as far as 1526 and Clement's abandonment of Filippo Strozzi to his Neapolitan jailers, followed by Strozzi's deal with the republicans in 1527.[3] Few could be trusted in Alessandro's world.

Tensions with the Strozzi were only the start. At the beginning of 1533, wrote Francesco Settimanni, an eighteenth-century historian of Florence whose sympathies were firmly with the republican cause, 'the citizens of Florence were most discontent with the government of Duke Alessandro.' They were troubled by the 'avarice and ambition' of his servants, many of whom came from outside the city. They feared the 'novelty and violence' of the government. Almost every day, and for the most minor of offences, some citizen came to a bad end. 'Though Pope Clement was well informed of Alessandro's actions, it was said of him that he had found a man after his own heart.'[4]

In his appointments to key offices around the Florentine territories Alessandro made extensive use of non-Florentine citizens. His chief secretary Francesco Campana, a veteran of Clement's administration, was one. Ser Maurizio, chancellor to the *Otto di Pratica*, was another.[5] This was not only a political gripe on the part of the Florentines. City office-holding had traditionally been a route to wealth and power for Florence's leading citizens. If these roles went to outsiders, such advantages were lost.

After the hints of relaxation in 1532, evidence that the exiles had been courting Charles (and doing so in an organised, collective fashion) prompted new measures against them. In 1533 a second round of confinement orders was issued, constraining opponents of the Medici to live in 'plague-ridden' places. If they broke their bounds, the regime would have licence to confiscate their possessions. Silvestro Aldobrandini, who had been confined for three years in 1530, now found his exile extended. The Florentine authorities selected 'the bitterest of places' to hold them, wrote Varchi. Many decided they would rather become rebels.[6]

Exile was not the regime's only weapon. For some months now there had been discussions about building a more substantial fortress in Florence, echoing Lorenzo de' Medici's plans back in 1518 for a castle in his duchy of Urbino. 'Although you may have fortresses, they will not save you if the people hate you,' Machiavelli had observed.[7] Perhaps Francesco Vettori had his friend's comments in mind when he explained the situation in a letter of October 1532: 'We're obliged to do everything possible to make ourselves safe, without respect to the hatred that might follow, though we shouldn't do anything that might make us hated without improving security. We've built a bit of a fortress, which won't be taken without artillery; it would be better to have another that can be defended against artillery.'[8]

Though plans for a larger fortress progressed only slowly, the smaller fortifications at the Porta alla Giustizia were now well established. The *Capitani di Parte Guelfa*, the city magistrates responsible for the project, spent significant sums on the fort. Carvings of Alessandro's coat of arms were erected over two of its gates and the larger of the pair was gilded.[9] The question that has taxed historians is how far the plan for a new fortress was perceived as an exercise in protecting Alessandro and his regime – and how far it was a reasonable project for the general defence of the city. Italy had, after all, endured a series of wars over almost forty years, and no serious government would leave itself unprepared for another. But under the circumstances, almost anything Alessandro did was subject to suspicion, and prompted accusations that he was putting his own private interests before those of Florence. Yet, as the Medici ally Luigi Guicciardini knew, there were others who had an interest in Florence too. For him, a strong regime led by Alessandro was far preferable to constant interference from the big powers, France and Spain. 'Nothing else can preserve the well-being of the city,' he wrote to his brother, 'our enemies being more determined and venomous than ever, and only awaiting their chance.' He continued: 'We need to keep our eyes open, and not stay our hands.'[10]

The state of Florence's fortifications was just one of the many security issues that Alessandro and his ministers had to address. Florence ruled a large part of what is now Tuscany, its territory stretching to Pisa in the west, Prato and Pistoia to the north-west. To the north and north-east were the Apennines and the villages of Scarperia and Borgo San Lorenzo, the road to Bologna snaking up through the Mugello to the pass over the mountains. Closer to the southern borders were Arezzo and San Sepolcro. Alessandro had to deal with the governors of neighbouring territories: Siena, Perugia, Bologna, the Romagna, and with his own duchy of Penne, far to the south. His letters give a sense of the variety of government. Within a few weeks he might write an appeal for clemency for a man accused of murder, a letter relieving a captain of his duties at one fortress, a recommendation for a servant and a request for a good supply of Greco di Tufo wine. He dealt with men impersonating priests and the transfer of prisoners from neighbouring states, and supported a request from his fiancée Margaret to the Pope, though for what we do not know. There was all manner of business to do in the city. Favourable tax arrangements were put in place to revitalise the local silk industry. Penalties for late payment of city taxes were waived. The reform of the *monte di pietà*, the city's public pawnbroker, was completed.[11]

Complementing these details from Alessandro's own correspondence is a book written in the 1560s, by Alessandro Ceccherelli, about his 'actions and sentences'. It was presented as an illustration of the Duke's virtues for the benefit of Alessandro's daughter Giulia. In an imagined dialogue, Ceccherelli's characters explain the Duke's role in insisting that city officials cut grain prices when there was a shortage, and in importing grain from Sicily after a poor harvest. They describe how he made sure one courtier paid his carpenter's bill, and another paid for a horse he had bought on credit. They testify that he defended the honour of women, if not in terms that would appeal today. Hearing that the daughter of a miller had been kidnapped and raped by two rich young men, he insisted that one marry her and the other pay a dowry of 3,000 *scudi*. They describe the Duke's benevolence towards a captain who had fought with the rebels. Advised by a servant that he should not employ him, Alessandro replied that if the captain had defended liberty with no care for his own life, 'he will know how to defend us'. 'You see well,' observes Ceccherelli's protagonist of Alessandro, 'that he was an honourable man.'[12] These tales of a prince doing good among his own people were, like the tales of Alessandro's wickedness, no doubt romanticised. But they reflect some real evidence in the official correspondence for Alessandro's clemency and willingness to intervene in the interests of his subjects. His was a political populism designed to appeal to the lower classes and avoid any groundswell of support for the enemies of the Medici.

15

Margaret of Austria left the Low Countries in 1533 to travel to Italy. She was headed for Naples, where she would spend the years until her marriage learning Italian and acquiring the necessary knowledge and polish to take up a role as Duchess-consort. Madame de Lannoy, wife of a former Viceroy of Naples, was appointed her guardian.[1] Her departure – three and a half years after the betrothal had been agreed – was a relief for the Medici. It confirmed Charles V's commitment to the match. Margaret was still only ten years old, though, and there was time yet for the Emperor to waver, especially in light of Clement VII's unwelcome pursuit of a French alliance for his niece Catherine.

Margaret arrived in Verona, just east of Lake Garda in northern Italy, on 18 March, where she was greeted by 'all the youth' of the city, who lined the streets from two miles out of town to welcome her. As she neared her lodgings, people peered out from balconies and doorways to catch a glimpse of this magnificent procession. Her clothes were stunning: cloth of gold lined with *pavonazzo* satin. Her hair was worn in Flemish style, beneath a close-fitting coif. She wore a jewel on her forehead surrounded by pearls, and a great diamond at her neck with a ruby and a white teardrop pearl.[2] The pressure for a quick marriage was already showing. Margaret had turned ten in the summer of 1532, but supporters of the match with Alessandro talked up her age. Clement told a Venetian ambassador that she had turned eleven the previous November. An observer of her entry to Verona described her as 'aged nine or ten'. But, he added, 'they say that she's twelve.' Margaret was, though, 'very small and thin', hence his suspicions. She did not resemble her father, except that she had, like him, 'quite large lips'. An account of her arrival in Florence also upped her age: she was 'about eleven', and would go to Naples for 'four or five years' until she was of age to be married.[3] Whether through deliberate deceit or wishful thinking, the Medici had every reason to add on as many months as possible to Margaret's true age.

After a stop in Mantua in mid March, where she was due to meet her guardian,[4] Margaret travelled on first to the papal city of Bologna and then to Florence. The preparations for her arrival had been tireless. Down in Penne, Alessandro's officials had been given the task of supplying a new silver service, commissioned in large part from merchants in Naples. Fifty-six rounded plates, in the French style, and thirty flatter ones made up the set. At banquets, silver services were displayed on shelves above a sideboard, often stacked to the ceiling, a visual expression of household wealth. Together these eighty-six weighed over 119 Florentine pounds (just over 40 kilograms or 90 modern pounds), making their average weight almost half a kilo, or one pound, each. They were dispatched to Florence in the care of three servants, with just one horse and a packmule between them. The journey, over 250 miles, took them fifteen days. With such a valuable cargo, it would have been a dangerous enterprise for the men involved. Hilly terrain, bad weather and bandits were serious risks for the sixteenth-century traveller.[5]

For Alessandro, the effort was well worth it. These festivities were an opportunity to show that Florence under his rule was a home fit for an Imperial bride. They needed to be truly magnificent. For the space of a week the entire resources of the Florentine court would be at Margaret's service.

Alessandro's court was a splendid affair. By 1535 it was over two hundred strong, not including visiting dignitaries. There had been significant changes of personnel since 1531.[6] The Duke had fourteen attendant courtiers, all but one with a personal servant. Four of them – Girolamo de' Santi, Matteo da Cortona, Pietropaolo and Aurelio – were described as chamberlains and probably attended to the Duke's dressing and valeting. There were five chaplains, sixteen under-chamberlains or pages and their master. Another twenty-two men were 'squires and officials' of the court: they included a furrier, an armourer, a tailor, a *spenditore* (paymaster and buyer of produce for the household), a *bottigliere*, responsible for wines, a mace-bearer (who had a ceremonial role carrying the Duke's staff of office but in practice might be allocated various duties at court), a cellar man, a *dispensiere* (custodian of items for table service), a shoemaker and a barber, besides four heralds and men responsible for fodder and firewood.[7] There were twenty-six staff responsible for the Duke's hawks and dogs and twenty-nine for the stables, an indication of the importance of hunting at Alessandro's court. He employed a fencing master, soldiers and messengers, not to mention separate kitchen staff for the servants' dining room, several musicians and a jester. Giorgio Vasari was in residence, with a servant, as was Domenico di Polo, a skilled gem cutter who produced cameos and other fine work for the Duke, and Benedetto, a gilder.

Many of these men came from outside Florence. There were staff from Bologna, Perugia, Parma, Ancona, Rimini, from Alessandro's own fief of Penne, from Milan, from Piedmont. Some came from well beyond Italy: France (musicians, and a rider), Flanders (a manservant, a falconer), perhaps even Greece (a herald), Albania (a falconer) and Muscovy, though patronymics like 'the Muscovite' – a page in Alessandro's household was described as such – are not a reliable guide to someone's origins: these may have been sons of old immigrant families, or simply nicknames. On the other hand Vasily III, grand prince of Muscovy, had sent an embassy to Pope Clement VII in 1525, and it is conceivable that one of its younger members stayed on for education at the Italian courts.[8] In short, this was a cosmopolitan establishment – though as we have seen, the presence of so many outsiders alienated some Florentines.

The quantity of food consumed was quite as impressive as the size of the court. In 1535, during an ambassador's visit, the daily food order for the ducal dining room was estimated as follows: 220 Florentine pounds (75 kilograms or 165 pounds) of veal, fourteen capons, twenty-four chickens, twenty-four pigeons and the 'usual antipasti'. Antipasti could be elaborate: figs and nuts, stuffed prunes, cold trout patties and capers, lampreys, calamari and veal tongue were among dishes recommended by Domenico 'Panonto' Romoli in his book of recipes and household advice. Another 17 kilos of unspecified meat was purchased for the servants' dining room and a further 13.5 kilos of

1. Raphael's portrait of Lorenzo, duke of Urbino, shows the luxurious fashions worn at the Medici court.

2. Raphael also painted Pope Leo X, accompanied by Cardinal Giulio de' Medici (*left*), the future Pope Clement VII, and another relative, Luigi Rossi.

3. This splendid map of Florence, known as the *Carta della Catena*, dates from the 1490s.

Key

1. Santa Maria Novella
2. San Marco
3. Santissima Annunziata
4. San Lorenzo
5. Palazzo Medici
6. The Duomo
7. Palazzo della Signoria (Palazzo Vecchio)
8. Santa Croce

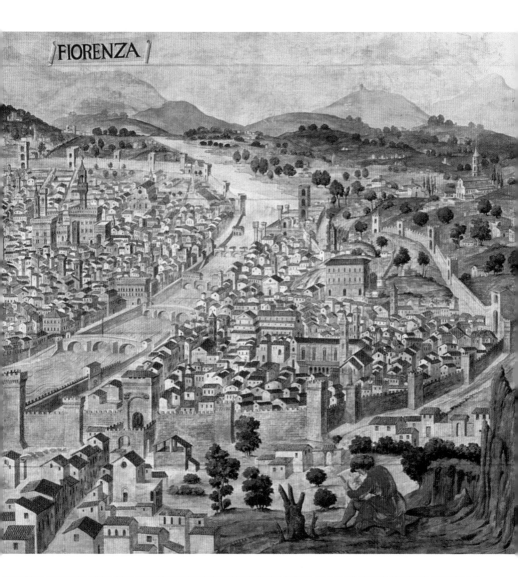

FIORENZA

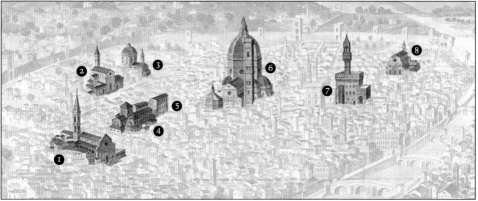

4. Piero di Cosimo's *Liberation of Andromeda* is an allegory for the return of the Medici to Florence.

5. This fresco by Benozzo Gozzoli, in the chapel of the Palazzo Medici, shows a black archer alongside many members of the Medici family.

6. Giorgio Vasari's decorative scheme for the Palazzo Vecchio immortalised key events of Medici family history, including Leo X's entrance to Florence in 1515.

7. Members of Alessandro's household appear in Nicolas Hogenberg's engraving of Charles V's coronation procession.

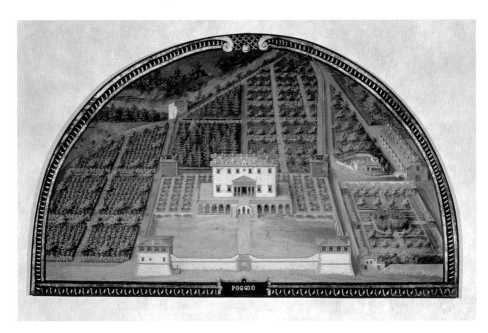

8. Alessandro's favourite country retreat, the villa at Poggio a Caiano, is depicted here by Flemish artist Justus Utens.

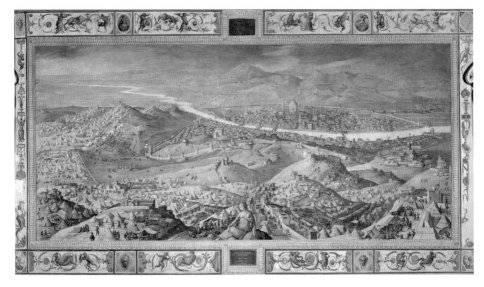

9. The victory of papal-Imperial troops in the 1530 Siege of Florence was another moment commemorated in the Palazzo Vecchio.

10. Florence's famous cathedral dominated the skyline in the 1530s just as it does today.

11. The Palazzo della Signoria (Palazzo Vecchio) was Florence's traditional seat of government.

12. Baccio Bandinelli's controversial statue of Hercules and Cacus can still be seen outside.

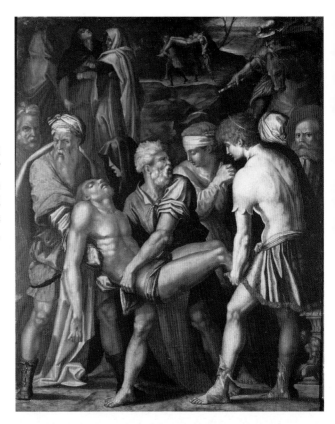

13. Alessandro acquired this *Entombment of Christ* by Giorgio Vasari, though it had been intended for his cousin Ippolito.

14. Jacopo da Pontormo's *Venus and Cupid* was painted to a design by Michelangelo. Alessandro insisted on having it.

meat was given out to officials and servants entitled to food as part of their wage but who didn't eat in. When there wasn't an important visitor the catering was a little less extravagant: only 27 kilos of veal, eight capons, thirty chickens or pigeons and the antipasti, plus 15.5 kilos of unspecified meat for the servants. The main courses of meat were accompanied by salamis and soups, with some added sauce or condiment: salsa verde, or capers, or anchovies. A more lavish menu might include a course of *fritti* – fried fish, eggs and vegetables – before concluding with fruits and cheeses: *marzolino*, pears, peaches, pistachio nuts, fennel or artichokes, sugared pine nuts and almonds.[9] On fast days, including Fridays and during Lent, the servants dined on eggs (220 per day), while those privileged to dine with the Duke enjoyed a share of 500 eggs and over 40 kilos of fish. The court as a whole consumed almost 33 kilos of bread, twelve barrels of wine, three barrels of oil and 5.5 kilos of cheese each day. Assuming that only the Duke, his courtiers and the chaplains ate in the Duke's dining room, that makes for 1.36 kilos (3 lb) of veal, or 2 kilos of fish each per day! The numbers may have been higher, and consumption correspondingly lower but this enormous consumption of meat and fish was typical of high-ranking men. Though we now know that such diets were responsible for the high incidence of gout and other health problems, at the time they were thought to be appropriate for the type of lives these men led, and appropriate to their constitutions.[10]

The night before her arrival in Florence, Margaret stayed in the Medici villa at Cafaggiolo. Up in the Mugello hills, some sixteen miles outside Florence, this was one of the oldest Medici properties. It had been in the family since the fourteenth century. In the mid fifteenth century, under Cosimo the Elder, it had been extensively remodelled to designs by Michelozzo, 'at great expense', as the Mantuan agent Giovanni Borromei put it. There, Margaret was greeted by Alessandro's fourteen-year-old sister Catherine and 'many gentlewomen, all very well dressed, and richly, and accompanied by many gentlemen and servants'.

Margaret's descent into Florence was no less spectacular. As she was carried in a litter down the winding hill roads, the streets were dressed with tapestries, there was music and dancing and tables covered with food and wine, both red and white. Some two miles outside the city, Margaret exchanged her litter to ride the remainder of the route on a jennet. With great 'pomp and solemnity' her party entered from the west at the Porta al Prato. They were greeted by three hundred of Florence's leading citizens – or perhaps five hundred, according to one observer – 'the greater part dressed in the richest of silks'. 'You would never have thought there had been war or siege in that city,' wrote Borromei. To shouts of 'Palle, Palle', to music and gun salutes, she made her way through the city streets. 'But what was the greatest marvel to the men was to see at the windows of the houses we passed such an infinity of women of every sort . . . all dressed according to their condition and quality.'

The procession passed along Borgo Ognissanti and the north bank of the River Arno, turning up past the church of Santa Trinità and Palazzo Strozzi and rounding the Duomo to head up Via Martelli to the Medici palace. 'Never had the city seemed richer or happier,' wrote one observer of the celebrations; for another 'neither words nor pen' would suffice to explain the city's great hopes in the Duke's betrothed.[11] The extravagance of the entry itself was a political statement, designed to impress observers both within and outside the city. The choice of entry route made a statement too. Previous state entries, like that of Pope Leo X in 1515, had passed the Palazzo della Signoria, the city's seat of government. Margaret's did not. Deprived of its great bell the year before, the Palazzo was now ignored in favour of a shorter route directly to the new seat of power: the Palazzo Medici.[12]

The plans for Margaret's stay were quite as lavish as her entrance. There would be fireworks, palios, hunts, bullfights, football, dances, jousting. Alessandro's French court composer Jacques Arcadelt may have written the madrigal *Giovanetta regal pur innocente* ('Little lady, royal yet innocent') for her visit. The city that Margaret entered did not just look magnificent: it sounded wonderful too. Alessandro's musicians included not only Arcadelt but two boy singers, five trumpeters, and four other players, including Antonio da Lucca ('an excellent player of the lute'), Giovanni da Lucca, Ludovico and a second French musician, Richard.[13] Around the time of Margaret's visit there were also two drummers at Alessandro's court: Giuliano and Giovanni. The latter, who came from Naples, was known as 'el Moretto', meaning 'the little Moor'. This may have been a nickname rather than a descriptor of origin, but African drummers were certainly in demand at the courts of Europe at this time. On one hand this points to a certain valuing of African culture, but music was also associated with negative images of Africans as unrestrained and uncivilised. Ippolito de' Medici was said to have learned to drum 'like the *barbari*', and African dancers were sought out for the court of Urbino. The pair were given velvet hats from the wardrobe on 30 April, just as Margaret was departing. Giovanni was still in Florence late the following year, when he came to an unhappy end. He stabbed a shoemaker in a fight at the Coronet Inn, was convicted of homicide and sentenced to death.[14]

Among the many grand entertainments arranged for Margaret in the course of her visit was a stunning religious spectacle. The *sacra rappresentazione* (holy representation) of the Annunciation to the Virgin Mary was held in the church of San Felice. Located on the south side of the Arno, near Palazzo Pitti, the church's rather plain exterior was beautifully dressed for the occasion. Inside it was transformed with stage machinery. This Annunciation spectacle had a long pedigree, going back to the early fifteenth century at least – when Filippo Brunelleschi, architect of Florence's great cathedral, had designed the apparatus – if not before. It often featured in entertainments for visiting foreign dignitaries. Many of the leading artists of the day worked on such festivals. Leonardo da Vinci was among them.

Niccolò Fabbrini, a contemporary observer with considerable experience of Florentine politics (not all on the Medici side), explained how it looked in a dialogue with Giovanni, perhaps a cousin. The spectacle played to various audiences. For 'contemplative persons', those who bothered to consider its meaning, it prompted reflection on the mystery of God. For 'simple people', on the other hand, who didn't appreciate the nuances, 'it seems such a wonder that they exclaim and are happy. Others, given to worldly things, content themselves with the apparatus, the melodies, sounds and music, and other delights, such that the one thing pleases everyone.'

For the performance itself, a stage was erected across the transept. On one side was the Virgin's chamber, a curtain drawn across it. The remainder of the space was left for other actors. 'At the start it seems empty,' Niccolò explained:

When the time comes to begin the festival, eight candelabra are lit with fireworks, and these last the duration of the event. An angel comes and announces the festival, exhorting everyone to pay attention. Then, one by one, he calls many prophets and sibyls, commanding that each tell what they know of the incarnation of the Son of God. When they come to the presence of the Son they sing in a single stanza what they have prophesied about the birth of the Messiah. That done, they go and sit in the empty stage above, which is beautiful to see. After the prophets, the sky opens, with dancing, playing and celebration and there is the Angel Gabriel in the middle of six angels exulting.

Reconstructions of the machinery have suggested it consisted of a wooden apparatus of circular design able to accommodate six actors dressed as angels. Niccolò's description also refers to lilies, to lights appearing above the Virgin's chamber, and 'many lights that go on and off' in the Angel's cloud. On seeing the Virgin, the Angel greeted her with the words of Luke the Evangelist, in which he announces to her (hence the term Annunciation) that she is to bear the Lord's child. It was, in short, intended as a good omen for the marriage of Alessandro to Margaret, and it was performed three times, 'so that as many people as possible could see it'. On Sunday, which was the 20th, Margaret herself went.[15]

The most curious of the entertainments devised for Margaret's visit was the *girandola* held in Piazza San Lorenzo the previous day. This piazza lies between the gardens of the Medici palace and the great church of San Lorenzo where the New Sacristy was still under construction. A great canopy was strung between the bell tower of San Lorenzo and the roof of the Medici palace, some eight *braccia* (fifteen feet) above ground. From it hung a construction some twenty *braccia* wide, showing scenes of the Underworld, devils, and 'that fable where Pluto seized Proserpina and carried her off to Hell'. Filled with hundreds of fireworks to create the effect of an inferno, it smoked and flamed 'so that it seemed the air was burning, a beautiful thing,' according to Niccolò Fabbrini. He was impressed that it was managed without injury to anyone present.[16]

The imagery of this entertainment is quite remarkable. The Rape of Proserpina is a classical story in which the beautiful Proserpina (or Persephone) is kidnapped by the god of the underworld, Pluto. According to the myth, her mother Demeter, goddess of the harvest, refused to feed the earth until she was returned. In the underworld, Proserpina was tricked into eating six pomegranate seeds, and because those who have eaten the food of the dead cannot return to the realm of the living, she was obliged thereafter to spend half of every year with Pluto. (One interpretation of Botticelli's celebrated painting *Primavera* (Springtime) is that the central, red-draped figure is Proserpina, returned from the Underworld to herald the spring.)[17] On one level the symbolism seems quite dramatically inappropriate as a celebration for a fiancée's visit; it is certainly open to the reading that Margaret was to be dragged down into a hellish Florence by her future husband. Yet perhaps, like Alessandro's Turkish costume, it was a riposte to the enemies of Medici rule: you call me a tyrant, I'll play God of the Underworld. Proserpina is also a goddess associated with fertility, symbolism more appropriate to a future marriage but also a reminder of the prospect of a Medici–Habsburg heir who would be the grandson of the most powerful man in Europe. Or – perhaps – the opportunity to play at fireworks was just too tempting.

These were only two of the events held in Margaret's honour during her week in Florence. On the Friday there had been athletics: races featuring men and children, and the quintain, a street game played on horseback in which a bell was hung on a rope across the road, and masked players tried to sound it with their lances. On Monday there was a bullfight in Piazza Santa Croce. On one account a bull jumped the fence and escaped. Tuesday's football was cancelled on account of poor weather, but on the Thursday morning there was a tournament, just as there had been in 1532 on Alessandro's elevation to duke. That evening the final event held in Margaret's honour was a banquet in the courtyard of the Medici palace. The palace was dressed for the occasion with arrases. Portraits of the Medici family hung in the loggia and courtyard: the Pope, his father Giuliano (murdered in the Pazzi conspiracy), Lorenzo the Magnificent, Cosimo the Elder, Alessandro himself, Cardinal Ippolito and their fathers, Dukes Lorenzo and Giuliano. The chamber was hung with cloth of gold, its antechamber with cloth of silver. It was said the furnishings had cost 5,000 ducats. The courtyard was transformed into a woodland scene, with a gallery of painted wood and hangings embroidered with ivy leaves. 'Wild men' appeared from the bushes. A pergola hung with vines and bunches of grapes completed the picture, and above the courtyard hung a sky-blue cloth, in its centre the arms of Pope and Emperor, Duke and Duchess.[18]

'Most memorable of all,' wrote the Mantuan envoy, 'was a banquet that His Excellency held on the Thursday before she departed and there were about sixty young gentlewomen in company with all the ladies and gentlewomen who had come with the Illustrious Lady, and no men except the Cardinal of Bari and Cardinal Cibo; and they were served by young gentlemen, all of the city, well arrayed.' There had been a banquet of ladies to welcome Duke Lorenzo's bride Madeleine de la Tour d'Auvergne to Florence, back in 1518. Now, once again, the city was playing host to a royal dynastic bride. 'On the table was every type of food it was possible to have, as well prepared and composed as possible, and as Your Excellency can imagine. And if Your Excellency had seen with what pomp all these gentle ladies comported themselves, both in dress and . . . in jewels I believe without doubt you would have marvelled.' Niccolò Fabbrini gave more precise numbers: seventy at the table in all, including two other prelates besides the cardinals; thirty young men to serve; forty-six courses, including one dish from which live birds appeared. It quite outdid the legendary feasts of Mark Antony, Sardanapalus and 'every other banquet described by historians or poets'. Followed by masquerades, dancing and a comedy, performed on a set beneath the loggia facing Borgo San Lorenzo, it lasted until four hours after sunset.[19]

On 2 May, Niccolò da Monteaguto, one of Alessandro's courtiers, handed over to Pretino the wardrobe master a series of masquerading costumes. Perhaps they had been worn at the Palazzo Medici banquet. There were two red gowns, with caps, a little cape of *pavonazzo* satin, a small white satin gown – perhaps for Catherine de' Medici, or another young lady of the court – along with little *pavonazzo* satin caps and pink stockings. The symbolism of the 'five dresses in the Spanish style in white taffeta and one in white damask', placed in the wardrobe three weeks later, is easy to decipher. Adopting the fashion of the visiting guest was a way to do Margaret honour. Yet that was a change from the celebrations for her predecessor Madeleine. At her banquet, the young ladies had dressed 'according to the customs of the city'.[20]

On the morning of Saturday 26 April, a miserable day, rainy and windy, Margaret left Florence in her litter. To the sound of gun salutes she set out on the road south to Siena, accompanied by a guard of fifty men in *pavonazzo* and white. A few days later Alessandro gave Cardinal Cibo a German matchlock gun, perhaps a gift from Margaret or one of her entourage; in any case a reminder of their Imperial alliance.[21]

It was rumoured that the Medici had tried to persuade Margaret to stay near Florence, citing the poor air in Naples that summer. Her guardian, Madame de Lannoy, was having none of it. If Naples was unhealthy, they would go instead to Abruzzo, likewise in Imperial territory. But first, Margaret went to Rome.

The 170-mile journey took about ten days and she made her entrance on 6 May, greeted by members of the papal guard and household, by her father's ambassador and by the ambassador of the king of Portugal. Alessandro rode post to join her, changing horses regularly to arrive on the evening of the 6th. Though not yet eleven, Margaret was already an Imperial representative. She received the Venetian ambassador, though it was left to Madame de Lannoy to make a formal response to his greetings. Alessandro, meanwhile, stayed with Ippolito in the Medici palace, and they went riding together through Rome.[22] In public, at least, their relationship seemed cordial. In private, it must have been tense. Only eight years before, Margaret had been touted as Ippolito's bride, and the closer Alessandro came to marriage, the fainter Ippolito's prospects of ruling Florence seemed.

Clement presented Margaret with a jewel said to be worth 5 or 6,000 ducats, a staggering sum, more than twice the annual income of some cardinals.[23] It may well have been one of the antique gems from the collection of Lorenzo the Magnificent, most of which ended up in Margaret's possession. The substantial gift was perhaps intended to smooth relations with the Habsburgs. Clement's plan for a match between his niece Catherine and a French prince had not met with Charles' approval, and the attempt of Henry VIII of England to dissolve his marriage – on which the Pope would soon have to pronounce judgement – was a further source of tension: Henry's wife Catherine of Aragon was Charles' aunt. Charles' empire, too, was not without its troubles. Religious conflict between the German states, both at the level of high politics and local radicalism, was a continuing problem. In the eastern borderlands the Turks were a threat, as were ambitious local noblemen who played Sultan against Emperor. Charles could not fight on all fronts, and Clement knew it. If the Medici could help maintain stability in Italy, that would be to Charles' benefit.

Across Europe there was intense interest in the match. The Venetian ambassador in London heard a rumour that Alessandro and Margaret had already consummated the marriage, but that this was being kept secret so that his relatives (presumably, Ippolito) would not find out. This seems quite unlikely, but there was such hostility to the Medici Pope in England that all manner of insulting rumour might pass for fact.[24]

16

Margaret departed for Naples on 13 May after a week in Rome, accompanied for the first day of her journey by Alessandro. Keen to ensure his fiancée did not forget him, Alessandro kept up the gift-giving, commissioning for her some works of art in gold from Benvenuto Cellini. Margaret arrived in Naples two weeks later and moved into the Villa di Pizzofalcone.[1] Located on a hill just to the west of the city, this was one of the first aristocratic residences built in the area. With views across the bay to Vesuvius and the island of Capri it was a sumptuous setting for its royal guest.

The festivities for Margaret's visit had been a chance for Alessandro to show off his generosity to the Florentine populace, and he kept up that effort in the next months. For six years, the palio – Florence's great annual horse race, named for the length of silk or woollen cloth that was traditionally given as a prize – had not been run. The tradition was centuries old. Writing at the beginning of the 1300s Dante had referred to it in his *Divine Comedy* as an 'annual game'; in the first decades of the 1400s Goro di Stagio Dati described the wonders of a festival attracting visitors from far and wide; a great holiday, the city adorned with flowers, blue hangings with yellow fleurs-de-lis, and the palio itself, of crimson velvet, fur and gold brocade. Such events were smart politics: Machiavelli had advised that the prince should 'at the appropriate time of year, keep the populace occupied with festivals and spectacles'. They maintained a sense of continuity. Alessandro restarted the tradition, to what a later historian called the 'incredible delight' of the people.[2]

The palio was the centrepiece of the celebrations of the feast of St John the Baptist, 24 June. It was run from west to east through the heart of the city, beginning from the church of San Pancrazio, near

Palazzo Rucellai, and continuing along the narrow and dangerous Via del Corso. Rumours of the race's revival reached Giovanni Borromei, the duke of Mantua's agent in Florence, in late May. The Duke prided himself on having one of the best stables in Italy, stocked with prime horses from North Africa and the Ottoman Empire. Borromei dashed off to ask Alessandro if the news was true. Alessandro told him yes, and that the Duke would be receiving an invitation to send a horse. Borromei kept his master updated with reports. So confident was he of victory that in mid June he proposed delaying a delivery of mozza-rella to Mantua so he could send it in a single consignment with the prize palio. In a preliminary race, a horse owned by Ippolito de' Medici – bred from Mantuan stock – triumphed. Almost thirty years later, when an inventory was taken of the Medici wardrobe, the compilers found 'two covers for barbary horses, of gold and silver embroidered velvet, with two gowns and helmets for boys, one with the livery of Duke Alessandro and the other of Cardinal Ippolito de' Medici'.[3] These races were splendid affairs, and often a round was run for young riders.

In the event, the main palio was a close-fought race. At first, Alessandro's horse was in the lead. But when the duke of Mantua's rider passed it, Alessandro's took an unexpected left. The Mantuan horse won, with Ippolito's coming in second. Alessandro's came in the length of a crossbow shot behind the others. Incensed at this outcome, Alessandro was all the more determined to win the following year. The rivalry between the Medici cousins was never-ending. Borromei duly dispatched the palio to Mantua with the delayed mozza-rella, a supply of Trebbiano wine and some straw hats.[4] His confidence had been justified.

Within a fortnight of the palio, there was bad news for Florentine taxpayers. The regime imposed a forced loan to raise 35,000 ducats. The money would pay for city defences, the purchase of grain and the maintenance of the River Arno's banks. Such loans were unpop-ular. Although theoretically they were supposed to be repaid – in this case with an interest rate of 12 per cent – few put their trust in such promises. Some suspected that the loan would be blown on Catherine de' Medici's trousseau. Even without such speculation the Florentine economy was still recovering from the effects of war. Florence, of course, was not the only city the Medici had to defend: the towns and villages of its wider dominion had to be considered too. In April 1533 Captain Fabio of Pisa received from the ducal wardrobe two large lances, two halberds and a Spanish-style helmet.[5] If there was no immediate prospect of invasion, there was no harm in being prepared. Alessandro and his ministers could only hope that the entertainments had left the taxpayers in a favourable mood.

The marriage of Catherine de' Medici to Henri, second son of the king of France, went ahead in October 1533 in Marseilles. Both bride and groom were fourteen. Alessandro clearly expected France to be cold: before his departure to attend the wedding he had his tailor make up some collars from a buffalo pelt, ordered a new Turkish-style cassock in red Venetian cloth, and took out from the wardrobe the silver small clock in its silver case, perhaps as a gift, perhaps to keep time on his journey.[6]

Catherine's wedding was a spectacular affair, from her entourage of attendants to her dress of cloth of gold. Caterina Cibo, Cardinal Innocenzo's sister, had helped prepare her trousseau and no expense had been spared. Clement gave her 100,000 *scudi* (perhaps double the annual income of the richest cardinals); he added another 30,000 in return for her renouncing any claim on the Medici family wealth and almost as much again in jewellery. This was funded by a loan from the Strozzi bank, secured against jewels and future papal tax income: advancing the funds put considerable strain on its Lyons branch. Filippo Strozzi went with her to France as papal nuncio. From her new father-in-law Francis she would have an annuity of 10,000 *livres* a year (5,000 gold *scudi*), and a château besides. Ippolito de' Medici, not to be outdone, turned up with an entourage of pages dressed as Turks. Francis presented him with a tame lion 'of exceptional height', said to have been obtained from the ambassadors of Hayreddin Barbarossa.[7]

Clement avoided travelling through Florence on his way to Marseilles, claiming he wanted to avoid incurring expense for the city, though he was more likely worried about a bad reception. The French match was a gamble. It risked damaging relations with Charles V, and it was rumoured that Charles planned to call off the marriage of Margaret and Alessandro.[8] Yet if Clement could call Charles' bluff –

and would the Emperor really turn down the influence in Italy that a Florentine match could win him? – Clement would have placed Catherine and Alessandro in marriages to the two greatest powers in Europe, and Ippolito in the most powerful single office besides the pope in the Catholic hierarchy: the vice-chancellorship of the Church. No previous generation of the Medici had married so royally.

Royal marriages, however, did not prevent trouble in Florence. Tales of the Duke's lavish spending and the rumoured diversion of funds to pay for Catherine's trousseau exacerbated hostility to the Medici regime. There were worries that the marriage celebrations in Marseilles might provide an opportunity for the exiles, some of whom were based in Lyons, to make trouble. In December 1533, two men from the hamlet of Vico di Val d'Elsa, just off the road to Siena south of Florence, were caught discussing Alessandro's murder. A servant of Gabriello de' Rossi had spoken 'very dishonest words about His Excellency the Duke, and the state, and the Pope' to his neighbour Orlando Bovarli. He said that the Medici needed to be finished off, and for real, suggesting that Alessandro might be targeted while out hunting. They were arrested and sentenced to beheading. Their goods were confiscated, punishing their families too.[9]

That such brutal punishment could be meted out simply for talking about opposing the Medici helps explain why accusations of tyranny against Alessandro easily gained traction. From the account given of this pair by Niccolò Guicciardini (Luigi's son), they were guilty of loose talk rather than serious conspiracy to murder. Still, it was quite plausible that a person might do some villainy to the Duke while he was away from the city, and Alessandro was genuinely fearful about the possibility of attack. Three days after Guicciardini wrote his letter, Alessandro retrieved from his wardrobe a new pair of fine chain-mail sleeves and gloves.[10] It was no time to go about unprotected.

There was a history of assassination attempts against the Medici. Pope Clement VII's father Giuliano de' Medici had been murdered, and his brother Lorenzo the Magnificent injured, in one of the most famous of all: the Pazzi conspiracy of 1478, in which the Pazzi, with papal backing, attempted to replace the Medici in Florence with a coup, attacking the Medici brothers at Mass. Giuliano was murdered in the cathedral. Lorenzo survived. Francesco de' Pazzi and his conspirators, including an archbishop, Francesco Salviati, were strung up from the Palazzo della Signoria. One observer told the gruesome tale of how, in his death agony, the Archbishop sank his teeth into Pazzi's body. In Florence, Botticelli painted pictures of the traitors on the wall of the Bargello. Elsewhere the consequences were not so happy. The Pope sequestered the assets of the Medici bank and only thanks to support from the king of Naples – and indirectly from Sultan Mehmet II, whose invasion of Otranto in Puglia concentrated minds on an external threat – did the Medici regain power in Florence. They held it for another fourteen years, until their expulsion in 1494.

Though the Pazzi conspiracy was fifty years in the past, the Medici were not likely to forget the murder of Clement's father. Nor were they likely to forget to take precautions against a possible attack now.

17

In the aftermath of the Pazzi conspiracy, the family's property had been confiscated. Their palace found its way into Medici hands and when Lorenzo the Magnificent's daughter Maddalena (sister to Pope Leo and cousin to Pope Clement) married Franceschetto Cibo in 1488 it became the Cibo residence in Florence. When Cardinal Innocenzo Cibo came to the city as Alessandro's chief minister it was the obvious choice for his home.

Not long after Cardinal Cibo took up residence in Florence to manage city affairs in Alessandro's absence, he was joined by his sister-in-law and lover Ricciarda Malaspina. By the middle of the year, Taddea Malaspina, Ricciarda's sister, had moved to Florence too. She was pregnant. The two sisters had a quite notorious reputation. Ortensio Lando, a poet, made a pun of their name (it means 'wicked thorns') to joke: 'I've found *malaspine* one can embrace at night, without giving offence, even with some delight.' A description of Ricciarda and her sister-in-law Caterina Cibo back in 1524, when they were visiting Rome, said they were 'ugly as devils, but they have a reputation for grandeur, all the more so for being courted by these lord cardinals'.[1]

The role of women in the courts of Renaissance Italy was very different from their role in Florence. By and large, women in a court society had much more scope to operate in public and political life than did their counterparts in republics. They might act as regents for husbands or sons – as Ricciarda did in Massa – without prompting the hostility that Alfonsina Orsini's role in Florence had done. A mistress might enjoy considerable political influence. Noble families, in short, needed women, not least to produce heirs: republics could simply elect a different man. That is not to say that women in republican Florence had had no role at all in politics: there is plenty of evidence for their involvement in some aspects of political life, such as the negotiation of marriage alliances between office-holding families. But the presence of Ricciarda and Taddea, two non-Florentine sisters, as the respective mistresses of the city's new Duke and the Pope's chief representative brought a new dimension to city politics. Ricciarda and her sister-in-law Caterina were, besides, unusually independent women for their time: the former was the effective ruler of Massa, the latter of Camerino. In Florence they became leaders of fashion, setting a trend for the use of carriages: their house became the setting for an informal side to the new court's social life.[2]

The sisters moved in to the former Palazzo Pazzi on the corner of Via del Proconsolo and Borgo degli Albizi around July 1533, perhaps following Margaret of Austria's departure. Both sisters were back in Massa in October, and it is possible they went there for Taddea's lying-in. A 'Giulio Giovanbattista Romolo' was baptised in Florence on 5 December 1533. The name of his father was not recorded in the baptismal register and it is very likely that this was Alessandro's son. Taddea seems to have divided her time between Florence, her family home in Massa, and other locations where she might see Alessandro. She travelled to Pisa for Lent 1534, and extended her visit, 'not lacking for entertainment, as Duke Alessandro is there'. That Easter trip prompted Francesco Berni, who had lately joined the Malaspina circle, to compose a satirical poem. He contrasted the courtiers' amorous fun with the poverty of Florence, concluding that the Florentines would be better off if the court stayed in Pisa.[3]

Alessandro regularly visited Taddea at the Pazzi Palace. Cellini records his presence there, probably around 1535. He 'often used to go there', according to the Cibo family memoirs; he was there 'every evening, usually,' according to Imperio Ricordati, a member of Cibo's household, writing in 1536.[4] Although no letters between Alessandro and Taddea survive, the evidence points to an ongoing liaison, characterised by frequent visits both within Florence and around Tuscany.

This apparently stable relationship with Taddea belies the posthumous accounts of Alessandro's rule, which almost all agree on one thing: the duke of Florence was a womaniser who abused his power to sleep his way around the city. While it is certainly possible that Alessandro had a regular mistress – Taddea – whom he saw frequently, while also seducing scores of virtuous young ladies on the side (as his enemies would have it), a careful look at the allegations suggests a more complex picture. With the exception of a reference to his having syphilis, from 1532, which looks to have been idle rumour (the tale was not repeated by later writers) the stories of Alessandro's abuses are remarkably unspecific. In his own lifetime his power probably ensured silence. but even in the posthumous histories not a single victim is named. Girolamo Ughi's account of Alessandro's sexual misconduct makes the point that while Alessandro seduced numerous women, he never did so by force.[5] His comment is important. It may be as much an observation on the women who accepted (or encouraged) Alessandro's attentions as a condemnation of the Duke's behaviour. It raises the possibility – ignored by writers of Alessandro's own day – that at least some of the women concerned may have sought the Duke's company. That is not to say there were never abuses, but the worst documented incident – in May 1531, five young men, including two of Filippo Strozzi's sons, Vincenzo and Roberto, kidnapped and raped a girl from Prato – involved not Alessandro himself but his associates, and happened before he had even arrived in Florence.[6]

In a court society sex with the prince was a route to favour. Around Europe, numerous women gained wealth and power through affairs, both short- and long-term, with royal men. Domenico 'Panonto' Romoli observed that it was very difficult to stop gatecrashers getting into court parties, especially when they included 'a number of attractive women'.[7] Diane de Poitiers, mistress of Henri II, is a prime example; Henry VIII's affairs are well known. The extramarital sex of Francesco II Gonzaga, marquis of Mantua, contributed positively to his reputation for virility. But there was a fine line here: too much female influence was thought to be troublesome. Political theorists like Machiavelli and Erasmus of Rotterdam argued that a prince ought to control his passions. 'What makes him hated above all else,' wrote Machiavelli of The Prince, 'is being rapacious and a usurper of the property and the women of his subjects.'[8]

In Florence, Taddea's family certainly took advantage of her relationship with the Duke. Alessandro used his influence to intervene on behalf of the Malaspina family with the authorities in Lucca, an

15. Giorgio Vasari's fantastic portrait of Alessandro in armour is packed with allusions to Medici power and the defeat of the Florentine republicans.

ALEX. MED. FLOR.   DVX I. LAVREN. F.

16. This small posthumous portrait of Alessandro was one of a series showing Medici family members made in Bronzino's workshop in the 1550s or 60s.

17. Ippolito de' Medici was portrayed in Hungarian costume by Titian around the time of his mission as Legate to Hungary.

18. The Holy Roman Emperor, Charles V, Alessandro's father-in-law, in a portrait by Christoph Amberger.

19. Alessandro's half-sister, Catherine de' Medici, portrayed by François Clouet, became queen of France.

20. Margaret of Austria, also portrayed by Clouet, married Alessandro shortly before her fourteenth birthday.

21. In contrast with Vasari's armorial portrait, Pontormo shows Alessandro in sober, civilian dress, engaged in the gentlemanly pastime of sketching.

ALEXANDER · MED· FLOR. D. I ·

22. Of all Alessandro's portraits, this posthumous image best conveys the splendour of his wardrobe.

23. This 1534 sketch by Jacopo da Pontormo may be the only surviving drawing of Alessandro from life.

24. Domenico di Polo's cameo follows a trend for objects in the classical style.

25. Cellini's portrayal of Alessandro on silver coins was a symbol of the new ducal regime.

26. In this letter of 8 April 1536, Alessandro thanks Isabella d'Este, marchioness of Mantua, for the gift of a puppy.

27. Alessandro's emblem, the rhinoceros, can be spotted in the decorations of the Palazzo Vecchio.

28. This luxurious Book of Hours features miniature portraits of Alessandro and Margaret.

29. Alessandro was buried in his father's tomb, beneath Michelangelo's sculptures of Dawn and Dusk.

30. Alessandro's illegitimate daughter Giulia is portrayed here with her guardian Maria Salviati.

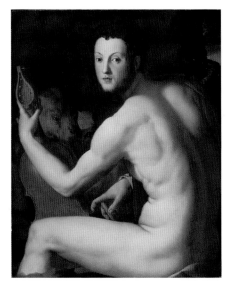

31. Cosimo de' Medici is shown here as Orpheus in this unusual nude portrait by Bronzino.

32. This striking portrait of Alessandro in fantastic classical dress is in the Palazzo Vecchio.

independent city some miles to the west of Florence, which bordered Malaspina lands (though he doubted the goodwill of the Lucchese officials). 'It was a most singular pleasure to be able to do you service,' he wrote to Lucrezia Malaspina, Taddea's mother, in May 1534. 'If I can be of service either regarding this or some other matter for Your Ladyship, let me know; I am at your disposal.' The relationship worked both ways. In February that year Alessandro had appealed to Ippolita Cibo Sanseverino, countess of Caiazzo and sister of Cardinal Cibo, on behalf of her major-domo Paolo Ferri. Ferri had evidently committed some 'errors' but Alessandro judged that they were 'nothing momentous' and asked the countess to pardon her servant.[9]

The sixteenth-century historians treat the young women of Florence as objects, unable to make their own choices about sex. In practice things worked differently. Ricciarda's open affair with her brother-in-law was only one of the most notorious examples. Yet beyond the satirical comment on the Cibo–Malaspina lifestyles, the sources are silent on how Florentine women might have related to this new court culture: the few surviving letters from the Malaspina sisters offer no clues. We might well wonder whether their libertine lifestyle shocked a city where women had traditionally lived more cloistered lives, but all we can say for sure about Alessandro de' Medici is that in 1534, his principal relationship was an ongoing liaison with Taddea Malaspina, and that they may have slept beneath a quilted bedcover of red and grey taffeta.[10]

18

In January 1534, Ippolito de' Medici was back in Rome, ill and brooding. He had an abscess on his leg that had to be removed. Surgeons of the period were well able to deal with such complaints, though infection was always a risk. Far worse for Ippolito, if true, was the rumour that he had syphilis. Hoping for a cure, he took allspice, known as 'India wood', a newish import from the Caribbean islands to Europe.[1]

Despite his poor health, he kept on with business. His correspondence is largely lost, perhaps destroyed, but a few letters survive. Among them is a request to the vice-legate in Perugia, dated July 1533, asking for his help in returning an escaped slave to Cardinal Pisani. The man was described as eighteen or nineteen, with a brown, pleasant face, reasonably tall and well built, wearing a grey and yellow livery. This brief reference is testimony both to the presence of slaves in Renaissance Rome and to the possibility of resisting enslavement, but running away was dangerous. Cardinal Pisani was from Venice, a city that enacted fierce penalties against runaway slaves and (unusually for this period) penalised black slaves in particular. The Venetian Senate offered a five-ducat reward to anyone capturing such a runaway; once recaptured, slaves would be publicly flogged. If they were killed in the course of capture, there would be no penalty for the killer.[2]

There is more evidence from around this time for Ippolito's own attempts to capture or otherwise acquire 'exotic' people. He wrote to the duke of Mantua to enquire about the fate of a Turk whom the Duke was said to have apprehended. He had wanted to get his hands on the man, and was trying to find out the name of the papal chamberlain who now had him in custody. This Turk (the word *turco* was used generically for Muslims and slaves and does not indicate a specific ethnicity)[3] may have been a prisoner whom Ippolito had saved from execution in 1532, while on campaign in Hungary. A correspondent described the scene in Regensburg following the soldier's detention:

> The whole square ran to see him, as he was dressed Turkish-style, with a turban on his head. . . . Yesterday they took him to the baths, where the Emperor was. It was believed that he would be beheaded, but today they've taken him to the house of the Most Reverend Medici, legate.[4]

We do not know whether this particular man became part of Ippolito's collection of non-European people and, if so, what he made of that fate.

Around this time Ippolito received from his friend Giulio Landi a description of the island of Madeira and its inhabitants.[5] Born in Piacenza in 1498, Giulio Landi studied philosophy, rhetoric and classics before graduating in law, and lived for a long period in Rome, where he was among Ippolito's circle of artists and writers. Landi had probably travelled to Madeira himself. The island had been settled by the Portuguese in the early fifteenth century, and its sugar plantations were worked by enslaved Africans, brought there from the coast of West Africa.[6] Landi's narrative follows a fashion at the time for descriptions of the 'New World'. It gives some intriguing clues as to how Ippolito and his friends might have perceived those of different ethnicities, conveying a sense of fascination and curiosity but also ideas about hierarchies of intelligence, and of compliance with European masters. Landi's schematic classification of slaves into Moors, Ethiopians and mulattoes was not strictly followed in Europe, where 'racial' descriptions were used far more loosely and where in the middle of the century the Arab traveller al-Ḥasan ibn Muḥammad al-Wazzān (Leo Africanus) would see no difficulty in writing about 'white Moors'.[7]

> All those who live in Madeira, or indeed in Portugal, are either free or slaves. The latter take the name for one of three reasons, either from the law, like those, who among [the Madeirans] are called Moors, because they observe the law of Mohammed, or from their colour, like the Ethiopians,

who they call blacks: or indeed from creation, like those who are born of a black man and a white woman, who are both slaves, or indeed from a black woman and a free man, or the contrary; and these are called mulattoes, as [they are] generated by the seed of another species; and they are neither white nor black but have an olive colour. Therefore one finds Madeirans and Portuguese who, leaving their wives, go out of their way to love these black women. And on the other hand there are free women, who willingly take their pleasure with these black men, because they are supposed to be more lustful.

I myself met in Ebora [Évora], a city of that realm, a young merchant gentleman, who (although he had a most beautiful wife, as I was told) nonetheless was on fire for a black servant woman. His wife not only didn't take this badly but she herself had fallen in love with a black slave. In such a way that, without seeming to disdain each other's love, they both happily went on with great pleasure. Among the Moors are to be found many who are wicked, and who run away from their owners. And it's no marvel that they suffer servitude badly, because they were previously free; but when they are captured in war they're immediately made slaves and are kept in chains. Those who are called blacks are for the most part good, and trusted, but of blunt intelligence. And they say that they're of such nature that if they aren't kept in continual work by their owners, and also sometimes beaten, they easily become useless and sluggards. That's why they make them lead a hard life, but don't keep them in chains, as with the Moors, except for some misdeed. The mulattoes, having nearly all been born in the household, are the best of all the other slaves and because they serve with gentility, many are freed.

Great diligence is used in buying and selling slaves: it's not sufficient for the buyers to test their dexterity and vigour through their appetite and running. They want to see minutely if they have any defect in their bodies, and if they're missing teeth, because they judge that those who are missing teeth are also weaker labourers, lacking the means of eating, from which strength is derived. When they have to put slaves on show for sale, they anoint them daily with oil, so that their bodies appear more lustrous and beautiful. As for free men, there are two sorts: that is, noblemen and plebeians. Nobles are those who have noble and illustrious ancestors. And if it happens that this purity of blood is joined with riches, they (as happens also in Italy) are highly esteemed.[8]

When Landi's work was translated from Latin into Italian, the translator cut out the words 'because they are supposed to be more lustful'. Perhaps he hoped to conceal the information from women readers, who were less likely to know Latin. But the existence of such a stereotype raises the possibility that there was a link between the rumours about Alessandro's ethnicity and the stories of his sexual conduct. Turks, as well, were stereotyped by Europeans as lascivious.[9] For a European nobleman, in contrast, self-control (or at least the image of it) was important.

Also in Rome around this time was Alessandro's distant cousin, Lorenzino, 'little Lorenzo', de' Medici. The cadet branch of the Medici to which Lorenzino belonged (sometimes known as the 'popolano' branch) had split from the main line almost a century before. Born on 22 March 1514 in Florence, and a couple of years Alessandro's junior, Lorenzino was the son of Pierfrancesco the Younger and Maria Soderini.[10] There was a history of conflict between the Soderini and the main branch of the Medici. Maria's great-uncle Piero Soderini had been *gonfaloniere* of Florence during the Medici exile, from 1502 to 1512. In 1517 Cardinal Francesco Soderini had been implicated, along with fellow cardinals Bandinello Sauli and Alfonso Petrucci, in the plot to assassinate Pope Leo X. Even within the cadet branch there was conflict. Lorenzino's mother Maria was fighting over the family inheritance with another Maria, Maria Salviati, widow of Giovanni de' Medici, mother of Cosimo and former guardian of Catherine de' Medici. In the tangled politics of Florence and the popes, Lorenzino's loyalties were surely mixed.[11]

From an early age, Lorenzino was interested in his studies. Pale-faced (or dark and melancholy, depending who you read), he was nicknamed 'the Philosopher' and by the age of eighteen was said to be fluent in Latin and Greek. Attractive, well-mannered and bright, 'everyone loved him'. Most of the surviving accounts of Lorenzino's youth were written after the assassination of Alessandro in 1537, and their glowing descriptions of his youthful achievements have a narrative function, but they are corroborated by the descriptions of contemporary observers: he was 'reputed to be most virtuous and very well lettered', wrote an agent of the duke of Urbino in 1532. All this, though, did not make him Clement's priority. He refused to repay in full a loan made by Lorenzino's uncle to the papal treasury. In 1533 Clement had granted Lorenzino the office of governor of Fano but within a few days had changed his mind and given it to Cardinal Benedetto Accolti of Ravenna instead. The Cardinal had paid seven thousand ducats for the office, a sum the cash-strapped Clement could hardly turn down.[12] The following year, their relationship worsened:

> Around the same time, he [Lorenzino] incurred the disgrace of the Pope, and the hatred of the entire Roman people, for this reason: finding one morning that at the Arch of Constantine, and in other places of Rome, there were many ancient statues without their heads, Clement was so furious that he ordered (not thinking that it might have been Lorenzino) that whoever had done it (with the sole exception of Cardinal [Ippolito] de' Medici) should be strung up without a trial. The Cardinal [Ippolito] went to the Pope, and excused Lorenzo as a young man, who had only wanted the antiques after the fashion of his elders, and who, with great effort, might change his ways, to which Clement agreed, only on the grounds that putting him to death would only be to the infamy and reproach of the house of Medici. Lorenzino had, nonetheless, to leave Rome. The local officials issued a decree that he could no longer stay in Rome;

the Senate proclaimed that anyone in Rome who killed him would not only not be punished, but would be rewarded.[13]

Lorenzino's vandalism became infamous. Francesco Maria Molza, a poet and Ippolito's secretary, denounced it in an oration to the Roman Academy. His words may have been genuinely felt. They also had the convenient effect of distancing his master from the affair.[14] Lorenzino fled to Florence, and to the court of his cousin Alessandro, greatly in Ippolito's debt after his intervention with Clement.

Lorenzino's delinquent behaviour was a minor irritation compared with Clement's political concerns. Far more important, in the bigger picture of Florentine politics, was the Pope's deal with Alfonso d'Este, duke of Ferrara, in February 1534. The Duke and the Pope had been at loggerheads since 1527, when the Este had occupied the city of Modena, part of the Papal States. The row was subsequently settled in the Este's favour, but Clement extracted a promise that the Duke would stop protecting the Florentine exiles, many of whom had flocked to his territories (such as Nardi and Benintendi, whom Cellini and Tribolo encountered on the road from Florence to Venice).[15] It was one more step towards securing the Medici regime. Clement also used his financial power as Pope to ensure support from the leading Florentine families at this time. The Strozzi bank, for example, was one of the principal lenders to the papacy. The financial mechanisms he deployed were complex but, at the simplest level, the bankers advanced money and, in return, Clement authorised them to collect particular taxes owing to the Papal States. These revenue streams could then be instrumentalised to provide a basis for the issue of further credit. But if a pope was slow to issue the formal authorisation to collect taxes (or failed to issue it at all and directed the money elsewhere), that could leave a bank overextended.[16] As their principal client, Clement therefore had a substantial hold over the Florentine banks, which depended on his goodwill to ensure timely repayments.

In Florence, plans moved ahead for new city defences. They would need an architect. Michelangelo had designed fortifications for the Florentine republic but he was spending more and more time in Rome and was no enthusiast for the new regime. He was afraid of Alessandro, said Vasari, and particularly reluctant to get involved in the fortress project. In March 1534, Alessandro approached Antonio Cordini da Sangallo, one of the leading architects of his day, whose projects had included fortifications for the papal town of Orvieto, where Clement had fled after the Sack of Rome. Now almost fifty, he had worked on the Castel Sant'Angelo in Rome, on fortresses at Bolsena and Civita Castellana, on cardinals' *palazzi* and on churches. In a cryptic note, Alessandro now invited Sangallo to Florence 'so that I might avail myself of your advice'.[17] All would be explained in person, once Sangallo arrived. These plans, at least for the moment, were not to be written down.

Discussions between Sangallo, other engineers and architects, and Alessandro Vitelli, commander of the city's defence force, continued with some urgency. Rejecting the eastern site at the Porta alla Giustizia, where an existing fortress had been rebuilt the year before, they settled on the Porta a Faenza, north of the Palazzo Medici, instead. The idea that Florence needed a new fortress may have originated with Clement, or even with Charles V. Some sources attribute it to Filippo Strozzi. Certainly Alessandro, at this stage in his rule, could not have proceeded without Clement's blessing.[18]

Shortly after the approach to Sangallo, Luigi Guicciardini wrote to his brother Francesco that the fortress would go ahead, 'but there've been no discussions yet about how to start it, or about the money'. Alessandro was not even in Florence: he had gone to Pisa with Taddea. Moreover, Luigi was worried about his health. The Duke had been indisposed owing to a lack of sleep which, Luigi thought, was a product of 'little valuing his person, both night and day'. The Duke's enjoyment of hunting and ball games – and late-night entertainments – was not helping matters. This was a repeated complaint. Two years later, Luigi would write again: 'I'm disappointed that His Excellency the Duke works himself so hard at *palla* as to do himself harm, because in fact His Excellency pushes nature too far: he needs to remember that we're made of flesh not iron.'[19] The game of *palla* was an early version of tennis, played in streets or courtyards with a small ball. (The well off would build a courtyard especially, hence the English name 'royal tennis'.) It was 'very suitable for the courtier to play,' observed one character in Castiglione's book of advice on good conduct, *The Courtier*. 'This shows how well he is built physically, how quick and agile he is in every member.'[20]

Alessandro evidently enjoyed ball games for their own sake, but there were political advanges to be had from them too. Besides *palla*, Alessandro played football (*calcio in livrea*). This historical version of the game is still played today in Florence's squares, and it resembles bare-knuckle fighting as much as modern football. 'He mixed with his young citizens,' wrote Ceccherelli, not wishing to be treated as other than their equal.

> Now once upon a time, in one of these tournaments, following a ball that had already been kicked, he encountered a youth and knocked him to the ground, and to show that he hadn't done him harm, he gave him his hand and helped him up. The game went on, and it so happened that another young man found the Duke on his feet and threw him to the ground, and in the fall he struck his nose somehow, and blood spurted out. The youth wanted to excuse himself, thinking he'd done ill, but the Duke said with a pleasant countenance that he wanted to play not as a superior but as an equal: and he shouldn't doubt it because he'd get him another time. And without more ado he got up on his feet and went to score. That done, he went off to a corner, wiped and washed his face, and once again returned to the game; and with a happy face he showed not only that he didn't take it badly, but, caressing the youth, made a sign that he was grateful that he was equal to everyone in the game.[21]

On the football pitch it was easy for Alessandro to play at being equal. He could cultivate an image of an athletic, populist ruler, ready for the physical challenge of warfare, should it come his way. Alessandro's successor Cosimo also knew the importance of football. Many years later he wrote about it in a letter to his son Francesco. Such 'justice and abundance' was vital to keep the support of the common people, who were the 'true treasure' for a regime.[22]

Through public festivals and games, Alessandro took care to be seen to attend to the interests of the people. But he was also said to be planning a more substantial series of reforms. He would ensure that legal contracts would be written in Italian, not Latin, so that everyone could understand them. He would insist that goods received on credit should be signed for by the purchaser, so there could be no dispute afterwards about who owed what. He would place a time limit on property litigation, so that after a certain period of possession owners could safely dispose of land without fear of long-delayed claims.[23] Even as the reforms to government sliced away at the power of the merchant elite, Alessandro took care to show sensitivity to their interests.

Meanwhile, Alessandro had been expanding the Medici art collection with a series of new commissions. Jacopo da Pontormo had already worked at the villa in Poggio a Caiano and now he was asked to prepare a huge fresco of naked men playing football. Commissioned in fact by Alessandro's elder relative Ottaviano de' Medici, this is sometimes said to allude to the football game played during the siege. If so, it would be a rather odd choice of pro-republican imagery. But perhaps this was a later gloss, and the desire was simply to have the Michelangelesque nudes for their aesthetic value.[24]

Other art works had political overtones, too. Having acquired Vasari's *Entombment of Christ*, Alessandro went on to commission a portrait of Lorenzo the Magnificent, perhaps the most celebrated member of the Medici family, from Vasari. It was an obvious choice of commission for the new prince, but it could be read too as a dig at Ippolito, who had adopted the title of Magnificent himself. In a letter of January 1533, Vasari described his plan for the Lorenzo painting. *Il Magnifico* was to be surrounded by a collection of bizarre masks, alluding to the triumph of virtue over vice.[25] Alessandro also employed Vasari to decorate a room in the Palazzo Medici – already stuccoed by Giovanni da Udine during the reign of Leo X – with scenes from the life of Julius Caesar. (Vasari was hoping not only for fame and honour from this commission, but to make a decent dowry for his sister.) In a letter to Pietro Aretino, Vasari observed that 'Our most

Illustrious Duke has such affection for Julius Caesar, that if he lives, and if I live to serve him, it won't be many years before this palace is full of all the stories of his every action.' One fresco showed Caesar swimming, his *Commentaries* in one hand, his sword between his teeth; another showed him burning Pompey's books, so as not to see the works of his enemies. A third showed him in stormy seas, revealing his identity to a helmsman; the fourth, never finished, was to show his triumph. The allusion to Caesar may well have been conceived as a homage to Pope Clement VII, whose given name Giulio is the Italian version of Julius.[26]

Yet in Florence frescoes of Caesar were bound to be a source of suspicion. A century earlier, Cosimo de' Medici the Elder, on whose financial and political acumen rested the family's success, had identified himself not with Caesar but with his assassin, Brutus. Cosimo had taken on the tyrannical Albizzi family, just as Brutus had taken on Caesar.[27] A fresco in the Palazzo della Signoria, painted by Domenico Ghirlandaio in the times of Lorenzo the Magnificent, portrayed the heroes of the Roman Republic: Brutus, Gaius Mucius Scaevola, Camillus, Decimus Brutus, Scipio and Cicero. The decision to celebrate Caesar the dictator, and no longer his republican opponents and assassins, pointed to a change in Florentine culture.

19

When, in 1534, Vasari came to paint a portrait of Alessandro himself, it likewise featured a fantastical scheme of allusions to the Duke's rule which, again, the artist went to some trouble to explain, this time in a letter to Ottaviano de' Medici. Employing a classical allusion typical of the Renaissance, Vasari said he hoped to do for Alessandro what the celebrated Greek artist Apelles had done for Alexander the Great. The enormous painting sums up Alessandro's triumph over his republican opponents. In the first armorial portrait of any of the Medici family – an evocation of their new, princely status – he is depicted 'prepared, for the love of the fatherland, for every public or particular defence'. Portrayed in profile, his dark, curly hair fades into background blackness, while his prominent nose – similar to Clement VII's – emphasises his Medici descent. In his hand he holds a gold staff, 'to rule and command as prince and captain'. The ruin of columns and buildings behind him alludes to the siege of 1530, and further in the background again the city of Florence 'seems to be resting, the air above it entirely serene'. The round stool on which Alessandro sits, having neither beginning nor end, represents his perpetual rule, while the three truncated bodies shown within it, with neither arms nor legs, are the Florentine people, submitting to his will. The red cloth over the seat refers to blood – not only of the Medici's enemies but also of old Giuliano and Lorenzo, killed and injured in the Pazzi conspiracy. The dried-out laurel trunk, sprouting a new branch, is the almost-extinct Medici family, growing once again through the person of Alessandro. The helmet burning on the ground represents eternal peace, which 'proceeding from the head of the prince through his good government, keeps his people full of happiness and love.'[1]

In his efforts to get Alessandro's armour just right, Vasari (who said the task was driving him mad) had consulted Pontormo, the artist responsible for the existing fresco of *Vertumnus and Pomona* at the Poggio villa, painted in around 1525–26, when both Ippolito and Alessandro had been living in Florence. Jacopo da Pontormo, properly called Jacopo Carucci, was some years Vasari's elder and one of the leading artists at the Medici court. Born in 1494, he had trained with Leonardo da Vinci, Piero di Cosimo and Andrea del Sarto and had begun work in Florence around the time of the Medici return in 1512. Besides the fresco at Poggio, Ottaviano had commissioned portraits of the two boys from Pontormo.[2]

Now he was duke, Alessandro was an acquisitive art collector, not afraid to use his position to upset other patrons. He insisted on having for himself a *Venus and Cupid* that Pontormo had painted from an initial design by Michelangelo for Bartolomeo Bettini, leaving Bettini with only the cartoon. Michelangelo was furious on Bettini's behalf, but it was a spectacular work and Alessandro's desire for it is quite understandable. A fleshy Venus sprawls across the scene, and in the corner are – once again – the masks of virtue and vice. The latter is unmistakably a portrait of the painting's designer, Michelangelo.[3]

It was to Pontormo that Alessandro now returned for a second portrait, of a very different style to Vasari's. Pontormo began by sketching his subject, and produced a small portrait that much later would hang in the wardrobe of Alessandro's successor. He then made a much larger work, showing Alessandro, pen in hand, drawing the head of a woman. Alessandro is dressed in plain, dark clothing; a black cap covers much of his hair. The Duke gave this version to Taddea Malaspina, and it probably hung in the Palazzo Pazzi for them both to see on the many evenings that he visited. While Vasari was always happy to explain the symbolism of his own work in detail, the meaning of the Pontormo portrait is less clear. Some have wondered whether Taddea is the woman whom Alessandro is sketching, but Vasari (who would have known what Taddea looked like) described it only as 'the head of a woman'. It may be a more abstract allusion to beauty and the appropriate artistic pursuits of an educated prince.[4]

Besides the paintings, Alessandro's image featured on many other objects. A cameo, now in the Victoria and Albert Museum, London, perhaps by Domenico di Polo, shows his profile in dark green chalcedony on a gold setting. The choice of a dark stone for this cameo is unusual and might be read as an allusion to Alessandro's dark skin, but another version of the same cameo, in the Museo degli Argenti, Florence, is cut from white stone, and a third, in the Hermitage, St Petersburg, is in a yellowish carnelian. Like the contemporary paintings, the cameos do not tell a straightforward story about Alessandro's ethnicity. Domenico, who was responsible for the production of Alessandro's ducal seal, may also have cut the gemstones for the gold ring with a carnelian and cat's eye that Alessandro placed in the care of the wardrobe master in April 1534. To gems was added glass. A stunning rock crystal vessel was finely engraved with portraits of Alessandro and Clement and the Medici arms.[5]

Pontormo's *Venus* may not have been the only artwork Alessandro de' Medici commandeered. Baccio Bandinelli's copy of the celebrated ancient sculpture of *Laocoön and his Sons,* originally intended for Francis I of France, found its way into the Medici palace gardens instead, erected in October 1531, not long after Alessandro's arrival in the city.[6] By May 1534, Bandinelli's statue of *Hercules and Cacus* was ready to go on display. It took ten pairs of oxen and an ingenious mechanism of rollers to shift it through the city streets to its place on the steps of the Palazzo della Signoria. There it stands to this day. Continuing the imagery of Hercules already employed for Alessandro's ducal seal, it conveyed an impression of strength, power and athleticism, but the critics were not enthused. As the eighteenth-century antiquarian Francesco Settimanni recorded, the marble of which it was made was 'one of the most beautiful pieces ever to be brought to Florence; but it was poorly worked, according to those who knew about sculpture'. On Cellini's account it had cost 5,000 ducats, but 'the universal judgement was that he'd ruined a beautiful piece of marble, and that the two giants were sad figures, with many defects, ugly even, and it was cursed by almost everyone who saw it.' Critics of the statue pinned satirical comments on its plinth, and if Vasari is to be believed the hostility to the work reached the point where Alessandro had to intervene. It was a public commission and criticism did not reflect well on the Duke, who had some of the worst offenders thrown into prison. But Vasari was concerned to elevate his friend Michelangelo's reputation above that of every rival sculptor; he may have been exaggerating the statue's poor reception. His relationships with fellow artists were not always easy. Cellini, for example, would later accuse Vasari of falsely claiming to Alessandro that he (Cellini) had insulted the Duke.[7]

Michelangelo himself had drifted away from Alessandro's court, more or less deliberately. Keen to secure his services to complete the New Sacristy in San Lorenzo, Clement VII had been prepared to overlook his associations with the republic of 1527–30, and had re-employed Michelangelo to finish the work. But from April 1532 onwards, Michelangelo spent more and more time in Rome, delegating work on the chapel to assistants, including Cellini's friend Niccolò Tribolo, Raffaello da Montelupo and Giovanni Angelo Montorsoli. Despite the best efforts of both Clement and the Florentine ambassador, after September 1534 he did not return to Florence.[8] When he left, the Medici chapel remained unfinished, but the great tombs for Dukes Lorenzo and Giuliano, with their sad, sombre sculptures of Dawn and Dusk, Night and Day, were ready. In a poem, Michelangelo imagined Day and Night speaking of Giuliano's death:

Day and Night speak: 'We killed Giuliano, with our rapid course:
It's fair he should make his vendetta. The vendetta is this:
We killed him, but he, now he's dead, has deprived us of light,
And closing his eyes has closed ours,
Which no longer shine down on earth.
What might he have done with us, if he had lived?'[9]

That question – what might Duke Giuliano have done with his life? – would have appealed to the Duke's son. Ippolito de' Medici was always keen to emphasise his father's popularity in Florence. Although Michelangelo no longer worked in Alessandro's Florence, he did consider producing work for Ippolito, who asked to look over some designs of Michelangelo's in September 1533.[10]

Alongside his art commissions, Alessandro continued to build a sumptuous collection of decorative objects for his home, often spending substantially more than he did on paintings. In April 1534 he sent once again to Penne for a consignment of silverware, to be commissioned from merchants in Naples. It included six great gilded silver flasks, equipped with chains, six silver candelabra for the table, a dozen gilded silver goblets, and twelve large silver dishes. The total cost of producing this set, including travel between Penne and Naples and its eventual transport to Florence, was more than 1,500 ducats: one silversmith alone received a payment of 1,253 ducats. In January 1535 Alessandro bought additional silver: twenty-four worked silver plates, weighing over 25 kilograms (55 lb) in total, plus two warming dishes and a flask weighing just under 17 kilograms.[11] The sideboard displays would be ever more extravagant.

Just as in previous years, new masks and costumes were ordered for Alessandro and his lieutenants for the Carnival of 1534. Mantles, gowns, shirts, breeches, habits, wigs and turbans were made up for the court in rich fabrics: gold and silver tissue, green damask with green and gold fringes, taffeta, crimson satin, gold brocade. A Spanish-style white damask dress, made for Margaret of Austria's visit the previous year, was recycled into two pilgrims' habits with matching hats. The costume list suggests the courtiers dressed up as rustics, peasants and gypsies. The *isbernia*, a type of cloak or coatdress mentioned in the wardrobe lists, is a standard Florentine garment but derives its name from a Sicilian word alluding to Arab women's dress. An 'eastern' setting for this masquerade is borne out by references to turbans and Levantine fabric.[12]

The reference to gypsies, a persecuted minority in early modern Europe, is particularly intriguing. Like Turks and Moors, they were outsiders to western Christendom. A German chronicler, Aventinus, writing in about 1522, described their arrival on the continent in the year 1439: 'At this time, that thievish race of men, the dregs and bilge-water of various peoples, who live on the borders of the Turkish empire and of Hungary (we call them Zigeni), began to wander through our provinces under their king Zindello, and by dint of theft, robbery and fortune-telling they seek their sustenance with impunity.' The Holy Roman Empire had expelled them as spies; Charles V had decreed that if caught wandering more than twice they could be 'seized and enslaved forever': those who failed to settle within two months could be sentenced to six years as galley slaves. Milan banned them from the Duchy in 1506, under threat of torture; Modena in 1524; other Italian states followed mid-century.[13]

In other political contexts, dressing up the court as a glitzy gang of peasants and gypsies might be a simple piece of fun, the social hierarchy temporarily turned upside down. But like his Turkish costume, in the context of Alessandro's illegitimacy and low birth, and his known favour for the lower classes, this masquerade can be read politically. It is as if Alessandro and his court were saying yes, we know what you say about us, and we don't care much.

Carnival 1534 was also the start of a sequence of events that would become part of Alessandro's mythology: the Luisa Strozzi affair.[14] A year on from the Strozzi youths' run-in with the Florentine authorities, relations between the Strozzi and Medici deteriorated. Late on the evening of Friday 13 March, riding home from the Palazzo Medici, Giuliano Salviati, one of Alessandro's courtiers, was attacked. Just past the cathedral, on the corner of Piazza delle Pallotole, three men set on him. They stabbed him twice, once in the face and once in the leg, leaving him permanently lame. Francesco Settimanni, who described the affair, insinuated that Giuliano was close to Alessandro on account of the latter's intrigues with Salviati's wife. 'Most displeased,' Alessandro went straight away to visit Salviati in an attempt to uncover who was responsible. Though Salviati could not name his attackers, the *Otto di Guardia e Balìa* quickly issued a decree that anyone failing to inform on the culprits would face heavy penalties. The following day Maso and Piero Strozzi were arrested, along with a member of the Pazzi family and several servants.

Suspicion had fallen on Piero Strozzi because the previous winter Giuliano Salviati had insulted his sister Luisa, a married woman of good reputation. The occasion for the insult had been a masked party, held to celebrate the wedding of Alessandro's courtier Guglielmo Martelli and Marietta Nasi. Alessandro and his party, Giuliano among them, had turned up dressed in matching costumes as nuns. Giuliano had sat himself down next to Luisa and said something – we know not what – at which she took offence. The following morning (it was, on one account, an all-night party), as she was trying to mount her horse to leave, he repeated his comments and she gave him 'the response he deserved'. Some months later, one Friday in March, she had gone out with some other ladies to visit the church of San Miniato al Monte. It was a fashionable trip at that time of year, when artisans set up stalls near the church to sell their wares, making a hilltop fair with views down over the city. Giuliano, standing by the stalls with a group of gentlemen, spotted Luisa passing. He repeated his comments from the party, and added that 'he'd like to give her one, at any rate.' Unfortunately for Giuliano, Luisa's brother Leone Strozzi overheard.

'I don't know if you realise that's my sister,' said Leone.

'I know that perfectly well,' replied Giuliano, 'but all women were made to lie with men, and that's why I'd like to lie with her anyhow.'

That remark – it was alleged – got him stabbed.

Questioned by the fearsome chancellor Ser Maurizio, Piero Strozzi refused to write his confession and instead (it was said) penned a sonnet against his interrogator. After a couple of weeks the three were freed from prison; their father Filippo was too important a man for them to be held any longer. Yet, like the arrests of 1533, it would be easy for the Strozzi to see this as one more insult to their family on the part of Alessandro and his regime. Luisa, after all, was Alessandro's cousin, and yet the Duke appeared to tolerate dishonourable behaviour towards her. The story could only worsen his court's reputation for licentiousness.

20

Though Piero Strozzi's well-connected family might get him out of trouble, there were tales of rougher justice. One told how, in May 1534, Alessandro Schiattesi, who lived near the Palazzo Medici, was playing *palla* in the palace courtyard with his son Ormanno. One of the Duke's servants, busy sweeping the courtyard, took exception to Ormanno's presence, and smacked him with a broom, at which the young man hit the servant in the face. When the latter complained to the Duke, Ormanno was arrested, taken to the Bargello, and sentenced to have a hand cut off.[1] No longer was Alessandro pulling his own knife to settle such household disputes, as he had in Brussels three years before. Now, such cases were a matter for the magistrates, and the regime made careful use of the official court procedures to investigate crimes and sentence offenders. Nonetheless, if the story is true this was brutal justice and incidents like this helped make Alessandro's reputation as a tyrant.

Alessandro constantly fielded requests from his commissars in the countryside to deal with tricky cases of justice and clemency. In April 1534 he wrote to Bartolomeo Valori, now papal governor of the Romagna, about the case of one Giovan Antonio Perlini of Forlì. Perlini had had words with a neighbour, Tyberio Nerini. When their argument turned violent, he had been 'forced to use a stiletto, which he carried, with which he wounded the said Tyberio and killed him'. In a society where knives were so common, it was easy for rows to escalate into injury and even death. The usual practice in such cases was for the offender's goods to be confiscated, but Alessandro intervened to ensure that the dowries of Perlini's mother and sister were protected. 'Your Lordship,' wrote Alessandro to Valori, 'should provide for justice so that the innocent do not suffer for those who have erred, but that they and their goods are preserved.'² In his book describing the Duke's virtues, Ceccherelli also has Alessandro providing dowries for poor families, but it was not only the lower classes who gained from the Duke's largesse. In June 1534 he agreed to grant Filippo Valori the sum of 700 ducats as a dowry for his eldest daughter, in recognition of many services rendered. The match was concluded the following year when Filippo's fourteen-year-old daughter Maria married twenty-year-old Niccolò Ginori. An alliance between the Valori and Ginori families was, presumably, more acceptable than the Valori–Strozzi marriage that Alessandro had vetoed.³

The business of government went on, with its usual combination of favours, fugitives and fortresses. The letters of these months tell a story of a culture slowly shifting towards a court society. 'If the Duke is our sun then we are his stars,' wrote Roberto Pucci in a letter of July 1534 to Francesco Guicciardini.⁴ Since his installation as duke, Alessandro had cultivated a benign, civil manner towards his subjects when he received them for audiences. Yet within the official correspondence there is often an undertone of anxiety. In March Alessandro wrote to the governor of Bologna and the vicar (a local rather than religious official) of Firenzuola regarding the transfer of a prisoner between them. Security and secrecy were paramount. The governor was to ensure the prisoner was well guarded during the transfer; once arrived in Firenzuola he must not be allowed to speak to anyone lest he be helped to escape, and Alessandro should be informed immediately so he could send for him. In neither of these letters was the prisoner named.⁵ The post was not a secure means of communication. The secretaries and couriers involved in writing and delivering letters might spy; correspondence might be stolen en route to its destination. If important details could be left out, on the understanding that both sender and receiver knew what they were discussing, so much the better.

The arrangements for handing over control of a fortress to Captain Giuliano de' Medici between March and May 1534 again show the sensitivities involved in holding the Florentine territories. In March Alessandro wrote to the Captain urging him to work with 'those people who will be faithful and suitable, as we told you in person'. The important business had been dealt with face to face. Another letter, dated 6 May, followed up on the message. 'I know that the bishop of Assisi, on my orders, told you in person how you should hold and take care of that fortress, above all with prudence.' But Alessandro was unhappy. 'It has come to my attention that you have been behaving uncivilly with the office-holders and others there in the area. In the future you should think about using your brain and consider the importance of that place, and your rank, and the manner in which for the future you might impress me so that I'd employ you in some greater capacity.' Keeping the subject towns secure was key to Alessandro's strategy for holding power. Local disaffection outside Florence might be exploited by shrewd exiles seeking a base for rebellion. It was not a new strategy for the Medici. Lorenzo de' Medici was supposed to have said that 'one keeps Pistoia through factions, Pisa in poverty, Volterra by force, Arezzo through its countryside and Cortona with grace.'6

The transition from conflict to stability was far from easy. Again and again, Alessandro urged his local officials to keep their eyes open for trouble, and efforts to strengthen the regime continued. A ruling of 15 May 1534 annulled attempts by exiles to sell property in Florence, a convenient means of attacking their finances. Late that same year, the exiles made an attempt to take the village of Pieve Santo Stefano, up in the Apennine hills, some miles from Arezzo. But when the locals denounced them, their leaders fled, pursued by Florentine agents. In this instance, Alessandro's approach to the subject towns had paid off.7

Since his arrival in Florence, Lorenzino de' Medici had become one of his cousin Alessandro's closest companions. Cellini describes them lounging together on Alessandro's bed after a 'debauch'.8 It is very difficult to know what Lorenzino thought of his cousin. Some accounts have him spying on Alessandro from the start, but that might simply be a way to rationalise his later actions. There may have been a genuine early friendship that went sour and was written out of Lorenzino's history so as to make his opposition to Alessandro seem consistent. On the other hand, Ippolito had intervened with Clement on his behalf, and perhaps Lorenzino's efforts to ingratiate himself with

Alessandro were a favour to Ippolito – all the better to find out information. After the Forum incident and his expulsion from Rome for
vandalism, Lorenzino had reason to be irritated with the Pope and,
by association, with his favoured nephew, Alessandro.

Once in Florence, according to Girolamo Ughi's chronicle of the
city, Lorenzino began cultivating a young, lower-class local, a man
'ready for any evil-doing'. For two years he befriended him with offers
of money and gifts. At the same time he kept frequent company with
Alessandro, spending lavishly to keep pace with the Duke. 'Day and
night they were together, now for adultery, now for some sacrilege
to a convent.' Ughi recounted how Lorenzino claimed he was spying
on the exiles for Alessandro, but in fact was only pretending to send
and receive letters. Other friends of Alessandro's warned him of
Lorenzino's duplicity. He laughed at them. What does seem certain
is that Lorenzino had money troubles. 'Rich and noble though he
was,' wrote Ughi, 'his incomes didn't match the excessive spending
he needed to keep up with such a duke.' Lorenzino's mother was
disappointed in him, 'all melancholy' at his poor manners and sad
spending habits. It is easy to imagine that Ippolito might have held
out to Lorenzino the prospect of a share in Florence's riches, should
he replace Alessandro in power. Certainly Clement, with his promise
and withdrawal of the governorship of Fano, had done Lorenzino's
finances no favours. Nor had Clement proved supportive of Lorenzino
and his mother in the cadet branch's internal dispute over money,
which was further reason for Lorenzino to resent the Pope.[9]

The 1534 palio was scheduled as usual on the feast day of St John the
Baptist. The duke of Mantua sent horses well in advance, and wrote
on 23 June in great expectation of news. The palio was run on the
24th, two hours before sunset, but it ended in chaos. Ippolito de'
Medici's horses jumped the starting horn. The duke of Mantua's jockey
was knocked off his mount thanks to another rider's carelessness.
After some deliberation the race was rescheduled for 29 June, the feast
of Saints Peter and Paul. The Mantuan horse led for most of the race,
only to be overtaken by Ippolito de' Medici's.[10] Once again, Alessandro
had lost out to his cousin.

In Rome, Ippolito was considering his options. He revisited the possibility of abandoning the cardinalate and marrying Giulia Varano, heiress of Camerino, a plan that had been touted two years earlier (before that, she had been a potential bride for Alessandro). Early in the summer of 1534, he sent a long-standing secretary and agent of the Medici, Gabriele Cesano, to Barcelona, to sound out the opinion of the Emperor and his ministers on a plan that would see Ippolito substituted for Alessandro as ruler of Florence. Charles' ministers, though, thought that Ippolito should stick to his role at the court of Rome, and were not prepared to countenance a change that would, without doubt, have brought the risk of political instability. Don Francisco de los Cobos, Charles' secretary of state in Castile, told Cesano that he would ensure Ippolito had 'the rank he deserved in Rome, and that Alessandro had the state, and that if the pair of them kept the peace, and showed the world that they were in real concord under the Emperor's protection, they would have nothing else to fear, and that the best road to ruin was discord.' He hinted that Charles would look favourably on Ippolito's promotion to pope. It was an inducement, if ever there was one, for Ippolito to remain a cardinal. Clement's health worsened in the summer of 1534, and for a while Ippolito seemed to come to terms with the idea of staying in the church. At least temporarily, he pulled back from plans for marriage, resolved, as Guicciardini put it, 'to be a priest'.[11]

Work on a fortress at Livorno, on the Tuscan coast, was completed on 1 April 1534 with the addition of a curtain wall and a supply of drinking water, a welcome addition to the security of Florentine territory.[12] In Florence itself, work on the new Fortezza began. It was an enormous project, its star-shaped walls covering a space of 100,000 square yards, the Medici arms carved into its stonework. Up to 3,000 men at a time were employed in its construction. Across Florentine territory, towns and villages were required to send men to work on the project; petty offenders in the city were forced to labour on the foundations as an alternative to paying fines. Construction was dangerous work. In one site accident alone six men died and fourteen were permanently injured. On 29 May, Carlo Borromei, a correspondent of the duke of Mantua, reported that 1,500 men were employed on the fortress. They were very willing, he commented, perhaps because of the bread and wine they received. (Three loaves and a flask of wine a day were the standard rations.) But the costs of construction weighed heavily on Florentine finances. Luigi Guicciardini worried that Alessandro would have to demobilise troops to cover the costs. The authorities clamped down on tax evasion. Borromei recounts how one of the duke of Mantua's messengers was detained by Florentine customs officials for failing to declare eleven bundles of silk he was taking out of the city. When Borromei appealed to Alessandro, the latter insisted on written confirmation from the duke of Mantua that the messenger's story was true and not some kind of fraud.[13]

On 15 July, the foundation stone of the new fortress was laid, 'with most beautiful ceremonies, earthly and heavenly'. In Alessandro's presence, before the entire court, an altar was set up and the bishop of Assisi said Mass. Two marble stones were laid, bearing the name Alessandro, duke of Florence. Carlo Borromei wrote to his master that the fortress had been given the name Alexandrina. He reported that Alessandro soon intended to move from the Medici palace 'and return to the Palazzo Grande as true *padrone* and just lord'. This was a reference to the Palazzo della Signoria, the traditional seat of government. Borromei praised Alessandro as a 'severe and just lord, and lover and defender of justice without respect to a man's birth,' and for his 'ready, spirited responses'. Such praise was cold comfort for the citizens of Florence who, two weeks later, received news of yet another forced loan to fund the new Fortezza's construction.[14]

The fortress could not be finished soon enough. Alessandro's regime was about to face its greatest challenge yet. By July 1534, Clement's health was failing. Could his nephew hold the state? Alessandro wrote to his lieutenant in Penne. 'Our Lord is gravely ill, and as we understand there is no other remedy but the help of God for his health. Here, thanks be to God, things are proceeding quietly and we hope for the same in the future, under the shadow and protection of his Imperial Majesty besides our own power and that of our friends.' To Bartolomeo Valori he sent a request to keep the fortress at Forlì, north-east of Florence on the far side of the Apennines, provisioned with both men and munitions.[15] He wrote again to Valori on 8 August: 'Your Lordship can feel hope and lightness of mind again with the good news that I bring you. Our Lord is, thanks be to God, much better and, according to his doctors, is out of danger.' Alessandro regretted that Valori found himself 'so troubled' in the area. 'I know that you rest neither day nor night to stop those restless souls,' he wrote in a reference to the exiles. Ferrante Gonzaga, Imperial commander and one of the leading generals of Italy, expected that on Clement's death the exiles would try for a coup d'état.[16] It was vital now for Alessandro to maintain the support of Clement's officials, especially those like Valori who had a strategic role in preventing any attack on Florence.

The situation did not stop Alessandro enjoying some respite out at Poggio, escaping the worst of the summer heat, indulging in his favourite pastime of hunting. When urgent business arose, Alessandro's counsellor Angelo Marzi had to send a rider out to him. He would be back tomorrow, replied Alessandro. Once returned, though, he had work to do. On 24 August, Alessandro dispatched orders to the governors of all his territories: Pisa, Pistoia, Prato, Arezzo, Cortona and beyond. More often than not, when a pope died, he wrote, there were 'many tumults and disorders'. They should do all in their power to prevent 'ill-living persons' from exploiting the situation. Men should be deputed for guard duty. Alessandro should be advised daily of developments.[17]

Quite apart from the Pope's failing health, Alessandro had other troubles. The fleet of the Ottoman admiral Hayreddin, known in Italy as Barbarossa, had been spotted off Salerno. The Duke had written to Chiarissimo de' Medici, his agent in Pisa, ordering him to stay vigilant, 'with your eyes open'. Elsewhere in the territories, the pro-Medici governors sought to ensure their provinces would stay loyal to Alessandro. Late in August, Alessandro wrote twice to Francesco Guicciardini. There were fears about a Turkish incursion into Calabria, and the Genoese had sent nineteen galleys to investigate.[18]

From Rome, there was bad news about Clement's health: the Pope had had a relapse; he was feverish, with little appetite, and the physicians were pessimistic. On 23 August Alessandro wrote that the doctors now 'had no remedy but the grace of God'. Every possible omen was analysed, astrological and otherwise. For now 'there was a full moon. The waning of which we await with great fear.' Behind the scenes, Guicciardini was making plans to secure Florence for Alessandro. That its citizens were already disarmed would help. So would the general peace in Italy. But extraordinary measures might still be necessary.[19]

In Rome, observers worried that Ippolito might seize his chance to act. Fabrizio Pellegrini, a Mantuan agent in Rome, said Ippolito and Alessandro 'would be ill-advised to squabble and behave like youthful hotheads rather than serious people'.[20] As Alessandro and his ministers awaited news of Clement's death, any hint of opposition to the Duke's regime was stamped on. On 5 September 1534, Tommaso di Bernardo della Badessa was brought before the *Otto di Guardia* charged with sedition. For his 'ignominious words against the dominion and duke of Florence', he was convicted and sentenced to beheading.[21] Clement's authority had reined in some opposition to Alessandro. Without it, his rule was undoubtedly vulnerable. Across Tuscany, Alessandro's captains and commissioners were prepared for trouble. Militiamen were drilled. In a letter of 1534 to Captain Matteo da Fabriano, Alessandro ordered him: 'It pleases us that with your prudence you should use diligence and select 500 of the best-qualified and suitable men for the militia, especially experienced ones.' The Captain should advise the quantity and type of arms needed, 'and everything will be provided'.[22]

The moon waned, and was almost full again when Clement VII died on 25 September 1534. As far as family politics went, he was a man who, dealt a very poor hand indeed, had played it brilliantly. If he had anything to fear on his deathbed, it was that his successors might lose his fortune. In the event the Tuscan militia was not required, but that came as a surprise.

A new pope was needed to succeed Clement, and the satirists quickly got to work speculating on the outcome. Anti-Medici feeling ran high in Rome. Clement's tomb was desecrated. Florence, in the description of one satirist, was champing at the bit to kill '*il mulazzo*', or kick him out of power. (This is a rare, perhaps unique, contemporary reference to Alessandro as 'mulatto', though in this context it may refer to his illegitimacy and does not necessarily have a racial overtone.) Another, considering the runners and riders in the papal election, had Cardinal Cibo down as one of a 'pair of dogs and whores', who'd treat the papacy like a brothel.[23]

The conclave opened on 11 October. It was unusually short. After only a single day of discussion, on the 13th the cardinals selected Alessandro Farnese. Cardinal Farnese (it was said) owed his promotion in the church to his sister Giulia's affair with Pope Alexander VI. His own life had hardly been pious. Still, he was sixty-six years old, and in failing health: a convenient stopgap, a compromise candidate. As a Roman citizen he would likely prove more popular with the local populace than had Clement and his avaricious ministers. Ippolito backed Farnese in the conclave. In return, Farnese promised him support for his campaign to regain Florence. But Farnese was no friend of the Medici and conclave promises were flimsy things.[24] The election of a new pope was never an easy moment for his predecessor's friends. The power relations of the Curia were shaken up. New alliances had to be made. The pontiff would have his own family and associates hovering around, ready to swoop down on chances for money and power. The new Pope – who took the name Paul III – quickly added two teenage grandsons to the College of Cardinals.

With the advantage of a cousin married to French royalty, Ippolito gathered around him French cardinals and friends. He hosted an impressive hunting party, hundreds strong, spending 2,000 ducats to lay on a lavish lunch, riding out on the barbary horse he had from Mantua, bringing home a great haul of game: ten wild boar, eight mountain goats, two deer and a fox.[25] The French were likely allies in any campaign to reduce Imperial influence in Italy – such as Ippolito's campaign against the Emperor's putative son-in-law Alessandro. Appearing too French, however, would risk any chance Ippolito had of securing Imperial support for the same endeavour.

In Florence, Cellini made a medal of Alessandro. On the reverse was a quotation from Virgil: 'Small solace for great grief.'[26]

Yet for all the entertainments, Ippolito was apprehensive. His position was not comfortable. Clement had left Ippolito the family property in Rome, but even with his ecclesiastical benefices, this was hardly enough to support the Cardinal's lifestyle.[27] The Florentine property went to Alessandro. It was a move that embittered Ippolito still further. He was now deprived of the status he had enjoyed as Clement's cardinal-nephew. The new Pope had his own family favourites to promote, sons and grandsons. It was all too tempting for Ippolito to look for power elsewhere – back in Florence – and to begin cultivating links with Alessandro's enemies.

Alessandro conferred with Francesco Guicciardini about how best to configure the embassy that was customarily sent to pledge obedience to a new pope. In the past Florence had sent multiple ambassadors, reflecting its status as a republic, but now Alessandro wondered whether he ought to follow princely fashion and send only one. He discussed with his advisers whether any special provisions needed to be made in Florence, but the city stayed quiet, and they concluded not. Yet, as Filippo Nerli wrote in his *Commentaries* on Florentine history, Clement's death left 'his nephews the most fervent enemies, and the state and government of Florence with many enemies outside it deemed rebels or exiles, and many of the leading citizens within it discontent.'[28]

This would be the greatest test of Alessandro's rule.

BOOK THREE
The Prince Alone

21

'Their eyes were veiled with ambition,' wrote Filippo Nerli of Alessandro and Ippolito in his *Commentaries*, 'so that they could not make out the righteous way, and walk on the straight road; through their discord matters deteriorated, and they diminished the reputation of their house and state.'[1] In the opening canto of Dante's *Inferno*, the narrator has also lost sight of 'the straight road': he is on his way to Hell. Nerli's readers would have known exactly what he meant.

The population of Rome rejoiced at the death of Clement. In Florence, and among the Florentine exiles, the mood was less certain. While Clement had been alive, he had been able to head off trouble between his nephews. Now, without their patriarch, the Medici were vulnerable. It was hard to see how a vicious struggle for power could be avoided. As the bells of Florence tolled for Clement, Alessandro made best use of his great advantage in the conflicts with Ippolito and the republicans: the control of the Florentine state that gave him power to pass laws, raise money, raise troops. Existing restrictions on the bearing of arms were extended. In 1534 the *Otto di Guardia e Balìa* banned the carrying of daggers or pointed knives within three miles of the city, under pain of a twenty-five ducat fine and three lashes. Fathers were obliged to pay their sons' fines. New fortifications were ordered for the port of Livorno. Work on the Fortezza in Florence itself was hurried on. Another forced loan was imposed on the reluctant citizens of Florence; workers were drafted in from across the ducal territories. Troops were raised to pre-empt any risings by supporters of the republic.[2]

The autumn of 1534 saw a series of arrests and trials for offences against the state. In October, Antonio Bonis was arrested for possession of eight illegal weapons: a halberd, two polearms, a half-pike, two large lances, one small one, and a spear. Under torture, he confessed that he hoped that one day the popular state would return. He was executed. Girolamo di Filippo Bonciani and Francesco di Piero Serragli were arrested after a man cleaning their former stable found a chest of arms concealed beneath the straw. Brought before the magistrates, it was found to hold an arquebus, its lead pellets, a flask of gunpowder, a mail doublet, sleeves and collar, and other banned weapons besides. The pair were fined 1,400 gold florins apiece. In November, Silvano di ser Silvano was hanged for sedition and possession of four illegal weapons. All his goods were confiscated. Francesco di Giovanbattista de' Nobili, who had gone on the run after the failed rising in Pieve Santo Stefano, was tracked down and arrested. The magistrates heard that Nobili had been to Venice, Ancona, Urbino, Pesaro and other places 'where many rebels were gathering'. According to letters intercepted by Florentine spies they were scheming to raise troops and take the town of Bagno, halfway between Rimini and Florence. Along with an associate, Francesco Graziani of Borgo San Sepolcro, he was sentenced to beheading. Their heads were put up on pikes as an example to others. Alessandro's regime made greater use of political execution than its predecessors in the republic, executing eleven members of the office-holding class between 1531 and 1536 (the republic had put four such men to death between 1527 and 1530).[3] For Alessandro and his ministers, this campaign of prosecutions was intended as a deterrent to anyone who sought to challenge the regime. For those challengers, it was indisputable evidence of Alessandro's tyranny.

Francesco Berni followed up his Easter satire on the ducal court with a poem about the ban on weapons:

> You who once bore sword and knife
> Rapier, dagger, steel and blade,
> Swordsmen, hotheads, robbers
> *Bravi*, thugs, tramps, wild men
> Now take a cane, a stick
> Or some lighter little wand
> Or a sparrowhawk in your fist
> The Eight don't want you to get hurt.
> Boys, and other folks who sing

> Don't sing 'The Bargello's watching'
> On pain of ten lashes.
> Here's the game, and you should fear it,
> Of their excellent Lordships
> Won by seven beans and a pod.
> Everyone keep your heads
> And if you want to live here
> We'll let you live in peace.[4]

The reference to beans here is to voting; the reference to the sparrowhawk has the same double meaning in Italian as the English 'cock'.

It was a risky business writing political verse. A priest in the Tuscan town of Pietrasanta had been put on trial in 1534 for writing poems about the town's captain. But perhaps in the libertine ambience of the Cibo household Berni had licence to mock; as Berni's biographer speculates, Alessandro himself might have laughed.[5] Cellini joked about the ban on arms too. Leaving Florence for Venice, his companion Tribolo asked him if he had wrapped his sword. Cellini, well aware of the dangers of travel, thought this was a ridiculous question, but Tribolo told him that 'it was the custom in Florence, because there was in office a certain Ser Maurizio who, for the merest trifle, would have whipped St John the Baptist himself; so one had to carry one's sword bound up till outside the gates.' Varchi, meanwhile, said it was certain that Maurizio, chancellor to the *Otto di Guardia*, planted weapons by night, only to 'discover' them the following day and arrest the supposed owners.[6]

Yet the records of the Eight suggest only a few such cases reached trial. Perhaps there was, nonetheless, a campaign of harassment, but Alessandro's regime always claimed to operate within the bounds of the law. That would be an important line of the Duke's defence against accusations of tyranny.

In December 1534 Luisa Strozzi died. In more ordinary circumstances the death of a young woman in Florence would have been sad but hardly noteworthy. In the charged context of Alessandro's conflict with his enemies, Luisa's story became a legend.

Luisa, the woman at the centre of the Carnival affair that had led to the arrest of the Strozzi brothers, had gone to dinner with her sister Maria, the wife of Lorenzo Ridolfi (brother of Cardinal Niccolò). Shortly afterwards she died: the doctors said she had been poisoned. 'It was said at the time,' wrote Settimanni, 'that she had been poisoned on the orders of Giuliano Salviati's wife, in revenge for the injuries Luisa's brother had done to Giuliano, and that Alessandro had known, and had rewarded the servant responsible.' Others thought she had been poisoned by her own relatives, fearing she had been seduced by Alessandro. Others still thought that Vincenzo di Rosso Ridolfi (a distant relative whose father had briefly been Alessandro's guardian) had happily done it, on Alessandro's orders, because Luisa had turned down the Duke's advances.[7]

Settimanni's account tells us little more than that there was a swirl of rumours around Luisa's death. Fears of poison were common at the time, and medical science was not so advanced that it was possible to be certain of a cause. But yet again – as with the death of Raffaello Girolami – this is a poisoning attributed to Alessandro through rumour when in fact the connection is tenuous. He is at least one remove from events. Despite the fact that Alessandro is said to be a shocking womaniser, here it is his courtier, Giuliano, who attempts seduction. It is telling that the only specific, detailed case of misconduct involving a woman that any of the more republican-minded writers recount is so inadequate as an indictment of the Duke's conduct.

As the Luisa Strozzi rumours circulated in Florence, Ippolito de' Medici saw a chance to build an alliance between the two groups opposed to Alessandro's rule: Medici supporters who preferred Ippolito as their leader, and outright republicans. In military dress, rather than his cardinal's robes, Ippolito met the exiled *popolari* in Rome in November 1534. He was well aware that they sought to use the alliance to gain power only then to double-cross him.[8] The frustrated Medici loyalists and the republican faction were hardly natural bedfellows, but on the principle of 'my enemy's enemy is my friend' they could unite for now.

Meanwhile, the movement against Alessandro gathered strength in another quarter. Filippo Strozzi had been unhappy with Alessandro's regime since the arrest of his son Piero earlier in the year (not to mention his earlier conflicts with Clement). He had never returned to Florence after his mission to France with Catherine in 1533. In autumn 1534 he refused an appointment as ambassador to the new Pope Paul III and, along with another important banker, Bindo Altoviti, broke entirely with Alessandro. Three Florentine cardinals – Giovanni Salviati, Niccolò Ridolfi and Niccolò Gaddi – joined them in their opposition to the Duke's regime. They all had their own motivations, wrote Giovanbattista Busini, one of Varchi's main informants, some years later. Ippolito was inspired by levity and vainglory, Ridolfi by envy of his brother Luigi, Strozzi by fear of the Duke.[9] Salviati and Ridolfi were legitimate descendants of the main line of the Medici family via their mothers. They owed their positions as cardinals to the Medici but like Piero Strozzi they had cause to resent the promotion of the illegitimate Alessandro. In the charged atmosphere of these months it was easy for the exiles to gild insignificant grievances. The Salviati were aggrieved by the conduct of Alessandro's officials in relation to their holdings around Pisa, a minor issue that in more ordinary times might easily have been resolved; Cardinal Salviati took offence at a perceived insult to his entourage at his sister's wedding to Ottaviano de' Medici.[10]

The link man between this *ottimati* group and the more radical *popolari* exiles was Jacopo Nardi, whose history of Florence describes a world of secret committees, late-night meetings and deals over money in Rome during the late months of 1534. The radicals did not trust the Ippolito–Strozzi clique, who they thought were more bothered about 'their own interests and grandness, than the liberty of the city'.[11] Strozzi's funding, however, was important for the enterprise, as was Altoviti's. While the *ottimati* hoped to persuade the Emperor to their cause, the natural allies of the *popolari* were the French. When Dante da Castiglione – he of the famous Bologna duel – disappeared on a trip to France, it prompted disquiet in Florence over what he might be planning. Meanwhile, others in the anti-Alessandro bloc were excited by reports from their man at the Imperial court that Charles was unhappy with Alessandro's conduct.[12]

Among the men recruited to the exiles' cause was Bartolomeo Valori, who had previously served Clement as governor of the Romagna. Deprived of this position after the Pope's death, he returned to Florence. There, he found that Alessandro 'did not account nor esteem him as he believed he deserved for the many wickednesses committed in the service of the House of Medici against the liberty of Florence'. Denied the role in Florentine government he thought he merited 'so that he could live as a gentleman, and satisfy his infinite appetites,' he began a secret correspondence with Filippo Strozzi. Office-holding had traditionally been a route to power for city families, and a sense that this was being unfairly denied to the Valori created resentment. Valori may also have been aggrieved at Alessandro's opposition to a marriage between his son Pagolantonio and a daughter of Filippo Strozzi. Whatever their individual reasons, Ippolito's presence in Rome created a focus around which all sorts of people discontented with Alessandro's regime might coalesce to oppose the Duke.[13]

The exiles were not the most effective force. They tried to win over one of Alessandro's agents in Rome, but it didn't go to plan. Information leaked: writing his commentaries on Alessandro's rule, Filippo Nerli reckoned the Duke was quite aware of Valori's activities. Staff proved unreliable: at the Imperial court, both Alessandro and Ippolito employed Pisan agents who proved more loyal to one another, and the interests of Pisa, than to their respective masters. Lorenzino de' Medici, too, played a double game, telling Alessandro he was liaising with the exiles only in order to gather information for him, telling the exiles he was honestly supporting them.[14]

At least in part, Ippolito's manoeuvres were prompted by financial troubles. Ippolito now faced difficulties at the Curia, where he no longer had the patronage of the Pope. Paul III had reason to marginalise the *nepoti* of the previous incumbent – and in particular Ippolito, whose benefices were substantial – in favour of his own. If Ippolito's military adventures led to his ruin, so much the better for the Farnese nephews of the Pope. But observers doubted whether he'd go so far as to encourage Ippolito's project. 'I'll believe that when I see it,' wrote the duke of Urbino's envoy, 'not wishing to believe such ill will of a pope.' Cardinal Ercole Gonzaga, brother of the duke of Mantua, was more cynical. He had worked with Paul III for a very long time. 'Anyone who knows him like me, and who's done business with him over the past forty years, knows that he's aiming to ruin this poor young Cardinal de' Medici so as to enrich his own.'[15] Just as Clement had seized the property of the deceased Cardinal Colonna for his nephew, Paul saw that if Ippolito could be manoeuvred out of the way, there was wealth to be had. He and Alessandro had some interests in common.

Yet as the plotting against Alessandro continued, there was one great barrier to the desires of Ippolito and the exiles. Charles V continued to support Alessandro in Florence. His ambassador tried to dissuade Ippolito from his plans, apparently extracting a commitment that he would make no move in Tuscany without discussing it first. Charles V's priority was a stable Italy, and rebellion in Florence was not welcome.[16]

The exiles took heart, though, from continuing tales of misconduct by Alessandro's courtiers. According to one story that circulated in Rome, a noble favourite of the Duke was accused of molesting a townswoman. When her brother challenged the nobleman in church, slapping him, the incident escalated and everyone fled in fear, even the friars. The rumour went round that the exiles were at the city gates; soldiers threw down their arms and ran to hide; and the Duke 'showed such fear that he seemed quite beside himself'.[17]

22

Despite the best efforts of the exiles, the news for Alessandro was not all bad. In March 1535 Don Pedro Zapata, an Imperial envoy, came to the court of Florence with news that Charles V planned to go ahead with the marriage of Margaret to Alessandro. The alliance would ensure that the city stayed loyal to the Empire and that it would be permanently at his disposal to whatever military ends Charles desired. There was even speculation that the match would shortly be consummated, though Margaret was not yet thirteen. Still, the situation was not calm enough for Alessandro to take off his chain mail. The same month, he ordered yet more.[1]

In the meantime, the government of Florence did not stop. There were reforms to government offices; a new committee was established to deal with the difficulties facing the Florentine countryside. New money was coined to a design by Benvenuto Cellini. Cellini made a two-*lire* coin, known as a *testone* (literally, big head) because it had Alessandro's portrait on one side and the heads of Saints Cosmas and Damian, favoured by the Medici, on the other. From March 1535, the old silver *grosso* (or groat; there were just over eleven *grossi* to a florin) was replaced by a *giulio*, which became the official money of account (its name comes from Leo X's predecessor as Pope, Julius or Giulio II). Cellini also designed a new half-*giulio* and a gold crown. They proved controversial. The Florentine lily, traditionally shown on the city's coins, was replaced on the new *giulio* with a Medici coat of arms. Step by step the duchy established its own iconography, sometimes replacing, sometimes adapting what had gone before, although there was a more prosaic reason for changing the coinage too: a serious case of counterfeiting had been uncovered the previous year.[2]

Cellini hoped his work on the new Florentine coins would bring him some reward in the form of an allowance and accommodation. But when the artist broached the subject with the Duke, Alessandro seemed preoccupied with his collection of firearms, weapons prohibited to most Florentine citizens:

> When I had finished these four sorts [of coin] I begged the Duke to make out my appointments and to assign me the lodgings I have mentioned, if he was contented with my service. He told me very graciously that he was quite satisfied, and that he would grant me my request. While we were thus talking, his Excellency was in his wardrobe, looking at a remarkable little gun that had been sent him out of Germany. When he noticed that I too paid particular attention to this pretty instrument, he put it in my hands, saying that he knew how much pleasure I took in such things, and adding that I might choose for earnest of his promises an arquebus to my own liking from the armoury, excepting only this one piece; he was well aware that I should find things of greater beauty, and not less excellent there. Upon this invitation, I accepted with thanks; and when he saw me looking round, he ordered his master of the wardrobe, a certain Pretino of Lucca, to let me take whatever I liked. Then he went away with the most pleasant words at parting, while I remained, and chose the finest and best arquebus I ever saw, or ever had, and took it back with me home.

The gift, however, did not convince Cellini to stay in Florence. To Alessandro's displeasure he left for Rome.[3]

He was not the only one. In April 1535 Giovanmaria della Porta, an agent of the duke of Urbino, reported on events in Rome:

> Filippo Strozzi has moved his entire household out of Florence and brought it here. They see that what with Duke

Alessandro stabilising things, Charles V coming to Italy and the fortress moving ahead, the enterprise [ousting Alessandro] will be much more difficult a year on . . . Ippolito, whom I don't see as often as I used too, is being rather reserved with me about his particular plans; and this after the news that the Emperor is resolved to give his daughter to Duke Alessandro.

Alessandro, according to della Porta, was keen to demonstrate to Charles that he enjoyed the support of the Florentine people. During the visit by Pedro Zapata, he left his bodyguard at home, 'to show that he wasn't so scared of the Florentine people as was said, and consequently not so hated as they've told His Majesty, though God knows whether it's a wise idea'. On one account, Alessandro had a 300-strong bodyguard, who went with him everywhere, though this may be later exaggeration.[4]

Meanwhile, men associated with the exiles were formally declared rebels: among them was Giovanbattista di Lionardo Bartoli, in late April, 'for having used in Rome many injurious words against the violent and tyrannical government of Florence'. Yet in these first months of 1535, as Alessandro began to feel more secure, prosecutions for illegal possession of weapons, and for sedition, seemed to ease off. The regime turned instead to diplomacy.[5] So did its enemies.

In May 1535, Ippolito and his allies decided to send an embassy to the Emperor to complain of Alessandro's behaviour. They took their case to Barcelona, where Charles' court was in residence. The coastal city was one of Spain's most attractive places, with its stone houses, myrtle, orange and cedar trees. This was a far grander delegation than the low-key mission to Charles' ministers in 1534. It included Filippo Strozzi's son Piero, one of the three arrested the previous year. Cardinal Niccolò Ridolfi, another Medici in-law, sent his brother Lorenzo. Cardinal Salviati sent a representative too. The exiles sent Paolo Antonio Soderini, whose family had a long rivalry with the Medici, Galeotto Giugni and Antonio Berardi.[6]

Though starry, the group was also split. There were effectively two embassies here: one from the *grandi* (Salviati, Ridolfi and Strozzi) and one from the more radical exiles (Soderini, Giugni and Berardi). The radicals' more natural alliance was with the French, while the oligarchs hoped to persuade Charles V to their side, not least by pointing out to him that he didn't want their temporary Francophile allies in charge. The oligarchs' laments were deeply self-interested. In the past, the house of Medici had treated citizens – especially the nobility and their relatives – as friends and companions in government, and not like slaves and servants, as the Duke would have it. (There is a little echo here of Machiavelli's comparison of the king of France, who ruled with his noblemen, and the Turkish sultan, whose ministers were all slaves.)[7] The *grandi* wanted their old role in government back. They left it to the radicals to complain of Alessandro's tyranny, his 'blasphemies, games and luxury', his cruelty, his easy resort to capital punishment.[8]

Charles, however, was preparing an attack on Tunis, and he was expected to depart in the middle of the month. The exiles had little time to make their case. Furthermore, Alessandro's ambassador Cherubino Buonanni was on hand in Barcelona to report (and spy) on their dealings. The republicans claimed that Alessandro also had spies around the residence of the Imperial ambassador Cifuentes. Back in Florence, meanwhile, Alessandro's companion Giovan Bandini had done his best to extract details of their enemies' mission from Bernardo Salviati as Salviati passed through Florence on his way to Spain.[9]

While in Barcelona Buonanni got much of his information about the exiles' antics from Andrea Doria, a veteran statesman of Genoa, now almost seventy, and admiral of the Imperial fleet. Doria had told the Emperor he needed to make a decision one way or the other: 'proceed with the marriage, or not'. Charles asked for his opinion. Doria, after all, had seen the many mutations of government in Florence: what was his view? Doria replied that he saw no other secure solution than to support Alessandro in Florence, to favour and help him, and that he seemed a person who deserved that.

At the same time, Doria tried to talk the exiles out of their plan. 'I was an exile too,' he told them, 'and I made plans, and schemes, which made it look easy to take back Genoa, and then they turned out not only difficult, but impossible.' The exiles' hope for French backing would come at a price, he explained: French dominance over Florence. If they won, they'd be 'out of the frying pan into the fire'. They'd end up with Catherine de' Medici's husband as lord and his noblemen to support. In Alessandro, at least, they had a Florentine lord. They would also do well to remember that Alessandro had access to the public treasury, while the exiles' enterprise could beggar Strozzi.

Lorenzo Ridolfi, meanwhile, told Doria that the exiles planned to take a nearby settlement as a base to 'molest' the Duke. His companions, displeased, told him to shut up. Doria told Charles of the plan, whose ministers told him in turn to pass it on to Buonanni. 'Remind him [Alessandro] to be diligent in guarding himself,' Buonanni wrote in a letter to the Florentine court, 'because it would be very damaging, if someone there were to secretly favour their [the exiles'] plan.'

More serious for the exiles was the mismatch between their politics and those of the Imperial court. Charles was 'naturally no friend of the people'. He had himself seen off a rebellion of Spanish cities fifteen years before. It seems unlikely that the exiles' complaints of ducal tyranny and high taxes played well with the Spanish noblemen in attendance on the Emperor either, many of whom would remember the *comuneros'* revolt. It was easy for Buonanni to denounce the exiles as motivated only by self-interest, their supposed love of liberty a fraud.[10] In addition, the enormous inconsistency between Ippolito's faction and the radicals cannot have helped matters. The former based their arguments at least in part on dynastic considerations (like Alessandro's illegitimacy). The latter had rather less interest in princely birth, because they didn't want a prince at all. Bernardo Salviati's denunciation of Alessandro as 'born of the basest slave, more likely the son of a coachman than of Lorenzo or Clement' was an argument founded on the presumption that suitability for rule was dependent on nobility of birth.[11]

When the exiles complained angrily that Alessandro had had one of their relatives executed for nothing more than possession of arms, Charles palmed them off with platitudes. He promised to look into the matter, but insisted that any settlement must wait until his return from the campaign in Tunis. In the meantime, Alessandro 'should guard his person well, and the state, and especially those places near the borders, where the exiles might have some schemes'. He should see the towns of his dominion personally.

As for the exiles, Pedro Zapata told Buonanni: 'While we keep them talking, the Duke should do his stuff. Supply the fortress, keep the other places well guarded, and wait for us. Once the Emperor gets to Italy he'll settle his business, and there'll be nothing more to say.'

Ippolito's case that he, not Alessandro, should rule Florence was set out in eight pages of instructions to his ambassador. Probably the product of collaboration between Ippolito and others in the exile circles in Rome, the arguments it contained would have roused fury among the radical exiles.[12] Ippolito's claim rested on Charles' concern for peace and stability in Italy. He held out the prospect that if Alessandro's regime fell, a more radical government might ally with the French. He, in contrast, was Charles' 'true and faithful servant' who with Charles' 'prudence and authority' could help avoid such problems. 'No city,' he went on, 'seems more likely to disturb his holy design than Florence.' Its citizens held Alessandro's government in such hatred that most men of rank had resolved to leave. Only Ippolito was holding them back, but he could not do that for long. If the Emperor would not help them reform the city, 'one must presume that they'll turn to the king of France.' The only way to prevent that, said Ippolito, was with a Medici ruler:

> Things being this way, and in such danger, there is no quicker or surer remedy, nor one more in Your Majesty's interests, except that you should be content that I should go to govern Florence, so that, even if the person is changed, the devotion to Your Majesty is not, and you will have a true and faithful servant.

He went on: 'It should come as no surprise to Your Majesty that there should be such great and universal hatred of the Duke, and love of me.' While Alessandro's father and grandfather had been hated in Florence, Duke Giuliano, Ippolito's father, 'had been loved by the whole city'. The gentlemen and goodmen of Florence could not tolerate Alessandro's 'violence and tyranny'. He treated them all 'like slaves, keeping them disarmed and deprived of property'. Their hatred for Alessandro 'is made all the greater, when they consider his birth, manifestly illegitimate on account of his mother, saying, as you have heard many times, that he is the son of a peasant, who at present lives near certain castles of Rome, poor, and a beggar, leading a miserable life'. The Florentines, wrote Ippolito, 'greatly disdain having to obey someone so base-born'. That was why Alessandro had to rely on foreigners for his services. The five great houses of the city, the Salviati, Ridolfi, Strozzi, Pazzi and Rucellai – old allies of the Medici – had deserted him.

Why did Ippolito focus on the present status of Alessandro's mother, as a peasant, rather than the story that she had been a servant or slave of Alfonsina's? One explanation is that he knew the circumstances of Margaret's birth to a servant in the Low Countries. He had an interest in marrying Margaret himself: roundly condemning servants' children as unsuitable might have been awkward.

His arguments went on. There was speculation about Alessandro's use of public funds. Patricians and plebs alike hated the Duke, so too did even his closest relatives. And now was the time to act. Florence was not fortified as it had been. Its bastions were broken and ruined. The enterprise would not be difficult. Even though Alessandro held fortresses outside Florence, in the past they had always followed the leadership of the city. Then he got down to money. There would be 100,000 *scudi* for the Emperor, agreement to enter the league arranged by Charles in Bologna, and a contribution to its expenses. While Alessandro had to spend much of the public revenues on guards, soldiers and fortresses, a less hated ruler would be able to save money, leaving more available to support Charles' enterprises. Alessandro's despicable government had men moving their money out of the city, to Rome, Venice or beyond. Fear had driven Florence's merchants away. Ippolito also had to deal with the awkward point that in 1527 *he* had been the ruler kicked out of Florence by its people. He had been young then, he wrote. He could not be blamed. The uprising was not about hatred of him, it was simply enemies of the Medici taking the opportunity that the Sack of Rome presented.

There were legal arguments too; in fact, legalities were central to the cases put by both sides. In 1529, Charles had agreed to restore Florence to the state it had been in before the expulsion of the Medici in 1527. 'That clearly shows the justice of my case,' wrote Ippolito:

> I being a true nephew of Lorenzo the Magnificent, and closer than the Duke, and older. On which account I should be restored to the rank and state that I had in 1527 when I was in Florence, and not Duke Alessandro, who lived outside. I was head of the office-holders, not the Duke. The reputation of the state resided in me, and not in the Duke, and so I should be restored to the state and government of Florence, not the Duke.

Alessandro 'was never brought up as, nor recognised as a prince of that state'. If Charles insisted on marrying his daughter to the Duke, 'everyone would despair of Imperial protection, and they would be forced to turn to the King of France for aid.' Ippolito would like to reconcile with Alessandro, but the latter's tyrannical ways made it impossible. If Charles would observe the agreement of 1529, he would win the hearts of many gentlemen hoping he would take pity on the city, and of many tyrannised citizens. 'I humbly recommend myself to Your Majesty,' he concluded, 'whose most true and faithful servant I will always remain.'[13]

The Emperor delayed. He agreed to hold hearings into the justice of Ippolito's claims, but only after his planned campaign in Tunis. But as Alessandro's fortress came closer to completion, his grip on Florence more secure, Ippolito and his allies feared that would be too late.[14]

On 31 May, one of the residents of the Palazzo Pazzi, Imperio Ricordati, sat down to pen a letter to Isabella d'Este, marchioness of Mantua. He was thinking of leaving town, he wrote. There was a 'murderous heat' in Florence.[15]

23

In the middle of May, Alessandro was out of Florence, perhaps following the Imperial advice to ensure he was seen around his dominions, perhaps enjoying the hunting at Poggio.[1] Within the city, however, hovering around the Cibo–Malaspina household was Francesco Berni. Writer of those satirical poems about Alessandro's court, Berni had for some years been associated with Caterina Cibo, duchess of Camerino. Berni had also spent time in Ippolito de' Medici's entourage but since 1533 had stayed mainly near Florence, where he enjoyed a living as a cathedral canon. But his connections to Ippolito and the exiles in Rome made him an ideal spy for Alessandro – and, perhaps, even an assassin. Years later Giovanbattista Busini told this tale: Berni had been commissioned by Cardinal Cibo to assassinate Giovanni Salviati, one of the Florentine cardinals scheming against Alessandro in Rome. The weapon of choice was poison. But Berni refused, and on 26 May he was found dead. Either he had taken the poison himself – or someone had given it to him.[2]

If the evidence for the Berni plot is slender, the evidence for other plots against Alessandro's enemies is strong enough to make one suspect there was some truth in it. Perhaps heartened by news from his agents in Barcelona, early in June Alessandro sent a party of assassins to Lombardy with orders to kill Piero Strozzi. The plot was discovered by Piero's relative Battista Strozzi, governor of Modena. He managed to arrest a Florentine captain named Petruccio, who revealed that the scheme involved nine men. He had been paid, so the exiles said, 100 ducats. Petruccio's confession was taken down and sent to Rome before he himself was freed, though he would later claim he was coerced at sword- and knife-point, and that he had sought only to intercept the messages Strozzi carried.[3] The *Otto di Guardia* accounts for these months record a payment of just over 100 florins to a spy for 'having travelled to various places outside the dominion on important matters'. The details of his mission were not written down, but perhaps this was Petruccio. His was one of twenty-six payments, totalling almost 600 florins, that the *Otto* made to 'secret spies' between May and August of 1535. Whether he was really sent to do murder, or whether his story was true, is a matter for conjecture.

Legal moves against potential rebels continued too. In June Girolamo di Ruberto de' Pepi was confined to the Rocca of Volterra for five years for having had discussions with exiles.[4]

In Florence the annual rituals continued as ever. The 1535 palio gave Alessandro the usual opportunity to host a popular festival in Florence. The duke of Mantua wrote at the end of April to enquire whether the event was scheduled. He made plans and, as usual, sent a horse towards the end of May.[5] But Alessandro and his courtiers had other things on their minds.

Pope Paul III encouraged Ippolito in his opposition to Alessandro. Paul played along with the Cardinal's schemes, allowing the exiles in Rome to bear arms and to begin raising troops. But his aim was to lever Ippolito out of his rich benefices. This could be accomplished in one or two ways: by shifting him into Florentine government as a replacement for Alessandro – or by sending him to his ruin.[6]

As hopes of action from the Emperor faded, Ippolito turned to more direct methods, and specifically to his old friend Giovanbattista Cibo, bishop of Marseilles, with whom he had caroused at Charles V's coronation five years before. Giovanbattista was brother to Cardinal Innocenzo Cibo and Lorenzo Cibo. He had access to the Cibo household in Florence, where Alessandro often dined with the Cardinal and the Malaspina sisters. And with that access, he had the means to do murder. The plan was this: they would choose an evening when Alessandro was due to dine at the Cibo house. Giovanbattista and his men would secretly place some barrels of gunpowder underneath the vault of the hall where they usually dined. They would light the fuse, and the way would be freed for Ippolito to take charge of the city. But in the middle of June, Alessandro's spies intercepted a letter from

Cibo to Ippolito's man Ottaviano della Genga. In it Cibo expressed his concern that Alessandro was well guarded. He asked for money to support the men he had with him. Its interception alerted Alessandro to the plot.[7]

Alessandro called in Cardinal Cibo, and told him what had happened. The Cardinal was 'so furious he seemed to have been gripped by a mania'. Cibo had little choice but to break with his brother. As the family memoirs recount, 'with his most fervent prayers, he begged the Duke to make a just vendetta, and to punish such wickedness.'[8]

Giovanbattista was arrested. On 21 June, under torture, he made this confession:

> I found myself, Giovambaptista Cybo, in Rome, last February, 1535. I was riding to Sollazo with the Most Reverend and Illustrious Cardinal de' Medici, and other gentlemen. And being in those uninhabited parts of the city near Termini and around about. Chatting to His Most Reverend Lordship about various things, he asked me whether I was going to Florence with my brother, the Most Reverend Cardinal, to which I replied that I wasn't sure. So, convincing himself that I was going, His Most Reverend Lordship said to me: 'Giovambaptista, you know that I have no other brother than you, nor anyone who I love better, and that we were brought up together,' and many like words. To this I responded that I was his servant, and that this ceremony wasn't necessary with me and that I wanted to serve him, as far as I could. So His Most Reverend Lordship asked me to promise not to tell anyone what he was about to tell me. And having said those words, His Most Reverend Lordship asked me if, once I was in Florence, I would kill the Lord Duke Alessandro. It seeming strange to me that he should ask such a thing, I responded neither yes nor no to his request. His Most Reverend Lordship, seeing that I wasn't answering his proposition for the moment, said nothing further to me, but leaving me a little way behind, started chatting to the other gentlemen in his

company about other things. And I likewise started to speak
with one of those who were following him . . . and nothing
more was said about that business of His Most Reverend
Lordship's.

Three or four days later, riding once again in his company,
he called me over, and said to me: 'Have you thought about
what we discussed the other day, killing the Duke?' He
added that if I did it, I'd be the master of that state, and
of him; and he made many other persuasive offers and
words, to convince me to do it. So I replied that I was happy
to do it . . . At that, His Most Reverend Lordship thanked
me, and told me that it would be easy to do it, going to
Florence with the said Cardinal, my brother, because His
Excellency wouldn't be watching out for me, so that I'd be
able to intrigue with the Duke, and go about in his company
day and night, at every hour, and that whenever seemed
best to me I'd be able to kill him.

Three or four days later, Count Ottaviano della Genga,
who was on the Cardinal's payroll and in his service, came
to look for me several times. When he found me he said
that Cardinal Medici had told him about the dealings that
he had with me to kill Duke Alessandro; and had asked
him to find me and by every possible way and means
persuade me to do it, reminding me that I'd promised His
Most Reverend Lordship that I'd do it, and telling me that
it would be easy to do it for the aforesaid reasons, adding
that I mustn't back out, because I'd be the master of all.

Count Ottaviano told Giovanbattista that he and Cardinal de' Medici
thought it best that he take a guard of seven or eight men with him
to Florence, who could support him in the assassination if necessary.
But as the Duke 'is hated by everyone, and because he has neither
relative nor friend there who loved him, and because the people are
all topsy-turvy and in confusion, they will quickly resolve to do what
is necessary.' And because Ippolito was so well loved in the city, once
Alessandro was dead, Ippolito would be the master of all – and
Giovanbattista would be the master of Ippolito. Count Ottaviano

repeatedly lobbied Giovanbattista on these lines, and to get him off his back Giovanbattista sent for three men who satisfied the Count of their ability to do the job. Sending the men ahead so as not to cause suspicion, Giovanbattista departed for Florence in the company of his brother, Cardinal Cibo. The Count continued to insist by letter that he go ahead with the murder. But when Giovanbattista wrote to Genga asking for money, he was caught. He told his interrogators he was planning to pull out of the plot.[9] His confession – and his powerful family – may have saved his life.

As the assassination plan unravelled, so did an attempt by the exiles to gather troops into Perugia, a papal town near the border with Tuscany. The Imperial envoys in Italy moved in to negotiate their dispersal.[10] The discovery of the plot also gave Paul III an opportunity to move against Ippolito de' Medici. He had Count Ottaviano arrested for homicide. Ippolito himself was thrown out of the papal palace and his mule confiscated on the pretext that he owed papal officials sixty *scudi*. The following morning, 22 June, Ippolito headed for the Castello Santo Angelo at Tivoli, some twenty miles east of Rome, in the company of Piero Strozzi and one of Cardinal Salviati's brothers. Following appeals from the Roman nobility and some negotiation, Ippolito was allowed to return to Rome, and Ottaviano was freed. Observers suspected that the superficial impression of reconciliation was a front.[11] Paul III had little interest in boosting Ippolito's reputation and every reason to undermine him.

The assassination scheme foiled, Alessandro's opponents put aside their differences and settled on a joint strategy to overthrow the Duke. The radical *popolari*, who had been seeking backing in France, agreed with Ippolito, Filippo Strozzi and the other *ottimati* that they would put their case to the Emperor. Despite their failure in Barcelona, they hoped with one last push to convince Charles V that Ippolito – perhaps governing in the old style as 'first among equals' in a tightly controlled regime of Medici allies – would be an improvement on his tyrannical cousin.[12]

'If he must take someone's life,' Machiavelli had advised his hypothetical prince, 'he should do so when there is proper justification and manifest cause.'[13] Behind the irony, there was some truth to that rule of vendetta, and now Giovanbattista Cibo's confession gave Alessandro good cause to move against his cousin. Circumstances favoured the Duke too. Ippolito was out of favour with Pope Paul III. He was in debt. That boded well for the chance of bribing underpaid servants. Expelled from the papal palace, he was more vulnerable to attack. And although Ippolito had in fact been allowed back to Rome, his return to the papal city had not lasted long. In July he left to travel south along the Via Appia, on some accounts to see his mistress, Giulia Gonzaga, on others to visit his bishopric at Monreale in Sicily. Frustrated at having to deal with the exiles, he hoped to meet the Emperor in person, either across the water in Tunis, or on Charles' return to Italy. He sent the duke of Mantua an ancient bust of the Emperor Augustus which had been highly praised for its quality, perhaps in an attempt to win diplomatic support for his contest with Alessandro (the Mantuans were Imperial allies, and might prove influential), or perhaps simply as one of those gifts that cemented friendships between the wealthy families of Renaissance Italy.[14]

A little more than halfway to Naples, Ippolito stopped off at the small town of Itri, just inland from the coast, where it was said that Giulia Gonzaga had taken refuge from pirates. He had a light meal of bread and chicken broth. On the evening of 6 August, in Itri's forbidding hilltop fortress, Ippolito de' Medici fell ill. He realised it was poison.[15]

24

As the doctors tried to save Ippolito, he accused his steward, Giovan Andrea of Borgo San Sepolcro. His entourage rounded on Giovan Andrea, smashed in his face with the handles of their daggers, and threw him in the castle dungeons. We know something of what happened there because the interrogators wrote down their version of events.[1]

At first, Giovan Andrea denied it all. He had not poisoned the Cardinal. He had not discussed poisoning the Cardinal. God preserve him, he had never thought such a thing, and knew nothing of what they were asking.

The interrogators strung him up by his arms, and raised him a little way from the ground. This was a standard method of torture in sixteenth-century Italy: the hands were tied behind the back, then the wrists raised and hung so that they bore the full weight of the prisoner, often dislocating the shoulders. In the first instance, torture was supposed to be just enough to inflict pain. It might be imposed for the length of a prayer, an Our Father or Hail Mary. Subsequent applications of torture might be double the length: in the most serious cases the prisoner could be strung up for up to an hour. That was the official advice, at least.[2]

The interrogators warned Giovan Andrea to speak the truth.

Giovan Andrea told them he was a gentleman and had been a good servant of the Cardinal's for seven years, and he had never done such a thing, nor knew anything about it.

Still strung up, he was warned again to speak the truth.

He said the same again. If the Commissioner would let him down, he would speak the truth.

Giovan Andrea was lowered, and warned again to speak the truth. He said the truth was that he, the accused, was not guilty, nor did he think the Cardinal's illness was of that type, and he understood that His Reverend Lordship was taking medicine, and he hoped it would be nothing.

He was strung up again. He was warned again to speak the truth.

He told them that he was guilty and had poisoned the Cardinal.

Where had he got the poison? He had bought it on their travels, at the Castello, near Rome. Yesterday morning he had put it in a soup for the Cardinal.

Why had he poisoned him? Because he wanted him to die.

At whose request? Of his own accord.

How much had he spent on the poison? A *grosso*.

What type of poison was it? He didn't know.

Giovan Andrea's answers did not satisfy the interrogators. Around noon they started again.

Had he given poison to Cardinal Medici? Yes.

When? Yesterday morning, with the soup.

What quantity? As much as he could get for a *grosso*; it was powdered.

What type of poison was it? He didn't know, but it was a yellow colour.

Who did he buy it from? From an apothecary near the Castello . . . He said he wanted it for mice.

How much did he buy? A *grosso*.

What quantity did he get for a *grosso*? A little sachet of powder.

Why did he give it to Monsignor yesterday morning? So he would die.

Why did he want him to die? Only because of the slights he had received.

What slights had he received from Monsignor? Some rebuffs, now and again.

What had happened to the rest of the poison? There was hardly any left; he threw away the little there was.

Had he tried to poison Monsignor other times? No, only this once.

The interrogators were set on implicating others in the plot. They asked Giovan Andrea who had told him to poison Ippolito. Giovan Andrea named names. While in Castello he had received a letter from one of his servants, Ercole, who had had it from a Messer Ottaviano of Borgo San Sepolcro. The letter had originated with a chamberlain of Duke Alessandro's called Matteo da Cortona, and in turn Matteo had claimed to be writing on the instructions of Messer Girolamo da Carpi. Girolamo had instructed Matteo to make use of Giovan Andrea in their scheme to have the Cardinal poisoned, and Matteo assured Giovan Andrea that Ippolito's death would be to the Duke's 'great pleasure', that he could expect 'great reward' and become a 'big man'.

How long ago was that letter written? About a month.

Where did he receive that letter? As soon as it arrived in Castello. Once read and understood he tore it up.

What greater advantage did he hope for besides what he already had, and daily expected to receive from the Cardinal? The Duke [Alessandro] was lord of Borgo San Sepolcro, where he was born, and would make him great.

Who had he got the poison from? In Castello there was a Bergamasque, a 'bastard' apothecary, that is, selling various things, and he had it from him, saying he wanted it for mice.

The interrogators stopped there, but three days after the deadly meal, on 9 August, as Ippolito lay close to death, they began again, the better to sort out the inconsistencies in Giovan Andrea's story.

Once again, Giovan Andrea was strung up, and hoisted as far as the rope would take him. 'Let me down,' he said. 'I want to tell the truth.'

They let him down and warned him to tell the truth. He said he had poisoned the Most Reverend Lord Cardinal de' Medici with poison that had been given to him.

When had he given the poison? Not yesterday morning, the day before, which was Thursday, in a soup of bread and broth, and he put it under the bread, before the broth was poured in.

When he had poisoned Monsignor, who else had been involved? No one was involved.

What type of poison had he given to Monsignor? It was white, tending to yellow.

The poison. What type and quality was it? He didn't know. Nor did he know the antidote.

What quantity had he put in the soup when he gave it to the Cardinal? Whatever a *grosso* would buy, and it was in powder: and so he mixed it in the soup.

Was the soup tasted before he gave it to the Cardinal? Neither he nor anyone else tasted the soup: true, the broth that went into the soup had been tasted by the cook in the kitchen.

Did the cook know anything about the poison in the soup? No.

Where had he got the poison? He had got it in Castello, from an apothecary who lived there, who was a Bergamasque who lived low down, by the gate.

How did he get it from this Bergamasque? He bought a *grosso*.

What quantity did he get for a *grosso*? As much as he'd put in the Cardinal's soup, the little that remained he threw away.

What quantity was it that he bought? It was like a little chestnut, white in colour, tending to yellow, and he ground it with two stones to make powder, and so he brought it from Castello.

Over and again, the same questions.

When he bought the poison, had he planned to poison the Cardinal? Yes, he bought it with that intention.

Why did he poison the Cardinal? He had a letter from Florence, from a Matteo da Cortona, who lived with Duke Alessandro, who wrote a letter to the accused on the orders and commission of Messer Girolamo da Carpi, assuring him that the witness being from Borgo San Sepolcro and a vassal of Duke Alessandro should poison the said Cardinal because the said Duke would see him right. [. . .]

Until, finally, the interrogators got some different answers. Asked again about the letters, Giovan Andrea added some new information.

Seven or eight days before they left Rome, he got a letter from Florence, from a Signor Otto da Monteaguto, who wrote, as Matteo da Cortona had done, that he must poison the Cardinal. Because this Signor Otto had had assurances from the Lord Duke that he would make Giovan Andrea a big man and of great worth. This letter was given to him by one Messer Carlo d'Arezzo. Having read it, he tore it up. It was true that the said Messer Carlo did not know that he had to poison the Cardinal.

Where did he keep the poison? In the pocket of his hose, so he could more easily get at it to poison Monsignor.

But the interrogators wanted more. They strung up Giovan Andrea as far as the ropes would take him. Again, they warned him to speak the truth.

What type of poison was it? Signor Otto sent him a little glass ampule full of greenish poison by Messer Carlo d'Arezzo in Rome, wrapped in paper and cotton. He had the ampule from Messer Carlo about eight days before they left Rome to go to Castello Santo Angelo.

Four days of questioning and torture had got the interrogators some of what they wanted. Giovan Andrea had directly implicated Matteo da Cortona and Girolamo da Carpi, members of Alessandro's household. But nothing he said could help them find an antidote.

On 10 August 1535, Ippolito de' Medici died.

25

The funeral of Ippolito de' Medici was a great spectacle for the city of Rome. Typically, on a cardinal's death, a 'castle of grief' was set up in his home church to house his bier. Draped with cloths and surrounded by torches it would provide a focus for mourning. Paolo Giovio, former adviser to Clement, explained:

> After his body was brought back to Rome, his funeral rites were honoured continuously for three days with the true tears of the people, and by persons of every condition, which in that impervious city had never happened to anyone. He had been brought to his palazzo in a great hurry on the shoulders of Africans and Moors, who did nothing but cry. Besides them, the most excellent minds of all the professions and sciences – deprived and abandoned by their most liberal patron, dead before his time – lamented the cruelty of fortune. Because Ippolito's house liberally received from all the peoples of the world men distinguished for virtue of mind or greatness of body; and there one saw men born under quite diverse skies, who, beating their chests and scraping their faces with their nails, showed the same grief, and the same sadness, for the death of their patron, but with a different face, and clamorous chatter.[1]

The literati of Italy scribbled down their epigraphs. Veronica Gambara, Venetian poet and lady of letters, mother of Alessandro's courtier Girolamo da Correggio, thought Ippolito 'would have done better to have lived and let live'. Pietro Aretino wrote an impassioned letter to the duke of Ferrara: 'I'm out of my mind hearing the horrible case of

Cardinal de' Medici. Alas, unchained desires to rule and get rich, to what will you not inspire minds burning with such cupidity?' To his friend Molza, Aretino lamented that he had not spent more time with Ippolito, praising his virtues. For Benedetto Varchi, Ippolito was 'courteous, of great mind, a lover of every type of virtue, with praiseworthy manners, an attractive person, but haughty and marvellous proud'.[2]

Some years later, writing his history of Florence, Filippo Nerli had to acknowledge that for Alessandro, Ippolito's death 'was the principal means of thwarting his enemies' designs'. Whether or not Alessandro knew the details of the plot, or had entrusted it to others, is an open question. And there was at least one other person who stood to gain from Ippolito's demise, Pope Paul III, who promptly redistributed Ippolito's many benefices to his own nephews. As the satirists put it:

> Don Paulino was Roman too
> And you'll see whose livings he took.
> Cesi, Medici, Spinola killed
> To give to his nephews, the crook.[3]

Whatever the more malicious authors might make of Paul's involvement, the Pope and his lieutenants did an excellent job of closing down discussion. Giovanmaria della Porta wrote on 20 August that 'suspicions that Monsignor de' Medici was poisoned are diminishing by the day. The common view is that his death was caused by nothing other than his own disorders, and the change of air, together with an ignorant doctor who let a large quantity of blood with little regard to standard practice.'[4]

The whole affair was thoroughly covered up. Cardinal Girolamo Ghinucci, one of Rome's most senior judges, ruled that Giovanni Andrea's original confession was invalid because it had been obtained under torture. The doctor was persuaded to declare that he had seen nothing in the autopsy that might indicate poison, contradicting his earlier statements. Released from custody, Giovan Andrea made his way to Florentine territories, evidence if anyone wanted it that Alessandro was prepared to protect his cousin's killer.

Other rumours circulated. A report from the court of France suggested that Ippolito's killer was a Moor, a tale that led to the sacking of the Dauphin's Moorish music instructor. It is of course possible that Giovan Andrea was of Moorish descent, though this is not referred to elsewhere; it is also possible that this is a garbled allusion to Alessandro's involvement. If so, it would be the earliest textual reference to Alessandro as a 'moro', but the letter is not clear enough to draw certain conclusions.[5]

Others were not so lucky as Giovan Andrea. Giulio Landi, Ippolito's friend, author of the treatise on Madeira, was arrested: Landi's crime was to claim that the Pope was involved. Only thanks to the intervention of Cardinal Ercole Gonzaga and other high-ranking clergy did he secure release, and a pardon the following year. Much later, in 1541, Girolamo da Carpi was arrested for saying the same thing.[6] If he was indeed part of the plot, as Giovan Andrea had claimed, Girolamo da Carpi would have been in a position to know the truth. Inside the back cover of the file containing all the records of Ippolito's death, the cover-up, the later arrests, someone – a clerk? – inscribed a Latin tag. *Tanquam magnus ductus ad sacrificium*: A nobleman led to sacrifice, as it were. Ippolito might have appreciated the epitaph.

It is impossible to say for sure whether the Pope was involved but Ippolito's death was very convenient for the Farnese family. Within a few months of Ippolito's demise, Paul III was intervening in Alessandro's favour in a dispute with the Orsini family over the Castello Santo Angelo in Tivoli, which Alessandro had inherited from his murdered cousin. The Orsini thought it should revert to them (as the castle, or at least the use of it, had come into the Medici family with the marriage of Alessandro's grandfather Piero de' Medici to Alfonsina Orsini) but in a papal brief of 16 December 1535 Paul III ordered them to return it to Alessandro.[7] This did not settle the argument, which dragged on in the courts for decades, but the timing is suspicious. Did Paul III have reason to be grateful to Alessandro?

In Florence, city life continued almost as if nothing had happened. Nothing could happen – for now. Alessandro's future hinged on his marriage to Margaret, and that hinged on Charles' agreement, which would be delayed until he returned from his expedition to Tunis. In the meantime, Alessandro moved on with the consolidation of his state. The militias established in Tuscany's various towns and villages in the summer before Clement's death were formalised and regulated, the duties of their commissars, captains and soldiers outlined in statute. The commissars enjoyed full military authority over their bands, and reported directly to Alessandro. They were not under the command of Alessandro Vitelli, whose jurisdiction was limited to Florence – a structure that had the helpful effect of constraining Vitelli's power.[8]

There were more mundane affairs of state to manage too. Alessandro's ministers oversaw a crackdown on smuggling in the area around Pietrasanta, north of Pisa on the Tuscan coast. Agostino the tailor was commissioned to make up some new masquerading costumes in red velvet for a wedding in the household of Alessandro Antinori, a wealthy merchant who despite the exile of some relatives had supported Alessandro's regime. Alessandro sent the duke of Mantua a Turkish horse, 'beautiful and good'; the Duke reciprocated with a gift of three colts. They were smaller than expected but the Duke reassured Alessandro that they were of excellent quality. Alessandro sought Mantuan help to protect El Spagna di Correggio, a brother of one of his servants, who had been arrested in Mantuan territory. The Duke regretted he could not assist. That did not stop him, later, asking for Alessandro's help in arresting a bandit who was hiding out in Pisa. So went matters of court and government in the last months of 1535.[9]

In November, the *Otto di Guardia*, a committee that now included the veteran Florentine statesman Francesco Vettori and Jacopo de' Medici (a distant cousin of the Duke), heard a case of kidnapping and rape. Sixteen-year-old Aurelia had been out collecting chestnuts when she was attacked by a group of men. The offenders were exiled, 'so that they might be an example to others not to molest women and girls,' and so that women might go about free from fear of assault. Irrespective of the merits of the case, it was a ruling that allowed Alessandro and his ministers to point to their defence of women.[10]

Alessandro continued to expand his art collection, acquiring the services of at least one man whom his cousin's death had left under-employed. In late 1535 Alfonso Lombardi (whom Ippolito had commissioned to design a tomb for Leo X and Clement VII) left Rome to return to his home city of Bologna. On his way through Florence, he gave Alessandro a beautiful marble head of Charles V. Lombardi had previously portrayed Ippolito (though only in wax or white stucco, not marble) and now made a portrait of Alessandro in relief. The Duke hoped to commission a marble version from Lombardi but the artist died in 1537 and it is not clear whether the work was ever completed.[11]

Sometime in the autumn of 1535, Taddea Malaspina gave birth to her second child. Giulia Romola was christened on 5 November 1535, her birth registered in the cathedral records, the name of her father 'not stated'.[12]

With the murder of Ippolito de' Medici, one remaining obstacle to a secure regime in Florence had been eliminated. Alessandro and his ministers seized their chance to crack down further on the exiles' schemes. On 30 August, Francesco di Antonio di Guglielmo de' Pazzi was declared a rebel 'for having plotted against the state'. On 7 December Niccolaso Bracciolini of Pistoia, who had talked with others about rebellion against the Duke, met the same fate. Their goods were confiscated. Pazzi was exiled on pain of death.[13]

The republican party, though, was still a threat, particularly if they could discredit Alessandro in the eyes of Charles V and win the Emperor to their side. Charles had agreed to hear their grievances and Alessandro's defence, and in December 1535 much of the Florentine elite set out for Naples to put their cases.

26

Before Alessandro's departure, the astrologers made their charts, found an auspicious date, and on 5 December, the very first garrison entered Florence's new fortress. Their entry was accompanied by a spectacular ceremony. Among the audience was Giorgio Vasari, who wrote to his friend Pietro Aretino, describing the day. Outside the castle, an altar was set up, facing into the north wind. Angelo Marzi de' Medici, the bishop of Assisi, donned his vestments and began the antiphon *Spiritus Domini*, which was followed by a Kyrie 'that seemed to be sung by celestial voices'. If the religious dedication of the fortress was important, the demonstration of power that followed was more to the point. Four by four the captains marched. At the end of their train came forty pieces of artillery, all brand new, marked with the ducal arms, each drawn by four pairs of oxen. Carts full of cannonballs followed, and mules laden with barrels of powder. It 'would have put fear into Mars,' wrote Vasari. As the ceremony ended, Alessandro de' Medici knelt before the bishop, with Paolantonio da Parma, the newly appointed castellan, to his left. Paolantonio swore that he would know no other master than the Duke. Should anything happen, he promised, the fortress would remain in the power of Charles V.

Exactly nineteen hours and three minutes after sunset the previous day (on a rough calculation, shortly before midday), the timing precisely calibrated with the astrological chart, the crowd heard a great roar of artillery, trumpets, arquebuses and shouts. 'It seemed as if heaven and earth and the whole world might end.' The horses bolted. It took an hour for the air to clear, such was the quantity of smoke. The new captain led the way to the castle. The first standard in the procession was the Emperor's. The Duke's followed, teased by a north-easterly wind. The soldiers went in four by four, arquebuses in hand. Vasari marvelled at the great lances 'that would have taken on Jove's thunderbolts' and at the number of pikes. Entering the fortress, he could look up at the walls and see the walkways full of soldiers. He had no doubt that this would put paid to the exiles' schemes. 'We can count ourselves happy,' he wrote, 'having seen in this worst of times the bit and tether, that already worked for horses and the like, now bind and bridle the feverish lion.' Aretino was in Venice, a magnet for the exiles. 'I think one needs to be where you are to hear the horrendous bellows of those who can't bear to hear the name of our ruler spoken. They're like a brand plunged into water. At first it smokes and sizzles but, brought into the air, it's eventually extinguished.'[1]

Two days later, Alessandro left Florence for Naples. Within the week, another of his enemies was arrested. Maso Strozzi, who had been implicated in the Luisa Strozzi affair, was charged with sedition and sodomy. The number of such controversial decisions made during Alessandro's absences from Florence may not be coincidence: Raffaello Girolami's mysterious death in custody took place when the Duke was away; Berni died in Alessandro's absence too. In Naples his advocates would claim he could not be blamed for any early errors of the regime, because he had been away in Flanders at the time. Alessandro had learnt from his great-uncle's decision to keep him away from the difficult first months after the siege. He was often one step removed from his agents' 'distasteful tasks'.[2]

Packing up for the trip to Naples was an elaborate and no doubt tiresome business. It was vital for Alessandro's court to convey the magnificence appropriate to a son-in-law of the Emperor. Some years before, a chief minister of Naples had written a series of books on the social virtues. Magnificence and splendour, he had noted, were virtues for private persons but vital for princes, whose hospitality ought not merely to be liberal, but magnificent and splendid too. The Florentine court was certainly that. When Alessandro left Florence, his entourage was dressed in black, mourning the death of Pope Clement.[3] But if his dress was respectfully dark, that could not be said for the extravagant textiles that would hang in his Neapolitan lodgings. There were cloth of gold hangings, red silk and *pavonazzo* 'in the eastern style'. The celebrations were expected to last through Carnival, so there were the inevitable masquerading costumes: two nuns' habits in silver tissue; two in rich cloth, probably silk; four mantles in gold brocade; seven shirts or chemises worked in gold; two more masquerade costumes in red velvet with two pairs of hose. Packed in the same box were the palios – the lengths of rich cloth won at horse-racing – of *pavonazzo* and red velvet, of red and ash-grey damask, of crimson satin. A second consignment of fabrics and furnishings went on to Naples in January. More hangings, in damask and cloth of silver. Silks and velvets in crimson, black, gold and peacock.[4]

On his way to Naples, Alessandro stopped in Rome, and on one account he brought with him three hundred horses and 'many Florentine gentlemen'. Others put the size of the entourage still higher: '500 select arquebusiers on horseback and fifty helmeted lancers with their lances at their thighs; beyond this he had five hundred other cavalry.' The horses' tack was in enamelled gold and silver; even their bits were gilded.[5]

Alessandro's entourage included leading figures of government: Francesco Guicciardini, Roberto Acciaiuoli, Francesco Vettori, Luigi Ridolfi and Bartolomeo Valori. Vettori at first declined to go, citing ill health (apparently to avoid conflict with Filippo Strozzi, who was a friend) but later agreed. Among the Duke's intimates was Niccolò da Monteaguto (a relative, presumably, of Otto, the courtier accused by the cook of involvement in poisoning Ippolito). From the family there was Lorenzino de' Medici and another cousin, the seventeen-year-old Cosimo. He, like Lorenzino, was from the cadet branch of the family. Young Cosimo travelled with his uncle Alamanno Salviati, a man whose sympathies might well be questioned, for the rest of the Salviati family had thrown in their lot with the exiles. His was not the only divided family. Alessandro's supporters also included Matteo Strozzi, cousin to Filippo, and Luigi Ridolfi was brother to the Cardinal. To the *ottimati* were added the gentlemen of Alessandro's chamber, the major-domo, the stable master, the butler, three cooks (one for each rank of the household) and their staff, a chaplain, the steward, the apothecary in charge of spices and medicines, the blacksmith, the cellar master, the shoemaker, the tailor, the swordsmith. There were guards, messengers, the musician Jacques Arcadelt and his ensemble. There were pages, trumpeters, the archbishop of Pisa and the bishop of Forlì.[6]

Even as Alessandro made his way through Rome, his opponents made political jibes. On the wall of his lodgings they chalked 'Long Live Alessandro of Colle Vecchio'. Benedetto Varchi, who told the story, explained that this was 'so as to underline the baseness of his mother who was, so it's said, a poor country girl, born in that place.' Alessandro made light of it. 'He laughed, saying he was greatly obliged to whoever had written those words, because they'd taught him where he'd come from, which he hadn't previously known.' Filippo Strozzi, now exiled in Rome, sent Alessandro a demand for repayment of the loan he had made for the construction of the Fortezza.[7]

Charles V had travelled to Naples following his campaign in Tunis, which had occupied him during the summer of 1535. At the end of May he and his fleet had set sail from Barcelona, heading for the north coast of Africa and Tunis, stronghold of Hayreddin Barbarossa. The expedition was framed in the usual language of crusading – and Charles would boast that he had freed twenty thousand Christian captives from imprisonment. But there was plenty of self-interest in play too. Charles' troops sacked Tunis on 21 July, and the local ruler paid him tribute, including in Barbary horses. (One made its way into Alessandro's possession, and the duke of Mantua instructed his ambassador to Charles to buy the best of them.) But Hayreddin escaped, sailed to Minorca, sacked the town of Mahón, acquired a new set of Christian captives and headed back to Algiers.[8] Nonetheless, it was enough for Charles to return to Italy in triumph. By mid August he was on his way to Sicily – just as Alessandro de' Medici's opponents were hearing of Ippolito's death.

From Charles' point of view the situation in Florence was far from the most pressing matter facing his empire. He had to deal with ongoing challenges from the Ottoman Emperor Süleyman in the east and south. In his own German states there was religious trouble from the Protestants and their princely backers. Francesco II Sforza, duke of Milan, had died at the beginning of November, without an heir.

The French had a claim on Milan and no sensible observer of Italian politics would rule out an invasion. 'Even if it should seem to His Majesty that the Duke isn't a suitable son-in-law, this is not the time to show it,' wrote Ercole Gonzaga.[9] He was right. The French would march on Italy in March 1536, right at the start of the fighting season. They would take Turin and try for Milan.

Charles' triumphant return from Tunis took him first to Naples. It was the first time he had visited the court and he took up residence in the Castel Capuano, an old royal fortress near the city walls. Naples was Imperial territory and was ruled on Charles' behalf by a viceroy, Don Pedro de (or Pietro di) Toledo. In his history of the Emperor's visit, Gregorio Rosso recorded the entertainments laid on for Charles. Among them was a lavish banquet, with accompanying theatricals, in the garden of the villa at Poggioreale, the residence of the Aragonese kings to the east of the old city. Agostino Landulfo, a poet, wrote a collection of stories set in those gardens and dedicated them to Alessandro de' Medici. Landulfo evokes a wonderful garden setting, in which Charles V took time to walk with his daughter Margaret, who had been living in Naples since 1533, and their guests. He describes cloisters and white marble columns, with the insignia of Aragon, a little orchard full of flowers and herbs, divided into cobbled paths, miniature myrtle trees, vermilion roses, white orange blossom, every type of plant that ever came from the East. There was a white marble fountain with marvellous carvings and, again, the arms of Aragon, and there was even space for a game of *palla*. Among the women present for the literary and musical entertainments were the poet Vittoria Colonna, Giulia Gonzaga (lover of the late Ippolito: one wonders what she made of proceedings), and members of the House of Aragon.[10]

Lacking their figurehead, Ippolito, Alessandro's opponents were divided. Silvestro Aldobrandini, who had been exiled in 1530, his sentence extended in 1533, had tried to ready the ground. He held a series of informal meetings with Charles but made little progress. The radicals suspected the oligarchs of 'seeking their own aggrandisement, and not the city's freedom'. Five of them, they believed – the cardinals Salviati, Ridolfi and Gaddi, the bishop Soderini and Filippo Strozzi – had met Charles and his officials secretly.[11]

Alessandro had come well prepared. His entourage included experts in law. This was a case that would be argued not so much in terms of Alessandro's own suitability to rule – however much his enemies might have liked that – but in terms of rights and jurisdiction. That is not to say all the tactics were above board. Alessandro and his ministers did everything they could to destabilise the exiles' plans. Antonfrancesco degli Albizzi, who was due to present the exiles' case to the Emperor, instead pleaded illness; he was said to have accepted a secret deal, allowing him to recover his property in Florence.[12]

Albizzi was replaced by the exile Jacopo Nardi, 'wise and eloquent', in the words of the Mantuan envoy. Nardi made his first oration to the Emperor before Alessandro had even arrived in Naples, on 3 January. It had not been easy for the exiles to get an audience. They had had to stop Charles as he was on his way from his chamber to Mass, and beg a hearing, which the Emperor granted. At the heart of their case was legal argument about the agreement made in 1530. When Florence had surrendered to Charles' troops, a duchy had not been part of the deal. But there was also political argument about what the Emperor should do now.[13] The exiles' case, put in a series of speeches, was wide-ranging. Alessandro, they complained, was making all the decisions about office-holding. He was helping himself to 20,000 ducats a year from public funds (this was far from the first time that the Medici had been accused of having their hands in the till). His government was full of foreign officials and churchmen. Criminal trials were being heard by his Milanese chancellor, Ser Maurizio, and the bishop of Assisi. He had banned arms, down to the smallest knife. He had built a fortress. The charges then moved on to specific attacks on individuals. Vincenzo Martelli had only narrowly escaped the death penalty for a sonnet implicitly criticising Alessandro. Members of the Bardi and Carducci families had been flogged and imprisoned for saying Alessandro's rule wouldn't last. L'Unghero, one of Alessandro's courtiers, had beaten a young nobleman to death in the public piazza.[14]

Francesco Guicciardini replied for Alessandro. 'It was notorious,' he said of the 1527–30 government, 'that Florence had never had a more pernicious or corrupt regime.' He was brutally clear about what the liberty of Florence did and did not mean: 'Liberty does not mean that the plebs should trample on the nobility, nor that the envious poor should destroy the property of the rich; nor that in the administration of the republic those ignorant and inexperienced in government should take a greater place than prudent and expert men.' He justified the 1533 confinements on the grounds that the exiles had violated the peace accords. As for the claims of injustice, those cases were not under the Duke's jurisdiction but had been decided with due process by the city magistrates. The accusations about Alessandro's behaviour with women were 'calumnies'. His reputation as a prudent ruler of good manners was sufficient response.[15]

But how strange the things that went unsaid. Alessandro's advocates did not mention the attempt on his life for which they had imprisoned Giovanbattista Cibo the previous summer. And though his opponents referred to the attempted murder of Piero Strozzi, they never once accused Alessandro of poisoning Ippolito. The court of Naples was an occasion for public politics, law and official justice. Private vendettas went on elsewhere.

One person was mysteriously absent from the hearings in Naples. According to Lorenzino de' Medici, the exiles had planned to take Alessandro's mother to Naples, 'to show His Majesty whence Alessandro was born'.[16] She never got there. Lorenzino said Alessandro had her poisoned. Lorenzino is far from the most reliable witness. Most of what he had to say was written as a justification of his actions in his *Apology* for assassinating Alessandro. On the other hand, he was close enough to Alessandro that he was in a position to know about any such plot. It is clear from the *Apology* that he knew about Ippolito's murder. He was one of the few people to discuss that openly. If Lorenzino was right about Ippolito, might he also be right about Simunetta? The chalking incident recounted by Varchi as an allusion to Alessandro's parentage suggests that the exiles saw him as politically vulnerable on that front. Writing in the 1560s, the French author Jean Nestor said it was in Naples that the exiles insulted Alessandro by calling his mother a 'Moorish slave'.[17] There is ample evidence from the Ippolito investigation that Alessandro was prepared to resort to murder. True, after the gunpowder plot, Alessandro had reason to take revenge on Ippolito. But if he saw his mother as a threat to his power – and bearing in mind that he probably hardly knew her – Lorenzino's allegation should not be dismissed.

While he does not make the claim of murder, Jacopo Nardi was sure that Alessandro hated Simunetta. 'He did not want to know his mother, on account of her baseness,' he wrote. 'As a matter of fact he so greatly hated her that he would not even deign to provide her with the necessary victuals, when she was deeply impoverished.'[18] There is good evidence that Alessandro conspired to murder one person. It is not inconceivable that he murdered two.

27

Charles refused to make a quick decision. The rounds of entertainment went on. There had been a bullfight on 3 January, and a joust on the 6th, when the Emperor appeared in Moorish costume, a nod to his victory in Tunis. The city seemed to turn itself around its visitors. Musicians played in the streets, and in the evenings the Castel Capuano became a site for dancing. Charles sometimes went out in disguise. It was a festive time, at least for those of the Imperial court who could avoid the Florentine controversies. Charles' flirtations with court ladies made some husbands jealous, but the stories of his conduct were lightly told and entertaining, as if this were all part of the ambience, in sharp contrast to the negative descriptions of Alessandro's supposed womanising.[1]

As the festivities continued, those on the margins of discussion watched and waited for news. On 4 January, Giovanni Agnello, a Mantuan diplomat, reported rumours that Alessandro had already kissed his bride – virtual confirmation that the marriage would go ahead, and that the exiles' cause was lost. Then came the denials. Kissing a fiancée was permitted by Flemish custom. It didn't mean very much. By the 10th, Agnello was hearing that Alessandro's business was going 'very well indeed'. By the end of the month, Alessandro was complaining to the Mantuan ambassador Nicola Maffei that Maffei had snapped up some prime horseflesh ahead of him. It was hardly the behaviour of a man contemplating political disaster.[2]

Frustrated by Charles' reluctance, the exiles came close to leaving Naples. They made a second case to Charles in mid January. By this time they were trying to negotiate a settlement that would 'constitutionalise' Alessandro's rule, returning the government of Florence to something closer to its old form. Strozzi mulled over strategy in secret night-time discussions with Bartolomeo Valori.[3] Alessandro, meanwhile, spent lavishly as he tried to win favour at Charles' court. In February he paid over 1,000 ducats for the manufacture of two gilded silver basins for hand washing ('in the Imperial style'), on which he had his coat of arms engraved. These may be the two golden vessels, each weighing over 8 kilograms (18 lb), that diplomats saw him present to the Emperor. He commissioned forty-six plates too, taking a personal interest in the look of this tableware: he asked that tin models be made up and sent for his approval. (His agent added just over a ducat to the bill to cover the cost of the models and some 'drinks for the lads in the workshop'.) Alessandro also gave a sword to Louis de Praet, a long-serving diplomat and adviser to the Emperor. Rumour had it that the Duke had spent 120,000 gold *scudi*, though he would hope for reimbursement via Margaret's dowry.[4]

The exiles kept trying. Their demands on Charles became ever slimmer. Abandoning their calls for governmental reforms they focused instead on the right to return to Florence and the restitution of their property. Margaret was still very young: she had turned thirteen at the end of 1535. The Strozzi hoped that Charles might be persuaded to delay the marriage. Jean du Bellay, the French ambassador, had it right when he wrote: 'the exiles are desperate.' They, too, turned to bribery. One report had them offering 200,000 ducats to the Emperor.[5]

One day, the rivalry flared into violence. Outside a city palazzo, an armed man accosted Alessandro's companion Giovan Bandini, star of the Bologna duel of 1530. 'He told him to get down from his horse, because he wanted to kill him.' Bandini got down. He ordered his servants not to move. He took his sword in both hands and attacked. Even without mail gloves, or a helmet, he managed to contain his opponent until Fernando de Alarcón, one of Charles' leading commanders, arrived and intervened.[6]

Alessandro was a target too. On 16 February, Lodovico de' Nobili, another exile, was spotted watching him from behind a great elm tree in the castle piazza. Nobili, it was said, was set on assassination, although he knew it would mean his own death. Francesco di Giovanbattista de' Nobili (presumably a relative) had been executed in 1534, his head put up on a pike. This was revenge. 'He had sworn to kill the Duke,' wrote Nicola Maffei. As Alessandro rode into the castle, their eyes met, though Nobili never moved. Fearing an ambush, he sent Giovan Bandini to investigate. No other men were found nearby. But Maffei had heard that four men had vowed to assassinate Alessandro. One, accused of betraying the others, had been murdered, but three remained. Alessandro put a price of 2,000 ducats on their heads. 'He lives in such suspicion,' wrote Maffei, 'and doubt of his state.'[7]

Much later, when Benedetto Varchi was writing his history of Florence, he told the story of an encounter in Naples between Piero Strozzi and Lorenzino de' Medici. Accused of betraying Piero, Lorenzino assured him that he would soon learn differently. He threw one of Alessandro's chain-mail jackets into a well of the Castel Capuano.[8]

Desperate assassination attempts aside, the exiles had failed. Antonfrancesco degli Albizzi had been bought off. Filippo Strozzi's secret meetings with Bartolomeo Valori had come to nothing, except to make Valori insecure enough about his position that he never returned to Alessandro's court. The others drifted away. Few took up Charles' offer that they might return to Florence without penalty.[9]

Charles' final ruling on the dispute had one real beneficiary: Charles himself. Alessandro was prohibited from proceeding against the exiles without the permission of the Imperial representative; the exiles agreed to stop their plotting against him in return for certain rights to reclaim their confiscated property. Alessandro conceded to his father-in-law enormous authority over Florentine affairs, promising to ratify whatever the Emperor ordered with regard to government or taxes. This was supposedly to bring the taxes back into line with historic custom and practice but it amounted to an unprecedented extension of Imperial power.[10] Charles did not at first declare Filippo Strozzi a rebel, hoping for compromise, but when Strozzi began bankrolling French troops the Emperor changed his mind and sequestrated the family's assets in Naples and Sicily. Filippo and his sons Piero and Roberto, along with Bernardo Salviati and Lorenzo Ridolfi, were now fully exiled from Florence.[11]

The deal done, the wedding of Alessandro and Margaret took place on 29 February 1536. This was the second of three stages in a Renaissance marriage, which began with the betrothal, then saw this ring ceremony, and concluded with Mass and the consummation of the marriage. Like everything in this Neapolitan visit, the wedding was staged in style. Three hundred noblemen gathered for the occasion. The feast featured sugar sculptures. It was said to have cost 1,000 *scudi*. Charles V joined in a joust for the occasion; he danced at a masked party.[12] It was, for Alessandro de' Medici, something very close to victory.

28

As Alessandro returned to Florence, so Benedetto Varchi wrote, a strange incident occurred on the road:

> On Friday 3 March, Duke Alessandro de' Medici left Naples with all his entourage of gentlemen and light cavalry, which had accompanied him, to return to Florence and prepare to receive Madama Margherita of Austria, his wife. But on his arrival at Capua a servant of one of those Neapolitan princes demanded quite haughtily that the Duke return a slave belonging to his master, whom he said had escaped and hidden among the light cavalry. The Duke responded that he should search among the soldiers, and to that effect, everyone removed his helmet. But this servant could not find the slave, despite which he continued to demand him in arrogant fashion, making a great ado, and Giovanni Bandini, who was beside the Duke, took a dagger to the servant's face saying 'you should learn how to speak to princes'. The beaten servant began to scream loudly, and to complain at the insult received, so that all the land awoke with the noise. At that the Duke, retiring with his men, who were of greater number and better armed than those of the area, turned towards the gate of the city, from which with little effort he made his exit and continued his voyage.[1]

This is a curious tale, and one wonders at the motivation for telling it. On the one hand, it emphasises the casual violence of Alessandro's courtiers. We are back in the world of Brussels, five years earlier, where Alessandro pulled a knife on his servant. Given the talk about

Alessandro's mother it is also possible that the story was intended to hint at Alessandro's sympathy for slaves, though that would run counter to the suggestion he had her killed. Perhaps, like Alessandro's alleged womanising, his protection of a runaway is another metaphor for his failure to enforce social order and govern well.

Alessandro arrived back in Florence on 11 March. It was the anniversary of Giovanni de' Medici's election as Pope Leo X, an auspicious day for the Medici. Perhaps reflecting on the attempted assassination in Naples, he ordered in a consignment of arquebuses from Ferrara,[2] and settled into preparations for the final stage of the wedding, planned for June.

A few days after his return, he spent the evening in the Cibo–Malaspina household. Imperio Ricordati, Cardinal Cibo's secretary, described the conversation in a letter to Isabella d'Este, marchioness of Mantua. 'Yesterday,' he wrote, 'the Duke found himself here in the house of Signora Taddea, where he usually comes in the evening.' Alessandro discussed his consort Margaret, 'and how much he cared about her, and how much she would delight in having some little dogs'. He asked Ricordati to write to the Marchioness, who was known for her excellent pedigree dogs ('the best in Italy'), and ask if she might send one to Florence, so that Alessandro could send it on to Margaret.[3] The care Alessandro took with this and other gifts suggests he was genuinely fond of his fiancée, at least within the confines of the expected aristocratic relationship.

His own letter to the Marchioness emphasises those expectations. 'Your Excellency must excuse me if I take too great advantage of your gentility. In truth if it were for anything other than satisfying my wife – in which Your Excellency knows how much is expected of a man – perhaps I would not have importuned you so.'[4] The little dog was not the only gift Alessandro obtained for Margaret. He had had Cellini make up some 'works of art in gold' for her too.[5] That affectionate courtesy towards Margaret, and the apparently committed relationship with Taddea, gives a very different impression of Alessandro's behaviour with women than the histories tend to suggest.

The personal gifts to Margaret were only one aspect of an enormous process of commissioning decorative objects, fashionable clothes and home furnishings prior to the wedding. Alessandro acquired exotic furs: a couple of panther skins, a saddle covered with tiger skin. He had a substantial collection of ceramics. Even his barbary horses were clad in gold tissue and dark grey silk. The Emperor had given Alessandro white velvet trappings, trimmed with gold, for his courser.[6] So costly were Alessandro's commissions for his new bride that in November 1536 Charles V authorised Alessandro to sell parts of the duchy of Penne and the barony of Rocca Guglielma in order to recoup the cost of his wedding.[7]

The Duke's tailors were kept busy in April and May producing numerous items for Alessandro's person and household. He had heavy-weight doublets made up in black satin and cloth of gold. He had another, lighter doublet made, this time in a velvet cloth of gold, combining gold thread and white cloth to create a pale shimmering effect. A fourth doublet was made of black velvet. The cobbler made two pairs of white velvet shoes; white velvet was used for the lining of scabbards too. This black-and-white style followed Imperial fashion (both Burgundian and Spanish) but it also showed off wealth. Charles V was criticised for preferring black, which was considered rather under-stated for his Imperial rank, but Castiglione's courtiers thought sober dress was appropriate for everyday fashion, and approved of Spanish understatement. Moreover, black was expensive, a difficult colour to dye and stabilise; white was a difficult colour to keep clean.[8] It was an indication of the court's extravagance that white velvet was used to line saddles. After Alessandro's wedding we see numerous commissions for the production of costumes in the 'Hungarian style' – Charles and his brother Ferdinand were trying to assert a claim to Hungary – but also *all'imperiale*, in the Imperial fashion. It was visual confirmation of Florence's allegiance to the Empire. Alessandro was not the only satellite prince to follow Charles' fashions in this way: Christian II of Denmark, husband of the Emperor's sister, did the same.[9]

There were other preparations for Margaret's arrival. On 20 March, five young men of Florence were appointed Alessandro's 'gentlemen': Guglielmo Martelli, Lionetto Attavanti, Luca Mannelli, Lorenzo Pucci and Filippo, son of Bartolomeo Valori. The role of 'gentleman of the chamber' had developed across the European courts in the previous two decades and was typically filled by young, high-born favourites of the monarch: Francis I had his *gentilhommes*; Henry VIII had appointed English equivalents so as to match the personnel of a 1518 French embassy to London; Charles V's court had a similar arrangement.[10] These appointments served two purposes for Alessandro. First, they created a court structure suitable for the rank and status of his new wife. Second, they might win over support among the young nobility of Florence. Alessandro had been criticised for having too many foreigners at his court: Cardinal Cibo was from Genoa, his mistress Taddea from Massa, important officials from Milan, Parma, Umbria. The appointments of Lorenzo Pucci and Filippo Valori might also reconcile their families with the Duke's rule now that the marriage was approaching and the challenge from Ippolito gone. Cardinal Pucci had been one of Ippolito's supporters; Bartolomeo Valori had wavered.

The Emperor's visit also brought good news for Giovanbattista Cibo, who had now spent ten months in prison for his role in the plot to murder Alessandro. Early in April he was released and went to stay with his sister Caterina, duchess of Camerino. This was a time for restoring harmony in Florence, for smoothing over past differences, even when those differences had been murderous. For the duration of Charles' forthcoming visit to Florence, Alessandro would allow the people of the city to carry arms.[11]

Charles left Naples late in March to travel north, with a company of 6,000 infantry and 1,000 cavalry. In Rome he was received with one of the most spectacular ceremonial entries of his time. Acclaimed as a new 'Africanus', a name that echoed the Roman general Scipio Africanus who defeated Hannibal in North Africa, he went in procession from the Via Appia in the south, through the gate of St Sebastian and on to the sites of ancient Rome: the Colosseum and the arches of Constantine, Titus and Septimius Severus. To the classical ruins were added new, temporary arches to commemorate Charles' triumph. He made his way through the city to St Peter's, where he was greeted by Pope Paul III.[12]

From Rome, he travelled to Florence, where the ducal court did everything it could to compete. Charles spent the first night of his stay at Poggio a Caiano. Looking over its fortifications, he observed:

'these are not the walls of a private citizen'.[13] On 28 April he made
his entrance to Florence. Along the route there were 'triumphal arches,
and arms and insignia and other ornaments of the city'. Entering by
the southern gate at San Pier Gattolini, the Emperor processed along
Via Maggio, crossed the river, and headed up past the church of Santa
Trinità towards the Duomo. The streets were grandly dressed with
hangings, arrases and carpets. From the Duomo, taking Via de'
Martelli, he went to the Palazzo Medici. Alessandro gave his own
house over to Charles, and stayed instead in the Palazzo Tornabuoni.

Preparations for the ceremony had not been easy. A strike by
Florentine workers left Vasari importing craftsmen from the rival city
of Arezzo. An equestrian statue of the Emperor remained unfinished.
Still, the show was impressive enough. On the left side of the Arno,
Niccolò Tribolo had created two colossal statues. On the corner of
Piazza San Felice, near the church where Margaret had watched the
Annunciation three years before, a triumphal arch alluded to the
Imperial defence of Vienna against the Ottoman army, to Charles'
victory in Africa and to triumphs in Asia yet to come, with images of
Turks and Moors, imprisoned and bound. His was to be universal
power. Nearby, Tribolo had portrayed Hercules killing the Hydra.
Along the banks of the Arno were other statues of river deities. As
Charles neared the Medici palace the images changed, to virtues such
as Prudence and Justice. One statue summed up the symbolism of
the day: that of Jason the Argonaut, whose name comes from the
Greek word for 'healer'. It alluded to the Medici, whose name meant
'physicians' and who might, with Charles' help, heal troubled Italy.
Above the Palazzo Medici gate were the words: 'Hail our great guest
Augustus.'[14] Augustus, the founder of the Roman Empire, had cultivated a reputation as a peacemaker.

For all the efforts at rapprochement and all the confidence that
Charles' support brought to the Medici and their allies, there were
still moments of panic. On the last night of Charles' visit, Cardinal
Cibo, his dinner guests and several servants took ill after a party. The
Cardinal vomited copiously and had 'great pain' in his head and heart.[15]
Rumours of poison spread within hours.

Ferrante Gonzaga, the Imperial commander, heard the news of Cibo's illness late in the evening. 'I sent to [Cibo's] house,' he wrote, 'to understand the particularities of the case and whether his life was in danger, but discovered that the illness was of no moment at all, having just been a little accident and alteration of the stomach, which had happened not only to him but to everyone who had dined at his table, though none of them were in danger.' Two days later, Imperio Ricordati, Cibo's secretary, gave more details of what had happened. It was not certain, he wrote, that it was poison. Some thought it was caused by the fresh *marzolino* sheep's cheese they had eaten. Others said it was the water. There was 'no firm judgement' so far.[1] Yet the fear of poison was understandable. After years of threat and counter-threat the possibility of assassination remained real.

Charles left on 4 May, apparently well satisfied that the city could offer a suitable reception to his daughter. Margaret now set off for Florence, making the journey from Naples to Pisa by sea before travelling overland to Poggio a Caiano, where she arrived on 28 May. Giorgio Vasari wrote an extensive (and probably embellished) description of her travels in a letter to Pietro Aretino. It was a 'glorious entrance', he wrote. On the road from Livorno, to Pisa, to Poggio and Florence the people had packed the streets, creating a beautiful pastoral scene, costumed as shepherds, with vines and wells decorated for the occasion. 'Even the smallest bakery along the way had tables out in the street, and the quantity of food would have eased the thirst of Tantalus . . . at every house or gate there were double fountains gushing wine and water; and so, to her own great astonishment and that of others, Margaret arrived on the twenty-eighth at Poggio a Caiano. Seeing such a building, she was stupefied.' There had been no building like it since the days of the ancient writer Vitruvius, an authority on architecture. 'Many rooms were adorned with gold silk cloth, other drapes and leathers.' The palace had been decorated with paintings of women from the chivalric tales of Orlando.[2] It was not only a visual feast, but a musical one too, with cornets, trombones, flutes, crumhorns, viols, guitars and lutes.

Margaret arrived in Florence itself on 8 June. On her way, she stopped at the convent of San Donato in Polverosa, about a mile from the Porta al Prato. There she was met by Cardinal Cibo, in pontifical vestments, and the nobility and leading citizens, some in velvet, some damask, some in shimmering gold Persian silk. There were about 250 people on horseback, who came four by four, the doctors of law and medicine bringing up the rear. Thirty-two young men of Florence bore a great cloth-of-gold canopy trimmed with tassels of *pavonazzo*, black and white. It was just after dark, and almost 200 torches were used to light the procession as it made its way to the cathedral of Santa Maria del Fiore. The dome, wrote Vasari, looked as beautiful as ever. At the front of the procession were two dromedaries, gifts to Alessandro from Charles V. Further down the line Baldo, Alessandro's mace-bearer, threw coins from two great saddlebags to the crowd, just as Alessandro had done during Charles V's entry to Augsburg five years before. It was a good way to win favour for the new coins that so controversially bore the ducal arms.

After a blessing at the cathedral, Margaret arrived at her lodgings in the house of Ottaviano de' Medici. Stepping down from her horse, she was greeted by fifty young noblewomen, all under twenty-five. The door to the house had been dressed with fake red marble, showing figures in relief, her own arms and those of her husband. Through the gate the entrance hall had been transformed into a Roman grotto, with the heads of gods and emperors; enormous figures of the ancient god of marriage Hymen and his wife completed the picture, their figures five *braccia* high. The decoration of Margaret's own rooms was no less stunning. Cloth of silver and gold, bas-reliefs, carpets, door hangings to keep out draughts, and two beds made from red pernambuco wood imported from Brazil. As Vasari concluded, it was the sort of show that the court of Heaven might have put on for a long-awaited soul.[3]

After the splendour of the entry, accounts of the marriage ceremony itself sound rather restrained. It took place on 13 June. Margaret and Alessandro heard the nuptial Mass in the church of San Lorenzo. It was sung by Cardinal Antonio Pucci, member of a family closely allied to the Medici and nephew of one of Clement VII's closest advisers. The wedding banquet ('most beautiful', according to Varchi) was held in Palazzo Medici, and was followed by dancing, a comedy and a mock battle in Piazza San Lorenzo. But what obsessed the historians of Alessandro's rule was the ill omen that marred the day. As we saw with the foundation of the fortress, astrology was a serious business in Alessandro's Florence. On the thirteenth of June there was a solar eclipse. It was said to predict unhappiness in the marriage.[4]

For the day of the wedding, Lorenzino de' Medici had written a comedy, *Aridosia*. Performed at the Weavers' Guild in Via San Gallo, next door to Ottaviano de' Medici's house, it had an elaborate and on one account not particularly stable staging built to a design by an artist known as Aristotile (Bastiano da Sangallo).[5] Set in Florence and packed with in-jokes, the play tells the tale of the avaricious old Aridosio, father to three children: Tiberio, Erminio and Cassandra. Aridosio's brother Marcantonio has no children, so he and his wife Lucrezia have been bringing up young Erminio. This arrangement, however, has led to some confusion about who exactly Erminio's father is. The parallel with Alessandro is obvious enough, and is reinforced by other aspects of the character that play on the gossip about the Duke. Erminio is only interested in 'horses, dogs and love'.[6] He has been having a fling with a young novice, 'Fiammetta', who lives in the convent of Santa Susanna. She's pregnant. 'Fiammetta' is presented as a member of the Ridolfi family – a joke no doubt at the expense of Alessandro's courtier Luigi, his enemy Cardinal Ridolfi, or both.

Tiberio's private life is no more respectable: he's pursuing Livia, a slave owned by a chap called Ruffo. Tiberio agrees a price of fifty ducats to buy Livia from her master, convincing Ruffo to settle for a down payment of twenty-five with the promise of the rest later. Ruffo agrees, but threatens to tell Aridosio if Tiberio doesn't come up with the cash within twenty-four hours. Tiberio and Livia head off to spend the afternoon in bed. Erminio, meanwhile, can't believe his girlfriend's pregnant: they've only had sex once. Cassandra has her own suitor, Cesare, but her father's too mean to put up a decent dowry. Aridosio, the father, loses a purse full of 2,000 ducats.

Act Two turns rapidly to farce. Lucido, the stock 'cunning servant' character, prevents Aridosio finding Tiberio and Livia by convincing him that the house is haunted by devils. He hires the best exorcist in Tuscany. In the convent, Fiammetta is about to give birth. In Act Three, Aridosio panics about the money he'll lose on the haunted house. Ruffo turns up and complains that Tiberio has stolen Livia, taken her virginity and tried to give him a fake ruby in payment. The ruby may be an in-joke too: Clement gave Margaret a jewel as security; in 1531, Margaret had given Alessandro a ruby pendant. In Act Four, Marcantonio takes Erminio to task for his conduct: 'there's no one, however wicked he may be, who isn't displeased by affairs with nuns. Leave religion be.' Tiberio's affair with Livia takes a turn for the better when it's discovered that she is in fact a noble girl from Tortona, wrongly taken for a slave – and her father's on his way to Florence. When the father, Alfonso, finally turns up, he despairs at the state of the city:

RUFFO	Could you tell us where Livia and Tiberio are?
LUCIDO	Easily.
RUFFO	Where?
LUCIDO	In bed.
ALFONSO	I'm starting to regret coming to Florence.[7]

It all ends happily ever after: Alfonso provides a generous dowry for Livia, so she and Tiberio can marry; Aridosio finally gets back a purse full of money he has lost; his daughter Cassandra can marry 'Cesare del Poggio' (a nod there both to the Emperor – Cesare is the Italian for Caesar – and to Alessandro's country villa).

Writing with hindsight, Giorgio Vasari suggested that Lorenzino was contriving to have a part of the set collapse on Alessandro, but fortunately for the Duke it did no such thing.[8]

The marriage was consummated, but because Margaret was still young, not yet fourteen, it was agreed that she and Alessandro would live apart. She took up residence in Ottaviano de' Medici's house, which was just a little way from the Medici palace and boasted attractive gardens. (On one account, Ottaviano had not had a great deal of choice in the matter.) The routines of court life continued with only minor interruptions. The duke of Mantua did not send his horses for the palio as usual. That irritated Alessandro, but this little contretemps did not disrupt the regular exchange of horses between the courts.[9]

Hundreds of miles to the north, though, the fortunes of the Medici took another curious turn. On 10 August 1536, Francis, duke of Brittany, eldest son of the king of France, died. He was eighteen. His brother Henri, husband to Catherine de' Medici, was now first in line to the throne: Alessandro's half-sister was set to be queen. There was, of course, talk of poison. Nothing was proven: tuberculosis seems as likely an explanation.

Five days later, there was nearly another death, this time on the streets of Florence. On the night of 15 August, the Feast of the Assumption, Lorenzo Cibo, husband of Ricciarda Malaspina, was taking a stroll through the city. While he was talking to an unnamed person, a gentleman of the Martelli family approached them. Unaware of the gentleman's identity, Cibo and his companion both drew their swords and attacked, stabbing the Martelli man 'many times'.[10] The Martelli were, in fact, one of the families whom Alessandro had courted earlier in the year, appointing Guglielmo Martelli a gentleman of his chamber. They were not the most obvious enemies. But like the alarm over the possible poisoning incident, the reaction of Cibo and his companion to this stranger's approach is indicative of the fear that persisted in Florence. Although Alessandro was now married and his rival Ippolito was gone, it was a little too soon to be sure that all was well.

But early in September 1536 there was welcome news for Alessandro and his backers. Margaret was pregnant.

30

A Medici–Habsburg heir, grandchild to Emperor Charles V and under his protection, would offer a new level of security for the regime. The news quickly circulated to the courts of Italy. 'It's believed that the Lady Duchess is pregnant,' wrote Imperio Ricordati to the duke of Mantua, 'on account of certain signs that usually come to women who find themselves in that position.' On 13 September Alessandro took from the wardrobe a piece of unicorn horn on a little gold chain. To Renaissance people, unicorn horn was a cure-all, good not only during pregnancy but for all manner of ailments. Most importantly, it was thought to expel poisons. Lorenzo the Magnificent had owned a unicorn horn about six and a half feet long (in fact a narwhal tusk).[1] Perhaps, after the panic over Cibo's banquet, Alessandro was feeling cautious.

Some of Alessandro's contemporaries either did not know about, or did not tell of, Margaret's condition. Their histories relate a quite different story. Filippo Nerli wrote that after Alessandro was married 'he threw himself entirely into pleasure-seeking' and in doing so 'made many more enemies'. Girolamo Ughi, in a less hostile account, conceded that Alessandro 'governed quite wisely' but took advantage of the relatively quiet state of Florence to turn to womanising, 'profaning and insulting convents, and women common or noble, now with one scheme, now with another, though never by force'. Although 'he used many virtues in his government, and showed himself quite favourable to justice; nonetheless for his disordered lusts he was hated, but feared.'[2]

There may be some truth in these stories, despite the evidence for a relatively stable relationship between Alessandro and Taddea Malaspina. His marriage to Margaret is less well documented, but the careful attention to gift-giving suggests a degree of marital affection. That does not rule out the possibility, indeed likelihood, that Alessandro had other affairs, but it should qualify the more hostile accounts. Some observers were more laid back than the republicans and clergy of Florence.

Marguerite of Navarre, sister of Francis I, excused Alessandro's liaisons on the grounds that they spared his very young wife his attentions. Satirist Pietro Aretino was unsurprised by the Duke's behaviour. 'Tell me,' he wrote to a friend, 'is love an abominable thing in a young man like Alessandro? What would the lowest slave do if he could freely satisfy his desires?' (Admittedly, Aretino was one of the most sexually explicit writers of the Renaissance, and several of his works were banned.) However, this letter does suggest he thought there was some truth in the tales about Alessandro, a view confirmed in another of his letters, some years later, to a courtesan named La Zufolina. In it Aretino recalled how Alessandro had wanted to have sex with La Zufolina so he could discover whether or not s/he was really a hermaphrodite.[3]

Reading the accounts of Alessandro's lascivious behaviour, we should bear in mind that most of them were written after his assassination. They fit the classical narrative of hubris, the idea that extreme pride or arrogance comes before a fall, in other words that Alessandro brought his murder upon himself. They reinforce an argument that Alessandro was unfit to rule, that his masculinity was compromised by the excessive influence of women.[4] It is remarkable how hindsight can change a picture.

If conceiving an heir was important to the Duke and Duchess, so was establishing a court for Margaret. Although Alessandro had commissioned numerous outfits and home furnishings prior to the wedding, the process went on. Luxury goods flowed in and out of the wardrobe. In July 1536 Alessandro gave two masquerading costumes in the style of nuns' habits (perhaps those from the notorious Strozzi party or the Naples trip) to his tailor Agostino, with orders to make them into a carriage cover. Margaret's wardrobe master, Messer Antonio, took from the wardrobe carpets for her bedroom, fifteen black velvet cushions 'for ladies', two red velvet chairs, two leather chairs, two more cushions in rich brocade; two further carpets, one for Margaret herself, a dozen red velvet cushions 'for ladies', 'for sitting on the floor'. We can imagine the young Duchess perched on a chair, surrounded by kneeling courtiers. There were covers for Margaret's mules and two satin door curtains with the ducal arms on them.

The tailors and other staff were issued with fabric for the production of further items: twenty-one *braccia* of *pavonazzo* velvet to make another carriage cover; twenty-eight *braccia* of red silk crushed brocade to make vestments for the chapel staff; fourteen *braccia* of red velvet for the underside of gold brocade cushions; twenty-four *braccia* of red velvet to make carpets for Margaret. New hangings depicting the story of Aeneas were commissioned. A crimson damask palio won at Verona was used to line a cover for Margaret's litter; other palios of red velvet covered cushions and chairs. Half a palio won at Pistoia – a piece of grey damask – went to make a dress for a woman variously described in the records as 'the duchess's dwarf' and 'the wife of Bibiliano the dwarf'. Just as Ippolito had kept people of various nations as curiosities in his household, so many noble families kept dwarves, often as jesters or fools.[5]

The lavish decoration of the palazzo interiors during the four years of Alessandro's rule is apparent from the number of items that were still in use almost two decades later when an inventory was taken in 1553. Half a dozen cloth hangings with a foliage pattern and Alessandro's arms then adorned the enormous Room of the Two Hundred in the Palazzo della Signoria; others hung in his successor Cosimo's chambers; another eleven hangings with the Duke's arms were in a little room; still others were stored in the wardrobe. Fourteen arras hangings with Alessandro's arms were in use by the court: they must have been of good quality to stand the test of time. No wonder Cosimo found little need to commission new domestic furnishings or artworks while he lived in the Palazzo Medici.[6] He could simply make use of Alessandro's. Add to these items what we already know of the art commissioned during Alessandro's rule – the frescoes of Julius Caesar in the Palazzo Medici; portraits by Vasari and Pontormo; Pontormo's take on Michelangelo's *Venus and Cupid* and Vasari's *Entombment* originally intended for his cousin and rival Ippolito – and we have all the makings of a thoroughly magnificent princely court, and a palace fit for an Imperial match.

Margaret's pregnancy proved difficult. On 4 October, Imperio Ricordati wrote to the duke of Mantua: 'All day yesterday people were frantic that Her Excellency the Duchess might lose her baby, but today the physicians, and women of that science, have high hopes that there are no ill effects, and that things will go well.'[7]

Married and relatively secure in government, Alessandro could afford to consider his long-term future. As for many princes of small Italian states, one promising option was a military career. Still only in his mid-twenties, Alessandro had plenty of opportunity to acquire fame and fortune on the battlefield. Paolo Giovio, to whom Alessandro had sent a gift of ecclesiastical dress in 1532,[8] recounted the story of how the Duke had asked him to design a suitable emblem.

> After the Cardinal's death, Duke Alessandro had taken to wife Madama Margherita of Austria, daughter of the Emperor. He was governing Florence justly, for which the citizens were grateful, especially when it came to property cases. Finding himself strong and powerful of person, he desired to become distinguished in warfare, saying that in order to acquire glory – and for the Imperial faction he would have boldly entered into any difficult enterprise – he thought to win, or to die. One day he asked me with great insistence if I might find him a pleasing emblem for his surcoats with this meaning. And I chose for him that proud animal, which is called a Rhinoceros, capital enemy of the elephant.

Back in the days of Pope Leo X, King Manuel of Portugal had sent a rhinoceros to Rome. He had already sent an elephant and it is possible the two were intended to fight. The rhinoceros, however, had drowned before it could be delivered. Giovio had read the ancient author Pliny's account of the rhinoceros, and had put it together with Portuguese descriptions. The rhinoceros was a fierce opponent. It never left its enemy before it had floored and killed it. Alessandro had the rhinoceros embroidered on the livery of the barbary horses he raced in Rome, with a motto in Spanish. *No buelvo sin vencer* meant 'I shall not return without victory'. The emblem so pleased Alessandro, wrote Giovio, that he had it engraved on the breastplate of his armour.[9]

Alessandro now set off for Genoa to make his farewell to Charles, who was finally returning to Spain. The Emperor had other matters of government to attend to. The task of managing an Empire that stretched from Spain to the Netherlands and east to Austria was challenging – some would say impossible. Charles' departure would leave Italy for the first time in many years without the presence of an Imperial army. Accompanying Alessandro was Francesco Vettori, who evidently remained in the Duke's favour despite his earlier reluctance to attend the hearings in Naples.[10]

With Alessandro away in Genoa, Margaret was left in Florence with her ladies-in-waiting. At some point during October she miscarried. On the 31st Imperio Ricordati reported in a letter to Isabella that 'the *Duchessina* is out of hope of being pregnant'.[11] The word *duchessina* – little duchess – hints at an explanation. Margaret was only fourteen and earlier accounts suggest she was petite. If the miscarriage was a personal tragedy for Margaret, it also meant that, for now, there was no Habsburg grandson to inherit the duchy of Florence. That was good news for Alessandro's enemies.

31

The night of Friday 5 January, the eve of Epiphany, was an opportune moment for assassination. Though Margaret had miscarried that autumn, there was every possibility that she might conceive again. A Habsburg duchess with an infant Medici heir might prove a formidable power in Florentine politics. But as yet there was no child. The Emperor had returned to Spain; there was no longer an Imperial army in Italy and Charles was preoccupied by conflict with France. Though there was a garrison in the Fortezza da Basso, the fortifications were not yet complete and Alessandro Vitelli, the commander, was spending Christmas in Arezzo.[1]

On Alessandro's return from Genoa, life at the Florentine court had continued much as usual. Agostino the tailor had been busy in December fashioning a new black satin doublet for Alessandro with fringing and slashes; the Duke's companion Girolamo da Carpi commissioned a black satin collar and hose in the Imperial style. Alessandro had a Venetian goldsmith, Guasparre, draw up designs for various pendants for Margaret, and a jewelled net, perhaps similar to the ones worn by Eleonora di Toledo over hair and décolletage in the famous portrait by Bronzino. On Christmas Day, Alessandro entertained Lorenzino de' Medici for dinner. Afterwards, they went out masquerading, dressed up as shepherds and riding donkeys. Imperial style was the order of the day too for Alessandro. On 2 January he ordered a black velvet cassock. On 5 January the tailor Agostino took out four *braccia* of black satin from the wardrobe to make the Duke another doublet.[2]

The doublet would never be worn.

There are various stories of how Lorenzino plotted the murder of his cousin. At first, it was said, he tried for a conspiracy with other young noblemen. But Alessandro's guards, and the care he took with his person, made such a scheme impossible. Instead, Lorenzino turned to a single accomplice, convincing this man to kill an unnamed enemy, revealing only on the night of the murder that his target was the Duke. He arranged things carefully so that no one would suspect the noise on the night. He obtained his safe conduct in advance, the better to flee after the fact. That night Lorenzino went with his companion, Scoronconcolo, to the apartments where Alessandro was waiting for the promised company of Caterina de' Ginori.

Swords flashed, knives cut. The murder itself cannot have taken more than minutes. It was two armed men against one unarmed.

If Alessandro really sank his teeth into Lorenzino's thumb – as the stories say – it was a last gesture of contempt. Biting one's thumb was a well-known insult. And yet, because the dead cannot speak, we have only the word of Alessandro's killers for what happened that night.

What exactly brought Lorenzino de' Medici to the point of murder on the night of 5 January mystified his contemporaries, and the assassin's thinking remains an enigma today. From hero of the republican cause to self-seeking celebrity killer, Lorenzino can be painted in all manner of ways. Varchi, who had interviewed Lorenzino, came away with no firm idea of his motives.[3] Some found prosaic reasons: Vasari, for example, settled on hatred and envy. Ughi noted that although Lorenzino was rich and noble, his resources did not stretch to the lifestyle demanded at Alessandro's court, and that Alessandro had refused to help him in a dispute with others in the family over money.[4] Not only had the cadet branch (Lorenzino's part of the family) lost out to the main branch (Alessandro's), but within the cadet branch Lorenzino was squabbling with Cosimo. The historians of his day found all sorts of motives for Lorenzino: in his complexion (melancholy), in his character (solitary). They found prophecies and predictions in the dreams of pages and the charts of astrologers. They found that Alessandro's courtiers had suspected all along, but the Duke had defended his friend. The most honest of them conceded that Lorenzino's motives were a mystery.[5]

The most shameless of them wrote himself into the story. On the day of Alessandro's murder, Benvenuto Cellini, back in Rome, had gone out to the Magliana, south-west of the city, to hunt. He and his companion Felice had shot some ducks and geese, and were heading home.

> We mounted, and rode rapidly toward Rome; and when we had reached a certain gently rising ground – night had already fallen – looking in the direction of Florence, both with one breath exclaimed in the utmost astonishment: 'O God of heaven! What is that great thing one sees there over Florence?' It resembled a huge beam of fire, which sparkled and gave out extraordinary lustre.
>
> I said to Felice: 'Assuredly we shall hear tomorrow that something of vast importance has happened in Florence.'

After he heard of Alessandro's death Cellini was taunted by two of the exiles, Francesco Soderini and Baccio Bettini, for his loyalty to the Medici. 'You blockheads,' he replied.

> I am a poor goldsmith, who serves whoever pays me; and you are jeering me as though I were a party leader. However, this shall not make me cast in your teeth the insatiable greediness, idiocy and good-for-nothingness of your predecessors. But this one answer I will make to all your silly railleries; that before two or three days at the longest have passed by, you will have another duke, much worse perhaps than he who now has left you.[6]

If Cellini's heavenly omens seem unlikely to be true, his observations on the politics of Florence show an acute understanding of the city's affairs.

Lorenzino had prepared his escape well. The city gates were locked at night, but Angelo Marzi, bishop of Assisi, held the keys. Ughi told a dramatic tale of Lorenzino dashing to Marzi's house after the murder, but in fact he had planned his escape in advance, asking beforehand for Marzi's permission to leave Florence with three horses, so he could go to see his brother Giuliano, who was gravely ill up at the villa in Cafaggiolo. With Marzi's pass in hand, Lorenzino, his accomplice Scoronconcolo, and a third man, Matteo 'the Arrow', left the city and headed for Bologna. There, Lorenzino had his injured hand treated. And he dispatched urgent letters to the Florentine exiles in France, Rome and Venice.[7]

But Lorenzino's news arrived too late for the exiles to act. His decision to flee the scene – and to lock away the evidence of his crime – gave Cardinal Cibo vital time. The murder was discovered only when Alessandro's men, Giomo and l'Unghero, wondered at the Duke's absence and confided their worries to Cibo. When Cibo heard from Marzi of Lorenzino's flight, he feared the worst.

He sent to his brother Lorenzo in Pisa, asking him to come quickly with whatever troops he could raise. He wrote likewise to Jacopo de' Medici in Arezzo and to Alessandro Vitelli in Città di Castello. To the city he pretended nothing had happened. Continuing with preparations for a planned joust, he had sand laid down outside the Palazzo Medici; he hosted the event with a smile, pretending to the contestants that Alessandro had partied all night and was sleeping all day. He sent word to Pietro Monferrati, Alessandro's wardrobe master, that a conspiracy had been discovered, that Alessandro had fled to the Castello, and that all his belongings should be moved that night from the Palazzo Medici to the fortress.[8] As Pietro and the servants moved the Duke's possessions, Cibo gathered together his closest advisers: Francesco Guicciardini, Roberto Acciaiuoli, Matteo Strozzi and Francesco Vettori. In great secrecy, they opened Lorenzino's chamber and, as Cibo had suspected, found Alessandro dead. His body was concealed in a roll of carpet, taken first to the church of San Giovannino, then to the New Sacristy at San Lorenzo.

The news broke on Monday morning, just as Alessandro Vitelli and his troops arrived in Florence. In the event they were not needed. The city stayed quiet. Writing much later, Benedetto Varchi struggled to explain the citizens' passivity in the face of such an opportunity to rise against the Medici. Perhaps it was because they had been disarmed, he speculated; perhaps they feared that Alessandro was not dead after all, and this was a plot to trick them into an uprising. More likely, the lack of an uprising was testimony to the effectiveness of Alessandro's

regime in closing down opposition within Florence. With a combination of populist appeals to justice, efforts to rebuild the city economy,
and a hard-line approach to political criticism he and his ministers had
demoralised any remaining opponents.

Cibo initially thought to put Alessandro's bastard son Giulio into
power with himself as regent. But Florence's small council of Forty-
Eight, meeting in urgent session in the Palazzo Medici, greeted that
suggestion with scorn, realising that it would concentrate power in
the Cardinal's hands. Others in the council argued that no decision
should be made until at least some of the exiles could return to join
in discussion. The Medici loyalists, however, quickly realised that there
was an alternative, more convincing solution: Cosimo de' Medici,
nineteen-year-old scion of the junior branch of the family, son of
Giovanni de' Medici and Maria Salviati. After Lorenzino, Cosimo was
the next male in the Medici line of succession, which meant that
according to the agreements with Charles V, he should take over. On
Ughi's account, it was Alessandro Vitelli's military threat that convinced
the Forty-Eight. 'He came in, and said: "You have to make a new
duke, or I'll have you cut to pieces." And he could have done it.'[9]

If Lorenzino had hoped his assassination would leave a power
vacuum for the anti-Medici party to fill, he had miscalculated. 'It never
entered my head,' he confessed, 'that Cosimo de' Medici would
succeed Alessandro.' Yet he insisted that even had he thought of it he
would have done nothing differently. The exiles were to blame, instead,
for their failure to liberate Florence. 'What fault is mine,' he asked,
'if I did not find them [the exiles] as eager and as ardent as they should
have been?'[10] Yet that lack of judgement would leave him exiled himself,
with a price on his head, for the next ten years. Alessandro's supporters
in the city could easily imagine the risks of their enemies coming to
power – that they would be out, exiled themselves, even imprisoned.
They had ample incentive to find a new figurehead.

Only on 9 January, a full three days later, did news of the murder
reach Rome. The duke of Urbino's ambassador wrote:

> The Lord Count sent for me in a great hurry and told me
> he had absolutely certain news from Florence that Duke
> Alessandro had been killed, having gone to visit a Florentine

gentlewoman . . . The Count could not tell me more particulars except that he had been led into the trap by one of his closest confidants: From some I have heard it was Ottaviano de' Medici.

But the right information quickly got through and the ambassador added a postscript identifying Lorenzino as the assassin and detailing his escape. In a second postscript he added for clarification: 'This Lorenzo di Pier de' Medici is the one who took the heads off the statues of Rome's triumphal arches.'[11]

Paolo Giovio, counsellor to the Medici and one of the great men of letters of the sixteenth century, summed up Alessandro's life in a letter written at the end of January 1537. 'He bore the burden of Clement's sins, not his own, and so ended the Medici comedy in tragedy.'[12]

Lorenzino fled to the tiny city-state of Mirandola, where he arrived on 12 January. Over the next few weeks he wrote his own justification for the murder and on 5 February sent a draft to a childhood friend. Soon afterwards he left for Istanbul, where he hoped to secure Turkish backing for a military offensive against Florence by the exiles and the French. A revised version of the *Apology*, as it became known, circulated in manuscript, copies exchanged between correspondents in Italy and beyond.[13]

I tell you that there is no one who doubts that Duke Alessandro (who called himself a Medici) was a tyrant of our fatherland, except those who got rich by favouring and backing him. The city of Florence has since ancient times been the property of its people, and it follows that anyone who rules there, without being elected to do so, is a tyrant.

Alessandro wasn't a jot inferior to Caligula in his scorn, mockery and torment of the people, with adulteries and violence, with loutish words and threats. Even in his short rule, so many citizens were driven out of their homeland, and persecuted, and many then died in exile; so many of them were beheaded without due process or good cause, only on the slightest suspicion, and for words of no importance. Others were poisoned, or killed at his own hands, or those of his followers, just so he should not feel ashamed before those who had seen the state in which he was born and brought up.

He was born of a woman of the lowest and basest rank, from Collevecchio, near Rome, who used to work in Duke Lorenzo's house. And that he never loved anyone, and hated everyone, is clear, because he hated and persecuted and poisoned those who should have been close to him, those who should have been dear: his mother, and Cardinal Ippolito de' Medici.

Alessandro did not forget – for shame – the piety and love he owed to his mother. He never had it. But thanks to his innate cruelty and savagery he made sure she was dead before she could be brought to the Emperor.

He never loved anyone at all, and nor did he ever trust me. And even if he had, I would not have been wrong to kill him. Tyrants, however they are slain or snuffed out, are better off dead.[14]

There was no tomb for Alessandro. His body was unceremoniously deposited in his father's sarcophagus, in the New Sacristy of San Lorenzo that Michelangelo had abandoned. The only clue to where he lies is a cursory mention in the Latin of a chapel inscription. He has lain there ever since.

32

Amid the chaos, Cardinal Cibo and Margaret of Austria fled to the fortress, 'with all her late husband's treasure'. Charles V laid claim to Alessandro's property: villas in Rome and Florence, moveable goods, including the rich set of jewels belonging to the Medici. The property he leased back to Cosimo. The jewels were never returned.[1]

Some jewels went missing altogether. Pietro Monferrati, Alessandro's wardrobe master testified:

> A few days before the Duke's murder, I was in His Excellency's chamber one evening. Messer Girolamo had a little French-style box open on the table in front of him, and was showing Lorenz[in]o all the rings, chains and other jewels that were in the said box. I saw about fifteen or eighteen gold rings, set with beautiful stones, for the most part diamonds and rubies, and I also saw jewels by themselves in a little box, the type that goldsmiths have.

He saw strings of pearls, crowns, enamelled chains, gold medals – all of which he had seen many times before. But after Alessandro's death, when his companion Girolamo da Carpi was asked to hand over the ducal jewels, Pietro saw neither rings nor the stones from the little box, nor chains, studs, and very few pearls. 'This is certain,' he said:

> I was there when Messer Girolamo da Carpi accounted for the jewels that the Duchess of Camerino received on behalf of Margaret . . . After Messer Girolamo had handed everything over that he had there, the Duchess asked if he had anything else. He replied that he had no other jewels of

Alessandro's. Then she replied that these were rather few
jewels, and asked if he had an accounting. He replied that
he had no other accounting, and that Alessandro used to
trust him.[2]

Lorenzino, of course, would have needed money for his escape, and
jewels are very easily portable, but Monferrati evidently considered
that Carpi might be to blame. And not just Carpi: Monferrati hinted
that Alessandro Vitelli had helped himself to property too.

Margaret mourned her husband. Among her possessions was a beautiful Book of Hours. Illuminated by Francesco Boccardi, the volume
included tiny images of Margaret and Alessandro. Alongside an image
of the *Annunciation* and the *Virgin and Child* were portraits of the
Duke in golden armour and the Duchess in a square-necked purple
gown revealing her long neck and pearls, her blonde hair pulled back
into a headdress, her new Medici–Habsburg arms on the diamond-
shaped lozenge used for women's heraldic insignia. But at the beginning of the prayers for the dead, in the right-hand illuminated border,
was a monochrome portrait of Alessandro, white on black, a skull
and crossbones above him in the border, another below. In an illuminated D at the start of the verse 'Dilexi, quoniam exaudiet Dominus
vocem orationis meae' ('I have loved, because the Lord will hear the
voice of my prayer'), a skeletal grim reaper, wearing a gold crown
and carrying a scythe, led away a woman in white to her fate, against
a starry black sky. Towards the end of the volume was another image
of Alessandro, now once again in colour, next to a small image of
St Margaret standing on a defeated dragon and holding a cross. It is
almost as if St Margaret's intercession might bring Alessandro back
to life. Even the satirists showed some sympathy for Alessandro's
widow, writing of her desperation, her run of 'fearful fortune'.[3]

On 21 February 1537, funeral rites for Alessandro were held in the
church of San Lorenzo. It was not unusual to delay such ceremony
for some weeks after a burial in order to make preparations for a
grand event. Thirty pairs of mourners came in long black gowns; two
standards with the Duke's arms followed, then the militia, a young

nobleman bearing the Duke's helmet aloft on a spear; finally a bier, draped with gold brocade, a wax effigy of Alessandro above it to represent his body, clad in armour with a tabard of gold brocade and the ducal cap. It was carried by the highest-ranking courtiers, with a great multitude of torches. Behind walked Duke Cosimo, dressed in dark clothes for mourning, then all his court, and that of Duke Alessandro, and afterwards the Medici household, the councillors, magistrates, guilds, and the whole citizenry sombrely dressed. The statue representing the body of the Duke stood on the funeral bier, amid numerous lights at the entrance to the Palazzo de' Medici, for as long as the procession took to pass. The mourners made their way through the city, past the churches of Santa Trinità, San Michele and the great cathedral of Santa Maria del Fiore. Their destination, the church of San Lorenzo, was filled with candles.[4]

There were real fears about what might happen next. The duke of Mantua wrote to his agents in Florence. Was anyone raising troops? How many? Cavalry or infantry? But the Duke had other reasons for writing, too. For all his condemnation of the 'atrocious' murder, he knew Alessandro had taken great delight in gyrfalcons. Might his envoys help him get his hands on one or two? The request seems insensitive, but Margaret did not take offence. 'I thought,' she wrote, 'to send Your Lordship three of the best falcons that belonged to the unhappy Duke, my consort, who is in glory.' She hoped they would prove satisfactory; the duke of Mantua, she wrote, had been one of the closest allies of her late husband. She went on: 'As I understand it, two falconers, who fled Pisa with hawks and horses after the horrendous event, are in Your Lordship's territory.' She asked if he might help track them down. There had evidently been a great deal of looting in the aftermath of Alessandro's death. Dating her letter 17 February at 'Castel Alexandrino' – Alessandro's fortress – she signed it 'La trista margarita daustria, D. di Florenza': 'The sad Margaret of Austria, duchess of Florence'.[5] Her letter conveys something of her grief.

Later that year, the exiles did raise a military force, but they were too late. Duke Cosimo readied his troops, and at the beginning of August he defeated them at Montemurlo. Bartolomeo Valori,

Antonfrancesco degli Albizzi and eleven others were captured and executed. Lorenzino's failure to alert the exiles to his plans had given the Medici time to prepare. Alessandro was gone, but his regime lived on. Filippo Strozzi was taken prisoner and held in the Fortezza da Basso (which no longer bore Alessandro's name). He was tortured and pressured to confess to involvement in Alessandro's murder. He died, probably by his own hand, leaving a suicide note that framed him as a defiant hero of Florentine liberty, though for most of his life he had been a loyal servant of the Medici.[6]

  Cosimo tried for Margaret's hand, but had to settle instead for Eleonora di Toledo. Daughter of Charles' viceroy in Naples, she was another Imperial bride to cement the diplomatic alliance. Among the paintings commissioned for their 1539 wedding was a triple portrait of Alessandro, Ippolito and Clement. Glossing over the vicious family rivalry, it later hung in Cosimo's apartments. Other works at the wedding showed Alessandro's dispute with the exiles in Naples, and his marriage to Margaret.[7] Although Alessandro's image was painted into the fresco sequence of the Palazzo della Signoria, Cosimo also hoped to win back at least some of the Medici allies who had turned to Ippolito. While Alessandro's arms were displayed on hangings around Cosimo's residences, Cosimo proved slow to apprehend Lorenzino.

  A picture of the 'vile traitor' Lorenzino hanging by one foot was painted above the gates of the Fortezza. The Florentine authorities put a price of 4,000 gold ducats on his head. The assassin – who would later acquire the nickname 'Lorenzaccio' ('bad Lorenzo') – spent ten years in exile, travelling between Venice, Istanbul and Paris, trying in vain to build a Franco-Turkish–exile alliance that might defeat the new duke of Florence. But Imperial spies were never far away, and in 1548 he was finally assassinated on the orders of Charles V.[8]

Lorenzino's *Apology* for the murder made him famous, a celebrity killer of the Renaissance. Queen Marguerite of Navarre wrote a story about Alessandro's assassination. Versions of the tale featured on the London stage. It lent itself to the genre of Jacobean revenge drama. There's nothing like a good stabbing to entertain a theatrical audience. Lorenzino featured in several stage plays, including one by Alfred de

Musset and another by Alexandre Dumas, author of *The Three Musketeers*. His blow for republicanism found favour with nineteenth-century writers and audiences. Luisa Strozzi's story featured in those plays, and in opera too, her encounter with Alessandro de' Medici mythologised in melodrama.[9] In popular culture, Alessandro was generally the villain of the piece.

Back in the sixteenth century the women of this story fared rather better than the men. Margaret of Austria was married off to the fourteen-year-old Ottavio Farnese, grandson of Pope Paul III. 'Sold off,' in the words of one satirist, to a little boy. Margaret notoriously refused to consummate her second marriage, and another satirical poem contrasted Ottavio's sexual reputation unfavourably to Alessandro's. Margaret, the 'Spanish mule', had been already been broken in, by a man armed with a 'strong spur': if Ottavio couldn't manage her then his 'spur' was clearly lacking. Behind the bawdy speculation, however, it may well be that the sad end of her first pregnancy explains her reluctance to entertain another: it was 1545 before she delivered a Farnese heir. The Habsburg–Farnese marriage was unhappy and the couple spent extended periods apart, but as duchess of Parma Margaret became one of the most powerful women in Europe, acting as governor of the Netherlands (twice) and Abruzzo. Even after her marriage to Ottavio Farnese, she always wanted news of Florence. Three years on she was to be found in dressed in black, looking sad and sweet, as she asked after those left behind in Poggio, Careggi and Castello.[10]

Taddea Malaspina moved back to Massa. She took with her the portrait of Alessandro by Jacopo da Pontormo. (Later the Medici sought to have it returned.) Their daughter Giulia was looked after by Maria Salviati, mother of the new duke, Cosimo. Pontormo painted a portrait of Maria and her charge, though at some point in its history, Giulia's image was painted out. It was only discovered in later restoration.[11]

Giulia married Bernardo, son of Ottaviano de' Medici, who became lord of Ottaiano in the kingdom of Naples; they named their son Alessandro. It was for Giulia that in 1562 Ceccherelli wrote his book about Alessandro's virtues.[12] At the end of the eighteenth century, when the line of the Medici descended from Cosimo came to an end, the Medici of Ottaiano made a play for power in Florence. They failed.

Giulio, Giulia's elder brother, became a knight of the Order of St Stephen, a naval order dedicated to combatting pirates and Turks.

At the court of France, Alessandro's half-sister Catherine de' Medici outdid them all. She became queen, then queen mother and regent of France. Among her counsellors was her cousin, Alessandro's enemy, Piero Strozzi, who married Lorenzino's younger sister Laudomia in 1539. And at Catherine's court, in the middle of the sixteenth century, a new story was added to the tales of Alessandro's low birth. In a book celebrating the illustrious men of the house of Medici, Jean Nestor wrote: 'Lorenzo de' Medici, duke of Urbino and father of Catherine de' Medici, had a natural son called Alessandro, born (so it's said, at least) to a half-Negro woman.'[13]

In Alessandro's lifetime, however, that rumour did not loom large at all. A few contemporaries referred to his mother's slave status, but thanks to chance and contingency Alessandro was able to trump his illegitimate status and rise to the highest level of society, just as his relative Giulio de' Medici, Pope Clement VII, had done before him. His critics certainly pointed to his bastardy and low birth, but they were just as concerned if not more so with his tyranny and with the political questions surrounding the shift to ducal rule in Florence.

How might Alessandro's history have looked, if it had been written by his friends? Among the hostility, there are little hints of the qualities they might have emphasised: intelligence, wisdom beyond his years, respect for the law and justice. A long and fruitful marriage might have laid to rest some of the worse tales of sexual excess.

It is testimony to the determination of the Medici popes that they managed to establish their nephew as a prince of Florence where other papal nephews (Cesare Borgia, for example) had failed to make their own dynastic states. They had the advantage over Borgia that they were retaking an existing state which their family had long dominated, but they were not without strong-minded enemies, and even their friends were often sceptical of their plans. None of Clement's close advisers had advocated making Florence a duchy when it was discussed in 1531–2. There was little enthusiasm for the Medici trajectory towards princely power. After Alessandro's assassination, perhaps it was convenient to blame him for the despised transition to absolute rule, for the arrests, the executions, the exiling of opponents, the ban on bearing arms, the growing power of Spain and the Empire in Italian politics, the end of the centuries-old Florentine republic, its traditions and offices stretching back in time.

On the other hand, there is much to suggest that Alessandro fulfilled the expectations of a Renaissance prince rather well. By most accounts he was charming and popular, accomplished in sports, a patron of the arts. He kept his hands clean and left the less salubrious aspects of his rise to power to others. If the womanising stories are true, it would hint at recklessness, but the limited contemporary documentation should lead us to wonder whether they are. Unlike his cousin Ippolito, he respected Pope Clement VII, the head of the family, and did what the house of Medici required of him. Had it not been for Lorenzino, Alessandro and Margaret might well have founded a Medici–Habsburg cultural centre in Florence to outshine even the glamorous court of Duke Cosimo and his wife Eleonora di Toledo.

During the reign of Alessandro's successor, Cosimo de' Medici, the first Duke was memorialised by his schoolroom companion Vasari in frescoes in the Palazzo della Signoria. Following through on the plan that Alessandro had floated, Cosimo had moved his ducal residence into the city's old seat of government, where he had new apartments constructed. Alessandro's larger-than-life image, in fantastic Roman dress, is on the same wall as the picture of Cosimo himself. In many ways the new duke had reason to be grateful to his predecessor. Alessandro had done much to establish a stable state and a splendid court during the short years of his rule.

AFTERWORD

Alessandro's Ethnicity: Historical Sources and Debates

The story of Alessandro's 'race' appeared in print in Paris in 1564, in a book entitled *Histoire des hommes illustres de la maison de Medici* (History of the illustrious men of the house of Medici). Written by Jean Nestor and published with a royal privilege, it was dedicated to Alessandro's half-sister, Catherine, by this point queen mother of France. It was part of a concerted propaganda effort to defend her from those in France pointing to her common roots.[1] (The Medici might have been wealthy, even popes, but they were merchants and not truly royal.) Nestor introduced the rumour in the opening sentence of his chapter on Alessandro and Ippolito. He did so in a neutral fashion, simply reporting the story. This was not a man aiming to damn the Duke's reputation. Quite the opposite: Nestor's account of Alessandro's rule was rather favourable. He mentioned the exiles' allegations that Alessandro poisoned Ippolito, but noted that the alleged poisoner was released and that the doctors put the death down to the 'change of air'.[2] He did discuss a derogatory allegation about Alessandro's mother: considering the exiles' conduct during the disputes in Naples, he wrote that they insulted Alessandro 'with defamatory libels and public harangues, calling him the bastard son of a Moorish slave, who had become an inhuman tyrant of the fatherland'. (It is not clear from the text whether Nestor thought 'half-Negro' and 'Moorish' were the same thing, or whether he was reporting two different rumours.) But if Nestor thought that the claims about Alessandro's race were *only* defamatory libel, why draw attention to them in the opening section of his chapter? This was, after all, a book dedicated to the virtues and nobility of the Medici.

Was Nestor in a position to know the facts of Alessandro's birth? There were people in Paris who might have known at first or second hand. Catherine de' Medici was one. Some caution is needed here, because Catherine was associated with both Piero Strozzi and Lorenzino. Both were hostile to Alessandro, but on the other hand they were close to the situation. Piero was Alessandro's cousin (his mother was Clarice de' Medici Strozzi, who had so vocally objected to the bastard nephews' promotion). He was around the same age as Alessandro and Ippolito, and had been brought up in close proximity to the Medici in Rome. He might well have seen Alessandro's mother. He could certainly have talked to people who knew her.

Some writers have called the story about Alessandro's race a malicious fantasy, invented by the Duke's enemies.[3] His later nickname, 'Alessandro il Moro', is not apparent in the early sources. Yet it is a strange tale to invent. It is plausible because it fits with the visual evidence. The image of Alessandro in his portraits is not consistent, but all the artists are clear on his dark skin and curly black hair. The most 'Africanate' portrayal of Alessandro, the small portrait on tin made in Bronzino's workshop, is posthumous. It is dated between 1555 and 1565, making it more or less contemporary with Nestor's description, but that later dating has prompted questions about whether it is true to life.[4] The depictions of Alessandro in Vasari's Palazzo della Signoria frescoes of the same period are more ambiguous, but certainly compatible with Nestor's story that Alessandro was one-quarter black African or 'Moorish'. Vasari's armorial portrait of the Duke, the Pontormo sketch in Florence's Marucelliana Library and Pontormo's portrait of Alessandro show a man less obviously African, but we should beware of assuming that the portraits painted in Alessandro's lifetime are any closer to his actual appearance than the posthumous ones. Technical research on the Pontormo portrait has shown that Alessandro's face was narrowed in the course of painting, and if Ceccherelli is right that Alessandro broke his nose playing football, that may have been another feature to be tidied up in the portraiture. These works of art were commissioned in the context of Alessandro's rule of Florence so there was reason for the artists to underline his dynastic claim to power by emphasising his resemblance to other members of the Medici family. On the other hand, it is possible that the painter of the later small portrait had heard that Alessandro's mother was a slave and consciously or subconsciously adjusted the image to fit that story. Slavery and blackness became more closely associated as the sixteenth century wore on and the Atlantic slave trade grew.[5] Perhaps that portrait offers more a metaphor of Alessandro than a strictly accurate depiction.

Alongside the visual sources there are textual allusions and absences from Alessandro's own lifetime. Lorenzino's reference to the Duke's 'innate cruelty and savagery' lends itself to a reading that his origins were somehow 'uncivilised'. It is notable that Contarini, the Venetian ambassador, commented on Ippolito's good looks and said nothing of Alessandro's appearance, perhaps because Alessandro's looks did not lend themselves to compliments by the standards of the day.[6] Ippolito's claim that Alessandro was 'manifestly illegitimate' might suggest his bastardy was visible. And the plot to bring Alessandro's mother to Naples and parade her before the Emperor would make more sense if her looks were in some way ignoble; it is interesting that no one tried to pretend that Simunetta was any more noble than in fact she was. The curious tale of the hunt for an escaped slave on Alessandro's return from Naples also makes more sense in the context of the claim that Alessandro's mother was a slave herself. Even the stunning nude portrait of Cosimo de' Medici as Orpheus, painted soon after his accession, might seem an assertion of his 'proper' pink-and-white skin, the most desirable complexion for a Renaissance ruler. A later biography made explicit reference to Cosimo's *candido colore*: his pale colouring.[7]

The first textual description of Alessandro's looks is Bernardo Segni's account, written in the 1550s. A member of an old Florentine merchant family, Segni went on to serve in Cosimo's administration. He would have seen the Duke at first hand, and his description – 'well-built, stocky, dark-coloured and with a large nose' – chimes with the visual sources. Segni also reports Bernardo Salviati's allusion to Alessandro's mother as a slave in 1535. Giovanni Cambi, another historian of Florence, referred to her slave status too, and since Cambi died in April 1535, we can situate the circulation of the rumour with some certainty during Alessandro's lifetime.[8]

The question of whether Alessandro's mother was in fact a slave remains open. The language of the period is ambiguous. Most of the educated people who wrote histories of Alessandro's rule used the Latinate *serva*, which in the sixteenth century could refer either to an enslaved woman or a free servant. Cambi and Segni, the latter reporting Bernardo Salviati's speech to the Emperor, use the word *schiava*, which is more explicitly associated with slaves. (Though it is also associated with Slavs, which leads to further confusion!) This could, however, be a back-formation from their observation of Alessandro's appearance. Either way, it is plausible enough that a low-ranking serving-woman in the Medici household might be of African descent: a slave herself, or a daughter of a former slave or migrant. Two Italian altarpieces from the turn of the fifteenth to the sixteenth century showing the Adoration of the Shepherds portray shepherds with significantly darker skin than other figures in the picture. Today, these men would probably be perceived as mixed-race. The complexion of Ercole de' Roberti's shepherd contrasts with the lighter skin of Mary and Jesus. This painting is linked to the Este family of Ferrara, whose acquisition of black slaves is well established. Amid the crowd of Luca Signorelli's *Adoration*, painted for Città di Castello in Umbria (home town of Alessandro Vitelli), is a dark-skinned man in a straw hat. His ethnicity is ambiguous but his looks clearly contrast with those of his companion.[9] It seems to me unhelpful to insist on categorising Alessandro's mother as either black (sub-Saharan) African or North African, as if people of these two groups never mixed. In reality they did, and for many centuries had mixed with Italians too.[10] Simunetta may not have been a slave herself, but the descendant of an African who had arrived in Italy decades before.

So long as historians stuck to the story that Alessandro was secretly favoured over Ippolito by Pope Clement on account of being Clement's son, the argument that he was the son of a mixed-race serving-woman was trickier to sustain. Clement was a clever politician. His own mother was a woman of low birth and he would have been well aware of contemporary feeling about the importance of nobility of blood. However, now that it is clear that Alessandro was incorporated into the family only as a last resort, the picture changes. We know that as a teenager Alessandro lived rather discreetly, out of Florence, that he was thrust into a princely role only because Clement unexpectedly survived his 1529 illness when he decided to make Ippolito a cardinal.

This was not a situation where the Medici made a positive decision to promote Alessandro: Clement did so because he could not see a viable alternative. Throughout, he operated according to the usual expectations of seniority by age and nobility of blood.

The role of Charles V is also relevant here. Would he have accepted a son-in-law of mixed heritage? This was, in fact, an issue with which the Spanish nobility was very familiar. Spain had had a long tradition of coexistence of Muslim, Jewish and Christian populations. Its southernmost region, Andalusia, had been under Moorish rule until the Christian 'reconquest' of 1492. Spain insisted that office-holders show 'purity of blood' which in practice could be awkward for many noble families whose ancestors had intermarried. It was even rumoured that Charles' grandfather, King Ferdinand of Aragon, had Jewish heritage.[11] The Emperor would have been familiar enough with gossip about undesirable ancestors, and with the strategies used by Spanish families to deny their existence.

The simplest explanation for the existence of a tradition that Alessandro was of African descent is that it was based on fact. The story that his mother was a slave may be true as well, or it may be an invention derived from the fact that Alessandro had dark skin. In turn, the simplest explanation for an illegitimate child having notably darker skin is that this was a product of his maternal heritage. Knowing the numbers of Africans who travelled or were transported to Italy in this period, that is well within the bounds of possibility. I suspect that Alessandro's appearance left some room for doubt, that those who needed to could convince themselves that the rumour was simply malicious. That was the route to dealing with problematic ancestries in Spain. Beyond that I am reluctant to try to read the specifics of ethnicity from artworks. Race is not a scientific fact: it is a social construction. If there is one thing that Alessandro's life teaches us, it is that 'black' is in the eye of the beholder.

The sixteenth-century suggestions that Alessandro's mother was of mixed race or Moorish were adopted by some historians, ignored by others. Writing towards the end of the century, Scipione Ammirato, Cosimo de' Medici's official historiographer, described Alessandro as 'of a brown colour, with large lips and frizzy hair'. (He may have derived this description from the Bronzino workshop portrait.) In seventeenth- and eighteenth-century works on the Medici, Alessandro's appearance was rarely mentioned.[12]

Alfred de Musset's play *Lorenzaccio*, published in 1834 but not produced for many years afterwards, highlights Alessandro's illegitimacy but gives him red hair. Another historical drama about Alessandro, printed in Paris the following year, borrows Segni's description of the Duke, 'of a dark colour', and calls the character based on his mother 'Faustina the Moor'.[13] Alexandre Dumas *père* wrote a play on the same theme. *Lorenzino* was staged in 1842 and reworked into prose as *One Night in Florence* in 1861. In the novel, although not the play, Dumas, who was himself of mixed descent (his father was the illegitimate son of a French nobleman and an enslaved African) made Alessandro's mother Moorish.[14] Dumas had lived in Florence, read Varchi and others on the story of Alessandro's life, and might well have seen the Duke's portrait. He might also, by 1861, have read one of the first historical accounts to describe Alessandro in implicitly racial terms.

Alfred von Reumont's book on the youth of Catherine de' Medici was first published in 1854 (and in French translation in 1866). By this time the discourse of scientific racism was firmly established. It was widely believed that there were innate differences between peoples of different 'races', that these related to intelligence, to character, to civility, and that they could be measured. That thinking is evident in the way von Reumont wrote about Alessandro and Ippolito de' Medici:

> Seeing the portraits of the two young men, one immediately recognises the difference in their natures. Ippolito, painted by Titian, is in a red velvet Hungarian costume, which he was in the habit of wearing as legate to the army against the Turks, and his fine, noble features have a serious and melancholy expression; Alessandro, in the hand of Giorgio Vasari, is in full armour; his hard stare, his frizzy hair and thick lips betray his origins.[15]

The most famous exposition of racial theory in Italian is probably Cesare Lombroso's 1871 book, *The White Man and the Man of Colour*.

Lombroso was a white supremacist who credited whites with all the significant achievements of humankind (including the liberation of slaves), and his work was the intellectual backdrop to later nineteenth-century commentary on Alessandro's ethnicity. It is pertinent here that Lombroso did not see North Africans as a sharply distinct ethnic category from black Africans. For example, he thought Berbers were a 'midway point between Negroids, Semites and Whites'. Those living to the south were 'black and almost woolly-haired', while those further north were olive-skinned.[16]

Writing in 1875, Italian historian Gino Capponi picked up Alessandro's story. The duke of Florence was 'born of a Moorish or mulatto slave'. He had inherited from his mother 'dark skin, thick lips and frizzy hair'. In that same year, Alessandro's tomb was opened. The reports of the eyewitnesses present make clear their interest in his 'racial' characteristics. Foresi, a physician, wrote: 'As soon as that skull was removed from the tomb, it was immediately recognised by Professor Paganucci, Niccolini, Cambi, Bianchi and the author to be Duke Alessandro's, because it looked close to the form of a skull of the Ethiopian race.' P. Ferrigni, a publicist present at the tomb opening, gave a different account, claiming that Alessandro's nose was small and not 'Ethiopian' in type.[17] Paganucci, an anatomist, was more cautious on the question of race but he too drew conclusions about the character of Alessandro and his father Lorenzo on the basis of their physiognomy: both were 'rapacious', 'usurping' types, Lorenzo perhaps more so than his son.[18] Other Italian scholars of the late nineteenth and early twentieth centuries worried more generally about the impact of earlier migration on modern Italian 'stock'. Corrado Avolio, in an 1888 study of slavery in sixteenth-century Sicily, noted that one twenty-fourth of the population were slaves. 'The greatest number were black,' he wrote, 'and it is very likely that some mulatto types [sic] were reproduced in the households of their masters.' This 'Negro blood' meant that even in the present day, now and again one might see individuals whose appearance reflected that heritage, 'especially among the lower social strata'.[19]

These ideas persisted into the mid twentieth century. In 1924–5, Gaetano Pieraccini, a doctor and politician, published a book entitled *The ancestry of the Medici of Cafaggiolo: an essay on research into the hereditary transmission of biological characteristics.* His conclusions on Alessandro, based on his study of the 1875 reports, drew not so much on Lombroso's ideas about race, but on his idea that some people were born criminals. 'Now, in Alessandro we find all the known features of the delinquent amoral constitutional type: proud, arrogant, selfish, sensual, thinks only of his own success and happiness. . . . The psychic lacuna, that made Alexander a born criminal, and therefore incorrigible, lay in his lack of "moral sense".' Pieraccini was reluctant to conclude that Alessandro was of mixed race but he conceded that the 'structural particularities' of his skull had led his contemporaries to call him a 'mulatto'.[20]

The story had already made its way into English. Colonel G. F. Young quoted Capponi approvingly in 1909; H. B. Cotterill, in a popular 1919 history of medieval and Renaissance Italy, wrote that Alessandro was 'probably a son of the Pope himself by a mulatto woman'. For Young, Alessandro was 'uneducated, incapable, vicious, and universally detested'; Ippolito was 'handsome, courteous, good-natured, highly cultivated, possessed of much ability and a universal favourite'.[21] This was history through the prism of racist stereotype: the tales of Alessandro's tyranny and his race became mutually reinforcing.

But around them society was changing, and with it attitudes towards black history, particularly in the United States. In 1931, Arturo Alfonso Schomburg published in *The Crisis* an article entitled 'Alessandro, First Duke of Florence, the Negro Medici'. *The Crisis* was the magazine of the National Association for the Advancement of Colored People, then edited by NAACP's co-founder W. E. B. Du Bois. Born in Puerto Rico in 1874, Schomburg had moved to New York and created one of the most important collections of sources for African history, now housed in a centre bearing his name at the New York Public Library. He was a co-founder of the Negro Society for Historical Research.[22] Musing on the Bronzino workshop portrait, Schomburg wrote of Alessandro's case:

> I think if this had happened in North America, the picture would have been removed long ago and by some plausible excuse relegated to the cellar or entirely discarded. But the Florentines lived up to the judgement of history. The truth

cannot be always concealed from the eyes of the world. So here is the unvarnished story of the picture: A young man of Negro descent was married to the daughter of the Emperor of Germany, King of Spain and King of Naples, and he [became] the first Duke of Florence.[23]

His article proved inspirational. At the 1933 annual meeting of the Association for the Study of Negro Life and History, W. Napoleon Rivers cited Schomburg in a speech on 'Why Negroes Should Study Romance Languages and Literatures'. Rivers taught languages at North Carolina Agricultural and Technical College and went on to collaborate on an edition of Alexandre Dumas' *Georges*. In his talk (later published) he noted as evidence for Renaissance Italy's contact with Africans 'the historical fact that the First Hereditary Duke of Florence was a Negro, Alessandro de Medici, of the powerful house of the Medici'.[24]

In 1947, Alessandro was featured in the second volume of Joel Augustus Rogers' book, *World's Great Men of Color*.[25] Rogers was a journalist and self-taught historian, and his works, including *100 Amazing Facts about the Negro*, sought to highlight the role of black leaders in history. He claimed African ancestry for several American presidents as well as figures such as Cleopatra, and although not all his arguments stand up to scrutiny, his work was grounded in carefully referenced research, drawing on material in multiple languages. In the American sphere, at least, the story of Alessandro de' Medici now had a new dimension. It stayed in circulation. In September 1963, twenty-five years after Schomburg's death, his article on Alessandro was republished in the *Negro Digest*.

For all the efforts of Schomburg and Rogers, though, Alessandro's story subsequently stayed remarkably hidden for the remainder of the twentieth century. When it emerged, most often at the edges of his sister Catherine's much-recounted life, there were still echoes of nineteenth-century racism. In a 1986 biography of Catherine de' Medici, French writer Jean Orieux described Alessandro as 'negroid, frizzy-haired and large-lipped. Intellectually, he wasn't bright, quite the opposite of Ippolito.' This despite the fact that two Venetian ambassadors and the hostile Nardi all agreed (in well-known and accessible historical sources) that Alessandro was an intelligent man. Orieux was not a one-off. In a 1999 biography of Margaret of Austria, Belgian historian Georges-Henri Dumont concluded, on the basis of Alessandro's appearance in the Bronzino workshop portrait, that his fiancée 'must not have found him very attractive'.[26]

Only in the twenty-first century has the question of Alessandro's race begun to attract more serious scholarly interest.[27] With a fuller account of his life now at hand, perhaps we may put paid to such ill-informed comment.

ACKNOWLEDGEMENTS

My thanks to Will Hammond, Henry Howard and Catherine Clarke; to all at Radio 3 Free Thinking and the AHRC/BBC New Generation Thinkers scheme; to Miranda Kaufmann, Michael Ohajuru, and the many contributors to the Black British History initiative for ideas and inspiration; and to colleagues at the Medici Archive Project, the Society for Court Studies, the Textual Ambassadors project, the Marrying Cultures project and the Diplomatic Ceremonial project for opportunities to discuss this research. Special thanks go to all the archive and library staff who helped me navigate the sources and to Karen Azaadi, Hugo Blake, Evelien Bracke, Lucy Byatt, Irene Fosi, Jean-Louis Fournel, the late Carl Hornsey, Lisa Kaborycha, John Law, Elisabetta Mori, Caroline Murphy, Mary Partington, Guido Rebecchini, Sheryl Reiss, Tim Shephard, Marcello Simonetta, Paco Smith, Andrea Spreafico and Faryal Velmi for hospitality, encouragement, and some very helpful observations. I'm particularly grateful to University of Sheffield students Emma Newman, Leila Yilmaz, Keir Shields and Bella Peniston, who worked with me on aspects of the project thanks to funding from the University of Sheffield Arts Enterprise and Festival of the Mind schemes. Any errors are, of course, entirely my own.

British Library Board, 144.g.3(1) page 13 • 9: Palazzo Vecchio (Palazzo della Signoria), Florence, Italy/Bridgeman Images • 10, 11 and 12: the author • 13: Vasari's House, Arezzo/Scala, Florence courtesy of the Ministero Beni e Att. Culturali 2015 • 14: Galleria dell'Accademia, Florence, Italy/Bridgeman Images • 17: Palazzo Pitti, Florence, Italy/ Bridgeman Images • 18: Musée des Beaux-Arts, Lille, France/Bridgeman Images • 19: BeBa / Iberfoto/Alinari Archives • 20: Lobkowicz Palace, Prague Castle, Czech Republic/Bridgeman Images • 21: Philadelphia Museum of Art/Art Resource/Scala, Florence 2015 • 22: Galleria degli Uffizi, Florence/De Agostini Picture Library/Scala, Florence 2015 • 23: Jacopo da Pontormo, 'Ritratto di Alessandro de' Medici', 1534. Biblioteca Marucelliana, Florence, Dis. I. 16. Further reproduction or duplication of this image, including partial, is expressly prohibited. • 24: Victoria and Albert Museum, London • 25: Museo Nazionale del Bargello, Florence, Italy/Bridgeman Images • 26: Archivio di Stato di Mantova, concessione no. 52/2015 • 28: Biblioteca Lincei e Corsiniana, Rome • 29: Museo delle Cappelle Medicee, Florence, Italy/De Agostini Picture Library/G. Barone/Bridgeman Images • 30: The Walters Art Museum, Baltimore.

BIBLIOGRAPHY

A NOTE ON SOURCES

The sources for Alessandro's life are not straightforward, so I offer these notes to readers who would like to understand the nature of the books and documents I have used in writing this book.

Only a small proportion of Alessandro's letters survive. Some are in the Florence State Archive (ASF); others in the archives of the rulers and individuals to whom they were sent. Some of his account books survive (mainly listed under Guardaroba Medicea, that is, the Medici Wardrobe), and these have provided many of the details of his clothing, gifts and furniture. Alessandro's ministers sometimes wrote about his doings, as did his enemies (these letters are also in the Florence State Archive, among the Strozzi Papers). Ambassadors and agents of other Italian states at Alessandro's court and at the papal court commented on Florentine affairs. The Venetian senator Marin Sanuto compiled thousands of diplomatic dispatches into his diaries, though not without introducing some errors in the process. There is almost certainly more to be found in the Spanish and French archives, but that would take another book.

Beyond the archive documents there are various histories of Florence written later in the sixteenth century. Each of these has its strengths, but all are partisan. Benedetto Varchi wrote his *Florentine Histories* on the commission of Alessandro's successor Cosimo. He had good access to the surviving archives, but during Alessandro's rule he had been in exile so he relied entirely on second-hand accounts. Jacopo Nardi, likewise an exile, is strong on the exiles' affairs but again had little first-hand knowledge of

Alessandro's court. Filippo Nerli served in Alessandro's government, as did Bernardo Segni, but neither was part of the Duke's inner circle.[1] Nardi's book was published in Lyons in the sixteenth century, but the other histories circulated only in manuscript for almost two hundred years, and were published in the eighteenth century thanks to the efforts of Francesco Settimanni, who also made his own highly selective compilation of Florentine memories.

Girolamo Ughi, a Franciscan chronicler not involved in Florentine government, is perhaps one of the more fair-minded commentators.[2] Cellini gives helpful details about Alessandro but they frequently serve to glamorise his own activities; Paolo Giovio has good inside information from Clement's court but is inclined to be loyal to the Medici. Other information comes from the memoirs of the Cibo family (there are two sets in the Massa State Archive, one published, one not), and from the correspondence of Imperio Ricordati, a member of Cardinal Cibo's household, with the marchioness and duke of Mantua. Ricordati has some of the best information about Alessandro's court that I have found. Ceccherelli's stories are heavily romanticised, but can be read in dialogue with the hostile accounts. Vasari's detailed descriptions of the art and ceremony of Alessandro's court are invaluable, if often coloured by his opinion of the quality of the artists involved, and by a desire to associate himself with the Medici dukes.

MANUSCRIPT SOURCES

Florence

Archivio di Stato di Firenze (ASF): Carte Strozziane (CS), serie I: 13, 16, 59, 61, 95, 100, 135, 335; Copialettere di Goro Gheri 4, 5; Ducato di Urbino, serie I: 132, 133; Guardaroba Medicea 2, 3, 4, 5, 6; Manoscritti (MS) 103, 125, 170, 433; Mediceo avanti il Principato (MAP) 107, 126, 132, 147, 157, 159, 164; Mediceo del Principato (MdP) 181, 630; Miscellanea Medicea 502; Notarile Antecosimiano 13243; Otto di Guardia e Balìa del Principato 5–11
Archivio dell'Opera del Duomo: Registri Battesimali 10, 229
Biblioteca Nazionale Centrale di Firenze (BNCF): Manoscritti, Nuove Accessioni (NA) 982
Biblioteca Riccardiana di Firenze (BRF): Manoscritti Riccardiana 1849, 1959

Mantua

Archivio di Stato di Mantova (ASMn): Archivio Gonzaga (AG) 440, 567, 812, 878, 880, 883, 1086, 1110–12, 1153, 1302, 1304, 1375, 1905, 2931, 2935–37, 2969, 2971–72

Massa

Archivio di Stato di Massa (ASMs): Archivio Cibo–Malaspina 477, 508; Appendice all'Archivio Cybo–Malaspina; Archivio del Cardinale Innocenzo Cybo 3; Memorie della Famiglia Cybo

Modena

Archivio di Stato di Modena (ASMo): Archivio Estense (AE), Carteggio Ambasciatori: Firenze 16; Carteggio Ambasciatori: Francia 11; Carteggio Ambasciatori: Roma 1356/33; Archivio Estense, Carteggio Principi Esteri 1152

Rome

Archivio di Stato di Roma: Tribunale del Governatore vol. 10, fasc. 3; Archivio Storico Capitolino (ASC): Archivio Orsini (AO): Pergamene II.A.23013, no. catena 766; Pergamene II.A.23,022, no. catena 722; Serie I, Corrispondenza 72, 93; Serie IV, Misc. Storico Genealogica, b. 43, fasc. 93; Biblioteca dell'Accademia Nazionale dei Lincei e Corsiniana: MS Corsiniana 55.K.16

Vatican City

Biblioteca Apostolica Vaticana: MS Vat. Lat. 12276; Archivio Segreto Vaticano (ASV): A. A., Arm. I-XVIII, nn. 3114, 3311, 6522, 6523; Armadio XL, 11; Camera Apostolica, Diversa Cameralia 84; Miscellanea, Arm. II, 49, 78; Segr. Stato, Principi 7; Segr. Stato, Vescovi e Prelati 6

Venice

Biblioteca Nazionale Marciana: Codices Italiani VII 1043 (=7616)

PRINTED WORKS

Adriani, Giovambattista. 1822. *Istoria de' suoi tempi*. 8 vols. Prato.
Albertini, R. von. 1970. *Firenze dalla repubblica al principato: Storia e coscienza politica*. Turin.
Aldobrandini, Silvestro, et al. 1857. 'Cartelli di querela e di sfida tra Lodovico Martelli, Dante da Castiglione e Giovanni Bandini, Rubertino Albobrandini

al tempo dell'assedio di Firenze.' Edited by Carlo Milanesi. *Archivio storico italiano*, nuova serie 4 (1857): 11–12.

Ammirato, Scipione. 1641. *Istorie fiorentine*. Florence.

———. 1642. *Opuscoli*. Florence.

Anzilotti, A. 1910. *La costituzione interna dello stato fiorentino sotto il duca Cosimo de' Medici*. Florence.

Aretino, Pietro. 1997. *Lettere*. Edited by Paolo Procaccioli. 6 vols. Rome.

Avolio, Corrado. 1888. *La schiavitù domestica in Sicilia nel secolo XVI*. Florence.

Azzolini, Monica. 2013. *The Duke and the Stars: Astrology and Politics in Renaissance Milan*. Cambridge, MA.

Baker, Nicholas Scott. 2007. 'Writing the Wrongs of the Past: Vengeance, Humanism, and the Assassination of Alessandro de' Medici.' *The Sixteenth Century Journal* 38: 307–27.

———. 2009. 'For Reasons of State: Political Executions, Republicanism, and the Medici in Florence, 1480–1560.' *Renaissance Quarterly* 62: 444–78.

———. 2010. 'Power and Passion in Sixteenth-Century Florence: The Sexual and Political Reputations of Alessandro and Cosimo I de' Medici.' *Journal of the History of Sexuality* 19: 432–57.

———. 2011. 'Medicean Metamorphoses: Carnival in Florence, 1513.' *Renaissance Studies* 25: 491–510.

———. 2013. *The Fruit of Liberty: Political Culture in the Florentine Renaissance, 1480–1550*. Cambridge, MA.

Bandello, Matteo. 1952. *Tutte le opere*. Edited by Francesco Flora. 2 vols, 3rd edition. Verona.

Bardazzi, Silvestro, and Eugenio Castellani. 1981. *La Villa Medicea di Poggio a Caiano*. 2 vols. Prato.

Bartlett, Robert. 2001. 'Medieval and Modern Concepts of Race and Ethnicity.' *Journal of Medieval and Early Modern Studies* 31: 39–56.

Bausi, Francesco. 2015. *Il Principe dalla scrittoio alla stampa*. Pisa.

Bawcutt, N. W. 2005. 'The Assassination of Alessandro de' Medici in Early Seventeenth-Century English Drama.' *The Review of English Studies* 56: 412–23.

Baxandall, Michael. 1972. *Painting and Experience in Fifteenth-Century Italy*. Oxford.

Belardini, Manuela. 2003. 'Margherita d'Austria, sposa e vedova del Duca Alessandro de' Medici.' In Mantini, 25–54.

———. 2008. '"Lontano da' sua parenti et suo paese": Margherita d'Austria; la costruzione di un'identità.' In Spinelli and Calvi, 169–94.

Beloch, Giulio. 1959. 'La popolazione d'Italia nei secoli sedicesimo, diciasset-tesimo e diciottesimo.' In *Storia dell'economia italiana: vol. 1, saggi di storia economica*, edited by Carlo Cipolla, 449–500. Turin.

Belozerskaya, M. 2006. *The Medici Giraffe: And Other Tales of Exotic Animals and Power*. London.

Benedetti, Francesco. 1995. *La madre del Moro*. Pescara.

Berni, Francesco. 1885. *Rime e poesie latine. Lettere edite e inedite*. Edited by Antonio Virgili. Florence.

Bestor, Jane Fair. 1996. 'Bastardy and Legitimacy in the Formation of a Regional State in Italy: The Estense Succession.' *Comparative Studies in Society and History* 38: 549–85.

Bindman, David and Henry Louis Gates, Jr. 2010. Eds. *The Image of the Black in Western Art*, vol. 3, pt. 1. Cambridge, MA.

Bono, Salvatore. 1999. *Schiavi musulmani nell'Italia moderna: galeotti, vu' cumpra', domestici*. Naples.

———. 2010. 'Schiavi in Italia: Maghrebini, neri, slavi, ebrei e altri (secc. XVI–XIX).' *Mediterranea: Ricerche Storiche* VII (19): 235–52.

Bourne, Molly. 2010. 'Mail Humour and Male Sociability: Sexual Innuendo in the Epistolary Domain of Francesco II Gonzaga.' In Matthews-Grieco, 199–221.

Brackett, John. 2005. 'Race and rulership: Alessandro de' Medici, first Medici duke of Florence, 1529–1537.' In Earle and Lowe, 303–25.

Bramanti, V. 1992. 'Il "Cartolaio" Ceccherelli e la fortuna del Duca Alessandro de' Medici.' *Lettere Italiane* 20: 269–88.

Brancato, Dario. 2013. 'Una "costituzione" dei fuorusciti: La silloge di Benedetto Varchi per Piero Strozzi e Lorenzino de' Medici.' In *Varchi e altro Rinascimento. Studi offerti a Vanni Bramanti*, edited by Salvatore Lo Re and F. Tomasi, 23–46. Manziana.

Bridges, Thomas W. 1982. 'The Publishing of Arcadelt's First Book of Madrigals.' Ph.D. diss., Harvard.

Bromfield, J. 1972. *De Lorenzino de Médicis à Lorenzaccio. Etude d'un thème historique*. Paris.

Bullard, M. M. 1980. *Filippo Strozzi and the Medici: Favor and Finance in Sixteenth-Century Florence and Rome*. New York.

Buonarroti, Michelangelo. 1983. *Carteggio*. Edited by Paola Barocchi and Renzo Ristori. 5 vols. Florence.

———. 1993. *The Poetry of Michelangelo: An Annotated Translation*. Edited and translated by James M. Saslow. New Haven.

Busini, G. B. 1860. *Lettere a Benedetto Varchi sopra l'assedio di Firenze*. Edited by G. Milanesi. Florence.

Butters, H. C. 1985. *Governors and Government in Sixteenth-Century Florence, 1502–1519*. Oxford.

———. 2010. 'Machiavelli and the Medici.' In *The Cambridge Companion to Machiavelli*, edited by John M. Najemy, 64–79. Cambridge.

Callard, Caroline. 2007. *Le Prince et la République: Histoire, pouvoir et société dans la Florence des Médicis au XVIIe siècle.* Paris.

Cambi, Giovanni. 1785–86. *Istorie di Giovanni Cambi.* Edited by Fr. Ildefonso di San Luigi. Florence: vols 20–23 of *Delizie degli eruditi toscani.*

Cambiagi, Gaetano. 1788. *Memorie istoriche riguardanti le feste.* Florence.

Campbell, Malcolm. 1985. 'Il ritratto del Duca Alessandro de' Medici di Giorgio Vasari: contesto e significato.' In Garfagnini, 339–59.

Capasso, Carlo. 1924. *Paolo III, 1534–1549.* 2 vols. Messina.

Cappi, Davide. 1995. *Del Lungo editore di Dino Compagni: Il problema del testo della 'Cronica'.* Rome.

Capponi, Gino. 1875. *Storia della Repubblica di Firenze.* 2 vols. Florence.

Capwell, Tobias. 2011. *Masterpieces of European Arms and Armour in the Wallace Collection.* London.

Carteggio inedito d'artisti dei secoli XIV, XV, XVI. 1839–40. Edited by Johan Gaye. 3 vols. Florence.

Castiglione, Baldesar [Baldessare]. 1967. *The Book of the Courtier.* Translated by George Bull. Harmondsworth.

Cazzato, Vincenzo. 1985. 'Vasari e Carlo V: L'ingresso trionfale a Firenze del 1536.' In Garfagnini, 179–204.

Ceccheregli [Ceccherelli], Alessandro. 1564. *Delle attioni et sentenze del S. Alessandro De' Medici primo duca di Fiorenza.* Venice.

Cellini, Benvenuto. 1889. *The Life of Benvenuto Cellini.* Translated by J. A. Symonds. 3rd edition. London.

Cherubini, Giovanni, and Giovanni Fanelli. 1990. Eds. *Il Palazzo Medici Riccardi di Firenze.* Florence.

Cipolla, Carlo M. 1989. *Money in Sixteenth-Century Florence.* Berkeley.

Cohen, Simona. 2014. *Transformations of Time and Temporality in Medieval and Renaissance Art.* Leiden.

Coniglio, Giuseppe. 1980. 'I Medici, i fiorentini e il Viceregno.' In *Napoli nel Cinquecento . . .,* 7–24.

Conti, Cosimo. 1893. *La prima reggia di Cosimo I de' Medici nel Palazzo già della Signoria di Firenze.* Florence.

Cortés, Hernán. 1972. *Letters from Mexico.* Translated by A. R. Pagden. London.

Cotterill, H. B. 1919. *Italy from Dante to Tasso (1300–1600).* London.

Cox-Rearick, Janet. 1964. *The Drawings of Pontormo.* 2 vols. Cambridge, MA.

———. 1982. 'Themes of time and rule at Poggio a Caiano: The portico frieze of Lorenzo il Magnifico.' *Mitteilungen des Kunsthistorischen Institutes in Florenz* 26(2): 167–210.

Crews, Daniel A. 2003. 'Spanish Diplomacy and the Mysterious Death of Cardinal Ippolito de' Medici.' *Mediterranean Studies* 12: 103–10.

Croizat-Glazer, Yassana. 2013. 'The Role of Ancient Egypt in Masquerades at the Court of François Ier.' *Renaissance Quarterly* 66: 1206–49.

Crum, Roger J. 2001. 'Lessons from the Past: The Palazzo Medici as Political "Mentor" in Sixteenth-Century Florence.' In *The Cultural Politics of Duke Cosimo I de' Medici*, edited by Konrad Eisenbichler, 44–62. Aldershot.

Cummings, Anthony M. 1992. *The Politicized Muse: Music for Medici Festivals, 1512–1537*. Princeton, NJ.

———. 2004. *The Maecenas and the Madrigalist: Patrons, Patronage and the Origins of the Italian Madrigal*. Philadelphia.

Dall'Aglio, Stefano. 2011. *L'Assassinio del Duca: Esilio e morte di Lorenzino de' Medici*. Florence.

D'Amico, John F. 1983. *Renaissance Humanism in Papal Rome*. Baltimore.

De Caesaris, G. 1929. 'Alessandro de' Medici e Margherita d'Austria, duchi di Penne.' *Bollettino della R. Deputazione Abruzzese di Storia Patria* 20–21: 165–265.

Decroisette, Françoise. 1980. 'Fêtes religieuses, fêtes princières au XVIe siècle: Les Médicis et la fête de l'Annonciation à Florence.' In *Culture et religion en Espagne et en Italie aux XVe et XVIe siècles*. Documents et travaux de l'équipe de recherche culture et société au XVIe siècle 4. Abbeville.

Del Vita, Alessandro. 1944. *Figure del Cinquecento*.

Della Porta, Giovanni. 1644. *Della fisionomia dell'uomo: libri sei*. Venice.

Devonshire Jones, Rosemary. 1972a. *Francesco Vettori: Florentine Citizen and Medici Servant*. London.

———. 1972b. 'Lorenzo de' Medici, Duca d'Urbino "Signore" of Florence?' In *Studies in Machiavelli*, edited by Myron P. Gilmore. Florence.

Di Stefano, Roberto, and Silvana Di Stefano. 1980. 'Il potere e lo spazio nella Napoli cinquecentesca.' In *Napoli nel Cinquecento . . .*, 77–124.

Dizionario biografico degli italiani (DBI). Online at http://www.treccani.it/biografico.

Dizionario del cittadino, o sia ristretto storico, teorico e pratico del commercio, vol. 1. 1781. Venice.

Dohrn-van Rossum, Gerhard. 1996. *History of the Hour: Clocks and Modern Temporal Orders*. Chicago.

Domenichi, Lodovico. 1564. *Facetie, motti et burle di diversi Signori et persone private etc*. Florence.

Dumas, Alexandre. 2013. *Une nuit à Florence sous Alexandre de Médicis*. Online at http://www.alexandredumasetcompagnie.com/images/1.pdf/UneNuitAFlorence.PDF.

———. 2014. *Lorenzino*. Online at http://www.alexandredumasetcompagnie.com/images/1.pdf/Lorenzino.PDF.

Dumont, Georges Henri. 1999. *Marguerite de Parme: Bâtarde de Charles Quint (1522–1586): Biographie*. Brussels.

Dumont, Jean. 1726. *Corps universel diplomatique du droit des gens*. Amsterdam.

Dunning, Albert. 1970. *Die Staatsmotette 1480–1555*. Utrecht.

Earle, T. F., and K. J. P. Lowe. 2005. *Black Africans in Renaissance Europe*. Cambridge.

Eichberger, Dagmar, and Yvonne Bleyerveld. 2005. Eds. *Women of Distinction: Margaret of York, Margaret of Austria*. Leuven.

Enenkel, Karl A. E., and Paul J. Smith. 2007. Eds. *Early Modern Zoology: The Construction of Animals in Science, Literature and the Visual Arts*. Leiden.

Epstein, Steven. 2001. *Speaking of Slavery: Color, Ethnicity, and Human Bondage in Italy*. Ithaca, NY.

Espinosa, Aurelio. 2009. *The Empire of the Cities: Emperor Charles V, the Comunero Revolt, and the Transformation of the Spanish System*. Leiden.

Ettlinger, Helen S. 1994. 'Visibilis et Invisibilis: The Mistress in Italian Renaissance Court Society.' *Renaissance Quarterly* 47: 770–92.

Fabbri, Mario. 1975. *Il luogo teatrale di Firenze*. Milan.

Fabre, Michel. 1993. *From Harlem to Paris: Black American Writers in France, 1840–1980*. Urbana, Ill.

Falciani, Carlo, and Antonio Natali. 2010. Eds. *Bronzino: Artist and Poet at the Court of the Medici*. Florence.

———. 2014. Eds. *Pontormo and Rosso Fiorentino: Diverging Paths of Mannerism*. Florence.

Ferer, Mary Tiffany. 2012. *Music and Ceremony at the Court of Charles V: The Capilla Flamenca and the Art of Political Promotion*. Woodbridge.

Ferrai, Luigi Alberto. 1882. *Cosimo de' Medici Duca di Firenze. Saggio*. Bologna.

———. 1891. *Lorenzino de' Medici e la società cortigiana del Cinquecento*. Milan.

Ferretti, J. 1929–30. 'L'organizzazione militare toscana durante il governo di Alessandro e di Cosimo I.' *Rivista storica degli archivi toscani*, 1: 248–75; 2: 58–80, 133–52, 211–19.

ffolliott, Sheila. n.d. 'The Italian "Training" of Catherine de Medici: Portraits as Dynastic Narrative.' Online at http://www.courtstudies.org/pdf/The%20Italian%20Training.pdf.

Firpo, Massimo, and Salvatore Lo Re. 2005. 'Gli occhi azzurri di Alessandro de' Medici. Note su una copia di un celebre ritratto di Iacopo Pontormo.' *Mitteilungen Des Kunsthistorischen Institutes in Florenz* 49: 413–26.

Flandrin, Jean-Louis, and Massimo Montanari. 1999. Eds. *Food: A Culinary History from Antiquity to the Present*. Translated by Albert Sonnenfeld. New York.

Foresi, A. 1875. *La tomba di Lorenzo e di Alessandro de' Medici aperta il 1° marzo 1875*. Florence.

Fragnito, Gigliola. 1993. 'Cardinals' Courts in Sixteenth Century Rome.' *Journal of Modern History* 65: 26–56.

Fraser, Angus. 1992. *The Gypsies*. Oxford.

Frick, Carole Collier. 2002. *Dressing Renaissance Florence: Families, Fortunes and Fine Clothing*. Baltimore.

Gaisser, J. H. 1999. *Pierio Valeriano on the Ill Fortune of Learned Men: A Renaissance Humanist and His World*. Ann Arbor, MI.

———. 2005. 'Seeking Patronage under the Medici Popes: A Tale of Two Humanists.' In Gouwens and Reiss, 293–309.

Gambara, Veronica. 1879. *Rime e lettere*. Edited by Pio Mestica. Florence.

Garfagnini, Gian Carlo. 1985. Ed. *Giorgio Vasari: Tra decorazione ambientale e storiografia artistica*. Florence.

Gattoni, Maurizio. 2002. *Clemente VII e la geopolitica dello Stato Pontificio*. Vatican City.

Gennaioli, Riccardo. 2007. *Le gemme dei Medici al Museo degli Argenti: Cammei e intagli nelle collezioni di Palazzo Pitti*. Florence.

Gianneschi, M., and C. Sodini. 1979. 'Urbanistica e politica durante il principato di Alessandro de' Medici, 1532–37.' *Storia della città* 10: 5–34.

Gilbert, Felix. 1935. 'Alcuni discorsi di uomini politici fiorentini e la politica di Clemente VII per la restaurazione medicea.' *Archivio storico italiano* 93, no. 2, 3–24.

Giordani, Gaetano. 1842. *Cronaca della venuta e dimora del Sommo Pontefice Clemente VII in Bologna*. Bologna.

Giove, Teresa, and Alessandro Villone. 1994. 'Dallo studio al tesoro: Le gemme farnese da Roma a Capodimonte.' In *Le gemme Farnese*, edited by Carlo Gasparri. Naples.

Giovio, Paolo. 1555. *The Historie of the Legation or Ambassade of Greate Basilius Prince of Moscovia to Pope Clement the VII*. London.

———. 1556. *Ragionamento di Mons. Paolo Giovio sopra i motti & disegni d'arme, & d'amore*. Venice.

———. 1956. *Lettere*. Edited by G. G. Ferrero. Rome.

———. 2006. *Elogi degli uomini illustri*. Edited by Franco Minonzio. Translated by Andrea Guasparri and Franco Minonzio. Turin.

Goldthwaite, Richard. 2009. *The Economy of Renaissance Florence*. Baltimore.

Gotfredsen, Lise. 1999. *The Unicorn*. New York.

Gouwens, Kenneth, and Sheryl E. Reiss. 2005. *The Pontificate of Clement VII: History, Politics, Culture*. Aldershot.

Grieco, Allen J. 1999. 'Food and social classes in late medieval and Renaissance Italy.' In Flandrin and Montanari, 302–12.

Guicciardini, Francesco. 1857–67. *Opere inedite*. 10 vols. Florence.

———. 1925. *Lettere inedite di Francesco Guicciardini a Bartolomeo Lanfredini dalla fine dell'assedio di Firenze al secondo convegno di Clemente VII e di Carlo V.* Edited by André Otetea. Aquila.

———. 1967. *Storia d'Italia.* 5 vols. Bari.

Hahn, Thomas. 2001. 'The Difference the Middle Ages Makes: Color and Race before the Modern World.' *Journal of Medieval and Early Modern Studies* 31: 1–37.

Hale, J. R. 1968. 'The End of Florentine Liberty: The Fortezza da Basso.' In *Florentine Studies*, edited by Nicolai Rubinstein, 501–32. London.

———. 1977. *Florence and the Medici: The Pattern of Control.* London.

Hankins, James. 1992. 'Cosimo de' Medici as a Patron of Humanistic Literature.' In *Cosimo 'Il Vecchio' de' Medici, 1389–1464*, edited by Francis Ames-Lewis, 69–94. Oxford.

[al-Ḥasan ibn Muḥammad al-Wazzān.] 1837. *Il viaggio di Giovan Leone.* Edited by Giovambattista Ramusio. Venice.

Hayward, Maria. 2007. *Dress at the Court of Henry VIII.* Leeds.

Heng, G. 2011a. 'The Invention of Race in the European Middle Ages I: Race Studies, Modernity, and the Middle Ages.' *Literature Compass* 8: 315–31.

———. 2011b. 'The Invention of Race in the European Middle Ages II: Locations of Medieval Race.' *Literature Compass* 8: 332–50.

Hernando Sánchez, Carlos José. 2007. 'Naples and Florence in Charles V's Italy: Family, Court, and Government in the Toledo–Medici Alliance.' In *Spain in Italy: Politics, Society, and Religion 1500–1700*, edited by Thomas James Dandelet and John A. Marino, 135–80. Leiden.

Heywood, William. 1904. *Palio and Ponte: An Account of the Sports of Central Italy from the Age of Dante to the XXth Century.* London.

Hibbert, Christopher. 1979. *The Rise and Fall of the House of Medici.* Harmondsworth.

Hirschman, Charles. 2004. 'The Origins and Demise of the Concept of Race.' *Population and Development Review* 30: 385–415.

Hogenberg, Nikolas. 1532. *Gratae et laboribus aequae posteritati Caesareas. . . .* The Hague.

Hurtubise, Pierre. 1985. *Une famille-témoin: Les Salviati.* Vatican City.

Hyde, Helen. 2009. *Cardinal Bendinello Sauli and Church Patronage in Sixteenth-Century Italy.* Woodbridge.

Jacquot, Jean. 1975. Ed. *Fêtes et cérémonies au temps de Charles Quint.* 3 vols. Paris.

Jurdjevic, Mark. 2006. 'The Guicciardinian Moment: The Discorsi Palleschi, Humanism, and Aristocratic Republicanism in Sixteenth-Century Florence.' In *Humanism and Creativity in the Renaissance: Essays in Honor of Ronald G. Witt*, edited by Christopher Celenza and Kenneth Gouwens, 113–40. Leiden.

——. 2008. *Guardians of Republicanism: The Valori Family in the Florentine Renaissance*. Oxford: Oxford University Press.

Kaplan, Paul H. D. 1982. 'Titian's *Laura Dianti* and the Origins of the Motif of the Black Page in Portraiture.' *Antichità Viva* 21, no. 1, 11–18 and no. 4, 10–18.

——. 2005. 'Isabella d'Este and black African women.' In Earle and Lowe, 125–54.

——. 2010. 'Italy, 1490–1700.' In Bindman and Gates, 93–190.

——. 2011. 'Black Turks: Venetian Artists and Perceptions of Ottoman Ethnicity.' In *The Turk and Islam in the Western Eye, 1450–1750: Visual Imagery before Orientalism*, edited by James G. Harper, 41–66. Farnham.

Kent, F. W. 1987. 'Palaces, Politics and Society.' *I Tatti Studies* 2: 41–70.

Kline, Jonathan. 2011. 'Botticelli's Return of Persephone: On the Source and Subject of the Primavera.' *Sixteenth Century Journal* 42: 665–88.

Kuehn, Thomas. 2002. *Illegitimacy in Renaissance Florence*. Ann Arbor.

Lach, Donald F. 1965. *Asia in the Making of Europe, Volume II: A Century of Wonder. Book 1: The Visual Arts*. Chicago.

Landi, Giulio. 1574. *La descrittione de l'isola de La Madera*. Translated by Alemanio Fini. Piacenza.

Lando, Ortensio. 1994. *Commentario delle piu notabili e mostruose cose d'Italia ed altri luoghi*. Bologna.

Landucci, Luca. 1883. *Diario fiorentino dal 1450 al 1516*. Florence.

Landulfo, Agostino. 1536. *Le cose volgare di Messere Augostino Landulfo*. Florence.

Langdon, Gabrielle. 2006. *Medici Women: Portraits of Power, Love and Betrayal*. Toronto.

Langedijk, Karla. 1981. *The Portraits of the Medici: 15th–18th Centuries*. Florence.

Lawrance, Jeremy. 2001. 'Europe and the Turks in Spanish Literature of the Renaissance and Early Modern Period.' In *Culture and Society in Habsburg Spain*, edited by Nigel Griffin, Clive Griffin, Eric Southworth, and Colin Thompson. Woodbridge.

Lazzi, G., and G. Bigalli Lulla. 1992. 'Alessandro de' Medici e il Palazzo di Via Larga: L'inventario del 1531.' *Archivio storico italiano* 150: 1201–33.

Lefevre, R. 1986. *'Madama' Margherita d'Austria (1522–1586)*. Rome.

Legislazione Toscana raccolta e illustrata da Lorenzo Cantini. 1800–1808. Edited by Lorenzo Cantini. Florence.

Leti, Gregorio. 1700. *Vita dell'invittissimo imperadore Carlo V*. 4 vols. Amsterdam.

Lettere di Principi. 1581. Edited by G. Ruscelli. 3 vols. Venice.

Levy, Allison. 2006. *Re-Membering Masculinity in Early Modern Florence: Widowed Bodies, Mourning and Portraiture*. Aldershot.

Lo Re, Salvatore. 2006. *La crisi della libertà fiorentina*. Rome.

Lorenzo de' Medici At Home: The Inventory of the Palazzo Medici in 1491. 2013. Edited and translated by Richard Stapleford. University Park, PA.

Lowe, K. J. P. 1993. *Church and Politics in Renaissance Italy: The Life and Career of Cardinal Francesco Soderini, 1453–1524*. Cambridge.

———. 2005. 'The Stereotyping of Black Africans.' In Earle and Lowe, 17–47.

———. 2013. 'Visible Lives: Black Gondoliers and Other Black Africans in Renaissance Venice.' *Renaissance Quarterly* 66: 412–52.

Luzio, Alessandro. 1900. *Un pronostico satirico di Pietro Aretino*. Bergamo.

Machiavelli, Niccolò. 1984. *The Prince*. Translated by Peter Bondanella and Mark Musa. Oxford.

———. 1985. *The Comedies of Machiavelli*. Edited and translated by David Sices and James B. Atkinson. Hanover.

———. 1989. *The Chief Works and Others*. Translated by Allan H. Gilbert. 2 vols. Durham, NC.

Mallett, Michael. 1971. *The Borgias: The Rise and Fall of a Renaissance Dynasty*. London.

———, and Christine Shaw. 2012. *The Italian Wars, 1494–1559*. Harlow.

Maltby, William S. 2002. *The Reign of Charles V*. Basingstoke.

Mantini, Silvia. 2003. Ed. *Margherita d'Austria (1522–1586): Costruzioni politiche e diplomazia, tra corte Farnese e monarchia spagnola*. Rome.

Marguerite of Navarre. 1967. *Nouvelles*. Edited by Yves Le Hir. Paris.

Martelli, N. 1992. 'Stanze sopra il Poggio del Duca di Fiorenza.' In *Il Giardino di Prato. Lieti convegni e molli amori dell'500 pratese e fiorentino nelle testimonianze poetiche di Nicolò Martelli e Bindaccio Guizzelmi*, edited by E. Bogani. Prato.

Martini, Ferruccio. 1972. *Lorenzino de' Medici e il tirannicidio nel Rinascimento*. Rome.

Masi, Bartolomeo. 1906. *Ricordanze dal 1478 al 1526*. Edited by G. O. Corazzini. Florence.

Matthews-Grieco, Sara F. 2010. Ed. *The Erotic Cultures of Renaissance Italy*. Farnham.

McClung Hallman, Barbara. 2005. 'The "disastrous" pontificate of Clement VII: disastrous for Giulio de' Medici?' In Gouwens and Reiss, 29–40.

McIver, K. 2006. *Women, Art and Architecture in Northern Italy: Negotiating Power*. Aldershot.

McKee, S. 2008. 'Domestic Slavery in Renaissance Italy.' *Slavery and Abolition* 29: 305–26.

Medici, Lorenzino de'. 2004. *Apology for a Murder*. Translated by Andrew Brown. London.

———. 2005. *L'aridosia: Comédie en 5 actes*. Translated and edited by Marina Marietti. Paris.

Medici, Lorenzo de'. 1995. *The Autobiography of Lorenzo de' Medici the Magnificent: A Commentary on My Sonnets*. Translated by James Wyatt Cook. Binghamton, NY.

———. 2007. *Selected Poems and Prose*. Translated by Jon Thiem. Philadelphia.

Memorie di casa Valori. 2007. Edited by Lorenzo Polizzotto and Catherine Kovesi. Florence.

Menchini, Carmen. 2005. *Panegirici e vite di Cosimo I de' Medici tra storia e propaganda*. Florence.

Meserve, Margaret. 2008. *Empires of Islam in Renaissance Historical Thought*. Cambridge, MA.

Montevecchi, Alessandro. 1989. *Storici di Firenze: Studi su Nardi, Nerli e Varchi*. Bologna.

Moretti, G. E. 1940. 'Il Cardinale Ippolito de' Medici dal trattato di Barcellona alla morte, 1529–1535.' *Archivio storico italiano* 98, 137–78.

Munby, Julian. 2008. 'From Carriage to Coach: What Happened?' In *The Art, Science and Technology of Medieval Travel*, edited by Robert Bork and Andrea Kann, 41–53. Aldershot.

Musset, Alfred de. 1995. *Five Plays*. Edited by Claude Schumacher. Translated by Donald Watson et al. London.

———. 1998. *Lorenzaccio*. Edited by Derek F. Connon. Bristol.

Muzzarelli, Maria Giuseppina. 1999. *Guardaroba medievale: Vesti e società dal XIII al XVI Secolo*. Bologna.

Najemy, John M. 2006. *A History of Florence, 1200–1575*. Malden, MA.

Napoli nel Cinquecento e la Toscana dei Medici. 1980. Naples.

Nardi, Jacopo. 1838. *Istorie della città di Firenze*. Edited by L. Arbib. 2 vols. Florence.

Navagero, Andrea. 1563. *Il viaggio fatto in Spagna et in Francia*. Venice.

Négociations diplomatiques de la France avec la Toscane. 1865. 6 vols. Paris.

Nerli, Filippo de'. 1859. *Commentari dei fatti civili occorsi dentro la città di Firenze*. 2 vols. Trieste.

Nestor, Jean. 1564. *Histoire des hommes illustres de la maison de Medici*. Paris.

Nicasi, Giuseppe. 1916. *La famiglia Vitelli di Città di Castello e la repubblica fiorentina fino al 1504*. Perugia.

Noble, Mark. 1797. *Memoirs of the Illustrious House of Medici*. London.

Orieux, Jean. 1986. *Catherine de Médicis, ou La reine noire*. Paris.

Paganucci, L. 1875. *Parere intorno alle individualità dei due scheletri trovati nel mausoleo, ecc.* Florence.

Paoli, C. 1886. 'Per la venuta di Alessandro de' Medici.' *Miscellanea fiorentina di erudizione e storia* 1: 28.

Partner, Peter. 1976. *Renaissance Rome, 1500–1559: A Portrait of a Society*. Berkeley.

Pasquinate romane del Cinquecento. 1983. Edited by Valerio Marucci, Antonio Marzo and Angelo Romano. 2 vols. Rome.

Pastore, Alessandro. 2010. *Veleno: Credenze, crimini, saperi nell'Italia moderna*. Bologna.

Pastoureau, Michel. 2001. *The Devil's Cloth: A History of Stripes and Striped Fabric*. Translated by Jody Gladding. New York.

Peloso, Silvano. 2004. *Al di là delle colonne d'Ercole: Madera e gli arcipelaghi atlantici nelle cronache italiane di viaggio dell'Età delle Scoperte*. Viterbo.

Pelù, Paolo, and Olga Raffo. 2007. *Ricciarda Malaspina Cibo, Marchesa di Massa e Signora di Carrara, 1497–1553*. Modena.

Pérez de Tudela, Almudena, and Annemarie Jordan Gschwend. 2007. 'Renaissance Menageries. Exotic Animals and Pets at the Habsburg Courts in Iberia and Central Europe.' In Enenkel and Smith, 419–47.

Pieraccini, Gaetano. 1924. *La stirpe de' Medici di Cafaggiolo. Saggio di ricerche sulla trasmissione ereditaria dei caratteri biologici*. 3 vols. Florence.

Pius II. 1988. *Secret Memoirs of a Renaissance Pope*. Edited by Leona C. Gabel. Translated by Florence A. Gragg. London.

Plaisance, Michel. 1975. 'La politique culturelle de Côme Ier.' In Jacquot, vol. 3, 133–52.

Pontano, Giovanni Gioviano. 1999. *I libri delle virtù sociali*. Edited by Francesco Tateo. Rome.

Quinones, Ricardo J. 1986. 'The New Dynamic of Time in Renaissance Literature and Society.' In *Time: The Greatest Innovator: Timekeeping and Time Consciousness in Early Modern Europe*, edited by Rachel Doggett, 25–37. Washington DC.

Randolph, Adrian W. B. 2002. *Engaging Symbols: Gender, Politics and Public Art in Fifteenth-Century Florence*. New Haven & London.

Rastrelli, Modesto. 1781. *Storia d'Alessandro de' Medici primo duca di Firenze*. 2 vols. Florence.

Rawlings, Helen. 2002. *Church, Religion and Society in Early Modern Spain*. Basingstoke.

Rebecchini, Guido. 1998. 'Fonti mantovane sul conflitto fra Alessandro de' Medici e i fuoriusciti fiorentini durante la visita a Napoli di Carlo V nel 1536.' *Archivio storico italiano* 156: 517–28.

———. 2010. 'Un Altro Lorenzo': Ippolito de' Medici tra Firenze e Roma 1511–1535. Venice.

———. In press. 'Vasari, Alessandro de' Medici, le arti e la politica della corte.'

Reiss, Sheryl E. 1992. 'Cardinal Giulio de' Medici as a patron of art, 1513–1523.' D.Phil. diss., Princeton.

Relazioni degli ambasciatori veneti al Senato. 1839–63. Edited by Eugenio Albèri. 3rd series; 15 vols. Florence.

Repetti, E. 1833–46. *Dizionario geografico–fisico–storico della Toscana.* 6 vols. Florence.

Reumont, Alfred von. 1866. *La jeunesse de Catherine de Médicis.* Edited by Armand Baschet. Paris.

Richardson, Carol. 2009. *Reclaiming Rome: Cardinals in the Fifteenth Century.* Leiden.

Ridolfi, R. 1964. 'Francesco Guicciardini e Cosimo I. *Archivio storico italiano* 122: 567–606.

Rivers, W. Napoleon. 1934. 'Why Negroes Should Study Romance Languages and Literatures.' *The Journal of Negro History* 19: 118–36.

Rogers, J. A. 1972. *World's Great Men of Color.* 2 vols. New York.

Romano, Dennis. 1996. *Housecraft and Statecraft: Domestic Service in Renaissance Venice, 1400–1600.* Baltimore.

Romoli, Domenico. 1560. *La singolare dottrina di M. D. Romoli sopranominato Panonto.* Venice.

Rossi, Agostino. 1896. *Francesco Guicciardini e il governo fiorentino dal 1527 al 1540.* 2 vols. Bologna.

Rosso, Gregorio. 1635. *Historia delle cose di Napoli sotto l'imperio di Carlo Quinto.* Naples.

Roth, Cecil. 1925. *The Last Florentine Republic.* London.

Rubin, Patricia L. 1995. *Giorgio Vasari: Art and History.* New Haven.

Rubinstein, Nicolai. 1995. *The Palazzo Vecchio, 1298–1532: Government, architecture and imagery in the civic palace of the Florentine Republic.* Oxford.

Rubys, Claude de. 1604. 'Sommaire discours de l'ancienne noblesse de la maison illustre des Medici de Florence.' In his *Histoire véritable de la ville de Lyon.* 516–527. Lyon.

Ruff, Julius R. 2001. *Violence in Early Modern Europe, 1500–1800.* Cambridge.

Ruggiero, G. 1985. *The Boundaries of Eros: Sex Crime and Sexuality in Renaissance Venice.* Oxford.

Saletta, Vincenzo. 1976. 'Il viaggio in Italia di Carlo V (1535–36).' *Studi Meridionali* 9–11: 286–327, 452–79; 78–114, 268–92, 420–42; 329–41.

Sandoval, Prudencio de. 1618. *Historia de la vida y hechos del Emperador Carlos V.* 2 vols. Pamplona.

Sanuto, Marin. 1969. *I diarii.* Edited by Rinaldo Fulin, Federico Stefani, Nicolò Barozzi, Guglielmo Berchet and Marco Allegri. 59 vols. Bologna.

Scalini, Mario, and Luisa Berretti. 2010. *Archibugi alla prova del Gran Principe.* Florence.

Schomburg, Arthur. 1931. 'Alessandro, First Duke of Florence, the Negro Medici.' *The Crisis* 38 (December): 421–22.

————. 1963. 'Alessandro, First Duke of Florence: The Negro Medici.' *Negro Digest* 12 (September): 24–27.

Schraven, Minou. 2014. *Festival Funerals in Early Modern Italy: The Art and Culture of Conspicuous Commemoration*. Burlington, VT.

Segni, Bernardo. 1830. *Storie fiorentine dall'anno 1527–1555 colla vita di Niccolo Capponi*. 3 vols. Livorno.

Segre, Arturo. 1912. *Un registro di lettere del Cardinale Ercole Gonzaga (1535–36)*. Turin.

Setton, Kenneth. 1976. *The Papacy and the Levant (1204–1571)*. 4 vols. Philadelphia.

Shearman, John. 1975. 'The Florentine Entrata of Leo X, 1515.' *Journal of the Warburg and Courtauld Institutes* 38: 136–54.

Sickel, Lothar. 2008. 'Ippolito de' Medici und das Problem seiner Geburt in Urbino.' *Quellen und Forschungen aus Italienischen Archiven und Bibliotheken* 88: 310–33.

Simoncelli, Paolo. 2003. 'Florentine Fuoriusciti at the Time of Bindo Altoviti.' In *Raphael, Cellini and a Renaissance Banker*, edited by Alan Chong, Donatella Pegazzano, and Dimitrios Zikos, 285–328. Boston.

————. 2006. *Fuoriuscitismo repubblicano fiorentino: 1530–54*. Milan.

Simonetta, Marcello. 2014. *Volpi e Leoni: I Medici, Machiavelli e la rovina d'Italia*. Milan.

————. 2016. 'Il ruolo di Francesco Guicciardini nel Tumulto del venerdi (26 aprile 1527) secondo alcune testimonianze extra-fiorentine'. *Laboratoire italien*. Forthcoming, issue 17.

Simons, P. 2008. 'Disegno and Desire in Pontormo's Alessandro de' Medici.' *Renaissance Studies* 22: 650–68.

Sinnette, Elinor Des Verney. 1989. *Arthur Alfonso Schomburg, Black Bibliophile and Collector: A Biography*. Detroit.

Siraisi, Nancy. 1990. *Medieval and Early Renaissance Medicine*. Chicago.

Soykut, Mustafa. 2001. *Image of the 'Turk' in Italy: A History of the 'Other' in Early Modern Europe: 1453–1683*. Berlin.

Spagnoletti, Angelantonio. 2003. 'Matrimoni e politiche dinastiche in Italia tra gli anni trenta e gli anni cinquanta del Cinquecento.' In *L'Italia di Carlo V*, edited by Francesca Cantù and Maria Antonietta Visceglia, 97–113. Rome.

Spallanzani, Marco. 1994. *Ceramiche alla corte dei Medici nel Cinquecento*. Modena.

———— and Giovanna Gaeta Bertelà. 1992. *Libro d'inventario dei beni di Lorenzo il Magnifico*. Florence.

Sperandio, Francesco Paolo. 1790. *Sabina sagra e profana antica e moderna*. Rome.

Spicer, J. 2012. *Revealing the African Presence in Renaissance Europe*. Baltimore.

Spinelli, Riccardo, and Giulia Calvi. 2008. Eds. *Le donne Medici nel sistema europea delle corti: XVI–XVIII secolo: Atti del convegno internazionale, Firenze, San Domenico di Fiesole, 6–8 ottobre 2005*. Florence.

Springer, Carolyn. 2010. *Armour and Masculinity in the Italian Renaissance*. Toronto.

Staffetti, Luigi. 1892. *Giulio Cybò-Malaspina, marchese di Massa. Studio storico, Etc.* Modena.

———. 1894. *Il Cardinale Innocenzo Cybo: Contributo alla storia della politica e dei costumi italiani, nella prima metà del secolo XVI*. Florence.

———. 1908. *Il libro di ricordi della famiglia Cybo*. Genoa.

Stephens, J. N. 1983. *The Fall of the Florentine Republic, 1512–1530*. Oxford.

———. 1976. 'Pope Clement VII, a Florentine Debtor.' *Bulletin of the Institute for Historical Research* 49: 138–41.

———. 1978. 'Giovanbattista Cibo's Confession.' In *Essays Presented to Myron P. Gilmore*, edited by S. Bertelli and G. Ramakus, 2: 255–69. Florence.

———. 1984. 'L'infanzia fiorentina di Caterina de' Medici, regina di Francia.' *Archivio storico italiano* 142: 421–36.

Stinger, Charles L. 1998. *The Renaissance in Rome*. Bloomington, IN.

Strehlke, Carl Brandon. 1985. 'Pontormo, Alessandro de' Medici, and the Palazzo Pazzi.' *Philadelphia Museum of Art Bulletin* 81: 3–15.

———. 2004. *Pontormo, Bronzino, and the Medici: The Transformation of the Renaissance Portrait in Florence*. University Park, PA.

Taylor, Valerie. 2005. 'Banquet Plate and Renaissance Culture: A Day in the Life.' *Renaissance Studies* 19: 621–33.

Tenhove, Nicolas. 1797. *Memoirs of the House of Medici*. Bath.

Tomas, Natalie. 2000. 'Alfonsina Orsini de' Medici and the "Problem" of a Female Ruler in Early Sixteenth-Century Florence.' *Renaissance Studies* 14: 70–90.

———. 2003. *The Medici Women: Gender and Power in Renaissance Florence*. New Hampshire.

Ughi, G. 1849. 'Cronica di Firenze o compendio storico delle cose di Firenze dall'anno MDI al MDXLVII.' *Archivio storico italiano*, I, Appendice VII: 97–274.

Vannucci, Marcello. 1984. *Lorenzaccio: Lorenzino de' Medici: Un ribelle in famiglia*. Rome.

Varchi, Benedetto. 1838. *Storie fiorentine*. Edited by L. Arbib. 3 vols. Florence.

Varillas, Antoine. 1685. *Les anecdotes de Florence*. The Hague.

Vasari, Giorgio. 1878–1885. *Opere*. Edited by Gaetano Milanesi. 9 vols. Florence.

Virgili, Antonio. 1881. *Francesco Berni*. Florence.

Waldman, Louis Alexander. 2004. *Baccio Bandinelli and Art at the Medici Court: A Corpus of Early Modern Sources*. Philadelphia.

Walker-Oakes, Vanessa. 2001. 'Representing the Perfect Prince: Pontormo's Alessandro de' Medici.' *Comitatus: A Journal of Medieval and Renaissance Studies* 32: 127–46.

Wallace, William E. 1994. *Michelangelo at San Lorenzo: The Genius as Entrepreneur.* Cambridge.

Weaver, Elissa. 1984. 'Inediti vaticani di Ippolito de' Medici'. *Filologia e critica* 9: 122–35.

Wilson, Stephen. 1998. *The Means of Naming: A Social History.* London.

Young, George Frederick. 1911. *The Medici.* 2nd edition. London.

Zecchino, Francesco. 2002. 'La Villa di Poggioreale, residenza degli aragonesi a Napoli.' *Delpinoa* 44: 3–16.

Zorzi, Elvira Garbero. 1987. 'Le "nozze" medicee del 1533 e le forme teatrali del principato.' In *La fête et l'écriture: Théâtre de cour, cour-théâtre en Espagne et en Italie, 1450–1530*, 277–91. Aix-en-Provence.

NOTES

NOTE ON MONEY

1. Cipolla. Fragnito, p. 46. Bullard, p. 161; Goldthwaite, pp. 364, 406, 568. Mallett and Shaw, pp. 209–10.

PROLOGUE

1. Most of this is a loose translation of the account in Varchi, vol. 3, pp. 185–88. It also incorporates material from Medici (2004), p. 13, Nerli, p. 287 and Ughi, pp. 191–92. For background: Dall'Aglio, pp. 3–10. • 2. Varchi, vol. 3, p. 182. • 3. Medici (2004), pp. 3, 9. For fuller discussion see the afterword. • 4. Heng (2011a), pp. 316–18. Bartlett, p. 44. • 5. Oxford English Dictionary, at www. oed.com. Landi (a modern edition of Landi is included in Peloso). • 6. Lowe (2013), pp. 415–19. • 7. Hirschman, pp. 399–400. • 8. Brackett. Attentive readers will note that I disagree with some aspects of this essay, but it nonetheless provides a valuable starting-point for discussion of Alessandro. • 9. See Bindman and Gates; http://www.vam.ac.uk/content/articles/a/africans-in-medieval-and-renaissance-art-duke-alessandro-de-medici [accessed 3 July 2015]; and Spicer.

1

1. ASF, Copialettere di Goro Gheri, 4, fol. 284r. • 2. ASF, Copialettere di Goro Gheri, 4, fols 289v–325r; 5, fol. 4v. • 3. ASF, Copialettere di Goro Gheri, 5, fols 13v–31v. • 4. ASF, Copialettere di Goro Gheri, 5, fols 46r, 47r. Butters (1985), p. 306. • 5. Giovio (2006), p. 887. • 6. Florentine coppersmith Bartolomeo Masi places him as Lorenzo's son (Masi, p. 243); so does Venetian diplomat Marco Foscari (*Relazioni*, ser. 2, vol. 3, p. 128); so does Florentine historian Giovanni Cambi (Cambi, vol. 22, p. 273, cit. in Pieraccini, p. 399). Masi makes Alessandro slightly older, with a birthdate in 1510, but Foscari and Cambi's accounts fit the 1511–12 dates. A contemporary report of the Treaty of Barcelona in Sanuto, vol. 51, col. 128, describes Alessandro as the pope's

nephew (in the generic Italian sense), as does the text of the treaty itself: see Dumont, vol. 4.2, p. 3. Even among the next generation of texts, the majority is still clearly with Lorenzo: Nardi, vol. 2, p. 11, Nerli, p. 140, and Varchi, vol. 1, p. 48, Guicciardini (1967), vol. 5, p. 261 and Adriani, vol. 1, p. 10 say Lorenzo. Segni, vol. 1, pp. 8, 163 is inconsistent: he first says Lorenzo but then suggests the question is open. A couple of letters allude to a relationship between Giulio and a courtesan at around the time of Alessandro's conception, but given the relative acceptance of clerical bastards in the period it seems unlikely that Cardinal Giulio would have gone to such elaborate lengths to pretend his own son was the child of another family member. Later on, the fact that Alessandro was acknowledged as Lorenzo's son made it easier to argue that he should follow his father as ruler of Florence, but in 1519 no one expected that. See Reiss, pp. 130–31, notes 123 and 124, for the letters. • 7. Giovanni Cambi, author of a history of Florence, has her as one of Lorenzo's slaves. (Cambi died in 1535 before Alessandro's assassination, which makes his account particularly valuable.) Cambi, vol. 22, p. 273; for date of death: *DBI*. Bernardo Segni, who entered Medici service during Alessandro's lifetime, wrote that his mother was a slave called Anna. Segni, vol. 1, p. 163. A Venetian ambassador, Antonio Soriano, writing in 1531, described her as a *serva* – a word that can mean either servant or slave. *Relazioni*, ser. 2, vol. 3, p. 281. (On the lack of distinction see the 1612 dictionary of the Accademia della Crusca, online at www.lessicografia.it, and Epstein, p. 43.) The assassin Lorenzino used the same description. Paolo Giovio, a particularly authoritative source on account of his closeness to Clement VII, also put her in Alfonsina's household, describing her in Latin as *ancilla*, a word that medieval dictionaries glossed as a female slave. Giovio (2006), p. 887; Epstein, pp. 20–21. Varchi, vol. 3, p. 287. • 8. Nardi, vol. 2, p. 276. Busini, p. 276. Varchi, vol. 3, p. 97. On Collevecchio and the Orsini: Sperandio, p. 153. • 9. Martini, p. 38. The date given in the letter is 1529 but if the writer followed Florentine style and dated from Lady Day (25 March) that would be 1528 modern style. • 10. Rossi was sceptical, vol. 2, pp. 187–88; so was Roth: 'a most curious human document if authentic,' p. 108, n. 3. It should be in ASF, MAP, filza 126. The letter was first published in 1882 by Ferruccio Martini, in a book that is deeply hostile to Alessandro. Martini claimed it was evidence for Alessandro's mistreatment of his mother, although it does not prove anything of the sort. Martini said he had been told about it by a fellow scholar, Isidore Del Lungo, who had found it in the Medici Archive. Del Lungo was a respected scholar who made many important contributions to Italian history, but he did not have the benefit of modern philological techniques used to identify the provenance of documents, on which see

Cappi. The letter was recorded in an inventory of the Archive in 1963, but has been missing since the digitisation project of 1997–99. In the absence of the original, and because modern scholarship has shown other transcriptions in Martini's book to be unreliable (Brancato, p. 25), I am wary about drawing too many conclusions from this letter. Even assuming it is what it seems to be, all it gives us is a name: the rest of the information in it can be derived from other sources for Alessandro's life. • **11.** ASF, MAP, filza 157, c. 107r. The word I have given as 'house-girl' is tricky to transcribe but I read it as 'la domi[cul]a': for definition see Romano, p. xxiv. • **12.** ASV, Miscellanea, Arm. II, 49, fol. 117r. • **13.** Kuehn, p. 142. Ruggiero, pp. 101–2. • **14.** Hibbert, pp. 95–96. • **15.** Bono (2010), p. 237; Bono (1999), pp. 35–36. Beloch, p. 496. • **16.** Epstein, pp. 167, 187–88. Bono (2010), pp. 246, 245, 240. McKee, p. 308, although this article deals principally with the period before 1500. Lowe (2013), p. 421. • **17.** Baker (2011), pp. 508–10. Two black figures can be clearly seen in the painting; the ethnicity of a third figure, in shadow, is indistinct. • **18.** Minnich, p. 283. • **19.** Rebecchini (2010), pp. 19–20. In a notarial document of December 1524 he was described as 'over fourteen, or a little younger such that it should not impede the oath below'. The caveat suggests he was not, in fact, yet fourteen. ASF, Notarile Antecosimiano, 13243, fols 280r–282r. • **20.** Rebecchini (2010), p. 21. • **21.** Partner, pp. 195–96; Stinger, pp. 97–98. ASF, MAP 107, doc 3, c. 3r–v. • **22.** Shearman, especially p. 141. • **23.** On Lorenzo in government, see Devonshire Jones (1972b). • **24.** www.newadvent.org/cathen/01206c.htm. • **25.** Sanuto, vol. 26, cols 368, 379; vol. 27, cols 144, 387 • **26.** ASF, MAP 159, doc. 642, c. 650 bis r. Background: Haas, pp. 130–53. • **27.** ASF, MAP, filza 132, c. 36v ASF, Copialettere di Goro Gheri 4, fol. 257r. Busini, p. 227, says Alessandro was never recognised by Lorenzo as his son, nor by Alfonsina as her grandson. Del Vita, pp. 130–1, citing Nardi. • **28.** Tomas (2000), p. 86; Butters (1985), p 279. *DBI* (entry for Lorenzo, duke of Urbino). • **29.** Baker (2013), p. 13. For background on the Medici women: Tomas (2003). • **30.** A copy of the legitimation document is in ASMs, Archivio Cibo–Malaspina, b. 477. See Sickel, p. 322, cited by Rebecchini (2010). • **31.** ASF, MS 433, cited by Kuehn, p. 174. Titled 'Spurii legittimati' and compiled around or after 1676, giving names of legitimised Florentine bastards, this includes Giovanni delle Bande Nere, Alessandro and Ippolito. Kuehn, pp. 167–205 deals with broader questions around legitimisation; for Venice: Romano, p. 53. • **32.** Sanuto, vol. 27, col. 283. • **33.** Sanuto, vol. 27, cols 298, 353. Leo had no motivation here to pretend that Alessandro was Lorenzo's son rather than Cardinal Giulio's. • **34.** Ceccherelli, fol. 42r. • **35.** Machiavelli (1989), vol. 1, 106–15, discussed in Jurdjevic (2006), pp. 119–21. For an introduction to Machiavelli's relations with the Medici, see Butters (2010). • **36.** Giovio (2006), p. 887. Busini, p. 227.

Alfonsina did not, however, leave Alessandro a legacy when she died in 1520: ASF, MAP, filza 157, c. 107r.

2

1. Partner, pp. 196–97, 118, 120–21. D'Amico, p. 42. • 2. Lowe (1993), pp. 104–13 and Hyde, pp. 131–48. • 3. Bausi. • 4. *Pasquinate*, vol. 1, n. 357. Written at the point of Adrian VI's election. • 5. Tomas (2000), p. 86. • 6. Castiglione, p. 291. Rebecchini (2010), p. 27. • 7. Sanuto, vol. 32, p. 326. • 8. ASC, AO, Serie I, Corrispondenza 93, fasc. 4, nn. 610, 682. Mallett and Shaw, p. 142. Guicciardini (1967), vol. 4, p. 84. Jurdjevic (2006), p. 126. • 9. De Caesaris, p. 169. Guicciardini (1967), vol. 4, p. 84, gives the figure of ten thousand. Reputation: Cambi, vol. 22, p. 273. The title is used in ASV, A. A., Arm. I-XVIII, no. 3311. • 10. Sanuto, vol. 35, col. 422. • 11. Sanuto, vol. 35, col. 255; vol. 36, cols 213, 268. • 12. Varchi, vol. 1, p. 64. Cambi, vol. 22, pp. 264–65, cit. Rebecchini (2010), p. 30. • 13. Kaplan (1982); Kaplan (2005), p. 134. Lowe (2005). • 14. Sanuto, vol. 38, col. 251; vol. 40, col. 554. • 15. ASF, Copialettere di Goro Gheri 4, fol. 359v. • 16. Rebecchini (2010), pp. 32–33. Vannucci, pp. 30, 37, 40–1. • 17. Varchi, vol. 1, p. 321 tells the story but notes there is no evidence that Michelangelo said such a thing. See Kent, p. 67; Stephens (1983), p. 224; Kuehn, p. 140. • 18. Vasari, vol. 8, p. 233. • 19. ASF, MAP, filza 126, cc. 107r, 108r, 109r, 110r. For background: Scalini and Berretti, pp. 5–11. • 20. ASV, Armadio XL, 11, fol. 34r, no. 46; fol. 35r, no. 49. • 21. Varchi, vol. 1, p. 65. Rebecchini (2010), p. 32, citing Rastrelli, vol. 1, p. 14. Nerli, p. 142. • 22. Rebecchini (2010), pp. 27–8. Gaisser (1999); Gaisser (2005). Vasari, vol. 5, p. 273. Both portraits are now lost. • 23. *Relazioni*, ser. 2, vol. 3, p. 129. • 24. Sanuto, vol. 44, cols 12, 472.

3

1. Hibbert, pp. 38, 37. Pius, p. 103. • 2. Pius, p. 102. • 3. Guicciardini (1857–67), vol. 3, p. 91. • 4. Najemy, p. 374. Stephens (1976), p. 139. • 5. Sanuto, vol. 44, col. 582. • 6. Sanuto, vol. 44, cols 580–83. Simonetta (2016). • 7. On Guicciardini's involvement see Simonetta (2016). Lo Re, p. 33. Roth, pp. 341–42. • 8. Sanuto, vol. 44, col. 583. • 9. Roth, p. 31 and p. 36 n. 84, citing ASF, MAP 126, c. 89r. • 10. Sanuto, vol. 44, cols 581–82. • 11. Baker (2013), pp. 269–70. Simonetta (2016). • 12. Varchi, vol. 1, p. 123. • 13. ASMs, Card. Cybo 3, insert 19; for Ridolfi see *Relazioni*, ser. 2, vol. 3, p. 280. Roth, p. 40. • 14. Simonetta (2014), pp. 279–85, 297–9. Varchi, vol. 1, pp. 128–36, vol. 3, p. 4. Roth, pp. 42–45. • 15. Varchi, vol. 1, p. 136. Stephens (1984), pp. 429, 433, and ffolliott. Vannucci, p. 45. • 16. Roth, pp. 45–50. • 17. ASMs, Card. Cybo 3; 17/5/1527; Rebecchini (2010), p. 50. Rastrelli, p. 32. Sanuto, vol. 45, cols 156, 278; Staffetti (1894), pp.

73–74. Unnumbered letter of 23/7/1527 in ASMo, Carteggio Ambasciatori, Firenze, b. 13. • **18.** McClung Hallman, p. 36. Sanuto, vol. 46, col. 347. Rebecchini (2010), pp. 49–50. Sanuto, vol. 49, col. 10. • **19.** Gaisser (2005), p. 307. Gaisser (1999), pp. 18–19. Rebecchini (2010), p. 51. • **20.** ASMn, AG 1375; 1528, Diversi; unnumbered letter of 2/9/1528. • **21.** ASF, MAP 126, c. 111r. ASMn, AG 1375; 1528, Diversi; unnumbered letter of 21/9/1528; AG 2931, lib. 295, n. 174 (c. 71v). • **22.** ASMn, AG 1375, 1528, Diversi; unnumbered letters of of 29/9/1528 (joint 'thank you' from Ippolito and Alessandro) and 15/10/1528 (Ippolito on hunting). • **23.** Ippolito's 'Exhortation to the Hunt' is in ASV, Misc. Arm. II 78, fols 317r–333v. Cellini, p. 116. • **24.** Sanuto, vol. 47, col. 359. McClung Hallman, p. 38. Sanuto, vol. 49, col. 218. • **25.** Pasquinate, vol. 1, pp. 368–69, n. 375. This must predate Armellini's death in January 1528. Background: Simonetta, pp. 195–96. • **26.** Biblioteca Nazionale Marciana, Codices Italiani VII 1043 (=7616), fol. 139v. McClung Hallman, p. 38, citing Sanuto, vol. 49, col. 218.

4

1. Sanuto, vol. 49, col. 328. ASMn, AG 878, c. 16r, cit. Rebecchini (2010), p. 56. *Lettere di principi*, vol. 2, fol. 155v. • **2.** Rebecchini (2010), p. 61. • **3.** Nardi, vol. 2, p. 162; Varchi, vol. 1, p. 379. *Relazioni*, ser. 2, vol. 3, p. 129. Moretti, p. 146. • **4.** Sanuto, vol. 50, cols 213, 320. Mirandas, at http://www2.fiu.edu/~mirandas/bios1529-ii.htm#Medici [accessed 13 June 2015]. • **5.** Cellini, pp. 108–16. Cellini places these events in 1529, but says this was not long after Alessandro's promotion to duke of Penne (1522). 1529 certainly seems more likely: Alessandro was in Rome early that year, and the idea of a sixteen- or seventeen-year-old Alessandro with a gang of bravi is more plausible than the idea that Alessandro as a ten-year-old had this sort of entourage. • **6.** McClung Hallman, p. 39. • **7.** ASF, MAP 159, c. 167 IIr. Some sources give a lower figure but it is 20,000 in the contract. Sanuto, vol. 51, cols 80, 98, 106, 107, 110, 128, 130, 137, 144; Guicciardini, vol. 5, p. 261. Lefevre, p. 39. • **8.** Dumont, p. 11; Lefevre, p. 23. • **9.** Ferer, p. 41; Eichberger, p. 49. • **10.** *Pasquinate*, vol. 1, pp. 381–82, n. 387. • **11.** Belardini (2003), p. 25; Lefevre, pp. 29–30. For background on bastard children and dynastic marriages in Italy see Spagnoletti, pp. 105–6; Bestor; Ettlinger. • **12.** Sanuto, vol. 51, col. 243, cit. Rebechini (2010), p. 63. • **13.** Sanuto, vol. 51, col. 414. • **14.** Sanuto, vol. 51, col. 515; vol. 52, cols 192, 262. • **15.** Giordani, p. 93. Guicciardini, vol. 5, p. 284. • **16.** Ruff, p. 123. Staffetti (1894), p. 140; Staffetti (1908), p. 295; Rebecchini (2010), pp. 64–5, citing ASMo, AE, Ambasciatori, Roma, b. 33, fasc. 215, ii, lett. 19, c. 3. • **17.** ASMs, Appendice all'archivio Cybo–Malaspina, Memorie della famiglia Cybo, fol. 58v. • **18.** *Pasquinate*, vol. 1, p. 398, n. 398; p. 372, n. 380; p. 399, n. 399. • **19.** ASV, Camera Apostolica, Diversa

Cameralia 84, fol. 98r–v. • **20.** Sanuto, vol. 52, col. 308. • **21.** ASMn, AG 1153, c. 168r. • **22.** Sanuto, vol. 52, col. 477. • **23.** Sanuto, vol. 52, cols 563–64.

5

1. ASMn, AG 1153, c. 232v; Sanuto, vol. 52, col. 604. • **2.** Sanuto, vol. 52, col. 628. • **3.** Sanuto, vol. 52, col. 639. Hogenberg, p. 13. • **4.** Giordani, p. 154; Leti, part 1, p. 481. • **5.** ASMn, AG 1153, cc. 19r, 38v, 45r–v. Roth, pp. 176–77. • **6.** ASMn, AG 1153, cc. 79v, 140r. • **7.** Guicciardini, vol. 5, p. 284; Giordani, p. 52; Moretti, p. 144. • **8.** Roth, pp. 176–77. • **9.** ASV, Miscellanea Arm. II, 78, fols. 291r–92v. Background: Weaver. On the Valori family and Bartolomeo's relationship with the Medici, see Jurdjevic (2008), esp. pp. 150–53. • **10.** Baker (2013), p. 128, citing Aldobrandini et al. (1857) and Ughi, pp. 156–57. Sanuto, vol. 53, cols 46–48. Varchi, vol. 2, pp. 230–26. • **11.** Varchi, vol. 2, pp. 274–75, p. 225. Knecht, p. 11. • **12.** Roth, pp. 264, 261. • **13.** Lo Re, p. 141; Simoncelli (2006), p. 18. For an English summary of Simoncelli's work see Simoncelli (2003). • **14.** Varchi, vol. 2, pp. 366–68; *Legislazione Toscana*, vol. 1, pp. 32–33; Nerli, pp. 244–46. • **15.** Varchi, vol. 2, p. 370. Guicciardini, pp. 278–99. Guicciardini (1925), pp. 3–4, cited in Devonshire Jones (1972a), pp. 230–31. • **16.** ASV, A. A. Arm. I-XVIII, 3114, fols 15r–17v (on some accounts the Italians had to settle for forty-six thousand); Devonshire Jones (1972a), pp. 227–28. Wage comparison: Mallett and Shaw, p. 210. • **17.** Lo Re, p. 144. Settimanni, fol. 61r. • **18.** Baker (2013), p. 138. Simoncelli (2006), p. 20; *DBI* (Silvestro Adobrandini); Varchi, vol. 2, pp. 405–10. • **19.** ASF, CS I / 335, fol. 82r. • **20.** Nerli, pp. 248–49; Baker (2009), pp. 463–64. • **21.** Sanuto, vol. 53, cols 514, 526, 543, 551.

6

1. Relazioni, ser. 2, vol. 3, p. 268. Nardi, vol. 2, p. 334. • **2.** Ceccherelli, fol. 58v. • **3.** Epstein, pp. 23, 105. Della Porta, p. 254. • **4.** Varchi, vol. 1, pp. 379–80. • **5.** Rebecchini (2010), pp. 67–68. Butters (1985), pp. 237, 265. • **6.** ASMn, AG 440, cc. 66v, 94v, 110r. • **7.** Sanuto, vol. 54, col. 97; ASMn, AG 440, c. 126r. • **8.** ASV, A. A. Arm. I-XVIII, no. 3311. Sanuto, vol. 54, cols 134–35. • **9.** *Négociations*, vol. 3, pp. 5–7. See also Simoncelli (2006), pp. 38, 184–85. • **10.** ASMn, AG 567, no. 2/I, unnumbered letter of 11/1/1531, also in Sanuto, vol. 54, cols 271, 275. • **11.** Maltby, p. 42; Lefevre, p. 51. ASMn, AG 567, no. 4; Sanuto, vol. 54, col. 300. Belardini (2008), p. 173. • **12.** ASMn, AG 567, letter no. 5 of 1/2/1531; also in Sanuto, vol. 54, col. 301. This 'Pan Onto' is probably to be identified with Domenico Romoli, Florentine author of a book on domestic economy published in 1560, who was known by that nickname. ASF, GM 3, fol. 4v. • **13.** Romoli, fol. 2r.

7

1. ASMn, AG 567, letter no. 7, 7/2/1531, Brussels. Cummings (1992), p. 140; Lo Re, p. 149. • 2. ASMn, AG 567, no. 11. • 3. ASMn, AG 567, no. 12; Sanuto, vol. 54, col. 342. • 4. Sanuto, vol. 54, col. 422. Castiglione, p. 116. ASC, AO, Serie I, Corrispondenza, b. 72, fasc. 2, no. 210, fol. iv. • 5. ASV, A. A. Arm. I-XVIII, no. 3311. Sanuto, vol. 54, cols 478–79. • 6. Sanuto, vol. 54, col. 478. ASF, MAP 159, c. 259r. • 7. ASMn, AG 880, c. 385r, cit. Rebecchini (2010), p. 187. • 8. Giovio (2006), p. 870. • 9. Cortés, pp. 110–11, discussed in Belozerskaya, pp. 149–52. Pérez de Tudela and Gschwend. • 10. Domenichi, pp. 171–72, cit. in Moretti, p. 140. • 11. Rebecchini (2010), pp. 68–9; Moretti, p. 147, citing for the quotation ASF, CS, Serie I, fol. 59, c. 323, letter of Niccolò Guicciardini, 28 April 1531. • 12. Sanuto, vol. 54, col. 411. Moretti, p. 148. • 13. ASV, A. A. Arm. I-XVIII, 6523, fol. 61v. Varchi, vol. 1, p. 67. Butters (2010), p. 70. • 14. Martinelli, MS Vat. Lat. 12276, fol. 156v, 15 April 1531; Moretti, p. 150, citing Rossi, vol. 1, p. 60, n. 3. • 15. ASC, AO, Serie I, Corrispondenza, b. 72, fasc. 2, no. 213, fol. 1r. Relazioni, ser. 2, vol. 3, p. 281. ASC, AO, Serie I, Corrispondenza, b. 72, fasc. 1, no. 152, fol. 2r. • 16. Relazioni, ser. 2, vol. 3, pp. 280–81, 285–6. • 17. ASMo, Carteggio Principi Esteri, 1152, no. 48; ASMn, AG 1110, c. 377r; ASV, A. A. Arm. I-XVIII, 6523 (dated 23 June 1530 but more plausibly 1531), fol. 68v; Sanuto, vol. 54, cols 481, 507. Paoli, p. 28. • 18. Varchi, vol. 1, p. 256. Ughi, p. 171. • 19. There are several accounts of these events. The detail of the speeches by Muscettola and Alessandro is taken from Imperio Ricordati's letter to Isabella d'Este: ASMn, AG 1304, cc. 38r–39v. Other details are derived from ASF, MS 170, fols 119v–121v and Sanuto, vol. 54, cols 491, 500. Hall of the Two Hundred: http://en.comune.fi.it/administration/municipality/rooms_pv.htm. On Buondelmonti: Butters (1985), p. 267. Salviati's letter: ASV, A. A. Arm. I-XVIII, 3114, fol. 13r. • 20. Sanuto, vol. 54, cols 519–20. • 21. Dunning, pp. 298–302, cited in Cummings (1992), p. 239, note 1. • 22. ASMn, AG 1304, c. 39v. Sanuto, vol. 54, col. 523. • 23. Aretino, vol. 1, book 1, no. 161, pp. 237–39.

8

1. Cellini, p. 197. • 2. Varchi, vol. 2, pp. 88, 55–81. Cipolla, pp. 47–48. • 3. Machiavelli (1984), p. 21. • 4. Ughi, p. 188; Nicasi, pp. 717–80. • 5. For the nickname, see ASF, CS I/95, fol. 34r. Varchi, vol. 2, pp. 439–40. For the title: Wilson, p. 179. Luigi Guicciardini had proposed a foreign commander for the Florentine guard in his opinion on the government of Florence. Jurdjevic (2006), p. 131. • 6. ASF, GM 2, discussed in Lazzi and Lulla. • 7. Martelli, p. 85, n. 149. • 8. Wilson, p. 179. • 9. Not the current staircase: see Rebecchini (2010), p. 42, citing Bulst 1993. • 10. Rebecchini (2010), p. 42. • 11. The ceiling tiles

are now in the Victoria and Albert Museum: inv. numbers 7632–1861 to 7643–1861 • **12.** There are some more details of what the palace looked like in Rebecchini (2010), pp. 41–47 based on a poetic description from 1525. It is hard to say what proportion of these furnishings were returned to the palace in the 1530s. • **13.** For the documentary sources see Waldman. The inventory record for Baccio's second room is not complete. • **14.** Segre, pp. 133–34. ASMs, Archivio Malaspina di Fosdinovo 14, fol. 1r. For background: Langdon, p. 43. • **15.** *DBI* (Ricciarda Malaspina); Pelù and Raffo. • **16.** Ricciarda in Rome: Sanuto, vol. 35, col. 423. Varchi, vol. 3, p. 196 says Giulio was not yet five. ASMs, Archivio Cybo–Malaspina 508, fol. 64v, makes him three. For the baptism date see Langdon, p. 42 and Archivio dell'Opera del Duomo, Registri Battesimali 10, fol. 14r, online photograph 27 at http://operaduomo.firenze. it/archivio/risorse-digitali. • **17.** ASMn, AG 1302, c. 145. See Bourne, 207–9, for discussion of a salacious 1494 account of the baths at Porretta.

9

1. Devonshire Jones (1972a), p. 239. Varchi, vol. 2, p. 410; Simoncelli (2006), pp. 21–22. • **2.** Devonshire Jones (1972a), p. 237; Simoncelli (2006), pp. 15–16. • **3.** Simoncelli (2006), p. 31. • **4.** Simoncelli (2006), pp. 24, 29, 34. • **5.** A play on Dante's famous line. Luzio, p. 11, cit. in Simoncelli (2006), p. 28. • **6.** See for example ASMs, Appendice Archivio Cybo–Malaspina, Card. Cybo, b. 3, insert 19, unnumbered letter of 6 May 1527; ASMo, Carteggio Principi Esteri, Cardinali, Roma b. 1356/88. • **7.** Payments to spies are included in the accounts at the back of each Otto di Guardia volume. For one payment of 104 florins in 1534, see ASF, Otto di Guardia e Balìa 7, fol. 159r. • **8.** Ceccherelli, fol. 55r. • **9.** For discussion of *The Prince* see Benner. • **10.** For background: Butters (2010); Jurdjevic (2006). • **11.** Simonetta (2014), p. 119. For the privileges and background information see: copy.law.cam.ac.uk/cam/tools/request/show-Record.php?id=record_i_1531 and copy.law.cam.ac.uk/cam/tools/request/showRecord.php?id=record_i_1531a. • **12.** *DBI* (Giulio de' Medici). Sanuto, vol. 55, cols 50–51. Hale (1968), p. 509. • **13.** *Pasquinate*, vol. 1, n. 396, p. 392. • **14.** ASMn, AG, b. 880, c. 218r, cited in Rebecchini (2010), p. 74. • **15.** Rebecchini (2010), pp. 71 and 74, citing ASF, Ducato di Urbino I/132, c. 545r (see also Moretti, p. 155), ASMo, AE, Ambasciatori, Roma, b. 33, unnumbered letter of 28 August 1531; ASMn, AG 880 cc. 210r, 239r–v. Shrugging shoulders: Varchi, vol. 2, p. 435. • **16.** ASF, Ducato di Urbino I/132, c. 546r. • **17.** *Négociations*, vol. 1, p. 8. Sanuto, vol. 55, col. 364. • **18.** ASF, CS, I, 100, fol. 44r. Sanuto, vol. 55, col. 72; Rebecchini (2010), p. 75, n. 77. *DBI* (Giulia Gonzaga). Segre, p. 150. • **19.** Cohen, p. 245; Cox-Rearick (1982), p. 170. • **20.** Bardazzi and Castellani, vol. 1, pp. 47, 51. The paintings were completed and enlarged later in the sixteenth century by Alessandro Allori. • **21.** ASMn, AG 2969, Lib. 46, cc. 77v–78r; ASMn, AG IIII, through this series, but especially cc. 18–59: the quotation is on c. 30r. ASF, MdP 630, fol. 5r ASF, CS, I, 100, fols 47v–48r. • **22.** Berni, p. 133. • **23.** ASF, CS, I, 100, fols 47v–48r. • **24.** Castiglione, p. 63. Medici (2007), pp. 31–42. Machiavelli (1984), p. 50. • **25.** ASV, Miscellanea, Armadio II, 78, fols 317r–333v, quotations on fols 318r–v and 320r. • **26.** Varchi, vol. 3, pp. 2, 110.

10

1. ASF, GM 3, fols 2r, 2v, 22r; Cellini, p. 141. • **2.** ASF, GM 3, fols 1r–2r. Background: Scalini and Berretti, pp. 8, 10, 11. Castiglione, p. 57. • **3.** ASF, MdP 630, fols 2v, 3r, 3v. Martelli, p. 85, n. 149. • **4.** Varchi, vol. 2, p. 438. • **5.** Lazzi and Lulla, pp. 1226–28; ASF, GM 2, pp. 66–71. For an English edition of the 1492 inventory see *Lorenzo de' Medici At Home*; for the Italian, Spallanzani and Bertelà. On the porcelain: Spallanzani. • **6.** Lazzi and Lulla, pp. 1228–30; ASF, GM 2, pp. 72–75. • **7.** ASF, GM 3, fol. 4v. On German clocks: Dohrn-van Rossum, pp. 121–23. • **8.** Landucci, p. 371; Varchi, vol. 2, pp. 84–86; Hayward, pp. 15–16; Frick, pp. 179–200; ASF, Copialettere di Goro Gheri 4, fol. 296v; Baker (2013), p. 126. • **9.** Varchi, vol. 2, pp. 449 and 370, latter cited in Gianneschi and Sodini, p. 6. • **10.** Varchi, vol. 2, p. 56. Segni, vol. 2, p. 363, cited in Gianneschi and Sodini, p. 9. This fortress is now demolished. • **11.** Anzilotti, p. 58; Gianneschi and Sodini, pp. 12–13 • **12.** Gianneschi and Sodini, pp. 13, 17.

11

1. The opinions are in *Archivio Storico Italiano*, ser. I, vol. 1, 1842. Vettori cited in Jurdjevic (2006), p. 127; Guicciardini cited in Baker (2013), p. 149. See also Anzilotti, pp. 26–29. • **2.** Baker (2013), p. 150; there are various archive records of the names. See for example BNCF, NA 982, fol. 148r–v. ASMn, AG IIII, c. 44r. Machiavelli (1984), p. 8. • **3.** ASMs, Appendice all'archivio Cybo–Malaspina, Card. Cybo, unnumbered insert, 27 April 1532. • **4.** Devonshire Jones (1972a), p. 252. Hale (1968), p. 505. Anzilotti, pp. 30–42. • **5.** Sanuto, vol. 56, col. 87. • **6.** Sanuto, vol. 56, col. 156. • **7.** Sanuto, vol. 56, cols 195–96. • **8.** BRF, MS Riccardiana 1849, fols 157r–168v; another copy in MS Riccardiana 1959, fols 89r–103v. Background: Rubinstein. • **9.** Cambiagi, pp. 90–91; Ceccherelli, fol. 16v; Settimanni, fol. 40r. • **10.** Sanuto, vol. 56, cols 227–28, 299–300. • **11.** Simoncelli (2006), p. 22. • **12.** Settimanni, fol. 43r; Varchi, vol. 3, p. 3. • **13.** Simoncelli (2006), pp. 21, 36. Mallett and Shaw, p. 162. • **14.** Cellini, pp. 166–67; Symonds gives an inoffensive version of 'Io ho in culo loro e il duca'. I have retranslated. This incident probably took place after December 1533, when Nardi broke his confinement. • **15.** ASF, Ducato di Urbino I/132, c. 600r, cited in Rebecchini

(2010), p. 89 and Moretti, p. 155. • **16.** Moretti, p. 156; Segre, p. 144; *Relazioni*, ser. 2, vol. 3, p. 380. • **17.** Rebecchini (2010), p. 79. • **18.** This was a second-hand account of a conversation between the Pope and Cardinal Ercole Gonzaga. Rebecchini (2010), p. 90, citing ASF, Ducato di Urbino, I/132, c. 648r–v; see also Moretti, p. 156. • **19.** Najemy, p. 374. ASF, Ducato di Urbino I/132, c. 611r. • **20.** Sanuto, vol. 56, col. 488. • **21.** Lefevre (1986), p. 52. ASV, A. A. Arm. I-XVIII, 6523, fol. 145v. • **22.** ASV, Segretaria di Stato, Principi, 7, fol. 157r–v.

12

1. Segre, pp. 144–46. Rebecchini (2010), pp. 90, 92. Moretti, pp. 152–53, citing Sanuto, vol. 56, p. 770. Ammirato (1642), p. 255. ASMn, AG IIII, cc. 22r 25v. ASF, GM 3, fols 3v–4r. • **2.** Rebecchini (2010), pp. 92–94. • **3.** Rosso, pp. 82–84. • **4.** Rubinstein, p. 96. Vasari, vol. 5, p. 384, fn 1; http://www.tesorodeimedici. it/index.php?it/65/percorsi-cosimo-i. The seal, reworked for Cosimo de' Medici, is in the Museo degli Argenti, inv. Bargello 1917 (II), n. 30. Randolph, p. 154. • **5.** ASF, GM 3, fol. 2v. Hayward, p. 17. Croizat-Glazer. • **6.** Meserve, p. 5. Simoncelli (2006), p. 80. Pastoureau, p. 39. • **7.** ASF, GM 3, fol. 3r. Ceccherelli, fols 55v–56r; 57v. Hayward, p. 20. • **8.** Vasari, vol. 7, pp. 655–56; vol. 8, pp. 233, 235–40; the *Entombment* is now in the Casa Vasari, Arezzo. For more on Vasari's work at the Medici court, see Guido Rebecchini, 'Vasari, Alessandro de' Medici, le arti e la politica della corte' (forthcoming): my thanks to the author for allowing me advance sight of this essay. • **9.** Rastrelli, vol. 1, p. 85. Butters (1985), pp. 279–80. • **10.** Settimanni, fols 48r, 51r, 52r, 54r, 55r. • **11.** Plaisance, vol. 3, p. 141, fn 42. • **12.** ASF, Ducato di Urbino I/132, c. 687v. Varchi, vol. 3, p. 5. ASV, A. A. Arm. I-XVIII, 6522, fol. 132r. • **13.** Knecht, p. 14. ASV, Segr. Stato, Principi 7, fol. 488r. • **14.** Varchi, vol. 3, p. 6. Settimanni, fol. 56r; Ughi, p. 171. • **15.** ASMn, AG IIII, c. 30.

13

1. Varchi, vol. 3, p. 9. Settimanni, fol. 59r. • **2.** *Relazioni*, ser. 2, vol. 3, p. 279. ASMs, Appendice all'archivio Cybo–Malaspina, Card. Cybo, Libro de' Ricordi, unpaginated, 'havendolo in luogo di padre' ('having him in place of a father'). • **3.** ASF, CS I/95, fols 39r–40r; Staffetti (1894), p. 137. *Pasquinate*, vol. 1, nos 208, 229, 257, 398, 423; vol. 2, no. 661. • **4.** Settimanni, fol. 60v; ASV, Segr. Stato, Principi, 7, fol. 568r. • **5.** Varchi, vol. 2, p. 396. Machiavelli (1984), p. 63. *DBI*: Raffaello Girolami. • **6.** ASV, A. A. Arm. I-XVIII, 6522, fol. 134r. For background: Hurtubise, pp. 164–65; 192–95. • **7.** Moretti, pp. 153–54; Guicciardini vol. 5, p. 306. Segre, p. 151. • **8.** ASF, Ducato di Urbino I/132, c. 726r. Segre, p. 152. • **9.** Rebecchini (2010), pp. 101–2. • **10.** Sanuto, vol. 57, cols 247, 250,

310. ASF, GM 3, fols 3r–v, 23r. The marginal notes in this manuscript may indicate the courtiers to whom these items were issued. • 11. Sanuto, vol. 57, cols 363, 366, 388. • 12. Varchi, vol. 3, p. 12. ASMs, Appendice Archivio Cybo–Malaspina, Card. Cybo, b. 3, insert 45. • 13. ASF, GM 3, fol. 6r. • 14. Capwell, p. 114. • 15. ASMn, AG 1110, c. 317r. • 16. Machiavelli (1985), p. 237. Castiglione, p. 119. • 17. Sanuto, vol. 57, cols 453, 467, 578. • 18. Guicciardini, vol. 5, p. 313. Sanuto, vol. 57, cols 403, 441, 568.

14

1. Varchi, vol. 3, p. 8. Settimanni, fols 63v–64v. • 2. Varchi, vol. 3, pp. 13–16; Settimanni, fol. 65r. • 3. Albertini, p. 203. Guicciardini (1857–67), vol. 9, p. 335. Nardi, vol. 2, p. 244. Nerli, p. 276. For background: Simonetta (2014). • 4. Settimanni, fol. 77r; Varchi, vol. 3, p. 5 gives a version of 'after his own heart'. • 5. Devonshire Jones (1972a), p. 252. • 6. Guicciardini (1857–67), vol. 9, p. 351. Simoncelli (2006), pp. 117 and 122; Varchi, vol. 3, pp. 46–47; for Aldobrandini: *DBI*. • 7. ASF, Copialettere di Goro Gheri 4, fols 167r, 251r. Machiavelli (1984), p. 73 • 8. To Lanfredini, cited in Gianneschi and Sodini, p. 9. • 9. Hale (1968), p. 502; Gianneschi and Sodini, p. 30, n. 61. • 10. Guicciardini (1867), vol. 9, p. 270. • 11. ASF, MdP 181. Varchi, vol. 3, pp. 21–29. • 12. Ceccherelli: help for poor: fols 8v–9v; 20v–22r, 48r–49r; dowry case: fols 11v–14r; honourable man: fol. 56v. See also Bandello's stories of Alessandro administering justice: vol. 1, pp. 815–19, 820–24.

15

1. Belardini (2003), p. 28; Sanuto, vol. 57, cols 403, 441, 516. • 2. Sanuto, vol. 57, cols 644–46. Lefevre, p. 61. • 3. Sanuto, vol. 58, col. 36; vol. 57, cols 644–46. BNCF, NA 982, fol. 152r. • 4. Sanuto, vol. 57, col. 644. • 5. ASF, MS 103, fols 26v, 28r. Taylor, p. 623. Weights: Cipolla, p. 139. • 6. ASF, CS I/13, fol. 13r. Compare with ASF, GM 2 for the personnel changes. • 7. For the household responsibilites see Romoli. • 8. Giovio (1555). • 9. Romoli. • 10. Grieco. • 11. BNCF, NA 982, 152r; ASMn, AG 1111, fols 85r–86v. • 12. Zorzi, p. 283. • 13. Cummings (1992), p. 239, note 4 (citing Bridges, pp. 42–43) and p. 157, citing ASF, CS I/13, fol. 13r, a list of the household in 1535. For more on Alessandro's music patronage see Cummings (2004), esp. Ch. 4, pp. 153–66. • 14. ASF, GM 4, p. 5; MdP 630, fol. 4v. Giovio (2006), p. 187; Rebecchini (2010), p. 177, citing ASF, Ducato di Urbino I/132, cc. 579r, 596r. ASF, Otto di Guardia 8, fols 95v, 98v. Lowe (2005), pp. 35–41. • 15. BNCF, NA 982, fols 164r–165v. I have abridged the text somewhat in my translation. The Bible verses are Luke 1:26–38. Background: Cummings (1992), pp. 142–3. Baxandall, p. 71. Zorzi, pp. 281–82, 287. • 16. BNCF, NA 982, fol. 168r–v. • 17. Kline. • 18. BNCF, NA 982, fols 167r–170r. • 19. ASMn, AG 1111, c. 86r.

Cummings (1992), pp. 145–47, citing BNCF, NA 982, cc. 170v–171r. • **20.** ASF, Copialettere di Goro Gheri 4, fol. 296v. • **21.** ASF, MdP 630, fol. 4r. • **22.** Sanuto, vol. 58, col. 77. ASF, Ducato di Urbino I/132: c. 848v. Rebecchini (2010), p. 104. • **23.** Sanuto, vol. 58, col. 194. Fragnito, p. 46. • **24.** Sanuto vol. 58, col. 607.

16

1. Belardini (2003), p. 29, citing Cellini, p. 141. The date of this commission is not known but it was during Margaret's residence in Naples. Belardini (2008), p. 174. • **2.** Heywood, pp. 7–8. Machiavelli (1984), p. 76. Ammirato (1641), p. 426, cited in Zorzi, p. 280. • **3.** Conti, p. 192. • **4.** ASMn, AG IIII, cc. 93r–99r. • **5.** Gianneschi and Sodini, p. 17; Hale (1968), p. 516, citing ASF, Capitani di Parte, 10 rosso, fols 89v–90r. ASF, MdP 630, fol. 4v. • **6.** Rastrelli, vol. 2, pp. 37–38. Clothes: ASF, GM 3, fol. 25v; GM 4, p. 7. ASF, MdP 630, fol. 4v, doc. 24891; GM 3, fol. 4v. • **7.** Knecht, pp. 15, 17. Giovio (2006), p. 873, fn 13, citing Giovio, *Historiae*, II, p. 256: 'Dedit et cupiditati Hippolyti Medicis Cardinalis, quum ingenuo pudore maiora dona repudiasset, mansuefactum leonem eximiae proceritatis quem a Mauritania Hariadenus Barbarussa cum legatis transmiserat.' • **8.** Varchi, vol. 3, p. 39. Nerli, p. 271. Rosso, p. 100. • **9.** ASF, CS I/100, fol. 66r. Discussed in Simoncelli (2006), p. 28; Guicciardini (1867), vol. 9, p. 276. • **10.** ASF, MdP 630, fol. 4v, doc. no. 24894.

17

1. Arrival date: DBI: Ricciarda Malaspina. See also ASMo, Carteggio Ambasciatori, Firenze, 16, letters of 5/7/1533 and seq. Lando, p. 70. Sanuto, vol. 35, col. 423. • **2.** Settimanni, c. 168v. Munby, esp. p. 51. • **3.** ASMn, AG 1304, fol. 57r. Langdon, p. 42; Archivio dell'Opera del Duomo, Registri Battesimali 10, fol. 14r, online at http://archivio.operaduomo.fi.it/battesimi/visualizza_carta.asp?id=10&p=26. ASMn, AG 1304, fols 97v, 102r. Berni, pp. 185–86. • **4.** Cellini, p. 134. ASMs, Archivio Cybo–Malaspina 508 (Memorie della famiglia Cibo), fol. 60r; ASMn, AG IIII, c. 277. • **5.** Varchi, vol. 3, p. 42. Syphilis: ASF, Ducato di Urbino I/132 c. 619r. Pieraccini, p. 402, finds another possible reference to syphilis in a 1530 mention of a venereal ulcer: ASF, MAP 126, c. 133v. Ughi, p. 181. • **6.** Baker (2013), p. 158. • **7.** Romoli, fol. 21r. • **8.** Bourne, p. 202. Baker (2010), pp. 451–52. Machiavelli (1984), p. 61. • **9.** ASF, MdP 181, fols 37v–38r, fol. 3r. • **10.** ASF, MdP 630, fol. 4r.

18

1. For background on contemporary treatments: Siraisi, p. 172. *Dizionario del cittadino*, p. 7; Rebecchini (2010), pp. 106–7. • **2.** ASV, Segr. Stato, Vescovi e

Prelati 6, fol. 198r. The term used to describe the runaway's status is ambiguous but the context strongly suggests he was a slave. Lowe (2013), p. 425. • **3.** ASMn, AG 2971, Copialettere riservati 1533–35, Lib. 51, c. 68v. Bono (2010), p. 238; Kaplan (2011), pp. 55–56. • **4.** Rebecchini (2010), pp. 98–99, citing Sanuto, vol. 56, col. 865. • **5.** Landi; for background, Peloso, pp. 128–33; Lowe (2005), pp. 31–2. • **6.** Newitt, pp. 6–8. • **7.** [al-Ḥasan ibn Muḥammad al-Wazzān], p. 15. • **8.** Landi; Peloso, pp. 206–11. • **9.** On black skin and sexuality see Hahn. On Turks and Arabs: Soykut, pp. 30–31, 75. Lawrance, pp. 30–31. Bartlett, p. 46. • **10.** This date is given in ASF, Misc. Med. 502, fol. 221r. • **11.** Lowe (1993), pp. 104–13 and Hyde, pp. 131–48; on the court case see the forthcoming *Brill Companion to Cosimo de' Medici* edited by Alessio Assonitis and Maurizio Arfaioli. • **12.** Varchi, vol. 3, p. 183. Ughi, pp. 185–86; Nerli, p. 286, ASF, Ducato di Urbino I/132, 611r. *DBI* (Lorenzino de' Medici). Sanuto vol. 58, col. 36. • **13.** ASF, Misc. Med. 502, fol. 222r–v. • **14.** Virgili, p. 489. • **15.** *DBI* (Alfonso d'Este); Varchi, vol. 3, p. 57. Simoncelli (2006), pp. 34–35. • **16.** Bullard, pp. 151–72. • **17.** Vasari, vol. 7, p. 205. *Carteggio Inedito*, vol. 2, p. 252. • **18.** Hale (1968), pp. 511–12; Nerli, p. 270. • **19.** ASF, CS I/100, fol. 52r; CS I/61, fol. 26r. • **20.** Castiglione, p. 63. • **21.** Ceccherelli, fols 26v–27r. • **22.** Cited in Zorzi, p. 279. • **23.** Varchi, vol. 3, p. 195, though these had not yet been enacted at the point of Alessandro's death. • **24.** Cox-Rearick (1964), vol. 1, pp. 285–87; Heywood, pp. 161–76. • **25.** Vasari, vol. 8, pp. 240–41. Rebecchini (2010), p. 33. • **26.** Crum, p. 54, citing Cherubini and Fanelli, pp. 120, 122 and Rubin, p. 10. Vasari, vol. 7, p. 656 and vol. 8, pp. 249–52. Reiss, p. 460. • **27.** Hankins, p. 86.

19

1. Vasari, vol. 8, pp. 241–42. For background: Springer, pp. 145–50; Campbell; Langedijk. • **2.** Vasari, vol. 7, p. 657; vol. 5, p. 273. • **3.** Vasari, vol. 6, pp. 278–79. Falciani and Natali (2014), p. 320 and Cropper, p. 20. • **4.** The two paintings are in the Art Institute of Chicago and the Philadelphia Museum of Art respectively. For debate on this work see Strehlke (1985); Levy, pp. 95–103; Walker-Oakes and Simons. • **5.** Gennaioli, p. 56. Victoria and Albert Museum, London, inv. no. CIS 7553–1861. Hermitage Museum, inventory no. И-4001. There is a fourth version in the Bibliothèque Nationale, Paris. ASF, MdP 630, fol. 5v, n. 24900. http://www.sothebys.com/en/auctions/ecatalogue/2013/treasures-princely-taste-l13303/lot.7.html. • **6.** Waldman, p. xviii. The sculpture is now in the Uffizi Gallery. • **7.** Settimanni, fol. 125r; Vasari, vol. 6, pp. 158–59; Cellini, pp. 175, 192–93. • **8.** Wallace, pp. 130–34; Michelangelo, vol. 4, pp. 44–45. • **9.** Cited in Cohen, p. 250; the Italian text is in Buonarroti (1993), p. 84. My translation. • **10.** Rebecchini (2010), pp. 236–37. • **11.** ASF, MS 103, fols 36r, 39v, 40r–41r. • **12.** ASF, GM 3, fol. 11r–v. • **13.** Fraser, especially chapter 5, pp. 85–129.

Here at pp. 85, 90, 100, 108–9. • **14.** Varchi, vol. 3, pp. 48–53. Settimanni, fols 118r–120r; 122r. Settimanni names Francesco Pazzi as the companion: the *Otto di Guardia* records have Jacopo Antonio Guglielmo de' Pazzi. Other names of prisoners freed on the same day were recorded as 'Antonius Luce de' Ricciardis', 'Jacopus Antonij de carrais' and 'Michael Franc. alias Papassino': they may also have been involved. ASF, Otto di Guardia e Balia del Principato 6, fol. 75r.

20

1. Settimanni, fol. 125v. The case is not apparent in the *Otto di Guardia* records for May 1534, but Settimanni's extracts of criminal trials (though selective) are mostly accurate, so it may be recorded elsewhere. • **2.** ASF, MdP 181, fol. 19v. Background: Ruff, pp. 122–23. • **3.** Ceccherelli, fols 26v–27r, 40v–41v. *Memorie*, pp. 147–48, and see above, chapter 14. • **4.** ASF, Carte Strozziane I/16, fol. 67r. • **5.** Varchi, vol. 3, p. 42; ASF, MdP 181, fol. 10v. • **6.** ASF, MdP 181, fols 13r, 23r. Ferretti, pp. 248–49, citing in n. 3 the Venetian ambassador in *Relazioni*, ser. 2, vol. 1, p. 73. • **7.** Simoncelli (2006), p. 32. Nerli, p. 276; see also Simoncelli (2006), p. 48. • **8.** Cellini, p. 142 • **9.** Ughi, pp. 186–89. • **10.** ASMn, AG 2935, c. 78r, n. 241; c. 90v, n. 281; AG IIII, cc. 155–57. • **11.** Moretti, p. 163, citing ASF, MAP, 147, doc. 19, and p. 160; Simoncelli (2006), p. 41; Rebecchini (2010), pp. 110, 112. • **12.** Gianneschi and Sodini, p. 16. • **13.** Hale (1968), pp. 516–18, citing CS, I/135, fol. 114v. ASMn, AG IIII, cc. 149v, 159v, 163r. • **14.** Cummings (1992), p. 148; ASMn, AG IIII, cc. 163r, 163v; Varchi, vol. 3, p. 62, cited in Hale (1968), p. 517. • **15.** ASF, MdP 181, fols 67v, 71r. • **16.** Simoncelli (2006), p. 43. • **17.** ASF, CS I/16, fol. 51r. ASF, MdP 181, fols 87v–88r. • **18.** ASF, MdP 181, fol. 78r. ASF, CS I/16, fols 64r, 40r, 41r. • **19.** ASF, CS I/16, fols 40r, 41r. Simoncelli (2006), pp. 39–40. • **20.** Rebecchini (2010), p. 109, citing ASMn, AG 883, c. 143r. • **21.** ASF, Otto di Guardia e Balìa del principato 8, fol. 12r–v. Settimanni, fol. 144r. • **22.** Ferretti, pp. 249–50, citing ASF, MdP 181, fol. 113. • **23.** Pasquinate, vol. 1, pp. 394–95, n. 398. Staffetti (1894), p. 136. • **24.** Simoncelli (2006), p. 42, citing Capasso, vol. 1, pp. 27–43 and 71–73. Rebecchini (2010), pp. 117–18. • **25.** Rebecchini (2010), p. 119, n. 5. • **26.** Museo Nazionale del Bargello, Florence. • **27.** Rebecchini (2010), pp. 114–15. • **28.** ASF, CS I/16, fol. 43r. ASF, MS 170, fol. 123r–v. Nerli, p. 273.

21

1. Nerli, p. 275. • **2.** Settimanni, fol. 168r. Gianneschi and Sodini, p. 16. Hale (1968), p. 523. Settimanni, fols 148v–149r. • **3.** ASF, Otto di Guardia e Balìa del Principato 8, fols 42r–43v, 44r–45r, 58v, 73v–74r. Settimanni, fols 152r, 154v, 159v.

Baker (2009), pp 463–64, 472. • **4.** Berni, p. 186. • **5.** Virgili, pp. 488–89. The Pietrasanta documents are in ASF, MdP 181, dated 21/11/1534, and in MdP Miscellanea 960. • **6.** Cellini, p. 134. Varchi, vol. 2, pp. 439–40. • **7.** Settimanni, fol. 162r–v, derived in part from Varchi, vol. 3, pp. 74–75. Segni, vol. 2, p. 424. • **8.** Settimanni, fol. 156r; Nardi, vol. 2, p. 248. Rebecchini (2010), p. 123; Moretti, p. 167. • **9.** Simoncelli (2006), pp. 44–48; Busini, p. 238. • **10.** Varchi, vol. 3, pp. 66–68. • **11.** Nardi, vol. 2, pp. 242–43, 247–48; cited in Simoncelli (2006), pp. 51–54. Varchi, vol. 3, p. 70. • **12.** Simoncelli (2006), pp. 54–60. • **13.** Settimanni, fol. 157r–v; Nerli, p. 301. Varchi, vol. 3, p. 65. • **14.** Nerli, pp. 279, 275. Ughi, p. 189. • **15.** Moretti, p. 169; Simoncelli (2006), pp. 59, 61. • **16.** ASF, Ducato di Urbino I/133, c. 4r. • **17.** Moretti, p. 170, citing ASF, Ducato di Urbino I/133; c. 148v.

22

1. ASF, Ducato di Urbino I/133, c. 4r. Simoncelli (2006), p. 62. ASF, MdP 630, fol. 6v. • **2.** Varchi, vol. 3, p. 73. Settimanni, fol. 203v; Ughi, p. 173; Cipolla, p. 7. ASF, Otto di Guardia e Balìa del Principato 8, fols 39v–41r. • **3.** Cellini, pp. 172–74. • **4.** ASF, Ducato di Urbino, I/133, cc. 148v, 155r. Segni, vol. 2, pp. 364–65. • **5.** Settimanni, fol. 206r; ASF, Otto di Guardia e Balìa del Principato 9, fols 103v–104r. For the decline in prosecutions, compare the *Otto di Guardia* prosecutions for September–December 1534 (vol. 8) with those to January–April 1535 (vol. 9). • **6.** Navagero, fol. 3r. Moretti, p. 168. • **7.** Machiavelli (1984), pp. 16–17. • **8.** Varchi, vol. 3, pp. 76–77. Simoncelli (2006), pp. 71–75. • **9.** ASF, Ducato di Urbino, I/133, c. 160r. Buonanni's letters are in BRF, MS Riccardiana 1959, fols 89r–103v. Simoncelli (2006), pp. 64–66 and p. 80. Varchi, vol. 3, p. 78. • **10.** Varchi, vol. 3, p. 166. Espinosa, pp. 65–82. Simoncelli (2006), pp. 83–84. • **11.** Segni, vol. 2, p. 420, cit. in Simoncelli (2006), p. 86. Simoncelli notes that Segni was very well informed about the oligarchs, referring to Ridolfi, p. 579. • **12.** Simoncelli (2006), p. 68. • **13.** ASV, Miscellanea, Arm. II, 49, fols 115r–123v. The full text runs to some five thousand words, with much repetition of the key points. I have given the gist. On the importance of the 1529 treaty wording see Moretti, p. 139, citing Nardi. • **14.** Moretti, p. 169. • **15.** ASMn, AG IIII, c. 246r.

23

1. ASMo, Carteggio Principi Esteri, Cardinali, Roma, b. 1356/88, letter of 19/5/1535. • **2.** Berni also had another connection to the Malaspina–Cibo household: his most famous work was a reworking in Tuscan dialect of one of Renaissance Italy's most celebrated epic poems, *Orlando Innamorato*

('Orlando in Love') and the author of the original *Orlando* was Matteo Maria Boiardo, a cousin once removed of Taddea Malaspina's late husband. McIver, p. 32, fn. 78. Busini, p. 262; Virgili, pp. 505–6; see also DBI (Francesco Berni). • **3.** ASF, Ducato di Urbino, I / 133, c. 227v; Moretti, p. 170; Settimanni, fol. 207r; Varchi, vol. 3, pp. 80–81, 148. Simoncelli (2006), p. 94. • **4.** ASF, Otto di Guardia e Balìa del Principato 10, fols 127r, 31v–32r. Settimanni, fol. 207v. • **5.** ASMn, AG 2936, lib. 312, cc. 43r, 58v, 85r–86r, 101v, nn. 116, 151, 177, 222, 250. • **6.** Rebecchini (2010), p. 125. • **7.** Moretti, pp. 171–72; published in Rastrelli, vol. 2, p. 77. • **8.** ASMs, Appendice all'archivio Cybo–Malaspina, Card. Cybo, Libro de' Ricordi, fol. 60r. • **9.** Rebecchini (2010), pp. 126–27 and Appendix 4; Ferrai (1891), pp. 179–81; Moretti, pp. 171–74. The Italian text of the confession is in Stephens (1978), pp. 255–69. • **10.** Simoncelli (2006), pp. 96–97. • **11.** Moretti, pp. 172, 177. • **12.** Simoncelli (2006), pp. 96–107. • **13.** Machiavelli (1984), p. 56. • **14.** Varchi, vol. 3, pp. 85–86. ASMn, AG 2936, lib. 313, c. 9r, n. 22; Rebecchini (2010), p. 128. • **15.** Nardi, vol. 2, p. 262.

24

1. Nardi, vol. 2, p. 262. The trial documents are in Archivio di Stato di Roma, Tribunale del Governatore, vol. 10, fasc. 3, discussed in Rebecchini (2010), pp. 131–35 and Pastore, pp. 19–21. • **2.** Dohrn-van Rossum, p. 276.

25

1. Giovio (1554), c. 282r, although Varchi, vol. 3, p. 95 says Ippolito was buried in Itri. On cardinals' funerals: C. Richardson (2009), pp. 440–42. • **2.** Gambara, pp. 221–25, cit. Moretti, p. 173fn. Aretino, vol. 1, Book 1, no. 50, pp. 103–4 and no. 51, pp. 104–5. Varchi, vol. 3, p. 92. • **3.** Nerli, p. 282. Varchi, vol. 3, pp. 93–94. *Pasquinate*, vol. 1, p. 531, n. 492. • **4.** Cited by Moretti, p. 178. • **5.** Segre, pp. 22, 27. ASMo, AE, Ambasciatori, Francia, b. 11, Domenico Ariano a Alfonso d'Este, 12 settembre 1535, cited in Rebecchini (2010), pp. 137–38, who describes the report as 'strangely deformed'. • **6.** ASR, Tribunale del Governatore, vol. 10, fasc. 3, fols 64r–66r. Rebecchini (2010), p. 144; *DBI.* Crews, pp. 109–10. • **7.** ASC, AO, Pergamene II.A.23,013, no. catena 766; for the subsequent manoeuvres see AO, Pergamene II.A.23,022, no. catena 722 and AO, Serie IV, Misc. Storico Genealogica, b. 43, fasc. 93. • **8.** Ferretti, pp. 251–56, citing ASF, MdP, filza 2355. • **9.** Gianneschi and Sodini, p. 17. ASF, GM 4, p. 23; MdP 630, fol. 33r. ASMn, AG 2936, lib. 313, nn. 117, 168, 170, 196, 260, 410. • **10.** ASF, Otto di Guardia e Balìa del Principato 11, fols 56v–59r. • **11.** Vasari, vol. 5, pp. 84, 91. • **12.** Langdon (2006), p. 42. Archivio dell'Opera del Duomo, Registri

Battesimali 229, fol. 46v, online at http://archivio.operaduomo.fi.it/battesimi/visualizza_carta.asp?id=229&p=91 • **13.** Settimanni, fols 217v, 222r.

26

1. Vasari, vol. 8, pp. 246–48; see also Hale (1968), p. 525 and Cummings (1992), p. 148. On astrological charts: Azzolini, pp. 53–64. • **2.** Nerli, p. 279. Hale (1968), p. 510. Varchi, vol. 3, p. 144. ASF, Otto di Guardia e Balìa del Principato 11, fol. 77r. Machiavelli (1984), p. 63. • **3.** Pontano, pp. 210–11. ASF, MS 170, fols 123v–124r. • **4.** ASF, GM 5 for wardrobe preparations; also GM 6. • **5.** Nardi, vol. 2, p. 268; Cummings (1992), p. 152, translating Giovio's quotation from Saletta, vol. 10 (1977), pp. 106–7. • **6.** Devonshire-Jones, p. 263; Simoncelli (2006), pp. 112–13; ASF, GM 5. • **7.** ASF, MS 170, fol. 124r. Varchi, vol. 3, p. 97. • **8.** Setton, vol. 3, pp. 397–400. ASMn, AG 1112, c. 62, 24/6/1537; AG 2972, Lib. 55, c. 50r–v. • **9.** *DBI* (Francesco II Sforza), Segre, p. 49, cited in Simoncelli (2006), p. 110. • **10.** Rosso, cit. in Cummings (1992), p. 153. Belardini (2008), pp. 176, 178. Landulfo. On Poggioreale see Zecchino. • **11.** Varchi, vol. 3, pp. 96–98; Simoncelli (2006), pp. 111, 114–15. • **12.** Varchi, vol. 3, pp. 91, 99. • **13.** Simoncelli (2006), p. 116 and fn. 44, citing Rossi, vol. 2, n. 2, pp. 92–93; Nardi, vol. 2, pp. 268–69. • **14.** The debates are edited in Guicciardini (1857–67), vol. 9; for the exiles' case see pp. 331–54, 375–78. For background: Simoncelli (2006), pp. 121–29. • **15.** Guicciardini (1857–67), vol. 9, pp. 354–74, 378–81. • **16.** Medici (2004), p. 9. • **17.** Nestor, p. 174. • **18.** Nardi, vol. 2, p. 276.

27

1. Cummings (1992), pp. 153–54; Rosso, p. 126. • **2.** Rebecchini (1998), pp. 522–24. • **3.** Simoncelli (2006), pp. 132–33. • **4.** ASF, Manoscritti 103, fols 65v, 71v. Simoncelli (2006), p. 136. ASF, MS 103, cc. 65v, 71v. Di Stefano, p. 108, n. 47. • **5.** Simoncelli (2006), pp. 138 and 142, citing Du Bellay, vol. 2, pp. 254–55. Rebecchini (1998), p. 524. • **6.** Rebecchini (1998), pp. 525–26, citing ASMn, AG 812, cc. 202r–203r; see also ASMn, AG 1905, c. 278v (a second-hand account); Varchi, vol. 3, pp. 108–9. • **7.** Rebecchini (1998), p. 526. • **8.** Simoncelli (2006), p. 144; Varchi, vol. 3, pp. 110–11; Busini, pp. 264–65. • **9.** Simoncelli (2006), pp. 143, 144, 147; Varchi, vol. 3, p. 167; and Nardi, vol. 2, p. 317. • **10.** Varchi, vol. 3, pp. 152–55 • **11.** Simoncelli (2006), p. 146, 150–51, 153. Nerli, p. 284. • **12.** Nerli, p. 283. Rebecchini (1998), pp. 527–28. Cummings (1992), p. 154.

28

1. Varchi, vol. 3, p. 167. Settimanni, fol. 302v. • **2.** Nerli, p. 283. ASMo, Carteggio Principi Esteri 1152, no. 55; the date of this document is not clear but 17

March 1536 seems the most likely reading. • **3.** ASMn, AG IIII, c. 277r. • **4.** ASMn, AG 1086, c. 133r. • **5.** Cellini, p. 141. • **6.** ASF, MAP 159, cc. 247–60. • **7.** Coniglio (1980), p. 12. No citation is given but references to the purchase of Rocca Guglielma are in ASF, MAP, filza 126, cc. 6r–15v. • **8.** Muzzarelli p. 164; Hayward, pp. 11, 20. Castiglione, p. 135. • **9.** Hayward, p. 21. • **10.** Settimanni, fol. 304v; Varchi, vol. 3, p. 168; Starkey, pp. 81–84. • **11.** ASMn, AG IIII, c. 281v. Varchi, vol. 3, p. 176. • **12.** Cummings (1992), p. 154; Setton, vol. 3, p. 398. • **13.** Bardazzi and Castellani, vol. 1, p. 21; Varchi, vol. 2, p. 61. • **14.** Ughi, p. 178; Rosso, p. 137; Nerli, p. 284; Vasari, vol. 8, pp. 252–53; Varchi, vol. 3, pp. 172–76; Cazzato, pp. 189–204. • **15.** ASMn, AG IIII, c. 363r.

29

1. ASMn, AG IIII, c. 296r. • **2.** Martelli, pp. 229–49, here at 238–42. • **3.** Vasari, vol. 8, pp. 263–65; discussed in Cummings (1992), p. 154; Belardini (2003), p. 31; Nerli, p. 285. • **4.** Varchi, vol. 3, p. 178. Nerli, p. 286; Segni (1805), vol. 2, p. 468; Adriani, vol. 1, p. 18 concurs. • **5.** Fabbri, p. 82, catalogue entry 6.3.1. • **6.** Medici (2005), p. 99, p. 6. • **7.** Medici (2005), p. 97. • **8.** Vasari, vol. 6, p. 440. Fabbri, p. 82, catalogue entry 6.3.1. • **9.** Varchi, vol. 3, p. 178. Segni, vol. 2, p. 468. ASMn, AG IIII, c. 371r. ASMo, Carteggio Principi Esteri, b. 1152, letter of 18/8/1536; Belardini (2003), p. 32. • **10.** ASMn, AG IIII, c. 313r.

30

1. ASMn, AG IIII, c. 320r. ASF, MdP 630, c. 8v. MAP doc. 24948. *Lorenzo de' Medici At Home*, p. 29. Knecht, p. 17. Gotfredson, p. 154. • **2.** Nerli, p. 286. Ughi, pp. 180–81. • **3.** Marguerite of Navarre, p. 82. Aretino, vol. 1, p. 164, no. 99; vol. 4, p. 235, no. 374. • **4.** Baker (2010). • **5.** ASF, GM 3, fols 15r–16r, 17r–19v; GM 4, pp. 23–31; GM 5, fol. 39v. ASF, MdP 630, fols 8r–9r. Lazzi and Lulla, p. 1213. • **6.** Conti, pp. 39, 83, 94, 117, 146, 230, 233. Crum notes Cosimo's inactivity as a patron of the domestic arts but does not link this to his inheritance from Alessandro. • **7.** ASMn, AG IIII, cc. 327r, 329. • **8.** Referred to in the text as 'pevialj', most likely 'pluviali': ASF, GM 4, p. 2; MdP 630, fol. 2, no. 24788. • **9.** Giovio (1556), pp. 36–38; for background, Lach, p. 167. • **10.** Settimanni, fols 328v, 331r; ASMn, AG IIII, c. 332r. • **11.** ASMn, AG IIII, c. 336r.

31

1. Ughi, p. 189. • **2.** ASF, MAP 159, c. 259r. Settimanni, fol. 334r. ASF, GM 3, fol. 18r. • **3.** Varchi, vol. 3, pp. 190–91. • **4.** Vasari, vol. 8, p. 269. Ughi, p. 186–87. • **5.** See also discussion in Simoncelli (2006), p. 169. • **6.** Cellini, pp. 194–96.

• **7.** Ughi, p. 192. Dall'Aglio, pp. 12–14. • **8.** ASF, MAP 159, c. 247r. • **9.** Varchi, vol. 3, pp. 192–96; Ughi, pp. 193–94. • **10.** Medici (2004), p. 18. • **11.** ASF, Ducato di Urbino, I/133, fols 601r–602r. • **12.** Simoncelli (2006), p. 163, citing Giovio (1956), p. 191. • **13.** Dall'Aglio, pp. 29–50. • **14.** My abridgement from Varchi, vol. 3, pp. 283–91. A full translation is in Medici (2004). For background: Baker (2007).

32

1. Nardi, vol. 2, p. 326; Giove and Villone, p. 31. Lefevre, pp. 104–5. • **2.** ASF, MAP, filza 159, c. 258v. • **3.** Biblioteca dell'Accademia Nazionale dei Lincei e Corsiniana, MS Corsiniana 55.K.16. The images are on fols 23v, 91r, 145v. Belardini (2008), p. 182, suggests that this was a wedding gift, though the lozenge could be used for widows' arms so it is possible it was a memorial commission. *Pasquinate*, vol. 1, p. 444, n. 429. • **4.** Rastrelli, vol. 2, pp. 205–7. Schraven, p. 88. • **5.** ASMn, AG 2937, Lib. 315, fols 116r–117r, nn. 341, 342; Lib. 316, fol. 20r; n. 54; ASMn, AG 1086, c. 316r. • **6.** Nerli, p. 289. Baker (2013), p. 186. Bullard, pp. 1, 176–77. Dall'Aglio, p. 78. • **7.** Conti, p. 86; Hernando Sánchez, pp. 138–89. • **8.** Simoncelli (2006), p. 225. Brancato. De' Medici (2004) includes an account of events by Captain Francesco Bibboni, one of the assassins, pp. 23–44. For Lorenzino's exile and Charles' role in the vendetta see Dall'Aglio, esp. pp. 72–76 and 243–57. • **9.** Marguerite of Navarre, pp. 82–88. For background: Bawcutt, Bromfield. • **10.** *Pasquinate*, vol. 1, p. 452, n. 436; p. 531, n. 491. Belardini (2008), p. 181. • **11.** Simons, p. 657; Cropper and Strehlke, p. 20. Langdon, p. 35. • **12.** On Ceccherelli: Bramanti. • **13.** Nestor, p. 174.

AFTERWORD

1. Callard, p. 183. • **2.** Nestor, fol. 187r. • **3.** Benedetti, for example, p. 13, n. 3. • **4.** Falciani and Natali (2010), pp. 144–46. Kaplan (2010), pp. 149–50. • **5.** Strehlke (1985), p. 7. Ceccherelli, fol. 26v. Firpo and Lo Re, pp. 417–18 and figure 5. Kaplan (2011), p. 52. • **6.** *Relazioni*, ser. 2, vol. 3, p. 268. • **7.** Filippo Cavriani, text edited in Menchini, p. 213. • **8.** Segni, vol. 2, p. 425, cited in Brackett, p. 310; 'persona raccolta, nerbuto, di color nero, e di naso grande'. For Cambi's dates see his *DBI* entry. • **9.** Ercole de' Roberti, *The Adoration of the Shepherds (The Este Diptych)*, c.1490, tempera on wood, 17.8 × 13.5 cm, NG1411.1 and Luca Signorelli, *The Adoration of the Shepherds*, c. 1496, oil on wood, 215 × 170.2 cm, NG1133, National Gallery, London. • **10.** Hirschman, p. 391. • **11.** Rawlings, pp. 4–5. • **12.** Ammirato, vol. 10 (1826), pp. 18–19, cit. in Bono (1999), p. 339; also Brackett. There appears to be no reference to Alessandro's appearance or parentage in any of Rubys, Sandoval, Varillas,

Noble or Tenhove. • **13.** Musset: 'Poils roux', rendered as 'tawny' in the recent English translation. Musset (1998), p. 81. Musset (1995), p. 184. The other drama is by Ghiglione, unpaginated. • **14.** Dumas (2013), p. 42. Dumas (2014). • **15.** Von Reumont, 1866, p. 134. • **16.** Lombroso, pp. 177–78; for background Hiller, pp. 235–36; Epstein, pp. 6–13. • **17.** Capponi, vol. 3, p. 167; Foresi; Pieraccini, vol. 1, p. 400. • **18.** Paganucci, pp. 6–7. • **19.** Avolio, p. 17. Epstein, p. 10. • **20.** Pieraccini, vol. 1, p. 410. • **21.** Young, vol. 1, pp. 439, 494–95. Cotterill, p. 444. • **22.** Schomburg (1931); Schomburg (1963); Sinnette, p. 111. See his entry in *the American National Biography*. • **23.** Schomburg (1963), p. 27. • **24.** Rivers, p. 121, citing Schomburg (1931). For his work on *Georges*, see Fabre, p. 135; for his position at the Agricultural and Technical College see *The Journal of Negro History* 18 (1933), p. 437. • **25.** Rogers, vol. 2, pp. 24–33. • **26.** Orieux, p. 44; Dumont, p. 19. • **27.** Brackett; Bindman and Gates; http://www.vam.ac.uk/content/articles/a/africans-in-medieval-and-renaissance-art-duke-alessandro-de-medici [accessed 3 July 2015] and Spicer.

BIBLIOGRAPHY: A NOTE ON SOURCES

1. For background: Montevecchi. • **2.** Baker (2010), p. 439.

INDEX